From "Euthanasia" to Sobibor

Published in Association with

THE UNITED STATES HOLOCAUST MEMORIAL MUSEUM

UNITED STATES
HOLOCAUST
MEMORIAL
MUSEUM

From "EUTHANASIA" to SOBIBOR

An SS Officer's Photo Collection

Edited by **Martin Cüppers,
Anne Lepper, and Jürgen Matthäus**

*for the Forschungsstelle Ludwigsburg of the Universität Stuttgart,
the Bildungswerk Stanisław Hantz e.V., and the Jack, Joseph and
Morton Mandel Center for Advanced Holocaust Studies of
the United States Holocaust Memorial Museum*

INDIANA UNIVERSITY PRESS

This book is a publication of

Indiana University Press
Office of Scholarly Publishing
Herman B Wells Library 350
1320 East 10th Street
Bloomington, Indiana 47405 USA

iupress.org

© 2022 by Indiana University Press

The assertions, arguments, and conclusions in the editorial emendations, commentary, and annotations are those of the volume editors and do not necessarily reflect the opinions of the Forschungstelle Ludwigsburg of the Universität Stuttgart, Bildungswerk Stanisław Hantz e.V. or the United States Holocaust Memorial Museum.

This is an English edition of *Fotos Aus Sobibor* (Metropol, 2020) and was made possible in part by funds from the Stichting Sobibor education and memorial foundation.

Manufactured in China

First printing 2022

Library of Congress Cataloging-in-Publication Data

Names: Cüppers, Martin, editor. | Lepper, Anne, editor. | Matthäus, Jürgen, editor. | Luft, Kathleen, translator.
Title: From "euthanasia" to Sobibor : an SS officer's photo collection / edited by Martin Cüppers, Anne Lepper, and Jürgen Matthäus for the Forschungsstelle Ludwigsburg of the Universität Stuttgart, the Bildungswerk Stanisław-Hantz e.V., and the Jack Joseph and Morton Mandel Center for Advanced Holocaust Studies of the United States Holocaust Memorial Museum.
Other titles: Fotos aus Sobibor. English.
Description: Bloomington, Indiana : Indiana University Press, [2022] | "Published in Association with the United States Holocaust Memorial Museum." | Includes bibliographical references and index.
Identifiers: LCCN 2022014256 (print) | LCCN 2022014257 (ebook) | ISBN 9780253064318 (hardback) | ISBN 9780253064325 (ebook)
Subjects: LCSH: Sobibór (Concentration camp)—Pictorial works. | Operation Reinhard, Poland, 1942-1943. | Nazi concentration camps—Poland—Pictorial works. | Holocaust, Jewish (1939-1945)—Poland—Pictorial works. | Niemann, Johann, 1913-1943. | Sobibor perpetrator collection (United States Holocaust Memorial Museum)
Classification: LCC D805.5.S63 F8613 2022 (print) | LCC D805.5.S63 (ebook) | DDC 940.53/180943843—dc23/eng/20220525
LC record available at https://lccn.loc.gov/2022014256
LC ebook record available at https://lccn.loc.gov/2022014257

Cover image: Gate of Sobibor killing center, spring 1943; USHMMA Acc. 2020.8.1.

Contents

Foreword

In 1996, representatives of the Bildungswerk Stanisław Hantz, a German educational organization dedicated to Holocaust memory, visited the sites of the Operation Reinhard (*Aktion Reinhard*) killing centers for the first time. It was there—in Belzec, Sobibor, and Treblinka—that at least 1.7 million Jews were murdered. These sites left a powerful impression and provided the incentive for us to offer educational trips to these largely unknown places where Germans committed their genocidal crimes during the Nazi era.

Our trips, which have taken place annually since 1998, generated diverse contacts and projects in the vicinity of each of the memorial complexes at these three sites. We have established cooperative projects with schools such as the Maria Konopnicka School in the town of Izbica. Among its various activities, this school now holds history competitions on the topic of the Holocaust. In 1942, Izbica—once a predominantly Jewish town, or shtetl—served for a short period as a transit ghetto for thousands of Jews from several European countries prior to their murder at Sobibor or Belzec. At the memorial site in Sobibor, a Bildungswerk initiative led to the creation of an Avenue of Remembrance in 2003. Memorial stones bordering the avenue recall individual victims, families, and communities murdered at this camp. Because it is constantly growing, the avenue serves as an organic place of remembrance. When construction work on the new memorial complex at Sobibor ends, the individual stones along the avenue, more than 300 in all, will form an integral part of the new site.

Over the course of more than twenty years of educational and memorial work, our colleagues have accrued extensive knowledge about the history of Operation Reinhard. We also have been fortunate to have had the opportunity to speak to survivors from Sobibor and Treblinka. We have met Poles who as children observed how Jews were hauled away to the killing centers, Poles who were the children of engineers who drove the trains to Treblinka. Moreover, we were able to establish contacts with people from small towns of eastern Poland who were "born after" but have taken an active interest in their community's Jewish history and readily shared their knowledge with us. We not only know the numbers, places, and facts of the killing operations, we have also seen the sorrow, rage, and despair connected with them and heard stories of betrayal and looking the other way. Above all, however, we have watched anonymous victims become human beings with names, faces, professions, hopes and dreams; dry, matter-of-fact documents have come alive.

In comparison with Auschwitz, the three killing centers of Operation Reinhard remain largely unknown to the general public, although it was there that more than a fourth of all victims of the Shoah were murdered. Outside of academia, hardly anyone knows the names of the perpetrators at these sites either.

Until now, the historical record did not include diaries, official reports, or letters belonging to any of the approximately 120 German men who organized and carried out the mass murder in Belzec, Sobibor, and Treblinka. We know of their journey through life primarily from their own sketchy, exculpatory, whitewashed statements to investigators. We know of their deeds from the invaluable testimonies of the few survivors.

Even for us, Johann Niemann, the deputy commandant at the Sobibor camp, whom Jewish prisoners bludgeoned to death with an axe during their uprising in October 1943, was a largely unknown Nazi perpetrator. Yet he was deeply involved in the murder of hundreds of thousands in the Holocaust and, prior to that, in the murder of tens of thousands of patients from sanatoriums and asylums throughout the German Reich.

In the autumn of 2015, Hermann Adams, a historian on northwestern Germany and a participant in one of our annual educational trips to the region of Lublin, presented the Bildungswerk with several photographs from Sobibor that he had received from Niemann's family. Adams turned them over to us, because he knew that the photo collection would enrich our work. He also put us in contact with Lothar Kudlasik, Johann Niemann's grandson. When we met Kudlasik, he showed us not just individual photos but two photo albums in which Niemann had documented the various stages of his career in the SS.

What was to be done with all these photos? We decided on a research project, which would lead to a related publication. Six colleagues from the Bildungswerk—Annett Gerhardt, Karin Graf, Steffen Hänschen, Andreas Kahrs, Anne Lepper, and Florian Ross—along with Martin Cüppers, academic director of Stuttgart University's Ludwigsburg Research Center, joined together to form a working group and editorial board. In the period that followed, we found additional photos, as well as documents, that had been lying unnoticed for years in crates and boxes, in cabinets, and in the attic.

For the first time ever, we were able to see in photos what had been known to us in broad strokes from sketches and descriptions: barracks, stalls, the fire lookout tower, a house where German perpetrators lived, the camp's fence interwoven with pine branches. Previously, the historical record was almost devoid of any photographic material from the Sobibor killing center. Some of the photos depict persons who could be identified by name and matched to persons familiar to us from other documents. The pictures reveal Johann Niemann in the company of other Germans from the SS. They show mass murderers cheerfully playing music in their leisure time, just a stone's throw from the killing facilities.

Viewed in its totality, this photo collection appears even more spectacular upon closer examination than at first glance. Over 350 photographs illustrate the life of a Nazi perpetrator, his familial and above all his professional history, in exhaustive detail and, to date, in singular fashion. In order to make these photos accessible to the public, we first had to learn how to read and understand them. The resulting publication presents the overwhelming majority of the collection's photographs and puts them into context by means of several scholarly articles.

Also found within this same trove, a few handwritten documents by Johann Niemann himself have now entered the historical record as well. The most important one is a letter, probably his last, to his wife Henriette in Völlen (East Frisia). It is a harmless text and as such all the more irritating. Niemann wrote it at Sobibor two months before his violent death. He reports his longing to see his two children and assures his wife that he is doing "very well personally."

In the Bildungswerk's work, we have always put great store on contacting survivors and hearing their testimony. It gave us great pleasure and filled us with gratitude that, within the framework of this project, we were able to meet with the last living witnesses from Sobibor. Semion Rozenfeld had been deported there from Minsk in the autumn of 1943. He viewed the photos in November 2017. At the time, he lived in a retirement home in Gedera, Israel. We are fortunate that we could include a report about our conversation with him in this book. Rozenfeld passed away in 2019.

Selma Engel, born Saartje Wijnberg, came from Zwolle in the Netherlands. On April 9, 1943, she was taken from Westerbork to Sobibor together with 2,000 other Jews. In 2017, Engel was the second survivor with whom we shared the photos. We visited her in the United States, where for years she had spoken about the Holocaust at schools and community centers. She passed away in December 2018. With the current volume, we hope to fulfill her wish that we never forget the Shoah, and that we go on informing the public about it.

Unfortunately, we could not show the Niemann photos to our friend Jules Schelvis, also of the Netherlands. He passed away in April 2016. We would have so gladly traveled to Amstelveen and discussed the pictures with him. Throughout his long life, he had concerned himself with the Sobibor camp and would have been of great assistance in analyzing the photos. Schelvis was originally from Amsterdam. The Germans had sent him and his wife, Rachel Borzykowski, along with her parents to Sobibor in May 1943. Upon his arrival in Sobibor, the Germans selected Schelvis for work. His wife and her parents were murdered. In 1993, Schelvis published a book about Sobibor that became an internationally recognized standard work about the killing center's history.

It was due to his initiative, in 2004, that we began organizing our trips to the sites of the Operation Reinhard camps together with the Sobibor Foundation (Stichting Sobibor) in the Netherlands.

We have worked with Jetje Manheim of Amsterdam, the former chairwoman of the Sobibor Foundation, for many years. Her grandfather, Mozes Manheim, and grandmother, Jettje Froukje Cohen, were murdered in Sobibor. For her, the photos of the perpetrators' village were most gripping. After all, her grandparents themselves had once seen the perpetrators' picture-perfect cottages and perhaps drawn hope from this idyll—but the idyll was deceiving. We are most grateful to Jetje Manheim for her contribution to this volume.

After a long period of research, writing, and debate among ourselves, we can now present Johann Niemann's photos to the general public. These photographs, taken together, form a singular visual record of the journey through life of a man whose deeds make the word mass murderer seem an understatement.

Bildungswerk Stanisław Hantz, April 2021

Preface

It was snowing the first time I went to Sobibor. As the roads narrowed with each turn and the heavy, snow-covered tree branches began striking the roof of the bus, I grew increasingly quiet and retreated into myself. When I stepped off the bus, my shoes sank deep into the snow and my thoughts wandered. I worried about my feet, now wet and ice-cold and likely to remain so all day. I was ashamed of myself for having such thoughts. After all, I was here to remember my family.

Sobibor felt like the end of the world, a place where one could fall off the edge of the earth. There was nothing but the silence and the trees. A small log house with a little museum inside stood at the start of an asphalt path. The path led to a circular open area with the so-called mound of ashes. Nothing recalled the 170,000 people who were brought here against their will and crammed into a gas chamber. Nothing evoked their lives. Nothing bore witness to the lives of the young people with dreams of the future, or to the lives of those who were too young or too old for dreams of the future. Only nature looked after the victims. The closer I came to my past, the less I could grasp that all that had really happened.

My parents were about twenty years old and had just fallen in love with one another when my father had to go into hiding in mid-1942. My mother and her best friend provided him with addresses where he could hide. His father—my grandfather—Mozes Manheim, born June 3, 1882, was a technical draftsman at an engineering firm in Amersfoort, the Netherlands. The day he received the summons to report for a transport, he bid farewell to each individual in his firm with a handshake and said, "I have to go." His boss, the firm's co-owner, offered him an address where he could hide. One of his colleagues also wanted to help him in the same way. But, as my parents told me more than fifty years later, he didn't want to avail himself of the opportunity, because he didn't want to put anyone in danger. His wife—my grandmother—Jettje Froukje Cohen, born January 6, 1889, was a nurse. She liked to work and had entrusted a nanny with bringing up my father during his first years. She would have gladly gone into hiding, but unfortunately, it didn't come to that.

And thus, in early 1942, Mozes and Jettje—my grandparents—were forced to leave their house in Amersfoort, a town in the middle of the country, and move to Amsterdam. There, they lived at no fewer than three different addresses, each place more cramped than the other, each with less and less privacy. They had to share their living space with four women, who were previously unknown to them, until they were seized during the last great raid in Amsterdam on June 20, 1943, and taken to

Westerbork. It was from there, on July 13, 1943, that they were sent away on a transport. They arrived in Sobibor on July 16, 1943.

My grandfather had three brothers and two sisters. None of them survived the war. My grandmother had four brothers and a sister. One brother survived. When my father came back to Amersfoort in May 1945 and found no one left, my mother's family took him in. A year later, my mother and father married. I was born in 1947, my brother four years later. At home, not a word has ever been spoken about my grandparents or our other murdered family members, but I bear the name of my grandmother who was murdered in Sobibor—Jetje Froukje. And I bear it with pride.

In 2003, five years after my first visit to Sobibor, the Avenue of Remembrance was opened. Retracing the probable route of the victims from the undressing area to the gas chambers, the Avenue of Remembrance had been the idea of the educational organization Bildungswerk Stanisław Hantz. It was created in cooperation with Marek Bem, who was at the time the director of the Sobibor Museum, and with support from Doede Sijtsma, who lives in the Dutch province of Gelderland. I was immediately excited by the idea; however, only years later did I understand just how magnificent the project really was—and that it was above all the engagement and determination of Marek Bem that made the plan a reality.

In Poland, remembrance of deceased loved ones is not limited to All Saints' Day. It occupies an important place in social life. Polish churchyards, where one always finds an abundance of flowers in bloom, stand out even from a distance. At the sites of the former killing centers, however, there is no remembrance of individuals. At most, there is some mention of the towns and villages from which the victims came.

If, during my first visit to Sobibor, I had missed any tangible form of remembrance of all the lives extinguished, I now found trees planted along the Avenue of Remembrance and, in front of every tree, stones bearing the names of families or loved ones so that victims could be remembered. In the museum, a cabinet with drawers was installed in which visitors can leave information about the persons named on the stones: a photo, a family tree, a biography. I had a memorial stone for my grandparents placed on the avenue.

Ever since the stones bearing the names of loved ones have been present, often supplemented with a short personal text, everything that happened here has become visible and perceptible amid nature's silence. I have been able to experience this myself, because as chairwoman of the Sobibor Foundation (Stichting Sobibor) in the Netherlands, I usually visited Sobibor twice each year. Thus, my fellow board members and I saw how the number of stones steadily increased and how healing a visit to Sobibor could be for those who came along with us and were able to remember their families at their memorial stones. I, too, always felt comfort and encouragement when I stooped to place a small stone and light a candle atop the memorial stone to my grandparents, whom I was never able to meet.

Other moving events have transpired, too. On one occasion, when representatives of the Sobibor Foundation were traveling in Poland with a group of persons interested in commemorating the victims of the Holocaust, we were surprised to find two teachers with a group of schoolchildren waiting for us at the synagogue in Włodawa, not far from Sobibor. The teachers asked whether we might take them with us. We adjusted our program accordingly and told the children the life story of the ten-year-old girl Selly Andriesse, whom a non-Jewish schoolmate commemorated with a stone. The day turned out to be a profound experience for the schoolchildren, their teachers, our group, and our board members.

In the period that followed, we established a strong bond with the teachers at this school. They and their young charges have accompanied us on our journeys to Sobibor every year since. Encouraged by their teachers, the children themselves have become active. During each visit to the grounds of the former camp, they would give our group a presentation and deliver fascinating reports about their research. Then, they would begin speaking to the next of kin "present" from among our group, which gave us hope for the future.

Over time, other schools have joined in. School classes regularly visit Sobibor on April 19, the day the Warsaw Ghetto uprising began in 1943. Without the Avenue of Remembrance and its stones, each of which tells a personal story, this would not have been possible. Things could not have developed this way.

On behalf of the Sobibor Foundation, I accompanied the twenty-seven Dutch coplaintiffs to the Munich trial of John Demjanjuk in 2009. On the day that the witnesses Jules Schelvis, Thomas Blatt, and Philip Bialowitz testified, it occurred to me that I was in the room with three persons who were in Sobibor at the time my grandparents arrived there. A feeling of horror shot through me. Perhaps Thomas Blatt had sorted their clothes, perhaps Philip Bialowitz had cut off my grandmother's long hair, while John Demjanjuk shut the door to the gas chamber. Never before had I been so close to the history of my grandparents.

I was overcome with the same emotion when I first set eyes on Johann Niemann's photos. So that's what they looked like, the fluttering SS banners, the cozy village cottages of the guards, the lovely house belonging to the camp commandant, the fire lookout tower. My grandparents had also seen all of this, assuming they had still been able to bring their attention to bear on such trifles after the strenuous 72-hour train ride. And once again, history, the history of my grandparents, came into view for a moment and overwhelmingly understandable.

Jetje Manheim, December 2020

Acknowledgments

This volume has profited greatly from numerous discussions with colleagues and friends whose valuable suggestions we, the participants in this project, would like to acknowledge.

Our sincere thanks go first to Lothar Kudlasik of Völlen, who decided to make his grandfather's photo collection available for scholarly examination and subsequent publication. His decision, one that by no means could be taken for granted, deserves our highest appreciation.

We are similarly indebted to regional historian Hermann Adams. It was he who first became aware of the photographs, sought with great dedication to establish contact with the Bildungswerk Stanisław Hantz, and personally introduced the project partners to Lothar Kudlasik. He was present at every one of the meetings in Völlen that followed and was immensely helpful as a facilitator.

We are grateful to the Baden-Württemberg State Office of Criminal Investigation, in particular its Image Comparison Branch at the Forensic Science Institute in Stuttgart, for its willingness to cooperate with us and for all the valuable information that emerged from our work together. We also would like to thank Semion Rozenfeld's son Mikhail Rozenfeld (Gedera), Daniel Hizkiyahu (Jerusalem), and Karina Martynova (Berlin) for all their translation work and support in the conversations with Semion Rozenfeld (who died in 2019). We also want to thank Alida and Tagan Engel (New Haven) for their assistance during our visit to Selma Engel (who died in 2018), their mother and grandmother, respectively.

We are grateful to all the employees of numerous archives and memorial sites who enabled us to access the holdings essential for a proper contextualization of the Niemann collection, now part of the archival collections of the United States Holocaust Memorial Museum (USHMM) and available there (and online) for further research. Among USHMM collections experts we would like to especially express our gratitude to Anatol Steck, Ron Coleman, and Radu Ioanid. At the German Federal Archives (Bundesarchiv) in Berlin, Regina Grüner, Mandy Dittrich, René Krüger, and Cornelius Sommer helped us a great deal, guiding us expertly through the search system and making large numbers of files available for our use. That applies also to Peter Gohle, Nadine Massag, Rainer Juchheim, and Sidar Toptanci of the German Federal Archives branch in Ludwigsburg who helped us with accessing important court records. For assistance with the archival work, we are grateful also to Jenny Gohr at the Archives of the Federal Commissioner for Stasi Records (Archiv des Bundesbeauftragten für die Stasi-Unterlagen), as well as the employees of the State Archives of North Rhine-Westphalia (Landesarchiv Nordrhein-Westfalen) in Münster and Duisburg and the Central State Archives of Hesse (Hessisches Hauptstaatsarchiv) in Wiesbaden.

We gratefully acknowledge the assistance of Tomasz Kranz and Jakub Chmielewski of the Majdanek State Museum (Państwowe Muzeum na Majdanku), Ewa Koper and Tomasz Hanejko of the Bełżec Memorial Site (Miejsce Pamięci w Bełżcu), Tomasz Oleksy-Zborowski of the Sobibór Memorial Site (Miejsce Pamięci w Sobiborze), and Krzystof Banach of the Jewish Historical Institute (Żydowski Instytut Historyczny) in Warsaw. Astrid Ley of the Sachsenhausen Memorial Site and Museum (Gedenkstätte und Museum Sachsenhausen), Ute Hoffmann of the Bernburg Memorial Site (Gedenkstätte Bernburg), Andrea Nepomuck, Stefan Wunsch and Jennifer Farber of the Vogelsang Nazi Documentation Center (NS-Dokumentation Vogelsang), and Sebastian Weitkamp and Kurt Buck of the Esterwegen Memorial Site (Gedenkstätte Esterwegen) provided us with valuable information that enriched our book. For additional suggestions and assistance, we thank Wenke Wilhelm of the Museum for Communication (Museum für Kommunikation) in Berlin, Dennis Bock in Hamburg, and Annika Wienert in Warsaw.

Over the course of the work on the German edition of this book, Eva Samuel-Eckerle compiled databases of significant excerpts and scanned court records at the Ludwigsburg Research Center (Forschungsstelle Ludwigsburg), thereby ensuring key information was available to the project. We are especially grateful to her for her valuable work. In addition, we received welcome assistance from Professor Michael Wildt in Berlin, who energetically championed the project. Professor Jan-Philipp Reemtsma, with a generous research grant from the Hamburg Foundation for the Promotion of Science and Culture (Hamburger Stiftung zur Förderung von Wissenschaft und Kultur), made it possible for us to travel to archives and to carry out many other substantial tasks related to the subject matter. We are very grateful to him and to the Foundation's staff members Matthias Kamm and Andrej Angrick. Last but not least, we want to express our thanks to Nicole Warmbold and Fritz Veitl of Metropol Verlag in Berlin, who quickly saw the value of the project and were immediately willing to include our book in their list, patiently supporting this edition with their technical skills. Klaus Viehmann, with great commitment and professional discernment, made an outstanding and clearly successful contribution to the layout and outward appearance of the book. Our thanks go to him as well.

The editors of this book would like to express their special gratitude to Kathleen Luft, who, in translating the German edition, demonstrated a high level of professionalism at all times. Important financial support for this translation was provided by the Stichting Sobibor in Amsterdam. We also thank the staff of the Jack, Joseph and Morton Mandel Center for Advanced Holocaust Studies, especially its director Lisa Leff, for supporting this project as part of the Mandel Center's activities. We are most grateful to Mandel colleagues Mel Hecker, Claire Rosenson, and Steven Feldman for their dedicated editorial work, and to David Miller and the staff at Indiana University Press for transforming our manuscript into a publication accessible to English-speaking audiences.

Last but not least, the editors would like to thank all those who made important contributions of one kind or another through their professional advice, intellectual engagement, and consideration in both their professional and private lives. This inspiring and valuable support facilitated the success of the project which, we hope, will contribute to a better understanding of Holocaust history and the people involved.

The Editors, April 2022

Abbreviations

AA	Auswärtiges Amt (German Ministry of Foreign Affairs)		BArch	Bundesarchiv (German Federal Archives), Berlin, Freiburg, Koblenz or Ludwigsburg
AIPN Lu	Archiwum Instytutu Pamięci Narodowej, Oddział w Lublinie (Archive of the Institute of National Remembrance, Lublin Division)		BStU	Behörde des Bundesbeauftragten für die Stasi-Unterlagen (Agency of the Federal Commissioner for Stasi Records), Berlin
AMMPB	Archiwum Muzeum-Miejsca Pamięci w Bełżcu (Archive of the Bełżec Museum and Memorial Site, a branch of the State Museum at Majdanek)		ECG	*Encyclopedia of Camps and Ghettos*, United States Holocaust Memorial Museum (USHMM)
APL	Archiwum Państwowe w Lublinie (State Archive in Lublin)		FSB	Federal'naia sluzhba bezopasnosti (Russian Federal Security Service), Moscow
APMM	Archiwum Państwowego Muzeum na Majdanku (State Archive of the Majdanek Museum)		Gekrat	Gemeinnützige Krankentransportgesellschaft (Charitable Ambulance Society)
AROPWiM	Archiwum Rada Ochrony Pomników Walk i Męczeństwa (Archive of the Council for Protection of Sites of Struggle and Martyrdom), Warsaw		Gestapo	Geheime Staatspolizei (Secret State Police)
			GFH	Ghetto Fighters House, Lohamei Hagetaot
			HHW	Hessisches Hauptstaatsarchiv (Hessen Central State Archives), Wiesbaden
AŻIH	Archiwum Żydowskiego Instytutu Historycznego (Archive of the Jewish Historical Institute), Warsaw		HSSPF	Höherer SS- und Polizeiführer (Higher SS and Police Leader)
			IfZ	Institut für Zeitgeschichte (Institute for Contemporary History), Munich

IKL	Inspektion der Konzentrationslager (Concentration Camps Inspectorate)
ITS	International Tracing Service (Arolsen Archives)
IMG	Internationaler Militärgerichtshof, Nürnberg (International Military Tribunal at Nuremberg)
JHI	Jewish Historical Institute, Warsaw
JuNSV	*Justiz und NS-Verbrechen*
KARTA	Fundacja Ośrodka KARTA (KARTA Center Foundation), Warsaw
KdF	Kanzlei der Führers (Chancellery of the Führer)
LAB	Landesarchiv Berlin (Berlin State Archive)
LNR	Landesarchiv NRW, Abt. Rheinland, Duisburg (North Rhine-Westphalia State Archive, Rhineland Division, Duisburg)
LNW	Landesarchiv NRW, Abt. Westfalen, Münster (North Rhine-Westphalia State Archive, Westphalia Division, Münster)
MfS	Ministerium für Staatssicherheit (East German Ministry of State Security)
NARA	United States National Archives and Records Administration, College Park, Maryland
Nbg. Doc.	Document(s) in evidence at the Nuremberg Trials
NIOD	Nederlands Instituut voor Oorlogsdocumentatie (Netherlands Institute for War, Holocaust, and Genocide Studies), Amsterdam
NL	Nachlass (posthumous papers)
NRW	Nordrhein-Westfalen (German state of North Rhine-Westphalia)

NSDAP	Nationalsozialistische Deutsche Arbeiterpartei (National Socialist German Workers' Party, the Nazi Party)
Ostfrsld.	Ostfriesland (East Frisia)
PBP	Peter Black papers, USHMM
RFSS	Reichsführer-SS
RKO	Reichskommissariat Ostland (German WWII civilian occupation regime in the Baltic states and part of the Belorussian SSR)
RM	Reichsmark(s)
RMbO	Reichsministerium für die besetzten Ostgebiete (Reich Ministry for the Occupied Eastern Territories)
ROPWiM	Rada Ochrony Pomników Walk i Męczeństwa (Archive of the Council for Protection of Sites of Struggle and Martyrdom), Warsaw
RSHA	Reichssicherheitshauptamt (Reich Security Main Office)
RuSHA	Rasse- und Siedlungshauptamts-Akte (Race and Settlement Main Office file)
SA	Sturmabteilung (Storm Troop or "Brown Shirts")
SD	Sicherheitsdienst Reichsführer-SS (Security Service of the Reichsführer-SS)
SDHA	SD-Hauptamt (SD Main Office)
SSO	SS-Offiziers-Akte (SS officer personnel file)
StAH	Staatsarchiv Hamburg (Hamburg State Archives)
StAM	Staatsarchiv München (Munich State Archives)
Stapo	Staatspolizei (State Police)

StAS   Staatsarchiv Sigmaringen (Sigmaringen State Archive)

Staw   Staatsanwalt(schaft) ([office of the] public prosecutor)

T.V.   Totenkopfverband (SS-Death's-Head unit)

USHMM   United States Holocaust Memorial Museum, Washington DC

USHMMA   USHMM Archives

VEJ   *Die Verfolgung und Ermordung der europäischen Juden durch das nationalsozialistische Deutschland* [a source collection]

WVHA   Wirtschaftsverwaltungshauptamt (SS Economic and Administrative Main Office)

YVA   Yad Vashem Archives, Jerusalem

YVS   *Yad Vashem Studies*

ZSL   Zentrale Stelle der Landesjustizverwaltungen, Ludwigsburg (Central Office of the State Judicial Authorities [for the Investigation of National Socialist Crimes]), Ludwigsburg

ŻIH   Żydowski Instytut Historyczny (Jewish Historical Institute), Warsaw

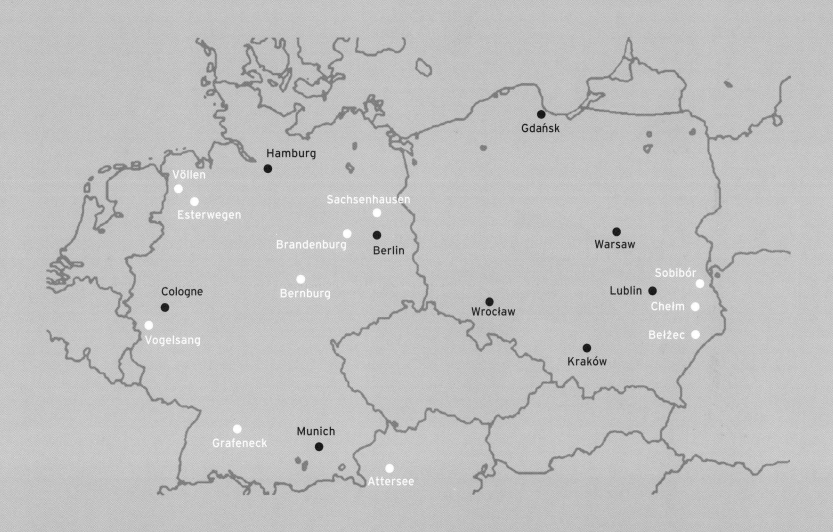

Map of Germany and Poland in their current borders. The locations marked in white identify places relevant to Johann Niemann's biography. The camps of Operation Reinhard were located in German-occupied Poland.

From "Euthanasia" to Sobibor

The Niemann Photographs

A Unique Collection from the Holocaust

MARTIN CÜPPERS

On October 14, 1943, several hundred Jewish men and a handful of Jewish women from various forced labor details at the Sobibor killing center launched an uprising and won their freedom. To signal the start of the revolt, axe-wielding inmates in the tailors' barracks bludgeoned to death SS-Untersturmführer Johann Niemann, the deputy camp commandant and duty officer on the day in question. In gaining their freedom, the Jewish women and men who survived the fighting established the basic precondition for securing their own future and for telling the world about the Holocaust and the ghastly nature of everyday life in this remote corner of German-occupied Poland.

More than seventy-five years later, the private photos that once belonged to this same Johann Niemann have surfaced. They are providing new insights into the world where the destruction of Europe's Jews took place, a world where the Nazi regime had in fact imposed a sweeping ban on photography. Niemann's photos reveal the everyday lives of men involved in the murder of institutionalized patients in Germany in 1940 and 1941 and the murder of Jews at Belzec and Sobibor in 1942 and 1943.

This collection, with its unprecedented concentration of source material, is also yielding extraordinary insights into the career of an important perpetrator of Nazi Germany's genocidal crimes, a figure hitherto deemed peripheral. Johann Niemann's collection introduces to the viewer his comrades, subordinates, and superiors; it includes views of numerous buildings and reveals other details of the places where he was deployed and where he committed his crimes. The photos show him going about his daily work routine, on excursions, and on vacation. And over and over again, they show Niemann himself, sometimes deliberately posed—as in one telling photograph on his horse atop the ramp where the deportation trains stopped inside Sobibor. A large number of the other photos are more spontaneous snapshots. A rather small number of pictures, from private and familial settings and featuring siblings or a circle of friends who are not always identifiable, supplements the visual evidence of Niemann's professional career.

Niemann's photos reveal what primarily only the perpetrators and Jewish slave laborers ever saw. However, these Jewish women and men, or other individuals subject to German persecution, appear here only as silhouettes in the background of a small number of photos. Apparently, Niemann did not wish to possess any visual evidence of his crimes, such as the images of tortured and humiliated people visible in numerous other photographs long known to researchers and the general public. Instead, the source of his photo collection seems to lie elsewhere. For Niemann, the collection was probably meant as visual testimony to assure himself and to remind him of his SS career as he saw it. It preserved for him, with varying degrees of intensity, the most important stages of his journey through life. Niemann himself revealingly wrote the word "Memento" (*Erinnerung*) along with his name and the date "5. September 1939" across a photo showing him in SS uniform. Not long thereafter, he received orders transferring him from the Sachsenhausen concentration camp to the Chancellery of the Führer (*Kanzlei des Führers*) in Berlin.[1] At his new post, Niemann found himself attached to the nascent program for the murder of institutionalized patients in Germany (see fig. 2.32).

What becomes visible from Niemann's photos is the start of his career as a Nazi perpetrator, when he assumed his duties as a guard at the Esterwegen concentration camp, some thirty miles from the Dutch border in northwest Germany. Transfer to the Sachsenhausen concentration camp, just north of Berlin, followed two years later, a posting that included at least one brief assignment for guard duty at the Nazi administrative training center (*Ordensburg*) Vogelsang, near the Belgian border. Some of the surviving prints from this early phase of his career provide hitherto unknown insights into the places named.

After joining the "euthanasia" program, Niemann collected an entire series of photos related to his service in the murder of physically and mentally disabled patients. In the course of this assignment, he worked at the killing facilities in Grafeneck (Württemberg), Brandenburg (Prussia), and Bernburg (Anhalt). Historians have long been aware of contemporaneous photo documentation for each of the six centers established for the mass murder of those deemed "unworthy of life."[2] What is unique about Niemann's photos is the sense of presence they create by showing one participant at three of these sites.

Niemann continued his career at the Belzec killing center. While there, he collected several prints originating in or near this killing center. Reassigned to Sobibor as deputy commandant, Niemann reached what would prove the zenith of his career. And it was from that key position of responsibility that Niemann left for posterity dozens of photographs of this camp, a place for which a mere two photos had been known before. The newly discovered photos do more than reveal previously unseen glimpses into the perpetrators' everyday life and their demeanor on-site. As historical sources of the first order, they are enabling scholars to reach new conclusions about the camp's physical layout, something that even the most recent archaeological excavations were unable to do with the same degree of clarity.

Through the career of one individual, this collection also reflects in exemplary fashion the radicalization of Nazi extermination policy: starting with the systematic crimes committed in the concentration camps, escalating with the murder of ostensibly "unworthy life" in the "euthanasia" operation, and culminating in the destruction of Europe's Jews during the Holocaust. Niemann's photo collection, supplemented by numerous written documents, ranks among the most important photo records of Germany's genocidal crimes known to date.

Origin and Photographic Content

For decades, Johann Niemann's photos and documents lay neglected in the household of his grandson Lothar Kudlasik. For at least some extended period of time, the collection seems to have held little significance for the family, as numerous prints were found rather thoughtlessly set aside among other highly diverse records pertaining to family history. Then some years ago the regional historian Hermann Adams learned of Niemann and his role at Sobibor. Over time, Adams's research in

Völlen, where Niemann was born, eventually led to conversations with the SS officer's grandson.

As a result of those discussions, Lothar Kudlasik decided to hand over the photo collection so it could be safely stored and made available for careful study. In the autumn of 2015, Adams turned over a large share of the photos in this volume to the German educational organization Bildungswerk Stanisław Hantz. This seemed to him appropriate, particularly in view of the group's twenty years of experience in organizing memorial and educational tours to Sobibor and other Holocaust sites in Poland. In January 2019, the editors of this volume secured additional pictures and documents in Völlen. In the course of two further visits, Lothar Kudlasik, Hermann Adams, and the author of this chapter ultimately found more than eighty additional photos, along with numerous written documents of significance.

In total, the Niemann collection encompasses 361 black-and-white photographs in varying formats and dozens of documents. Among the items preserved are two thematically cohesive photo albums. The first of these is bound in artificial leather and embossed in Fraktur lettering that states Niemann's unit: 2nd SS Death's Head Formation Brandenburg (*2. SS T.V. Brandenburg*). This album consists of 116 photos depicting above all Niemann's early SS career at the Esterwegen and Sachsenhausen concentration camps, his everyday work routine at the Nazi training center Vogelsang, as well as numerous scenes of family life. Among these photos are also images of Niemann during his stint at the Operation T4 (*Aktion T4*) killing centers in Grafeneck, Brandenburg, and Bernburg.

The second album—smaller in format and green in color, with a sailing ship for decoration on the front cover—originated much later, in the summer of 1943. Its eighty photos document a remarkable trip organized to reward men who had "distinguished" themselves in the course of Operation

Reinhard (*Aktion Reinhard*), the plan for the mass murder of Poland's Jews. On this occasion, Niemann traveled from occupied Poland to Berlin and Potsdam in the company of two other SS men (one each from the Sobibor and Treblinka killing centers) and twenty-two "Trawnikis," auxiliary guards recruited mostly from Soviet prisoners of war. The purpose of the trip was to meet important superiors, go sightseeing, rest and recuperate, and engage in jovial rounds of drinking.

Apart from the two albums, the Niemann collection encompasses a larger bundle of unsorted photos showing above all Sobibor and members of its personnel. Moreover, it was also possible to identify four photos from Belzec, more images from Niemann's assignment with the T4 program, private photos of family life, and, concluding chronologically, fourteen prints of his funeral and his grave in Chelm (Polish: Chełm), twenty-three miles south of Sobibor. The latter photos were made by an unknown photographer and subsequently sent to his widow.

This extraordinary collection is supplemented by personal documents such as Niemann's marriage certificate, various promotion-related documents issued by the SS, and his death certificate. In addition, the family held on to an informative private letter from Niemann to his wife, as well as historically valuable written records from the Chancellery of the Führer that document, among other things, the Nazi party's efforts to care for Niemann's widow.[3]

Photos from the Holocaust—Dissemination and Significance

In at least 146 photos within this collection, Niemann himself is visible—which raises the question of who took the pictures. In light of the varying edge cuts and formats, there can be no doubt that the photos originated from several photographers. Examination of the collection yielded no conclusive evidence that Niemann ever owned or used a small-format camera, something corroborated by the fact that no negatives from the Nazi era were found among family records. That private photography was apparently not commonplace in his East Frisian peasant family between the world wars may also explain why no photos of Niemann's childhood exist. Only as an adult does Niemann seem to have obtained and collected prints of photos from acquaintances and friends. Tellingly, Niemann's collection even includes a scene of SS personnel viewing photos on a terrace in Sobibor (see fig. 6.27).

On occasions such as these, interested parties could order prints directly from a photographer or choose from an available series of pictures those images that seemed interesting for their own personal visual record. The viewers of the photos on display in the aforementioned terrace scene in Sobibor probably ordered prints afterward from the photographer concerned.

Apart from the numerous prints, Niemann acquired several picture postcards as an additional form of photo documentation. He sent two to his wife in 1943 and retained others without attaching postage or writing on them, thereby emphasizing all the more his interest in visual memorabilia. Whenever Niemann was unable to find any available prints, he simply bought a postcard and integrated it into his collection.[4]

Niemann's photos generally reflect the significance of private photography as a mass medium in Germany starting in the mid-1930s. Nazi propaganda ushered in a new "visual age" in which photos and motion pictures reached unprecedented levels of distribution and were thus able to have an entirely novel effect on society.[5] The photographs and newsreels of the "Führer," the Nuremberg rallies, modern weapons, sporting achievements, and Nazi party formations marching shoulder to shoulder in goosestep on all kinds of occasions created an iconic historical record of a Germany that had regained its strength. The visual presence of these photos and films left an indelible mark on the Nazi "community of the people" (*Volksgemeinschaft*).

At the same time, the production of inexpensive, sturdy cameras enabled private households to create their own photographic memories on a massive scale. Peering through their own viewfinders, Germans began imitating the visual stylistic devices of Nazi propaganda. At the same time, the Ministry of Propaganda, by means of newspaper and magazine articles, offered advice as to how amateur photographers could acquire a suitable photographic language.[6] By some estimates, around 10 percent of Germany's population of 80 million owned a camera at the start of the Second World War, suggesting in turn that millions of cameras were in use for at least some period between 1939 and 1945.[7]

During the National Socialist era, a considerable number of hobby photographers were taking pictures of private and official life, the home front and occupied Europe, the theaters of military operations and the rear areas. In doing so, amateur photographers often violated a sweeping ban on photography, which, with regard to Germany's genocidal crimes, provided for severe punishment for breach of confidentiality. This applied especially to those who worked at the three killing centers of Operation Reinhard. Such persons had to sign a declaration stating explicitly that they had been instructed "regarding an express ban on photography in the camps of 'Operation Reinhard,'" before simultaneously committing to strict adherence to the ban.[8] Nonetheless, once a photographer had developed pictures made in violation of this ban, offers of prints were soon making the rounds. Niemann, therefore, would not have been the sole recipient of such pictures. Others involved in Nazi Germany's genocidal crimes possessed identical prints as well.

Kurt Franz, the deputy camp commandant at Treblinka, acquired some of the photos made during Niemann's trip to Berlin. In doing so, he was evidently compiling a means of preserving his own memories of everyday life during the implementation of Nazi extermination policy.[9] In October 1945, investigators discovered a photo of Niemann and fellow SS man

Gottfried Schwarz near the T4 killing facility in Bernburg in the possession of Schwarz's widow. The very same print also appears in Niemann's first photo album (see fig. 3.11).[10] The back of a print in Niemann's Berlin album bears the inscription "*30 Stck*," meaning thirty copies. This makes it clear that, besides Niemann, a good number of his traveling companions and other interested parties obtained this photo and others.[11] Such details serve to show that many prints taken in the course of Germany's crimes originally circulated, before such photos were forgotten or disposed of in the course of postwar criminal investigations.

Both as an accomplice to murder at T4 facilities and as deputy commandant at Sobibor, Niemann chose a very specific form of visual reminder from an undoubtedly wider range of photos on offer. Apart from supposed idyll, semblances of military camaraderie, and enjoyable scenes of recreation, his selections included military drill and Nazi rituals. Notably missing from his choices were images of his crimes or his victims, although such pictures likewise existed despite the ban on photography.[12]

Upon receiving his prints, Niemann seems to have assembled them himself in a carefully composed narrative. In other cases, the perpetrators' wives often did this. In placing his photos, Niemann by no means adhered to a chronological order. Instead, he usually combined photos on the basis of unmistakably aesthetic motifs. For example, after a photo of himself in his SS uniform and a studio portrait of his wife, Niemann begins his first album not with memories of his early career at the Esterwegen concentration camp but with those of the Nazi training center Vogelsang, photos made only years later. Prints from the T4 killing facilities during 1940 and 1941 then alternate with family photos or with prints that originated much earlier in Esterwegen, Sachsenhausen, and Vogelsang.

Niemann sometimes dedicated entire album pages to certain stages of his career, such as the Esterwegen concentration

camp or the training center Vogelsang. In other cases, he seems to have arranged his images on a single page without any particular theme in mind. Page 23 (see app. 1 fig. 1.14) of the Brandenburg album displays an assortment of six highly diverse photos of varying significance. Next to a snapshot of two young women in a meadow (a holiday photo from 1934, according to the inscription on the back) is a picture of Niemann and four other "euthanasia" perpetrators clowning around on the premises of the Brandenburg killing facility. A winter landscape near the T4 center in Grafeneck then follows alongside a photo of the bear enclosure from Bernburg Castle, not far from the T4 killing site in that town. The page then concludes with comparatively harmless photos, one in connection with a "Moselle cruise," as Niemann himself noted in the caption beneath it, and the other a panoramic view of the Eifel region. The selection of images on the following page is similar. Four larger prints of the Nazi training center Vogelsang and a landscape portrait of the surrounding area dominate two smaller prints. Of the latter, the upper one shows Niemann and two fellow SS men sitting on a paddleboat near the T4 facility in Brandenburg, while the lower middle photo portrays a family member who cannot be identified with certainty (see app. 1 fig. 1.15).

While the prints in the first album cover the period from the summer of 1934 to September 1941, the Berlin album contains photos that must have originated within a single week in 1943. As the condensed timeframe might suggest, the photos from the Berlin trip appear to stem from just two photographers, while the Brandenburg album clearly contains photos taken by numerous photographers and selected from many series. The number of photos glued into the first album is higher, with a total of 116 prints, but the Berlin album, with its 80 mounted photos and 8 individual prints, indicates just how much was photographed that week and how much Niemann himself was concerned with compiling a thematically diverse photographic record of the trip (see The Berlin Album and Additional Travel Pictures following ch. 8).

The 1943 photo album resembles the first in terms of its loose chronological structure and the aesthetic impressions on display. In the prints from the Berlin trip, the viewer sees the presumed photographers for once, each through the lens of the other: a tour guide from the Chancellery of the Führer and Herbert Floß, who served at the Operation Reinhard camps. Their 35 mm cameras reflect the range of models available in Nazi Germany at the time. In the mid-1920s, the Leitz Company had launched the Leica, an affordable, easy-to-use 24 mm × 36 mm viewfinder camera. Companies like Zeiss and Agfa developed their own products in the early 1930s. Such models dominated the amateur photography market for years. Most known private photos taken during the Nazi era were made with such affordable devices. Floß, for example, seems to have owned a fairly modern Leica IIIc, while the official acting as tour guide used another make.

The amateur photographer Floß aside, Sobibor had three trained photographers on staff: the brothers Franz and Josef Wolf and Thomas Steffel. During the murder of the patients in Germany's sanatoriums and asylums, all three men had been entrusted with the photographic documentation of the victims. It therefore seems quite possible that someone from within this circle also took photographs in private in the Sobibor camp and then passed the prints on to Niemann, that is to say, to one of his superiors, as well as to other comrades.[13]

The Niemann Collection and Other Photos from the Holocaust

Several important photo collections from the Holocaust and Nazi extermination policies in Europe have long been available to researchers. Comparison with them helps assess the historical value of the Niemann collection and facilitates a better understanding of the importance of amateur photography in the Nazi era. Just taking into account the nature and scope of such historical records reveals major differences. While other collections suitable for comparison are available as individual albums or only as a series of photos, the Niemann collection boasts two albums, numerous individual photos, and supplemental documents.

The historical record that is thematically most closely related to the Niemann collection is the aforementioned photo album belonging to Kurt Franz, the deputy commandant at Treblinka. West German investigators confiscated it during a search of Franz's home in 1959. In it, Franz had titled pages with photos from Treblinka in his own hand using such catchphrases as the contemptuous "The Good Old Days" (Schöhne [sic] Zeiten) or the banal "Our Camp" (Unser Lager).[14] In addition to an abundance of landscape portraits from excursions and travels, this album includes at least thirty-three images from the Treblinka killing center. Ten photos, distributed over two pages, show the two excavators used to dig up corpses for cremation starting in early 1943. By including such photos, Franz provided at least some scenes of the area of Treblinka where the mass killing took place. This stands in contrast to Niemann's Sobibor photos, which do not reveal the sector with the gas chambers. Moreover, Franz's album contains photos of the Treblinka zoo, built by Jewish slave laborers, as well as some other rather innocuous-looking images. While the Niemann collection holds numerous pictures of Niemann in Sobibor, only one photo of Kurt Franz in Treblinka appears in the Franz album. There, Franz is standing with his superior, Commandant Franz Stangl, at the entrance to a barracks building.[15]

The Franz album also contains a number of photos from Berlin and Potsdam that researchers have hitherto interpreted as private photos from his own travels and given no further attention. Only in comparison with the Niemann collection does it become clear that his Berlin album and Franz's album share sixteen identical prints from the former's trip to the German capital in the summer of 1943. Franz, however, was not among the participants. Instead, he appears to have acquired the images afterward out of a personal interest in the sights and glued them into his album.[16]

Most unlike Niemann's collection, the Franz album also illustrates the perpetrators' interest in denying any responsibility for the mass murder they committed as well as in defacing private memorabilia that suggested otherwise. For example, Franz removed from his album several apparently incriminating photos and replaced them with seemingly harmless images. This retroactive falsification of the record dramatically changed the photo album's original character and diminished its value as evidence. With regard to Niemann and his photos, such tampering with the evidence could not arise given his death in 1943.

Posterity may lack an album for Belzec, but more than a dozen photos from the camp are known to exist. In what is probably the most famous of these images, some of the camp's SS personnel are standing in front of the commandant's office.[17] Moreover, a series of nine prints features members of the German camp staff, numerous Trawnikis, and individual members of a Jewish slave labor detail outside of barracks within the camp. In addition, individual photos of Belzec and the surrounding area portray other Trawnikis deployed there.[18] The four Belzec-related pictures contained in the Niemann collection now supplement this historical record. There are no duplicates.[19]

By contrast, only two photos of Sobibor during the mass killing operations were previously known to exist. One print shows several members of the camp's staff gathered around the first commandant, Franz Stangl, and two subordinates, the notorious Gustav Wagner and Erich Bauer, enjoying a drink together, inside the former Polish post office that housed SS personnel.[20] The second photo, taken in what was called Camp I, depicts two barracks for Jewish slave laborers, near which several people, discernible only as silhouettes, are standing.[21] Sobibor, until recently the Nazi crime scene with the smallest number of visual records, has now become the killing center with the most extensive photographic documentation, with sixty-two prints in all, consisting of forty-nine different images along with thirteen duplicates.

An additional photo collection that lends itself to direct comparison with Niemann's photos is the Karl Höcker album, which is archived in the United States Holocaust Memorial Museum and was published in 2016. Höcker had served as adjutant to Richard Baer, commandant of the main camp at Auschwitz (Auschwitz I).[22] Among the photos found in this album is an important series portraying German personnel at Solahütte, an SS recreation facility twenty miles south of Auschwitz, in the summer of 1944. They are apparently celebrating the end of the operation that murdered more than 380,000 Hungarian Jews.

Like the Niemann collection, the overwhelming share of the photographs in the Höcker album are snapshots made mainly to preserve private memory. The photos here depict numerous key figures from the killing center at Birkenau (Auschwitz II). Unlike Niemann's Sobibor photos, however, Höcker's photos were not taken at the place where these men committed their crimes but outside the Auschwitz camp complex, at best on its periphery. That said, some of the images in the Höcker album do recall subject matter found in the Niemann photos when it comes to collectively experienced leisure time. For both Karl Höcker and Johann Niemann, photos of social settings with people eating and drinking in what appears to be a relaxed atmosphere obviously had a particular appeal. This likely lay in the contrast of such settings with the murderous nature of their everyday work routine in Auschwitz-Birkenau or Sobibor, a truly unbearable contrast from today's perspective.

Serving as a supplement to the context of the Höcker album's content is another photo album that originated at Auschwitz-Birkenau.[23] Survivor Lily Jacob discovered this album shortly after her liberation at the Mittelbau-Dora concentration camp in Thuringia. Taken with the camera's gaze fixed on the victims, the photos in this album give a completely different kind of perspective than those of the Niemann collection. They convey detailed impressions of the arrival of transports of Hungarian Jews in Birkenau in the summer of 1944, the selections on the notorious ramp at the camp railroad station, and the final walk to the gas chambers.

The photographers, probably Ernst Hofmann and Bernhard Walter, both of the camp's SS personnel, took up special vantage points, climbing on top of a train and later moving about the victims unabashedly as they waited in front of the gas chambers. As a consequence, these photographs, which look somewhat professional, possess a distressing intensity. This album clearly is made up of photos that were not for private use. Rather, they were supposed to document operations in Birkenau. In doing so, this album and its 193 photos acquire an official function, something entirely different from those intended for private use. And while the assignment by its very nature entailed preserving images of the victims on film, Niemann strove to obscure the victims at his camp.

Many of the photos from the so-called Stroop report on the suppression of the Warsaw ghetto uprising in the spring of 1943 also portrayed Jews through the lens of German perpetrators. They therefore convey a perspective similar to that of the photos in the album discovered by Lily Jacob.[24] Very much unlike the Niemann photos, numerous images from the Stroop report likewise show Jewish women and men, including captured members of the Jewish resistance, in the streets of the embattled ghetto. Furthermore, they also feature German perpetrators, such as SS-Brigadeführer Jürgen Stroop, in the ghetto as well.

This important photo documentation of the murderous operation directed against Warsaw's Jewish insurgents also performed an official function. With his final report and the photos contained therein, Stroop was providing an account of his assignment to combat and quell the uprising. That official function highlights the most important difference between the Stroop report and the Niemann collection, whose chief purpose was to preserve private memory.

The interest in preserving personal memory likewise distinguishes a large part of the amateur photos that have become known since the mid-1990s through two exhibitions sponsored by the Hamburg Institute for Social Research (Hamburger Institut für Sozialforschung). The purpose of these exhibitions was to illuminate the role of the Wehrmacht in Nazi Germany's war of annihilation against the Soviet Union. Unlike Niemann's photos, a large number of these photos focus even voyeuristically on the tortured and murdered victims.[25]

It probably should come as no surprise that the images taken by Nazi-era hobby photographers sometimes came to resemble one another to startling effect. A scene from the Niemann collection depicting SS men and Trawnikis in a tour bus during their stay in Berlin looks just like another photo showing an entirely different group of T4 personnel from the Hartheim killing center on an excursion.[26] Two photos from the Höcker album also exhibit clear similarities to individual prints from the Berlin trip.[27] And by photographing their comrades during a cheerful round in the outer camp or various Trawnikis in front of the hidden area with the gas chambers, the photographers at Sobibor were drawing on the same photographic language demonstrated and recommended not least of all by Nazi propaganda—just like countless other hobby photographers elsewhere in the Reich or German-occupied Europe, when they took pictures of their leisure time or daily work routine.

Such comparisons underscore the unique nature of the Niemann photos as a source not only for Operation Reinhard and Operation T4, but also for National Socialism and its criminal character. Unlike any other collection known to date, the photos here reveal the nature of everyday life for the actors who carried out these crimes. It is thus by far the most comprehensive visual record of a perpetrator directly involved in this area of Nazi extermination policy.

With regard to the Sobibor camp's topography and personnel, the photos provide valuable historical insights as well. As will be explained in detail in the articles that follow, these photos allow scholars for the first time to investigate in detail the different phases of the camp's construction. They shed light on the Germans and non-Germans involved. And they offer fleeting glimpses into the social standing of the perpetrators and their interaction with one another in the killing centers. Not least of all, no other photo collection summarizes so precisely the career of an important Nazi perpetrator, from his seemingly insignificant beginnings as a journeyman painter, to his gradual professional advancement as an SA stormtrooper and concentration camp guard, to his membership in SS Death's Head formations and his integration into the Nazi regime's criminal policies, right up to his demise as duty officer in Sobibor on October 14, 1943.

This volume takes up first and foremost those questions that examine how the photos published here reflect the intersection of Johann Niemann's biography with Nazi Germany's crimes. Nonetheless, the editors could address only peripherally certain aspects of Niemann's early career at Esterwegen and Sachsenhausen. Owing to a lack of time and space, the editors were also unable to devote as much attention to some topics as might

be desirable, for example, the relevance of photography in documenting the Nazi era.

The essays here represent only a first foray into analyzing this unique collection of photos. Other scholars with their own specialized knowledge and experience will soon assess these prints for themselves and bring their own perspectives to bear. Over time, the Niemann collection will be integrated into articles and books in a variety of fields. One such area of study will certainly involve comparisons with contemporaneous photographic records of everyday life and analyses of image composition and choice of subject matter. The Niemann collection could also offer further insights into the history of everyday life, gender history, and material culture, as well as the field of habitus formation.[28]

Structure of the Volume

In both Holocaust research and the culture of remembrance, Operation Reinhard remains underrepresented. Throughout most of the postwar era, Auschwitz-Birkenau has been the killing center that received the greatest amount of attention. This emphasis is likely due to the fact that, until now, there was hardly any compelling photo documentation for the genocidal crimes committed in Belzec, Sobibor, or Treblinka. The discovery of Niemann's photos now provides an opportunity to make up for this neglect and to grant the nearly two million victims of Operation Reinhard a more adequate place in Holocaust remembrance culture.

The editors of this volume depict, with a series of articles, Niemann's biography and the planning and implementation of Nazi extermination policies. By elaborating at length on questions of history, geography, personnel and institutions, and biography, these articles aim to guide readers through the complexities of Operation Reinhard, as well as the T4 program, in the hope of facilitating an understanding of the photos that follow each text.

After a foreword from the educational organization Bildungswerk Stanisław Hantz as the coeditor of this volume, a preface by Jetje Manheim, the former chairwoman of the Dutch foundation Stichting Sobibor, and this introduction, there follows a survey of Niemann's journey through life, from his birth as the son of peasants in northwest Germany to his own violent death as an SS officer at Sobibor.

The next article explores the murder of institutionalized patients in Operation T4 and the murder of Poland's Jews during Operation Reinhard. This article conveys basic information about these essential chapters in the history of Nazi extermination policy and introduces key figures and participating institutions.

There follows an article about Belzec, the first Operation Reinhard camp, represented by four photos in the Niemann collection. Another article presents the history of Sobibor, from its construction to its dismantling. With respect to Sobibor, Niemann's collection has massively expanded the number of known photos from two to sixty-two. These articles provide the context for what the photos reveal and help fill in gaps with regard to what they do not show.

One of the most obvious recurring themes in Niemann's photos from Belzec and Sobibor is his working relationship with the auxiliary guards known as Trawnikis. Their numbers and brutality ensured that the Operation Reinhard camps functioned with considerable efficiency despite frequent desertion. This article explores how many of the circa five thousand Trawnikis served in the killing centers and considers the scope of action they had between repudiating their service with the SS and embracing atrocity and murder.

The extraordinary photo album that Niemann subsequently compiled to document his trip to Berlin is preceded by an article that examines the trip's significance and the tour group's composition.

The prints taken at Niemann's funeral in October 1943 provide a fitting opportunity to reflect on how Sobibor's prisoners tried to resist the Nazis. The editors present the many forms of refusal and resistance and give special attention to the Jewish uprising. This outstanding act resulted in the killing of Niemann and other Germans and the escape of many of the Jewish inmates.

To round out the thematic articles, the editors also included a text about Niemann's wife Henriette. Drawing on an array of sources beyond the Niemann collection itself, they have managed to construct a revealing narrative about the woman at Niemann's side. Here, the editors pursue questions concerning her development and personality, her knowledge of and possible complicity in her husband's crimes, and her life after National Socialism.

Despite this volume's heavy focus on sources generated by the perpetrators, the postwar accounts of Sobibor's survivors in particular provided basic knowledge to decipher those documents. Without these testimonies of the survivors we would know far less about Sobibor, Belzec, Niemann, and his accomplices. In the process of developing this volume, the editors were granted the opportunity to visit Semion Rozenfeld, a veteran of the Sobibor uprising, and to show him Niemann's photos. Passages from the two days of discussions in Israel at the end of 2017 are also published here, edited for clarity, as a contribution to this volume. Rozenfeld passed away on June 3, 2019.

All of the texts, especially those that explain Germany's genocidal crimes and their background, require conceptual accuracy. For the sake of clarity and readability, the mass murder of the physically and mentally disabled, including persons merely considered socially nonconformist, is described in this volume as the murder of institutionalized patients. The editors' use of the Nazi term "euthanasia" occurs only with quotation marks. The victims were "unworthy of life" only from the National Socialists' point of view, and the way they died was anything but the "easy death" implied by the ancient Greek word. In a similar vein, it was only the Nationalist Socialists' definition of a Jew that led to the persecution and death of thousands of Holocaust victims who did not identify as Jews.

In texts and captions, geographical names such as Bełżec appear, as does the spelling Belzec. Likewise, Sobibór also deviates at times from Sobibor. This is done to differentiate between Polish place names and the German killing centers or other places where the Nazis committed their genocidal crimes.

A village in the Lublin area is still called Trawniki—the place after which the non-German guards trained there were named. Various designations for these auxiliaries circulated at the time, such as "Ukrainians" or "black ones" (for the color of their uniforms), but these are in fact misnomers. In the interest of brevity, the term "Trawniki" is used here instead of "Trawniki man."

In drawing on source material, the editors took quotes from original documents, along with any divergent spellings and stylistic defects. The English translation strives to reflect the integrity of the source material to the greatest extent possible.

In the sections of illustrations following the articles, the editors have added explanatory captions to Niemann's photos. Over the years spent preparing this volume, a significant amount of time and effort went into identifying all of the persons who appeared relevant. Despite a great deal of success, open questions remain. To minimize such cases, photo experts from the Forensic Science Institute of the State Criminal Investigation Police of Baden-Württemberg in Stuttgart assisted in the analysis of numerous Niemann photos. This remarkable cooperation between historical research and modern investigative police

work made it possible to correct some earlier assumptions and to confirm other important findings.

Aside from identifying individuals, the editors faced the additional challenge of determining many of the locations visible in the prints. Contrary to the adage that "a picture is worth a thousand words," it often happens that additional information, sometimes extensive research, is needed to decipher a photo whose original significance is known only to the photographer or the photo's owner. Only the specific context of an image endows a photograph with historical significance. For example, one of Niemann's photos shows a mountain panorama with people strolling along not just any idyllic shoreline but that of the Attersee, an Austrian lake where T4 and Operation Reinhard technicians could vacation in a recreation facility run by the Chancellery of the Führer. In another photo, Niemann appears wrapped in a winter coat in front of not just any building but at the entrance to his quarters at the T4 facility in Bernburg, close to the wing that housed the gas chamber. Such examples make clear how crucial the exact attribution of a photo can be and how proper attribution can lead to a more adequate historical understanding of visual records.

This volume includes the vast majority of prints contained within the Niemann collection. Duplicates aside, the editors have included all of the photos from Niemann's early career at the Esterwegen and Sachsenhausen concentration camps, all of the photos taken in the course of the T4 and Reinhard operations, as well as all of the photos made on the trip to Berlin. With respect to Niemann's first album, the editors decided after much deliberation to select for enlargement only those photos bearing directly on his biography and to reproduce the full Brandenburg album in a smaller format in the appendixes.[29] This will allow viewers to gain an overall impression of the album and to see how he arranged the highly diverse photos of his SS career and family life. A separate reproduction of every single image of a military drill or parlor photo from Vogelsang would have placed an undue burden on the book's format and possibly distracted from the collection's historical value. For the same reason, the editors chose to omit some photos showing family members or friends who could not be identified.

Of the 361 photos in the Niemann collection, 291 are published here, including all of the photos contained in the two albums. The entire Niemann collection is available as digital reproductions via the United States Holocaust Memorial Museum's online collections catalogue at https://collections.ushmm.org/search/

The editors hope that this volume will reach a broad audience and provide the general public with greater knowledge of the murder of institutionalized patients in Nazi Germany during the T4 program and the murder of Jews from throughout Europe in German-occupied Poland during Operation Reinhard.

With this in mind, the editors dedicate this volume to the prisoners of Sobibor who fought for and won their freedom on October 14, 1943, and to the hundreds of thousands of others who did not survive the genocidal actions of Johann Niemann and his accomplices.

Notes

1. As of early 1939, the Chancellery of the Führer, headed by Philipp Bouhler, primarily handled Hitler's personal correspondence with the Nazi party and the general public. Its official address was the New Reich Chancellery, but it operated out of a nearby building. See Kershaw, *Hitler*, vol. 2, pp. 257–258. This chancellery is not to be confused with the Reich Chancellery under Hans Heinrich Lammers, the National Socialist Party Chancellery led by Martin Bormann, or the Presidential Chancellery run by Otto Meissner.

2. The other three centers were Sonnenstein (Saxony), Hartheim (Austria), and Hadamar (Hesse).

3. Some of these documents are reproduced in the appendix.

4. There is a postcard of Berlin that Niemann wrote but never mailed. The collection also includes a card that Danida Floß, the wife of another perpetrator from the T4 and Reinhard operations, sent her parents in September 1941. It shows a mountain summit near the T4 recreation facility on the Attersee. Floß, also widowed in October 1943, probably brought it with her when she visited Henriette Niemann in 1944.

5. For details, see Paul, *Zeitalter*, pp. 216–305; idem, "Kriegsbilder", pp. 39–46.

6. See Bopp and Starke, *Fremde*, pp. 10–23; Paul, *Zeitalter*, p. 238.

7. Starl, *Knipser*, pp. 95–98.

8. "Dienst- und Geheimhaltungsverpflichtung v. 18.7.1942," published in *VEJ*, vol. 9, p. 336.

9. See Franz's photo album, LNR Duisburg, RWB 18244. This album includes 16 prints of images from Berlin identical to photos found in Niemann's Berlin album.

10. See also BStU, HA IX/11-ZAST K 154/3 (Erna Schwarz).

11. The inscription is on the back of appendix 1 figure 1.26 in the upper left-hand corner.

12. Survivors testified that some of Sobibor's SS personnel photographed the violent excesses that ensued when deportation trains arrived (see statement of Philip Bialowitz, May 15, 1963, NIOD, 804/13).

13. Figures 6.24–6.26 seem to suggest this context. While the same group of five is depicted in front of the new staff club and on the adjoining terrace, Franz Wolf appears in a photo that seems to have been taken shortly thereafter. Wolf could have taken the previous photos and then handed the camera to a comrade so that Wolf himself would appear in a photo.

14. Franz photo album, LNR Duisburg, RWB 18244. Thirteen pages of the album are reproduced in Wienert, *Lager*, pp. 40–45, see also Klee et al., "*Schöne Zeiten*," pp. 222–225.

15. The Franz album aside, just two additional photos of Treblinka are known. The first depicts the German perpetrators Bredow, Mentz, Möller, and Hirtreiter, likely on the premises of the camp (LNR Duisburg, RWB 18250, fol. 15). The second, a photo taken in a studio, shows four German perpetrators from Treblinka together with three noncommissioned officers from the ranks of the Trawnikis. This photo was found in the possession of Willi Mentz, who served in Operation T4 and at Treblinka (BArch, B 162/30386, Bild 8098). The author of this

chapter will soon publish a volume about the Franz album and other photographic sources on the T4 and Reinhard operations.

16. Interrogation of Kurt Franz, February 26, 1960, LNR, Rep. 388/796, in which the accused tried to deny his personal responsibility for the extremely incriminating album.

17. See Kuwałek, *Vernichtungslager*, p. 95

18. Five prints from the series are published in Wienert, *Lager*, pp. 25–27. The origin of the photos has not been clarified unequivocally.

19. See Niemann's Photos from Belzec following ch. 5 in this volume.

20. Three other pictures supposedly depicting Hubert Gomerski of Sobibor actually show his cousin, in a completely different and quite innocuous context; see photos published in Webb, *Sobibor*, pp. 399–401. In addition, there is another photo incorrectly attributed to Sobibor that supposedly depicts various SS personnel at the camp (ibid., p. 403). In fact, it shows unidentified persons from an entirely different office.

21. The photo is reproduced in Schelvis, *Vernichtungslager*, p. 51.

22. See Busch, Hördler, and van Pelt, *Höcker-Album*.

23. Gutman and Gutterman, *Auschwitz Album* and recently Bruttmann, Hördler, and Kreutzmüller, *Inszenierung*.

24. On these photos, see Wirth, *Stroop-Bericht*. In this context, the Katzmann report on the murder of the Jews of District Galicia is also important; see Bodek and Sandkühler, *Katzmann-Bericht*.

25. Regarding these photos, see Hamburger Institut für Sozialforschung, *Vernichtungskrieg*; idem, *Verbrechen*.

26. See figure 8.6 and Kepplinger and Leitner, *Dameron Report*, p. 295 top.

27. Busch, Hördler, and van Pelt, *Höcker-Album*, pp. 225–226.

28. For the source of inspiration here, see Krauss, *Welten*. Petra Bopp has made valuable contributions to the study of private WWII photo collections; see Bopp, *Images*.

29. In the appendix, individual photos that could be clearly identified as having been torn from the "Brandenburg" album are marked in red.

2

Johann Gerhard Niemann

From Völlen to Sobibor, Part I

KARIN GRAF AND FLORIAN ROSS

Childhood and Social Environment

When Johann Gerhard Niemann was born in Völlen on August 4, 1913, his three sisters Johanna, Henriette, and Luise and his brother Gerhard were already sitting at their parents' table. The eldest child was seven, and the youngest had just turned two. Johann was only one year old when his sister Margarethe joined the family, and she was followed by three more brothers: Karl, Bernhard, and Johannes. The father of this swarm of children was Claas Johann Niemann, born in 1882, a farmer and milk delivery man; their mother, Bilda Johanna Niemann, born in 1879, was a housewife and shared in the farming duties.[1] With nine children in all, the family far exceeded the German national average of three to four offspring.[2] In the years that followed, the Niemann siblings continued to live in the region of their birth. The brothers worked as laborers, farmers, and craftsmen, and the sisters married men from the same milieu.[3]

Thanks to the parents' small farm with half a dozen cows, the family table was adequately laid—but no more than that. The father supplemented his small-scale farming income by driving a milk delivery wagon. Day after day, often accompanied by one of his children, he picked up the full milk cans from every farm in the three villages of Völlen, Mitling, and Mark and delivered them with his horse and wagon to the dairy in Ihrhove, six miles (ten km) away. Farmer Niemann's work was a back-breaking job, but it secured a good extra income for the family.

Johann Niemann attended elementary school for eight years, and after graduation in 1927, he learned the trade of house painting from Ahlrich Harms, the local master painter, who in those days was already a convinced supporter of the Nazis.[4] In 1931, Niemann passed his journeyman's examination with a score of "good."[5] According to his statements about the occupations of his brothers and sisters, he was thus the only child in the family who completed training in a skilled trade.[6] His qualification did not help him, as there was a gap of two and one-half years in his life history, likely due to unemployment that forced him to help out on the family farm.[7]

The Emsland region, sparsely populated in the early 1930s, was one of the poorest areas in Germany, a section of the country that was not easily accessible and lacked a connection to major transport routes.[8] More than one hundred towns and villages could be reached only via unpaved roads through marshy or sandy land. As recently as 1930, the municipality of Esterwegen had opposed connection to the electrical grid. Poor climate conditions, low-fertility soil, undeveloped stretches of fenland, and a dearth of land devoted to agriculture were the causes of a poverty that had been obvious for decades. In 1929, the average income of gainfully employed persons in the communities in the Hümmling hills near Völlen was only 50 percent of the national average. Small-scale farming and peat extraction brought in too little. The local populace simply lacked the means to build up commercial operations; as a result, the region was left far behind. In 1933, one-fourth of the working population of the Emsland region was employed in industry and related sectors; in nearby Papenburg, unemployment was at a level of 22 percent despite the town's important shipyard.[9]

Political and Antisemitic Environment

In the last year of his vocational training, Johann Niemann clearly expressed his enthusiasm for the increasingly strong Nazi movement. In September 1931, one month after his eighteenth birthday, he joined the Nazi party (NSDAP) and received the membership number 753836. Days after joining the local storm troop (SA) group in Völlen in October, Niemann traveled to Brunswick (Braunschweig), where more than one hundred thousand SA members cheered Adolf Hitler at a mass rally. The 1931 Brunswick Rally was the largest gathering of paramilitary groups in the Weimar Republic. It was accompanied by bloody street fighting between SA stormtroopers and communists.[10] The young journeyman painter most likely returned to Völlen with lasting impressions and confirmed in his positive attitude toward National Socialism.[11]

In Niemann's native region, the Nazis quickly attained a position of dominant influence as they focused their attention specifically on the rural areas and enhanced the role of the peasantry.[12] Success did not fail to materialize. By the time of the 1932 elections to the Reichstag, the NSDAP had emerged as the strongest political force in East Frisia.[13] After the takeover in January 1933, 50.1 percent of the eligible voters in Völlen

voted for Hitler's party in the March elections to the Reichstag. In the district assembly (*Kreistag*) elections that followed, 55 percent of those entitled to vote cast their ballots for the NSDAP, a proportion that was almost 6 percent above the national average.[14] In the Emsland region, as everywhere, impressive demonstrations on May 1, 1933, provided an outward sign of the change of government.

The Nazis promptly implemented their plans for reorganization of the political order in East Frisia as well. Suspect officials and other public servants were replaced with regime loyalists; in the administrative district of Aurich, this measure affected 60 percent of the personnel in some sectors.[15] Rudolf Janssen, a seventy-one-year-old building contractor who had served as mayor of Völlen for thirty years—not an NSDAP member—was soon replaced with Johann Doeden, an SA functionary.[16] In the district town of Leer, twelve miles (twenty km) away, Mayor Erich von Bruch had refused to dismiss Social Democrats from their positions and had denied the NSDAP permission to use the livestock hall because he feared for the safety of the Jewish cattle dealers. After the occupation of the town hall by SA stormtroopers and the mayor's short-term arrest, he was subjected to wholesale accusations and severe threats during the weeks and months that followed. On May 7, 1933, the dedicated municipal leader shot himself in his apartment in the town hall.[17] In the Emsland region, as everywhere in the Reich, the subsequent period was marked by Nazi demonstrations and repressive measures, often supported by SA detachments, targeting Social Democrats, communists, unionists, and members of other organizations declared "hostile to the state." Niemann, as a member of the SA, was possibly involved in such operations.

In this agrarian-oriented region, antisemitic rabble-rousing, violence, robbery, and marginalization challenged the traditionally strong role of Jews in the economically significant cattle trade. Two months after the transfer of power, and four days sooner than in other parts of the German Reich, the boycotting of Jewish-owned shops began in East Frisia. During the November 1938 pogroms, the synagogues in Aurich, Emden, Esens, Leer, Norden, and Weener were burned down. By September 1939, there were only 697 Jewish citizens still living in East Frisia, down from 2,336 in 1933. In February 1940, the Gestapo demanded that the last remaining Jews leave East Frisia.[18]

The Esterwegen Concentration Camp

In March 1933, when the Prussian Ministry of the Interior under Hermann Göring decided to build concentration camps, among the sites chosen was the remote, sparsely populated northern part of the Emsland region, near the Dutch border. Between 1933 and 1945 the Nazis built, to the right and left of the River Ems between Papenburg and Rheine, fifteen barrack camps in succession. Three of them—Börgermoor, Neusustrum, and Esterwegen—were state-run concentration camps for the confinement of political adversaries. Between the summer of 1933 and 1936, approximately ten thousand persons were imprisoned there.[19] Initially, from August 1933, the three camps served as concentration camps for the deterrence and "re-education" of opponents of the regime. The most prominent prisoner there was pacifist journalist Carl von Ossietzky, who received a Nobel Prize in 1936 and died in May 1938 from the effects of his imprisonment in Esterwegen.

Beginning in 1934, increasing numbers of so-called delinquents, the socially marginalized, and Jews were imprisoned in Esterwegen, and by summer of that year, the camp had as many as one thousand inmates. From late 1933, stormtroopers from the region were shown preference in the hiring process for the guard force. In the early phase of the camp's existence, there were scarcely any guidelines for performance of guard duty in Esterwegen; instead, improvisation, violence, and arbitrariness became the dominant approach to action.[20]

In May 1934, Johann Niemann, still a minor at the age of twenty, volunteered to serve as an SA guard in the Esterwegen concentration camp. His enthusiasm for the Nazi system manifested itself here once again. "Although my civilian occupation promised me a bright future after I had passed the journeyman's examination, I wanted to be a soldier on active duty. My wish was fulfilled when I was hired to work at the Esterwegen penal camp [*Justizlager*],"[21] Niemann wrote in 1943, looking back on the course of his life. The pay was in line with the pay scale for the urban police (*Schutzpolizei*), which meant that an unmarried guard was entitled to the less-than-lavish sum of 96 Reichsmarks each month. More than 80 percent of the guard personnel, like Niemann, were among the so-called Old Fighters, who had joined the Nazi movement before the transfer of power and had already gained a great deal of experience in the violent treatment of political opponents.[22]

Only one month after he opted for a career as an SA concentration camp guard, top-level internal power struggles within the Nazi regime forced Niemann to take another look at his decision. In early 1934, the SA under Ernst Röhm—with a membership numbering four million, characterized by ruthless violence and extreme radicalism and, above all, intent on completing the National Socialist revolution—had become an unpredictable factor for Hitler, one he sought to curtail. The "Führer" had the support of Heinrich Himmler's SS, still nominally subordinate to the SA. Himmler, in turn, was eager to emancipate himself from Röhm. On June 30, 1934, SS forces fanned out in an extensive operation involving arrest and murder. The term introduced by the press, the "*Röhm-Putsch*," suggested merely a reaction to a planned SA coup d'état. In fact, however, it was nothing other than a painstakingly orchestrated removal of internal competition.[23]

Overnight, the SA had thus lost a large part of its power, a fact that prompted Niemann to turn to other, more opportune, alternatives with better potential for advancement. He decided to leave the SA behind and opted instead for Himmler's SS, which, as the self-proclaimed Nazi elite, had come out on top in the most recent power struggle. Of the approximately 250 SA members who had hitherto been part of the Esterwegen guard force, around half made the same decision as Niemann and switched to the SS.[24] The other half were mostly kept on by the penal camps. While the Esterwegen concentration camp was placed under SS control in the early summer, Neusustrum and Börgermoor, as prison camps (*Strafgefangenenlager*), passed to the authority of the state justice system.

Beginning on October 19, 1934, Johann Niemann belonged to an SS Death's-Head battalion: SS-Totenkopfsturmbann "Ostfriesland." From then on, he wore the SS uniform and the belt buckle with the SS motto, "My honor is loyalty." The decision in favor of the SS had far-reaching consequences for him and was perhaps the most crucial choice of direction in his life. In his life history, he wrote that he was "taken on" by the SS. In fact, however, this was not something he underwent passively; rather, it was an active declaration of his will.

In early July 1934, Theodor Eicke, the former commandant of the Dachau camp, assumed command of the Nazi concentration camps. As head of the Inspectorate of Concentration Camps (*Inspektion der Konzentrationslager*, IKL), Eicke oversaw the reorganization and standardization of the camp system, based on the model of Dachau, during the following months and years. The precedent-setting historical process had significant changes in store for Niemann too, deeply affecting his professional socialization and further career. Essential elements of Eicke's "Dachau model" were, first, the training of the SS guard units. In the training program, which was tailored to military standards, the men were conditioned with strict discipline, drill, absolute subordination, and tough punishment. Second, a camp disciplinary and penal code (*Lagerordnung*) was introduced in the Esterwegen concentration camp also.

The code simulated legality and projected a calculable system of rules for the prisoners, while in reality unceasing violence and arbitrariness continued to prevail.[25]

The restructuring of the camps was intended to create an effective apparatus of repression, with correspondingly unscrupulous personnel who were prepared to use violence, including murder and manslaughter. For guarding the facilities, the SS put together special units, characterized by increasing military professionalization. These forces later formed the nucleus of the Waffen-SS, the military branch of the SS. The training of the SS Death's-Head units encouraged use of violence and unconditional harshness, designed to instill a strong sense of belonging to an elite, in combination with a profound contempt for the prisoners. The result was a highly committed body of troops who supported and protected each other. For Esterwegen, that entity was the IVth SS Death's-Head Battalion "East Frisia." The concentration camp became a training site and cadre-training center for these Death's-Head units and frequently served as a springboard for SS careers in other concentration camps.[26] In the years that followed, the violence of the guard forces behind the fences of the camp also spread to life outside the camp gates. At rallies and gatherings, the number of politically motivated scuffles and brawls increased. In the southern part of the Leer administrative district, the guards from Esterwegen consistently participated in riots and acts of violence.[27]

With the introduction of the Dachau model and the new disciplinary code as defining features of the concentration camp system, the indiscriminate use of violence against prisoners became habitualized, ranging from draconian punishment all the way to execution. The notorious prisoner labor in the peat bog lost its previous significance and increasingly served the purpose of sheer punishment and harassment. From 1935/36, the procedures for classifying and identifying the prisoners were expanded and gradually systematized. Beginning in

1938, inmates in all concentration camps under the control of the IKL were required to wear prisoners' garb with triangles of different colors stitched on to indicate the reason for their imprisonment. In addition, the perfidious system of "prisoner self-administration" was expanded.

In Esterwegen, Johann Niemann must have witnessed and actually taken part in all the agonizing and frequently fatal measures used on the prisoners. Right on schedule and in the context of a relatively common career, he was made an SS-Sturmmann on August 1, 1935, followed by promotion to SS-Rottenführer on March 1, 1936. Niemann spent slightly less than two and a half years in Esterwegen.

The Sachsenhausen Concentration Camp

During the final phase of the Esterwegen concentration camp, the remaining prisoners were moved to Oranienburg, near Berlin, and utilized there to build the Sachsenhausen concentration camp. On July 12, 1936, an advance party of one hundred SS men and fifty political prisoners from Esterwegen arrived in Sachsenhausen. They were initially accommodated in temporary barracks.[28] Johann Niemann, who was stationed in Sachsenhausen as of August 10, certainly also took part in building the camp, which was completed after a construction period of twelve months. After its completion, those in authority were full of praise for their achievement of constructing a concentration camp in a forested area. A small town with approximately one hundred buildings, enclosures, a water supply, and a sewage system had come into existence, and the architect characterized Sachsenhausen as the "most modern, most beautiful, and biggest camp of this kind in the German Reich."[29] In reality, Sachsenhausen signifies the death of several tens of thousands of human beings who fell victim to SS terror between 1936 and 1945. The prisoners were subjected to arbitrary

punishment and brutal individual abuse by members of the SS; they died in executions and shootings, from hunger, disease, and exhaustion, in the course of medical experiments, and in a gas chamber.[30]

In September 1936 the last prisoners and leading SS men of the IVth Death's-Head Battalion "East Frisia" transferred from Esterwegen to Sachsenhausen, and along with them went the commandant, Karl Otto Koch, who now became the first commandant of the Sachsenhausen camp.[31]

By combining the SS men from East Frisia with the Vth Death's-Head Unit "Brandenburg," the 2nd SS Death's-Head Regiment "Brandenburg," with a strength of 1,375 SS men, was established in April 1937. Johann Niemann became affiliated with this regiment as of December 1, 1937.[32] The training of the SS guard units resembled the training in Esterwegen. Here too, the professed educational goal was to teach the men to be hard on themselves and on political opponents; such toughness was practiced in the labor detachments with experienced SS men. Many of the guards played an active role in the mistreatment and murder of prisoners.[33] The acts of terror against the prisoners did not motivate a single member of the Death's-Head units to leave the SS-run concentration camps.[34]

Men under the age of thirty were in the majority in the noncommissioned officer corps. Like Niemann, they frequently came from the lower middle class and, although most of them had only elementary or lower secondary schooling, they had hopes of a career in the Death's-Head units. In fact, the camps and the SS opened up careers for these men which civilian life could not have offered.[35] In their statements, former Sachsenhausen prisoners characterized the younger SS men as more brutal and ruthless than the older ones. Niemann too is to be included in this ambitious, career-oriented group of men who were sold on the system. Evidently he had acquitted himself well enough in his four years of service in two concentration camps that he was made a member of the headquarters staff at Sachsenhausen as of May 1, 1938, which implied a substantial advancement. Possibly the appointment to the staff was related to Hermann Baranowski's commencement of his duties as the new commandant at about the same time.[36]

While the regular guard units were supposed to take on the external guarding of the camp along the lines of the Dachau model, the members of the headquarters staff were responsible for guarding the camp's interior.[37] They implemented the reign of terror against the prisoners within the camp, in direct contact. There were five sections in total: commandant's office/headquarters, political section, protective custody camp, administration, and camp and station physician.[38] It is not possible to reconstruct Niemann's exact task in his new position. The statements of Sachsenhausen prisoners, who often were able to remember the names of their immediate tormentors, contain no direct reference to the SS man from Völlen.

The headquarters staff initially consisted of forty SS men, and the increasing numbers of prisoners brought it to 172 members by the end of 1938.[39] This group, still relatively small, also included Niemann's later accomplices in the murders of patients and in Operation Reinhard (Aktion Reinhard): Siegfried Graetschus and Josef Oberhauser. The pathway into the staff led, with very few exceptions, only through several years of service in the SS guard force. The individual testing in guard service gave superiors ample time to get an idea of each SS man. This trial period made it easier to decide whether he was "reliable" and "ideologically stable" and thus suited for the duties in the headquarters staff. Also significant were holding early memberships in the Nazi formations, opting out of the church, and having intact family circumstances.[40] Johann Niemann met all the preconditions, apart from his status as a man who was still single: he had left the church in March 1937. His early participation in the NSDAP had earned him the "Honor Chevron for the Old Guard" (Ehrenwinkel für alte Kämpfer).[41]

Niemann's transfer to the headquarters staff was followed three months later by his regular promotion to SS-Unterscharführer. The formative period in Sachsenhausen ended for him on October 1, 1939.

Johann Niemann at the Ordensburg Vogelsang

During the early days in Sachsenhausen, Battalion IV of the SS Death's-Head Unit "East Frisia" had already been ordered to supply the guard detachments for the Ordensburg Vogelsang in the Eifel region. The guards were replaced every three months. The photos in Niemann's Brandenburg album tell us that he was detailed to serve in the guard detachment in Vogelsang at least once (see figs. 2.16–2.29). His tasks included normal guard duty as well as setting up an "honor guard" for official visits. The men detailed to Vogelsang regarded participation in this honor guard as a sign of distinction. Anyone who was not assigned to guard duty took part in the classes for the cadets, who were known as Ordensjunker.[42]

Robert Ley, the Reich Organizational Leader (Reichsorganisationsleiter) of the NSDAP, brought into being three large NS-Ordensburgen (National Socialist Order Castles), all located near the borders of the Reich. These facilities were designed to serve as cadre training centers for up-and-coming NSDAP members: Krössinsee in Pomerania, Sonthofen in the Allgäu region, and Vogelsang in the Eifel region.[43] After completion of the first construction phase between March 1934 and April 1936, the training of the hand-picked cadets began. These Ordensjunker were to be trained as "political leaders" both for the NSDAP and for the state administration; later on, they were supposed to provide the midlevel bureaucracy. The training focused on unconditional obedience to the "Führer" and a steadfast belief in Nazi ideology. There was a wide gap between aspiration and reality with regard to the would-be future elite of the National Socialist state. The attempt to recruit the desired personnel did not succeed, nor did the training accomplish its ambitious goals. The three Ordensburg centers, in the three years of their existence, trained around 2,200 Ordensjunker in total by the fall of 1939.

Johann Niemann devoted 43 of the 116 photos preserved in his Brandenburg album to this NSDAP showcase project, which obviously had made an impression on him. The complex of buildings included modern accommodations, a parade ground, utility buildings, lecture halls, a library, and facilities for recreation and sports. Its architectural features reinforced the Nazi regime's self-stylization: a "sacred space" (*Kultraum*), huge sculptures made of wood and stone, a fortified tower, and an event stage known as the *Thing-Stätte*. New rituals were practiced at solstice celebrations, harvest festivals, May Day celebrations, and marriage consecrations. Even people from the region, members of the cadet group and the staff, school classes, business tour groups, and individual day-trippers exhibited keen interest in the mysterious installation on the hillside overlooking a lake, the Urftsee.[44]

Besides training the students, the Ordensburg served as an imposing setting for receiving guests from Germany and abroad, and as a conference center for the new nomenklatura. High-ranking officials such as Heinrich Himmler, Joseph Goebbels, Rudolf Heß, Generalfeldmarschall Werner von Blomberg, Reichsjugendführer Baldur von Schirach, Hermann Göring, and Reichsleiter Alfred Rosenberg used Vogelsang as a stage. Several photos from Niemann's album document visits by high-ranking Nazi officials during his time at Vogelsang (see figs. 2.9, 2.20, 2.21, app. 1 figs.1.5, 1.6) and testify to their effect on the young SS man.

The Year 1939

For Johann Niemann, 1939 was an eventful year in many respects. While he had climbed an important rung on the SS career ladder in Sachsenhausen in the spring, in the private sphere he realized his desire to start a family. Two and one-half months after his promotion to SS-Scharführer on May 1, Niemann sent a letter from Sachsenhausen to the Race and Settlement Main Office (*Rasse- und Siedlungshauptamt*, RuSHA), requesting the forms for a marriage application. This SS organization, in existence since 1933, was the institutional foundation for Himmler's National Socialist *Volkstumspolitik*. A standardized approval process for marriages of SS men was intended to safeguard the racial purity and "high quality" of the SS "community of kinship" (SS-*Sippengemeinschaft*).[45] Niemann wanted to marry his boyhood sweetheart, Henriette Frey. She had just reached the age of eighteen three weeks before. He himself had turned twenty-five on August 3, the age at which it was officially possible to seek approval for marriage.[46] Frey was born in Völlen on June 27, 1921, and, like Johann Niemann, attended the primary school there for eight years.[47] They had known each other since childhood. She stated that, after finishing school, she had worked in a shop as a temporary helper for two years. Like her future husband, Henriette Frey came from a rural milieu. Her family was respected in the town, and her parents' farm, with a handful of cows and a corresponding amount of land, offered a secure existence. After her mother had "an accident" that left her virtually unable to work, Henriette, still a teenager, had to take over the running of her parents' farm household.[48]

In August 1939, when Johann Niemann submitted his marriage application based on the required proofs of descent, his wife-to-be was already in the seventh month of pregnancy. That led Niemann to request that his application be processed expeditiously, so that his child would "be born in wedlock, as desired." The process went smoothly, and on September 21, 1939, Niemann was authorized to become engaged and to marry. His son, August, was born on October 8, 1939, but the young couple did not marry until the day after Christmas 1939, in Völlen.

From that time on, the shared home of the married couple was the farm of Henriette Niemann's parents.

On his home leaves, Johann Niemann regularly returned to his young family in East Frisia. In this way, the families also may have become privy to the Nazis' extermination policy. At the time of his marriage, Niemann had already changed his place of employment. Until October 1, 1939, he was a member of the SS Death's-Head Regiment "Brandenburg," and after that date he was detailed to the Chancellery of the Führer (*Kanzlei des Führers*).[49] In November 1939 in Berlin, the young father was let in on the plans for so-called euthanasia, and was sworn to strict secrecy with regard to his role in what was later called Operation T4 (*Aktion T4*), the Nazi "euthanasia" program. At this time, his son August was approximately one month old.

Notes

1. Transcript of conversation with historian Hermann Adams, Ihrhove, January 21, 2019. We thank Hermann Adams for his valuable cooperation. He provided us with his extensive preliminary work and diverse information on the biography of Johann Niemann and was always available to answer our questions.

2. Birg, *Bevölkerungsrückgang*, p. 50.

3. Insert sheet for extended family, BArch, RS Niemann.

4. Adams, conversation.

5. Curriculum vitae by Johann Niemann, BArch, RS Niemann.

6. Marriage records of Johann Niemann, BArch, RS Niemann.

7. Curriculum vitae by Johann Niemann, BArch, RS Niemann.

8. Weitkamp, "Machtsicherung," p. 28. On the region see Reyer, *Ostfriesland*.

9. See Roitsch, *Zaungäste*, pp. 58–61.

10. Rother, *Sozialdemokratie*, p. 244.

11. Like all other participants, he received a badge of honor in Brunswick. See Personnel record, BArch, SSO Niemann.

12. See Roitsch, *Zaungäste*, p. 76.

13. Eimers, "Eroberung," p. 14.

14. See "Ergebnisse der Reichstagswahl," in: *Leerer Anzeigenblatt*, March 6, 1933; "Die Ergebnisse der Kreistagswahl," in: *Leerer Anzeigenblatt*, March 19, 1933.

15. Reeken, "Elitenrevolution," p. 30.

16. Adams, conversation. Doeden, who was from a reputable and well-to-do farming family, married a woman from Völlen and built a house there. He was arrested after the war and imprisoned in Esterwegen-Börgermoor for two years.

17. See Hensmann, *Dokumentation*,, pp. 51–53.

18. Lokers, "Boykott," p. 82.

19. For an overview see Knoch, "Emslandlager;" *ENC* vol.1, "Esterwegen, IKL," pp. 64–68.

20. Knoch, "Emslandlager," p. 540.

21. Curriculum vitae by Johann Niemann for his SS file, 1943, BArch, SSO Niemann.

22. See Reinicke, "'Moor-SA,'" p. 146.

23. On the events Kershaw, *Hitler*, vol. 1, pp. 629–657.

24. Sofsky, *Ordnung*, p. 116.

25. See Orth, *Konzentrationslager-SS*, pp. 33–37; Riedle, *Kommandanturstab*, pp. 43–49.

26. Sofsky, *Ordnung*, p. 122.

27. Reyer, "Bedrohlicher Alltag," p. 84.

28. Morsch, *Sachsenhausen*, p. 25.

29. Ibid., p. 44.

30. Morsch, *Exzess- und Direkttäter*, p. 57.

31. *ECG* vol.1, "Esterwegen, IKL," p. 66.

32. Riedle, *Kommandanturstab*, p. 44; Certificate of service, BArch, SSO Niemann.

33. Riedle, *Kommandanturstab*, p. 46.

34. Morsch, *Sachsenhausen*, p. 87.

35. Ibid., pp. 90–91.

36. Morsch, *Exzess- und Direkttäter*, pp. 199–201.

37. Riedle has pointed out that this division of tasks was far from absolute, however (Riedle, *Kommandanturstab*, p. 46).

38. Ibid., p. 48.

39. Ibid., pp. 48–49.

40. Ibid, pp. 253–254.

41. Personnel record, BArch, SSO Niemann.

42. See Heinen, *Ordensburg*, p. 47; on the Ordensburg centers also Ring/Wunsch, *Herrenmensch*.

43. Additional Ordensburg centers were in the planning stages, but were never built.

44. The construction of the buildings planned at Vogelsang was never completed, but outwardly, the Ordensburg achieved its purpose and provided magnificent images. When the war began, almost all the Ordensjunker were called up for service in the Wehrmacht. Several hundred were later deployed as territorial commissioners, or *Gebietskommissare*, in the occupied Polish and Soviet territories. There they organized the occupation administrations, as well as the robbery and suppression of the local population, and were also willing helpers in the murder of the Jewish population. Sixty-nine percent of the fanatical Ordensjunker did not survive their wartime deployment (Heinen, *Ordensburg*, p. 119).

45. In total, 240,000 of these marriage applications were filed, see the section "Rassenauslese und Heiratsgenehmigungen in der SS," in: Heinemann, *Rasse- und Siedlungshauptamt*, pp. 50–62.

46. Schwarz, *Frau*, p. 33.

47. For details about Henriette Niemann, see chapter 10 in this volume.

48. Handwritten curriculum vitae by Henriette Niemann, BArch, RS Niemann.

49. Curriculum vitae by Johann Niemann, BArch, SSO Niemann.

Photos from the Niemann Collection, up to 1942

Figure 2.1. Johann Niemann in SS uniform, probably in 1939, and Henriette Frey, presumably in the fall of 1939. The couple married on December 26, 1939. The two photos are glued on the first page of the early album with embossed cover, "2nd SS Death's-Head Unit 'Brandenburg'" ("*2. SS T.V. 'Brandenburg'*").

Figure 2.2. Niemann (*right*), possibly during his training as a journeyman house painter, undated.

Figure 2.3. Henriette Niemann, presumably in 1940. Labeled "Henny" by her husband in his album.

Figures 2.4 and 2.5. Nazi symbolism in the area of the commandant's office at the Esterwegen concentration camp, between May 1934 and the summer of 1935. Niemann labeled both photos "Esterwegen" in his album.

Figure 2.6. Housing area for the guards in Esterwegen, between May 1934 and October 1936. A similar fence made of birch branches in front of the barracks appears in Niemann's photos from the Sobibor death camp, taken in 1943.

Figure 2.7. SS marching formation near Esterwegen, between 1934 and 1936. Labeled "Marching out" by Niemann in his album.

Figure 2.8. SA formation, probably in 1934. In his album, Niemann labeled the photo "Awarding the honor dagger at Esterwegen."

Figure 2.9. Visit by Heinrich Himmler (*center*) in Esterwegen on March 6, 1935. To his left, his adjutant Karl Wolff; in civilian dress, Reichsleiter Martin Bormann. *Far right*, the camp commandant, Hans Loritz. Niemann's label in the album: "Himmler in Esterwegen."

Figure 2.10. The Esterwegen concentration camp, between May 1934 and August 1936. Niemann's label: "Drill."

Figure 2.11. SS recruits peeling potatoes in front of kitchen barracks, between May 1934 and August 1936. Labeled in the album: "Esterwegen."

Figure 2.12. Tine to unwind for the guard personnel in Esterwegen, between May 1934 and August 1936. Niemann is in the third row, at far left. His label: "Colorful evening [*Bunter Abend*]."

Figure 2.13. Members of the guard force between October 1934 and July 1935. *First row, far right*, Niemann as a low-ranking SS man. Label in the album: "Esterwegen."

Figure 2.14. Reenacted scene of a slaughter, presumably during the period in Esterwegen between May 1934 and August 1936. Kneeling, with a pail, is Johann Niemann. Beneath the photo, he wrote "Butchering." The can is marked "trash."

Figure 2.15. *Left*, Niemann, with the rank of SS-Rottenführer, between March 1936 and August 1938. In the album, he noted: "Excursion."

Figure 2.16. View of Ordensburg Vogelsang, a Nazi training center for future leaders, around 1937. Photo caption: "Vogelsang."

Figure 2.17. View of the tower building, the so-called assembly hall, with an auditorium and dining hall, around 1937. Niemann noted in his album: "Vogelsang Castle."

Figure 2.18. The honor guard in the Adlerhof, the central area of Ordensburg Vogelsang, view to the south, presumably taken in the spring of 1937. Label in the album: "Vogelsang, changing of the guard."

Figure 2.19. Two guards at the entrance to the Adlerhof, view to the east. Niemann noted under the photo: "Post 17."

Figure 2.20. Welcoming Adolf Hitler in the Adlerhof of Ordensburg Vogelsang on the occasion of a Gauleiters (Nazi district leaders) conference, November 20, 1936. Half concealed by flowers, behind Hitler, is Richard Manderbach, the commandant of the Ordensburg; to the right, Robert Bauer, commandant of the Nazi Ordensburg Sonthofen. Niemann's inscription: "The Führer at Vogelsang."

Figure 2.21. Ordensburg commandant Richard Manderbach (*center*) with a delegation of the Italian Fascist Balilla youth organization, in 1937. Caption in the album: "Visit of the Italians."

Figure 2.22. Looking west at the large outdoor stage, the "Thing-Stätte" of the Ordensburg, and the athletic field behind it, around 1937. Under the photo, Niemann noted: "Harvest festival."

Figure 2.23. The grandstand for the outdoor stage during the celebration on May 1, 1937, simultaneously the topping-out ceremony for the facilities. Labeled in the album: "Vogelsang, guard mount."

Figure 2.24. *Left*, Niemann at Vogelsang, probably in the spring of 1937.

Figure 2.25. *Standing, fourth from the right*, Niemann, probably in the spring of 1937. Photo caption: "Target practice, Vogelsang."

Figure 2.26. Vogelsang, probably in the spring of 1937. Niemann, standing at the very back against the light, is on the left. Photo caption in the album: "In the guardroom."

Figure 2.27. Presumably during the time at Vogelsang in the spring of 1937; Niemann is on the right.

Figure 2.28. Staging of a joke scene, presumably in the spring of 1937. At the center, bending over and with his arm pulled in, is Johann Niemann. His label for this photo: "Vogelsang, farewell."

Figure 2.29. Guard personnel in a barracks room at the Sachsenhausen concentration camp, between September 1938 and the fall of 1939. At the back, standing, is Niemann, now with the rank of SS-Unterscharführer.

Figure 2.30. Niemann (*second from left*) in the headquarters area of the Sachsenhausen concentration camp, between September 1938 and the fall of 1939. Label in the album: "Oranienburg." Inscription on the photo: "As a friendly memento, your friend Jonny."

Figure 2.31. Henriette Frey and Johann Niemann. Because he is not wearing a wedding ring and she has a ring on her left hand, the photo presumably was taken in 1939 before the couple married.

Figure 2.32. Niemann as an SS-Unterscharführer. Studio photograph taken between September 1938 and April 1939. His inscription: "Memento, Johann Niemann, September 5, 1939."

Figure 2.33. Studio portrait of Henriette Frey, in the summer of 1939 at the latest. She used the same print for the personal information form in her marriage records for the Race and Settlement Main Office (*Rasse- und Siedlungshauptamt*, RuSHA). Caption in the album: "Henny."

Figure 2.34. The couple's first child, April 1940. Caption: "August, 6 months."

Figure 2.35. The brothers Johann, Karl, and Bernhard Niemann (*left to right*), between August 1941 and August 1942.

Figure 2.36. Studio portrait of Johann Niemann as an SS-Oberscharführer, between August 1941 and August 1942.

3

Johann Gerhard Niemann

From Völlen to Sobibor, Part II

KARIN GRAF AND FLORIAN ROSS

Berlin

In November 1939, Johann Niemann walked into the Chancellery of the Führer (*Kanzlei des Führers*, KdF) on Voßstraße in Berlin. He had been detailed for a special mission. Hitler's personal chancellery had just begun to carry out the Nazis' "euthanasia" program, the systematic murder of people alleged to have mental and physical disabilities.[1]

On this day, along with Niemann, the Waffen-SS members Kurt Franz, Herbert Floß, Fritz Jirmann, Josef Oberhauser, and Gottfried Schwarz received information about their future activities. Franz, Floß, and Jirmann had been detailed for this work from the Buchenwald concentration camp, Oberhauser came together with Niemann from the Sachsenhausen concentration camp, and Schwarz had previously been deployed in Dachau. The six SS men were shown a propaganda film that presented patients from mental hospitals. Following this, they were told that these people were a burden on the "racial community" (*Volksgemeinschaft*) and had to be killed. This program was a "top secret matter," they were informed, and the SS men had to sign a "red certification," a statement binding them to secrecy with regard to their future work.

Johann Niemann had learned on this day what his specific tasks in the planned program of murder would be. For him, the day must have begun with a sense of curious anticipation. Eight years after he had joined the SA in the East Frisian province and two months into the Second World War, he was summoned to a control center of power in Nazi Germany. Senior officials were looking after him, wanting him to take part in a "top secret matter," together with important physicians and other actors representing the interests of the state. What Niemann was thinking when he left the KdF building remains an open question. His SS comrade Werner Dubois, called to Berlin for the same reason, described the situation in an interrogation after the war: "Furthermore, we were told that gas chambers would be built, in which the victims would be gassed, and that the victims would be cremated afterward. We were supposed to help with that."[2] Dubois characterized his thoughts after the swearing-in without ambiguity: "After Blankenburg had given me the explanations about the 'euthanasia' program, I was shocked, to be sure. But because I had joined the SS voluntarily and given my oath of allegiance, it was also clear to me that I had to obey. That's why I thought that there was no way out for me."[3]

45

Signing the pledge of secrecy also meant that Niemann took off his SS uniform. Now he was no longer outwardly identifiable as a member of the SS, but rather was part of a conspiracy to commit murder. In the department store Peek & Cloppenburg, and accompanied by a coworker from the "euthanasia" program, he was furnished with civilian clothing. In the weeks that followed, he and his five SS comrades lived in a boardinghouse, Pension Kunz, in the Hallesches Tor area of Berlin. At midday, the group dined together in the Lucullus restaurant.[4] They stayed in Berlin for a few weeks, waiting for their marching orders.

Grafeneck

Before Christmas 1939, Johann Niemann was detailed to the Swabian Jura region and moved into his quarters in the Samaritan Foundation's Grafeneck Castle, around thirty miles (fifty km) from Tübingen. In early October 1939 the castle had already been appropriated "for purposes of the Reich" and then expanded and developed as a future killing center, the Grafeneck Regional Mental Hospital (*Landespflegeanstalt Grafeneck*). Approximately 220 yards (200 m) from his quarters was the place where Niemann—in days to come known as a "burner" or "disinfector," euphemisms for the men tasked with cremating the victims—would perform his daily duties. In a utility building, a gas chamber was erected, with the appropriate installations, and a newly constructed barracks building housed a crematorium with three mobile ovens. The mass murder in Grafeneck began on January 18, 1940, with the violent death of twenty-five patients from the Eglfing-Haar Mental Hospital, in Bavaria, in this gas chamber.[5] For Niemann, the special assignment given him in the abstract in Berlin thus became a reality and a daily routine. He pulled the bodies of the murder victims out of the gas chamber and incinerated them in the ovens. What that meant in concrete terms was described

in 1945 by Vinzenz Nohel, who performed the same function at the Hartheim killing center near Linz on the Danube: "Once the ventilation was done, we stokers [burners] had to [...] carry the corpses away from the gas chamber and take them to the mortuary. Moving the corpses from the gas room to the mortuary was a very difficult and nerve-wracking job. It was not always easy to untangle the corpses, which were all twisted together, and drag them into the mortuary. This work was hampered at first by the fact that the floor was uneven, and when they poured a concrete floor, it was rough and bumpy. Later on, once the floor was tiled, we poured water on it. That made it considerably easier to move the dead bodies. In the mortuary, the corpses were stacked up. Next to the mortuary was the furnace. It was equipped with a so-called pan, which could be taken out of the oven. The dead bodies were laid onto this pan and pushed into the furnace, just the way it works with a baker's oven, and put down inside. [...] The work continued day and night, if necessary. Before the dead bodies were incinerated, the stokers extracted the gold teeth of those deceased who were designated with a cross. After the corpses were cremated, the bone fragments that had fallen through the oven grate were put into a bone mill and ground to fine particles there. Because the work was very strenuous and, as I said before, nerve-wracking, we got a quarter of a liter of schnaps per day."[6]

At the Grafeneck killing center too, the "working ability" of the "burners" was ensured by means of alcohol, as Heinrich Unverhau, detached to Operation T4 (*Aktion T4*) as a medical orderly, reported during the investigations in preparation for the Grafeneck trial in 1948: "For example, I can still remember that the people who operated the combustion ovens, that is, Schwarz, Oberhauser, etc., drank like fish. But huge quantities of alcohol were made available to them, too."[7]

While emotions were numbed by alcohol, the ideological stance was supposed to be reinforced by political indoctrination. Unverhau continued: "In general, to ease our conscience, they frequently gave talks to us, in which they tried to use statistics, examples, etc., to make clear to us the necessity of this operation. Lectures of this kind were also given on various occasions by directors of mental hospitals. Economic statistics played a special role in the lectures. For example, speakers pointed out how many houses could be built for the money it cost to take care of the mentally ill, or told us how many parentless and destitute children could be educated, etc. They also tried to convince us that this method of doing away with people was the most humane one imaginable, as the patients would just fall asleep while breathing the gas and cease to feel anything more."[8]

Alcohol and political indoctrination, however, did not conceal from the men the fact that they were involved in systematic murder. Some of the T4 men were mindful that they, as coperpetrators and accessories, might themselves be done away with after the murders of patients were at an end. Heinrich Gley, also involved in the "euthanasia" program, said during his interrogation: "The rumors that the members of T4 would themselves be liquidated after the 'euthanasia' operation was ended, to get rid of witnesses or for other reasons, [such as] the reputation of the NSDAP, of the Third Reich, after the final victory, was already making the rounds at Grafeneck in 1940. According to the rumors, the members of T4 would be loaded onto trucks and then intercepted by a Sonderkommando and liquidated immediately. A second rumor alleged that the relatives of the participants in the 'euthanasia' program would be sent on a KdF [here *Kraft durch Freude*, Strength through Joy] boat trip, and then the boat, with all hands aboard, would be sunk."[9]

Cracks in the edifice of loyalty also become visible in the efforts made by the T4 participants to arrange transfers for themselves. Johann Niemann's SS comrades Josef Oberhauser and Gottfried Schwarz allegedly refused, after around three months at Grafeneck, to continue working as burners. As a result, they had to report to Viktor Brack at the Chancellery of the Führer and subsequently were transferred to the Brandenburg killing center, also part of the "euthanasia" program.[10] More than a year later, in June 1941, Oberhauser made a fresh attempt to obtain a transfer back to his previous duty station, Sachsenhausen. Apparent here is an endeavor to keep his own risk manageable, as personal consequences for the SS men could not be gauged at this point in time. Oberhauser wrote to the administration of the Bernburg killing center: "With the present letter, I venture to request my transfer back to the headquarters staff of the Sachsenhausen concentration camp in Oranienburg. The reasons are as follows: The task assigned to me here, which I have had to perform for almost 2 years now, has been so difficult for me lately because of my health that I think I must request to be replaced, if my health is not to suffer harm. In so doing, I note that I am forced to observe a significant weight loss, despite good meals and a work load that is not excessive. I am a career soldier, and my sole wish is to be permitted to return to my unit."[11]

In view of these efforts to be released from the murder program, it is necessary to mention that it was precisely SS men such as Schwarz and Oberhauser who, like Niemann, became central actors at the subsequent deployment sites in Poland, key figures in the implementation of the extermination program.[12] How Johann Niemann came to terms with his involvement in the "euthanasia" murders, whether he had doubts or played his part without perceptible conflicts, remains unclear. In the photos from the Grafeneck period, Niemann and his co-perpetrators Gottfried Schwarz and Siegfried Graetschus pose in the snow in front of the castle (see figs. 3.1–3.5). The images bear witness to the effort to document the SS men's "normal life" beyond the daily routine of murder.

With his work in Grafeneck, Niemann now entered into a period of intensive learning. He gained experience in the methods of murdering people in a gas chamber as quickly and efficiently as possible and then cremating their bodies in ovens.

Along with his SS comrades, Niemann thus belonged to a small group of men who possessed this practical knowledge. The idea of deploying these experts, with their specialized know-how, to construct and start up additional killing centers immediately suggested itself. Josef Oberhauser, during interrogation, described this function as a kind of advance construction squad: "In Grafeneck we were housed in an old castle that had previously served as a children's home. Around 660 feet [200 m] from the castle, the men on detached duty at Grafeneck then erected approximately 6 barracks. Even while building these barracks, we wondered what their purpose might be [. . .]. Then, a short time later, the first transports of mental patients also arrived, and they were exterminated in the barracks we had built [. . .]. From Grafeneck, I went with my detachment to Brandenburg [. . .]. In the Brandenburg jail, we enlarged the existing cells by breaking through the walls and restored other facilities; the pipelines for the gas chambers were laid again by the special detachment of the RSHA [*Reichssicherheitshauptamt,* the Reich Security Main Office]. [. . .] In Bernburg, a wing in the local asylum was provided with gas chambers; the warden there, Professor Entke, refused at first to let these gas chambers be installed in the asylum and thus managed to drag out the construction of the gas chambers by about 4 weeks. In the end, however, he had to relent, and the gas chambers were fitted out here too, like the ones in Brandenburg."[13]

The tasks of this advance detachment were not limited to construction projects; quite probably they also included familiarizing other actors with the trade of killing, all the way to the burning of corpses. The existence of this group of experts in the "euthanasia" program is not described in any documents, as those responsible practiced extensive concealment and later got rid of files and records; nonetheless, it can be deduced from the statements of former perpetrators. To ensure that the process of murder went without a hitch, it ultimately stood to reason that the construction of a new "euthanasia" center should be carried out and supervised by experienced operators. This circle of proven men also included Johann Niemann. His path, comparable to that of Josef Oberhauser, led him from Grafeneck to Brandenburg and from there to Bernburg. Also indicative of the functioning of the small advance unit is the fact that the SS men who gathered again in Poland in the late fall of 1941 were the very ones who, two years earlier in the Chancellery of the Führer, had jointly been engaged for the "euthanasia" program. Their activities in the "euthanasia" institutions predestined them later for the construction of the killing centers of Operation Reinhard.

Brandenburg

Three photos from the Brandenburg "euthanasia" center testify to the presence of Johann Niemann there (see figs. 3.6–3.8). The premises of the former jail were compact and cramped. The pathways of the personnel were short, functional, and reduced to eating, sleeping, and killing. At least seventeen active SS men worked in Brandenburg.[14] Walter Stephan, a driver in those days, said in his statement that an SS detail was responsible for the gassing and incineration, and he emphasized its partial isolation and aloofness with respect to the other employees: "These were all enlisted men, with whom we otherwise didn't come into contact; also, they were very reserved in their dealings with us."[15] Visits by the T4 men to the inns that were just opposite were not encouraged by those in charge. For entertainment, social evenings were arranged. The special role they played in Brandenburg resulted in a close-knit collective with strongly developed esprit de corps.

From February to October 28, 1940, 9,972 persons were murdered in the Brandenburg "euthanasia" center. The oldest victim was an eighty-seven-year-old man, a long-term psychiatric patient from the Berlin-Buch Mental Institution; the youngest victims were four two-year-old children from the Brandenburg regional institution in Görden.[16]

Around 330 feet (100 meters [m]) from the accommodation building for the T4 men was the institution's barn, with the gas chamber disguised as a shower room and the separate room with the poison gas stored in steel cylinders. The victims were killed on the very day of their arrival. In Brandenburg too, it was the job of the SS men to pry out the gold teeth of the dead and then bring the corpses to the combustion furnaces.[17] The mobile ovens were installed right next door. The driver Walter Stephan described the difficulties of keeping the killing center a secret in the midst of the small town of Brandenburg. The arriving transports could easily be observed from the neighboring houses, and flames and smoke rose every day from the chimneys, which lacked the proper height. This soon led to speculations among the local population. The locals lodged protests, as did the guardianship judge at the Brandenburg District Court, Lothar Kreyssig, and various church dignitaries.[18] According to Stephan, in early July 1940 an employee of the local Criminal Police (Kriminalpolizei) paid a visit to the "euthanasia" center, though he was "energetically" denied entry.[19] In the summer of 1940, the burning of the corpses was transferred to a facility in the village of Paterdamm, around four miles (six km) away, strictly guarded and well disguised as a chemical and technical testing plant.

As indicated by the photo of Johann Niemann and two of his SS comrades on the banks of the Niederhavel during their free time (see figs. 3.7–3.8), he was presumably on-site in Brandenburg in the line of duty at the time of this reorganization. From then on, the corpse transports were specially arranged during the early morning hours, but the killing center nonetheless proved unsuitable for long-term use because of the rumors circulating among the locals and the substantial added expense

for incineration of the corpses. On October 28, 1940, therefore, the Brandenburg killing center was closed, and the personnel relocated to Bernburg an der Saale, around 120 miles (200 km) away.[20]

Bernburg

Here, in a separate part of the Bernburg Regional Sanatorium and Mental Hospital, a new "euthanasia" center began its terrible work on November 21, 1940. It was located at the edge of the small town in the vicinity of Dessau and included several buildings within a spacious hospital area. By August 1941, 9,385 persons who were ill or in need of care—men, women, and children—from close to forty welfare and care facilities were killed in Bernburg. In total, around 140 men and women worked at the killing center. At peak periods in the spring of 1941, there were approximately seventy to eighty people working there at a given time.[21] The Niemann collection includes ten photos from his time in Bernburg. They show the twenty-seven-year-old SS-Scharführer in front of and inside his communal living quarters at the killing center and on walks during his free time (see figs. 3.9–3.18).

One of the photographs even shows Niemann's wife, Henriette, among the T4 perpetrators at Bernburg. She apparently came on a visit from Völlen, almost 250 miles (400 km) away, and thus was amazingly close to a scene of the "euthanasia" crimes. Other relationships were just beginning during the "euthanasia" program. Niemann's companion Gottfried Schwarz met his future wife Erna in Bernburg, where she worked in the killing center as a so-called caregiver. Johann Niemann's photos suggest that at all his places of employment, including Bernburg, the men and women working for the T4 organization constituted an insular and closed community.[22] Contact with the local population or the employees of the adjacent Anhalt

Clinic for Nervous Diseases was undesirable. For leisure-time activities, the personnel were provided with a recreation building, known as the staff club, and sports facilities.

Erna Schwarz, indicted after the war for her actions in Bernburg and prosecuted in the Magdeburg Regional Court in 1948, recalled Niemann, who was also deployed as a "burner" at this killing center: "The burning of the corpses was carried out by SS men who had been specially detailed by the SS for precisely that purpose. There were five men, one of whom later became my husband. These five SS men were Johannes [sic!] Niemann from East Frisia, Josef Oberhauser from Munich, Gottfried Schwarz (my husband), who was killed in action in 1944, Karl Tötzingen, and Siegfried Graetschus."[23]

The workplace of Johann Niemann was located in the basement of a nondescript building on the grounds in Bernburg. The killing process was strictly screened off from the rest of the operations at the facility. The victims were taken by Reich Postal Service buses into a wooden garage located just opposite, and led through a closed corridor to the ground floor of the building. As a general rule, the killing took place immediately after arrival. After the intake procedure on the ground floor, the people, already undressed and draped in old military overcoats, were taken to the rooms in the cellar.[24] The caregivers forced them—often despite their fierce resistance—into the gas chamber. The floor slab of the room had been elevated to reduce the volume and optimize the effect of the gas. Post-war accounts frequently ascribe the handling of the gas supply to the physicians present in the facilities, but it is likely that the SS men assigned as "burners" often carried out this task. Inge Schellenberg, employed as a T4 stenotypist in Bernburg, testified that it was even the rule that the T4 men took on this duty. She stated that two shifts, headed by Schwarz and Oberhauser, had this responsibility on a rotating basis.[25] Niemann, along with other "burners," waited on a wooden bench in a small room directly next to the gas chamber. Women, children, and

men died a horrible death behind the door. Inge Schellenberg reported that she had learned in conversations with nurses who were present that "the gassing took 20 to 30 minutes."[26] Together with the ventilation of the chambers, the entire killing process lasted approximately one hour. Then the actual work of Johann Niemann and his colleagues began. They sprayed the corpses with water, heaved them across a step into a tiled corridor about 50 feet (15 m) long, dragged them to the incinerators or the mortuary in the cellar, and burned them.[27]

In connection with the continuing protests by bereaved family members and from church circles, the murders of patients were officially halted in August 1941 at Hitler's direction. The KdF organizers, however, assumed that it was to be only a temporary interruption. Richard von Hegener, a Chancellery official with the party political rank of chief area leader (*Hauptstellenleiter*) who was involved with the murders of patients, recalled that he had "continued to work for this operation [. . .] to a certain extent for quite some time [. . .] as we assumed with confidence that the halt would soon be called off again and the operation would go on."[28] In anticipation of a resumption of the "euthanasia" program after the war was over, if not sooner, those in charge tried hard to keep the well-practiced personnel of the gassing centers available to them. Since April of that year, other groups of people had come into the focus of the Nazis' program of murder, and there was a desire to take advantage of the experience available at the "euthanasia" killing centers in Hartheim, Pirna-Sonnenstein, and Bernburg. Under the identifier "Operation 14f13," physicians who had already worked for T4 as evaluators were now screening prisoners in the concentration camps, separating out those who were deemed "unfit for work" or "racially undesirable." At Johann Niemann's deployment site in Bernburg, five thousand concentration camp prisoners were murdered, beginning in August 1941.[29] In recognition of his services, Niemann was promoted to Oberscharführer that same month. In his autobiographic notes, he stated that from September 1, 1941, he found "further use in deployment in the East."[30] Because this follow-on deployment in Poland quite probably began only some time later, however, it can be assumed that Niemann actually stayed a few weeks longer in Bernburg and presumably also undertook his tried-and-tested duties at the beginning of Operation 14f13.

Three photos from Austria's Attersee in the photo collection (see figs. 3.19–3.22) document in addition the fact that, together with his wife, Henriette, and another couple, Herbert and Danida Floß, he spent several days in September 1941 in Villa Schoberstein, the T4 rest and recreation facility.[31] What Niemann paraphrased as his new "use" ultimately took him in the fall of 1941 to District Lublin in occupied Poland.

Construction of Belzec

In the late fall of 1941, old acquaintances gradually gathered in the small town of Bełżec: Josef Oberhauser, Friedrich Jirmann, Gottfried Schwarz, and Johann Niemann. They all had been members of the "euthanasia" staff from the outset and had been involved, at their respective deployment sites, in the development of the killing centers. This group of SS comrades was joined by Lorenz Hackenholt. Together, they were tasked with creating a "test camp" for the murder of Polish Jews. That required both the building of the camp infrastructure and the development of a suitable method for the killings. The five men could do the job at hand only by exhibiting a talent for organization and improvisation and, above all, a great deal of personal initiative. During the first few weeks in Bełżec, Niemann and the others lodged with Polish families in the village. In December 1941, the SS men confiscated two buildings belonging to the Polish railway, which still stand directly along the road connecting Lublin and Lviv (formerly Lwów). In those days, they were approximately 550 yards (500 m) from the grounds of the subsequent killing center. During the months after their

move, the Germans built their housing and administrative area here.

Two images from Johann Niemann's photo collection show him on the grounds of the commandant's office in the winter of 1941/42 (see figs. 5.2–5.3). One of the buildings was used exclusively as accommodations. Here, Niemann temporarily shared a room with Werner Dubois, his SS comrade from the days of the murders of institutionalized patients in the territory of the Reich. Using Polish craftsmen and Jewish forced laborers as a workforce, the SS men acquired the necessary materials and organized the construction of the new killing center. In the process, they initially drew on their experience in the "euthanasia" program. Over the course of several weeks, they experimented with carbon monoxide from gas cylinders, which were brought from Lwów. Eventually Niemann and the others had refined the principle of the "euthanasia" facilities and designed a gas chamber into which gas produced by a tank engine could now be channeled.[32]

Beginning of Operation Reinhard

Shortly before the killing operation began, just over a dozen additional T4 men came to Belzec to join Niemann's original group of participants in the camp's construction. In the period that followed, there were never more than twnety Germans deployed in the camp at a given time. In all, we know the names of thirty-seven German perpetrators who took part in the murders in Belzec. The Germans were supported by a group of so-called Trawnikis, consisting of as many as 120 men. For the most part, they were Soviet POWs who, after a short training course in a camp located in the nearby village of Trawniki, had entered into the service of the Germans and were subordinate to the SS- and Police Leader in Lublin, Odilo Globocnik.[33] Trawnikis were used in the General Government during the liquidation of ghettos and in various camps, including the three Operation Reinhard camps that were activated, one after the other, in 1942. In Belzec they were under Niemann's command during the construction and start-up phase.

The mass murder in Belzec on March 17, 1942, marked the beginning of what was later known as Operation Reinhard. In the morning, a deportation train from the ghetto in Lwów arrived at the camp, followed in the afternoon by one from the Lublin ghetto. In the next four weeks, approximately seventy thoussand Jews were murdered in the new gas chambers of Belzec, a volume of destruction never before achieved in the context of a Nazi camp structure. After further modification during the initial phase, the death camp was spatially divided into two separate areas, linked by an access point. Camp I, also called the lower camp, housed the Trawnikis used as helpers and the Jewish prisoners selected for forced labor in the camp. Also located in this area were workshops, a camp kitchen, and additional barracks that were part of the camp's infrastructure. In addition, a rail spur ran from the railroad station directly into the lower camp, where the journey of the death trains ended at the so-called ramp. The second part of the camp was known as the upper camp. Here the victims were killed in the gas chambers and their corpses were hastily buried in mass graves. In the formal camp hierarchy, Camp II belonged to the sphere of responsibility of the deputy commandant, Gottfried Schwarz.

According to the postwar statements of members of the camp staff, although Schwarz was basically responsible for both areas, it was Johann Niemann who actually was the head of the upper camp. In the view of SS man Robert Jührs, Niemann even "worked exclusively in the gassing area."[34] A detailed report on this work area of Niemann's by one of the few survivors of the Belzec camp has been preserved. Rudolf Reder had been deported from Lwów to Belzec on August 16, 1942.[35] On the ramp, he was selected for work in Camp II. After the war he described his daily routine in Belzec: "With every transport it went the same as with mine. They were ordered to undress, the belongings were left in the yard, Irrman [sic] always gave his deceitful speech, and always the same one. People always cheered up at that moment, I saw the spark of hope in their eyes. The hope that they were going to work. But an instant later, the little ones were torn away from the mothers, the old and the sick were thrown onto stretchers, men and little girls were prodded with rifle butts further and further along the fenced-in path leading straight to the chambers, and the naked women were steered just as brutally to the second barracks where their hair was shaved off. I could tell precisely at which moment everyone understood what was awaiting them, and the horror, despair, cries and horrible moans mingled with the notes of the orchestra. The men were driven in first with bayonets, stabbed as they ran to the gas chambers. The askars [a reference to the Trawniki guards] counted 750 into each chamber. By the time they filled all six chambers, the people in the first chamber had been suffering two hours already. Only when all six chambers were so tightly packed with people that it was difficult to close the doors, was the motor started. [. . .] The machine ran for twenty minutes by the clock. They shut it down after twenty minutes. Right away the doors of the chambers leading to the ramp were opened from the outside and the corpses were thrown on the ground, making a huge mound of corpses several meters high. [. . .] The calling for help, the screams, the desperate wailing of the people locked in and being smothered in the chambers lasted ten to fifteen minutes, horribly loud, later the groans got quieter and at the end everything quieted."[36]

Besides the gas chamber, there was another killing center in Camp II. At the side of a pit cynically named the "hospital," the old or feeble Jews, those who no longer could walk into the gas chambers on their own two feet, were shot every day.

Apart from the postwar statements indicating Niemann's responsibility for the killing area at Belzec, there exists no detailed evidence of his actions in the camp. Whether Niemann himself took part in the murders there remains just as unclear as his conduct at the entrance to the gas chamber when the naked victims were unwilling to go inside. Without giving a specific name, the Trawniki Aleksandr Zsemigodow described the situation before the murder: "In these cases, the Germans and also a few guards took action and forcibly herded these Jews to their death. They used the bayonet and also whips for this."[37]

In the spring of 1942, after he had carried out his duties in Belzec for a number of weeks, Johann Niemann was temporarily detailed to assist with the building of Sobibor. The knowledge he had acquired in Belzec and previously in the T4 program, was now to be utilized for the construction of the second Operation Reinhard killing center. This allows conclusions to be drawn about the specialized know-how for which Niemann was now well regarded. Among other things, during those weeks in Sobibor along with Erich Fuchs, he procured the engine for the gas chambers there. After that, he returned to Belzec for the time being. In the questioning of the Belzec perpetrators in the West German courts, it is conspicuous that Niemann is mentioned rather seldom and then only peripherally, although he obviously played a significant role in the death camp. From the fragments of statements concerning Niemann, however, it is possible to reconstruct the fact that he held a leading position in the hierarchy of the German camp personnel. Thus, it seems conclusive that Niemann, in the memory of former comrades, maintained a close work relationship with his boss, Christian Wirth, and "was entrusted with special assignments" by him, as the SS man Erich Bauer testified after the war.[38]

During his affiliation with the camp staff at Belzec, Niemann was involved in the killing of approximately 250,000 Jews. He had entered a "space of violence" that was in no sense comparable to the dimensions of the "euthanasia" program. While a bus had taken fifty people to Grafeneck, Brandenburg, or Bernburg, a single train now brought as many as five thousand persons to Belzec. In carrying out his duties, Niemann

doubtless exhibited leadership qualities. In Belzec, he had proven his ability to guide the killing process in Camp II, and at the same time he had the social skills to lead the men under his command. In September 1942, a new step on the career ladder presented itself. He was transferred to another death camp and once again moved into a higher position.

Sobibor

The initial organization of the Treblinka killing center in the summer of 1942 gave rise to an exchange of personnel between the German staffs of the Operation Reinhard camps. The former commandant of Sobibor, Franz Stangl, assumed the same post in Treblinka. Kurt Franz also left Belzec for Treblinka and became deputy commandant under Stangl. Johann Niemann, in turn, was ordered back to Sobibor and was named deputy camp commandant there.[39] Immediately after commencing his duties, he even acted as commandant for a short time, because the actual new head of the camp, Franz Reichleitner, had not yet arrived. Niemann's central role in the camp from this point on has been underappreciated in past accounts of the camp's history. Both the Jewish survivors and Niemann's German comrades described him in his new function as an actor with a sweeping presence in the camp's daily routine. Erich Bauer, for example, said that Niemann was "in the know about everything."[40] Heinrich Unverhau, a member of the German camp staff at Sobibor in the summer of 1943, conveyed in one of his postwar statements the impression that the "commandant in Sobibor was a man named Niemann."[41] With respect to daily life in the camp, the statements of Sobibor survivors paint the picture of a perpetrator who "did not meddle in all the small details" but was more inclined to "stand in the background and give orders."[42] The survivor Regina Zielinski recalled that Niemann rarely took part in "unnecessary cruelty" toward the Jewish prisoners outside the context of the work routine and thought it possible that Niemann did not want "to get his hands dirty." Referring to the performance of his murderous mission, however, she described him as "cold and cruel."[43]

Individual cases of direct violence on the part of the deputy camp commandant have been concretely described by survivors. In one instance, he administered corporal punishment for the purpose of maintaining "order" and ordered individual shootings. Kalmen Wewryk of Chełm testified that he had "once been beaten with a whip [. . .] by Niemann single-handedly. He struck me 25 times."[44] The Sobibor survivor Aleksej Waizen told how the SS man from Völlen reacted with absolute callousness in a particular situation: "The neighbor of Neuman [sic] had been brought to the camp. Neuman knew this woman well, he knew her family, and he knew that she was a German by nationality. At first Neuman separated her from the group of prisoners, but later she was shot nevertheless."[45] Hela Weiss, a Jew, recalled especially clearly how Niemann had set dogs on the Jewish prisoners to entertain the German SS members.[46] Another survivor, Selma Engel, who was deported to Sobibor from the Netherlands, said that she had feared the notorious German perpetrators of violence Hubert Gomerski, Karl Frenzel, and Gustav Wagner but had also "been especially afraid" of Niemann.[47]

Johann Niemann repeatedly stood with his comrades at the ramp when the transports arrived and the Jews were forced out of the freight cars. The deportees arrived in a state of high anxiety and agitation at this remote railway siding in a strange environment. To calm them and make their imminent murder a smoothly running process, a member of the German camp staff stood before the crowd of people and gave a speech. This task too appears to have been performed by the deputy camp commandant at times. He greeted the Jews with the lie that "they were going to the Ukraine to work, would get appropriate clothing here for that purpose, and should therefore leave their clothes and everything they had with them here, before they

went to the baths."[48] To lend greater credence to his words, for his speech Niemann, like the other German perpetrators in this function, donned a white coat of the kind physicians wear. His "appearances" at the ramp led some of the Jewish prisoners to award him the nickname baldarsher, a Yiddish term meaning "itinerant preacher; lecturer."[49] Niemann was forced to learn at the ramp that not all the incoming Jews passively acquiesced to their fate. The SS man Karl Frenzel described Niemann's brutal and merciless reaction to such an attack: "It was in 1943, when Barracks 23 and 25 had already been built. Where this transport came from, I don't know. Niemann had made a speech and was attacked. At that provocation, he took a Ukrainian's rifle from him and fired a shot through a window. Niemann had fired into the barracks that contained the Jews who had attacked him."[50]

Some of the statements and reports also provide an insight into Johann Niemann's personal attitude toward mass murder and his Jewish victims. Selma Engel recalled that, along with Karl Frenzel and Franz Wolf, he had made fun of the deported victims.[51] One other personal detail was reported to a fellow sufferer by Johanna Koch, a Jewish kitchen worker at the German staff club in the front compound. During a festivity held by the camp SS, Koch had heard Niemann talking to his "comrades" about the deportation transports expected from the Netherlands in February 1943: Niemann informed them that fresh "salad greens" would arrive in Sobibor in the next month.[52]

In accordance with his new position in Sobibor, Johann Niemann now emerged officially as the organizer of the mass murder. In Camp III, the sector of the camp where the gas chambers and the pits for burial of the dead bodies were located, he was omnipresent, as Karl Frenzel recalled. Frenzel testified later that "Untersturmführer Niemann was in control of everything in Camp III."[53] In the killing area, the Trawnikis were also under Niemann's command.[54] Moreover, he had extended his authority to the other labor detachments too and actively intervened in the so-called selection process. He was present in person at the daily roll calls of the Jewish prisoners and accepted the results of the head-count after review. If the Jews were no longer "fit for work," then they had lost their right to exist, in the Germans' view. Niemann went into the barracks and earmarked sick Jewish prisoners for death. "That's too much! Off to the hospital with them!" he said, according to the statement of Ada Lichtman.[55] Ilona Safran, the only German survivor of the camp, was forced to work in the sorting barracks. She too remembered the central role of the deputy camp commandant, and testified that she "had dealings in particular with Niemann."[56]

The portrayals by the witnesses make it clear that Niemann's actions went far beyond a mere carrying out of orders. He used his comprehensive knowledge of the various areas of operations in the killing center to make the workflow even more efficient. The SS man Kurt Bolender was deployed in Sobibor at the corpse pits where the dead were hastily buried. Niemann, he said, had told him "immediately after the first walkthrough" that "many things in Sobibor still had to be changed."[57] Niemann made purposeful use of his powers and scope of action as deputy commandant in Sobibor, and gave his superiors proof of his leadership skills at decisive points. He obviously had the gift of being able not only to acquire the requisite knowledge for his duties as a manager but also to recognize where and when he needed to step in.

Niemann's superiors acknowledged that, with his abilities and motivation, he played a leading part in the implementation of Operation Reinhard. With his move from Belzec to Sobibor, he was promoted to the rank of SS-Hauptscharführer. Finally, in March 1943, along with his old SS comrades Oberhauser, Schwarz, and Franz, he was put forward for promotion to SS-Untersturmführer. They had been "deployed in Operation Reinhard from the outset and acquitted themselves excellently,"

Odilo Globocnik wrote in his justification of the corresponding application.[58] In June 1943, Niemann officially became an Untersturmführer, the entry-level rank for an SS officer.

In the everyday routine of Sobibor, as is evident in the photos that have survived, Niemann presented himself as a dashing German officer. For him, that obviously included good clothes and symbols of power such as a horse, a dog, and gloves. Various descriptions of him make reference to this and confirm that "he had a well-groomed appearance and was always on horseback."[59] Jakob Biscubicz recalled that Niemann "often [walked] through the camp with a dog, a wolf, a German shepherd."[60] In like manner, Ajzik Rotenberg described Niemann's central position in the camp: "He was a tall man, he always rode his horse through the camp and gave orders to the Germans."[61]

While Johann Niemann mercilessly tore families apart at the ramp in Sobibor and steered men, women, and children to their death, with respect to his own kin, he showed himself to be a caring and protective family man, even at a distance. In many statements, survivors describe how the SS men shamelessly enriched themselves from the belongings of the victims and shipped objects of all kinds to the territory of the Reich. Ada Lichtman recalled: "We prepared parcels, clothing parcels, for almost all the officers, and included in the parcels were very lovely things, also dolls for their children [. . .] In particular Frenzel, Wagner, and Naumann [sic], who wanted dolls for their children."[62] It is conceivable that Niemann not only supplied his wife and two children—his daughter Johanne had been born on May 25, 1942—with clothing but also bestowed gifts on his eight siblings and their families. On August 20, 1943, Niemann took the time to write a letter to his wife, "Dear Henny." Immediately after asking whether "all is well at home," Niemann told his wife that he was doing "very well, personally." In addition, he wrote that he had been informed by Berlin that he was "going to Italy in 5 weeks, and specifically to Trieste." Writing in platitudes, he commented on his announced transfer: "But Henny, what can you do, we have to do our duty wherever they put us."[63] For Niemann, ever since his agreement to be part of the "euthanasia" program in the fall of 1939, this duty consisted of a central and active role in the murder of thousands of human beings in Grafeneck, Brandenburg, and Bernburg, and then in the killing of hundreds of thousands of Jews in occupied Poland at Belzec and Sobibor.

It was Niemann's weakness for elegant clothes and his proclivity for personal enrichment that were to be his fatal undoing on October 14, 1943. Jewish prisoners in Sobibor had been planning an uprising for months. On the afternoon of October 14, they struck out, launching an attack on the SS men. Johann Niemann was to be the first. The Dutch Jew Jules Schelvis stood on the ramp in Sobibor in May 1943. Together with 80 other men, he was selected for work in the Dorohucza labor camp. He survived the Holocaust and the war and returned to the Netherlands. Decades later, he wrote a standard work on the history of the Sobibor killing center. In his book, he reconstructed the last minutes in the life of Johann Niemann.

"In order to lure Niemann into the tailors' barracks, one of the messengers had gone over and told Niemann just before 3:30 pm that he had been sent by Mosche Hochman, the tailors' foreman. 'I must pass a message from him to you, Herr Untersturmführer, to let you know that he is making a very fine leather coat for you. He thinks you should try it on first before he can continue working on it, though.' Niemann, who had a penchant for nice clothes and well-tailored uniforms, said he would be over as quickly as possible. Fifteen minutes later, having collected his horse from the stables, he came riding across at a leisurely pace, his whip elegantly tucked under his arm. As he dismounted his horse near the barracks, he noticed Srulek, the baker. He ordered him to hold the reins until he returned. Niemann then strolled in his customary fashion, hands behind his back, to the tailors' barracks. He probably saw himself already in the beautiful coat, going home on his

next leave and showing it to his wife. Of course, he would not tell her he was serving at a death camp and that the coat had belonged to a murdered Jew. Any thought may have crossed his mind at that point but probably not that these were the last steps he would ever take. As he entered the barracks, the man at the door called out the obligatory 'Achtung!' which made everyone jump to attention. Niemann responded with his customary 'Weitermachen!' (Carry on). [. . .] The first thing he sat his greedy eyes on after entering the fitting room was the beautiful leather coat lying on the table. Subserviently, Hochman asked, 'If you like it, would you mind trying it on, Herr Untersturmführer? I am sure it will really suit you.' Sjoebajew [Sjubajew] then stepped forward to gauge whether this was the right time to make his move. Niemann looked at him as he stood there holding his axe. He asked: 'What is that man doing here?' Hochman replied that he had had to make some alterations to the hat-maker's table. Niemann unbuckled his sword belt and took off his uniform jacket. [. . .] Hochman helped him put the coat on, while Niemann was prattling on about how nice it was. Then the tailor asked him to turn around so that he could see if anything needed altering at the back. When Niemann complied, he finally stood in the desired position. At that moment Sjoebajew [Sjubajew] leapt at him with his axe, which landed with a mighty thud on Niemann's head. He managed to scream once, but then was dealt the fatal blow. The body was quickly shoved under a table. The first SS officer had been eliminated according to plan."[64]

Besides Johann Niemann, ten other men from the German camp staff and two Trawnikis were killed by Jewish prisoners during the uprising in Sobibor. Four days later, they were buried in a German military cemetery near Chełm. The Sobibor killing center ceased operations after the revolt. Niemann left behind his young wife, Henriette, age twenty-two, his three-year-old son, August, and his one-year-old daughter, Johanne.

Notes

1. On the role of the Chancellery of the Führer in the "euthanasia" program and Operation Reinhard, see the contribution in this volume by Martin Cüppers.

2. Interrogation of Werner Dubois, September 15, 1971, BArch, B 162/3173.

3. Werner Dubois, September 7, 1961, NIOD, 804/47.

4. Interrogation of Kurt Franz, LNR, Gerichte Rep. 388, No. 743.

5. By December 1940, 10,654 men, women, and children had been killed in Grafeneck. For an overview see Stöckle, *Grafeneck*.

6. Cited in Klee, *"Euthanasie,"* pp. 146–148.

7. Interrogation of Heinrich Unverhau, May 20, 1948, StAS, Wü 29/3 T1 Nr. 1758/03/10.

8. Ibid.

9. Letter from Heinrich Gley, January 23, 1963, StAM, Staw 33033/13.

10. Interrogation of Josef Oberhauser, April 26, 1966, LNW, Q 234/4471.

11. Letter from Oberhauser, BArch, SSO Oberhauser.

12. Schwarz and Oberhauser were first deployed in the Belzec killing center and then assumed a leading role in the Old Airfield (Lublin) and Dorohucza labor camps, which were part of Odilo Globocnik's newly established camp system following the closing of Belzec. See Berger, *Experten*, pp. 261–269.

13. Interrogation of Josef Oberhauser, February 26, 1960, BArch, B 162/3167. By "Brandenburg jail," Oberhauser meant the T4 killing center in the "Old Jail" there.

14. Ley/Hinz-Wessels, *Brandenburg*, p. 141.

15. Interrogation of Walter Stephan, January 26, 1950, BStU, HA IX/11 AS 58/67.

16. For an overview see Ley/Hinz-Wessels, *Brandenburg*.

17. Ibid., p. 77.

18. Klee, *"Euthanasie,"* p. 180.

19. Interrogation of Walter Stephan, January 26, 1950, BStU, HA IX/11 AS 58/67.

20. Friedlander, *Weg*, p. 190.

21. Schulze, *Bernburg*, pp. 134–144.

22. Klee, *"Euthanasie,"* p. 223.

23. Interrogation of Erna Schwarz, July 15, 1966, BStU, HA IX/RF 23428 T.2, Nr. 23428 T1.

24. Schulze, *Bernburg*, p. 34.

25. Copy of interrogation of Inge Schellenberg, January 26, 1948, BStU, HA XX, Nr. 4357.

26. Ibid.

27. Schulze, *Bernburg*, pp. 34–35.

28. Hinz-Wessels, *Tiergartenstr. 4*, p. 93.

29. In total at all three places, as many as 20,000 persons. See Hördler, "Zwangsarbeiter," pp. 232–243.

30. Autobiographic notes by Johann Niemann, BArch, RS Niemann.

31. See the chapter on Henriette Niemann in this volume.

32. On the expansion phase and history of the Belzec killing center, see the contribution by Florian Ross and Steffen Hänschen in this volume.

33. On the origin and function of the Trawniki men in Operation Reinhard, see the contribution by Martin Cüppers in this volume.

34. Interrogation of Robert Jührs, October 11, 1961, StAH, LG NSG 213-12, 0039-042; also interrogation of Werner Dubois, September 15, 1971, NIOD, 804/47.

35. Reder successfully escaped in November 1942 during a work deployment for procurement of various materials for the camp.

36. Reder, "Bełżec", pp. 125 ff.

37. Kuwałek, *Vernichtungslager*, p. 187.

38. Interrogation of Erich Bauer, October 10, 1961, LNW, Q 234/4465.

39. See Berger, *Experten*, pp. 91–162.

40. Interrogation of Erich Bauer, October 10, 1961, LNW, Q 243/4465.

41. Interrogation of Heinrich Unverhau, July 21, 1960, StAH, LG NSG 213-12, 0039-042.

42. Statement of Dov Freiberg, December 23, 1965, LNW, Q 243/4470.

43. Statement of Regina Zielinski, March 15, 1983, LNW, Q 234/4406.

44. Statement of Kalmen Weweryk, March 30, 1984, NIOD, 804/20.

45. Statement of Aleksej Waizen, March 12, 1984, LNW, Q 234/4393.

46. Statement of Hela Weis, March 13, 1975, LNW, Q 234/4481.

47. Statement of Selma Engel, October 21, 1965, LNW, Q 234/4469.

48. Statement of Abraham Kohn, January 18, 1977, NIOD, 804/16.

49. Ibid. Hermann Michel is most frequently mentioned in connection with the speech to the new arrivals.

50. Interrogation of Karl Frenzel, October 10, 1966, LNW, Q 243/4625.

51. Statement of Selma Engel, October 21, 1965, LNW, Q 234/4469.

52. Statement of Hela Weis, March 13, 1975, LNW, Q 234/4481; also Selma Engel, October 21, 1965, LNW, Q 234/4469; letter of Kurt Thomas, December 15, 1949, LNW, Q 234/4481.

53. Interrogation of Karl Frenzel, February 4, 1974, LNW, Q 243/4416.

54. Interrogation of Hubert Gomerski, September 20, 1961, and December 9, 1949, LNW, Q 243/4466.

55. Statement of Ada Lichtman, May 19, 1959, LNW, Q 234/4475. In Sobibor too, the "hospital" was the term used for a pit at whose edge Jews who were old and no longer fit for work were shot.

56. Statement of Ilona Safran, November 8, 1965, LNW, Q 234/4623.

57. Interrogation of Kurt Bolender, October 2, 1963, LNW, Q 234/4293.

58. Copy of promotion nominations, Personal Staff of the Reichsführer-SS, March 29, 1943, BArch, SSO Niemann.

59. Statement of Hela Weis, August 2, 1983, LNW, Q 234/4415; similarly, statement of Dov Freiberg, December 23, 1965, LNW, Q 234/8229.

60. Statement of Jakob Biscubicz, November 11, 1965, LNW, Q 234/4418.

61. Statement of Ajzik Rotenberg, January 18, 1983, LNW, Q 234/4411.

62. Statement of Ada Lichtman, March 3, 1964, LNW, Q 234/4569.

63. Letter from Johann to Henriette Niemann, August 20, 1943, USHMMA, Acc 2020.8.1.

64. Schelvis, *Sobibor*, pp. 161 ff.

Photos from the Niemann Collection from the Period of Operation T4

Figure 3.1. Siegfried Graetschus (*right*) with an unidentified man in front of the T4 killing center at Grafeneck Castle. Graetschus, like Niemann, came to the T4 program from the Sachsenhausen concentration camp. This photograph and the following ones date from early 1940.

Figure 3.2. Siegfried Graetschus on the terrace in front of Grafeneck Castle.

Figure 3.3. Niemann in the foreground, with Gottfried Schwarz, beside a horse and cart on the grounds of the T4 killing center at Grafeneck.

Figure 3.4. Niemann (*left*) on the road leading up to Grafeneck Castle.

Figure 3.5. The Marbach railroad station, located below Grafeneck Castle. Niemann wrote "Grafeneck" under the print in his album.

Figure 3.6. A playful photo on the grounds of the T4 killing center in Brandenburg/Havel in the spring of 1940. The scene staged here seems to refer to the Gold-Ass in a fairytale by the Brothers Grimm. *Far right*, probably August Hengst, and next to him, Kurt Bolender. Niemann, wearing a chef's toque, is second from left. He wrote "Brandenburg" below the photo in his album.

Figure 3.7. Sitting on a canoe (*left to right*) are the "burners" Karl Pötzinger, Johann Niemann, and Siegfried Graetschus; behind them is the fence of the Brandenburg T4 facility. Visible in the background of this photo, taken in the summer of 1940, are the municipal baths. Below the print in his album, Niemann noted: "Brandenburg."

Figure 3.8. Niemann (*right*) with Willi Wendland in a canoe in Brandenburg/Havel, summer of 1940.

Figure 3.9. Niemann (*center*) with his wife, Henriette, near the old sluice in Bernburg. This photo, like the following ones, was taken in the winter of 1940/41. *Right, behind Niemann*, T4 driver and "burner" Otto Schmiedgen.

Figure 3.10. Niemann (*left*) und Schmiedgen near the Bernburg killing facility. The photo in Niemann's album was captioned "Bernburg."

Figure 3.11. Niemann and Schwarz near the Bernburg T4 facility. For this print too, Niemann chose the caption "Bernburg."

Figure 3.12. Niemann (*right*) with two unidentified men, presumably on the premises of the T4 killing center in Bernburg.

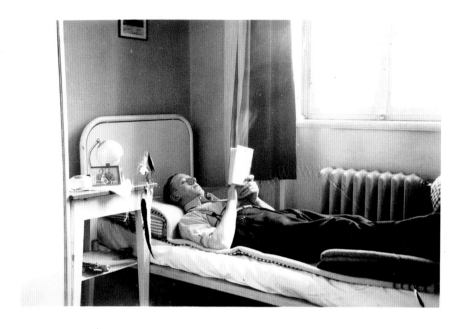

Figure 3.13. Niemann at the entrance to the wing where his quarters were located at the Bernburg T4 facility.

Figure 3.14. Niemann in his room in Bernburg. Note the family photo on the bedside table turned toward the photographer. His caption in the album: "Bernburg, bedroom."

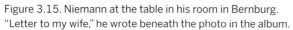

Figure 3.15. Niemann at the table in his room in Bernburg. "Letter to my wife," he wrote beneath the photo in the album.

Figure 3.16. Niemann in his room in Bernburg on the premises of the killing center.

Figure 3.17. Niemann in the courtyard of Bernburg Castle; both statues stand in other locations today.

Figure 3.18. The bear pit at Bernburg Castle.

Figure 3.19. Danida and Herbert Floß with Henriette Niemann (*left to right*) on the shore of the Attersee lake near Weißenbach in September 1941. The T4 recreation facility is close by. Niemann might have taken the photograph with Floß's camera.

Figure 3.20. Weißenbach on the Attersee in September 1941. Slightly right of center, the two-story building known as Villa Schoberstein is visible; it was used by the Chancellery of the Führer as a recreation facility for the T4 personnel.

Figure 3.21. The Attersee, presumably in September 1941.

Figure 3.22. The Wolfgangsee, only a few miles south of the Attersee, with a view of St. Wolfgang, probably in September 1941.

4

Realizing the Unthinkable

Operation T4, Operation Reinhard, and Their Actors

MARTIN CÜPPERS

Recent research into National Socialism and its genocidal crimes is providing insights into certain mechanisms and structures that have significantly refined some of the assumptions about the Nazi era that dominated in the past. These new insights are also relevant to classifying and evaluating the photos that once belonged to Johann Niemann. The Nazi regime did not consist solely of the seemingly omnipotent dictator Adolf Hitler, on the one hand, and the legion of loyal followers implementing his vision and orders, on the other. By now we have a great deal of reliable knowledge about factors and methods of operation that require appropriate consideration: above all, the war provided the decisive operational framework that enabled the Nazis to put their inhumane ideology into deadly practice. With the start of the war in September 1939, the initial phase of the extermination policy began, as early genocidal campaigns of mass murder targeted people dismissed as "unworthy of life" in the German Reich and members of the social elites in Poland.[1]

Additionally, the Holocaust and other Nazi genocides were by no means realized solely on the basis of detailed advance planning and a simple logic of command and obedience. Rather, a wide array of functionaries at the regional and local levels, acting on their own initiative and emboldened by the scope of action granted them under ever-changing circumstances, also helped pave the road to genocide. This is important because systematic murder on such a scale had never been attempted before. The responsible officials therefore lacked any kind of experience to draw on for adequate planning. To remedy this, they simply tested approaches to determine which ones might be feasible and what had to be excluded as unrealistic in practice. What we perceive in retrospect as gigantic, rigorously implemented genocidal campaigns began on a rather small scale and initially encountered various problems and took numerous wrong turns.

It was precisely such trial runs that made it possible not least of all to gauge the scope of action and to create suitable networks of personnel to implement those actions. In the process, the officials who initiated this program had the opportunity to evaluate their subordinates' willingness to kill. Parallel to the testing of technical solutions and procedural sequencing needed for mass murder, the early stages yielded important insights into the question of whether the men deployed would be willing to commit in practice the violations of civilizational norms that were based on ideology and envisaged in theory.[2] As already described in his biography, Johann Niemann was directly involved in the murder of patients in the German Reich, as well as in the killing of Jews in Poland. This chapter summarizes how German officials developed and implemented these mass crimes.

Operation T4—Killing "Unworthy Life"

Soon after the transfer of power to Adolf Hitler in January 1933, evidence began to mount that Germany's physically disabled and mentally ill, even people who seemed merely socially nonconformist, faced a threat to their right to exist. Schools of thought that classified individuals based predominantly on considerations of utility for the nation had emerged in numerous other nominally civilized countries since the late nineteenth century.[3] Only in Nazi Germany, however, did such ideas lead to a program of mass murder organized by the state. One of the first steps in this direction was a new "Law for the Prevention of Offspring with Hereditary Diseases," which took effect in July 1933. As a consequence of this legislation, 250,000 people were forcibly sterilized, 5,000 of whom died as a result of such surgery. By resorting to criminal means and a massive violation of inalienable personal rights, the Nazi state had taken action against people who it merely assumed could beget children with physical or mental anomalies in the future. This law was a clear indication that from then on persons with mental or physical disabilities were especially at risk.[4]

Postwar statements indicate that as early as 1935 Hitler had entertained the idea of killing disabled persons in the event of a new war, if not sooner. Four years later, a married couple wrote the "Führer" a letter in which they wished for the death of their disabled child. It was this couple's letter that enabled a first breach of taboo. Hitler personally approved this individual murder. And immediately thereafter, he endorsed the registration of comparably severe diagnoses throughout the Reich

by means of a notification system. This effort led to the killing of more than five thousand children by 1945.[5] Thus Nazi Germany embarked on its first systematic program of mass murder by targeting vulnerable children. Not long thereafter, but still before the German invasion of Poland, attention shifted in the summer of 1939 to adults deemed "unworthy of life" because they deviated from National Socialism's understanding of what was physically, mentally, and socially normal.

Karl Brandt, Hitler's attending physician, and Philipp Bouhler, head of the Chancellery of the Führer (*Kanzlei des Führers*, KdF), led the new program of murder. The KdF, a comparatively small, non-state agency beholden to Hitler alone, possessed good prerequisites for a discreet, unquestioning implementation of this program. Within the KdF, responsibility for the realization of the project lay first and foremost with Main Office II, which oversaw state and party affairs and was run by Oberdienstleiter Viktor Brack and his deputy, Oberbereichsleiter Werner Blankenburg. In consultation with the Ministry of the Interior and other agencies, Brack and his men developed an organizational structure, which then implemented the murders of patients under the classification "top secret [political]" (*Geheime Reichssache*).

Compared with the "euthanasia" project for children, the new group of victims was considerably larger and required a much greater degree of administrative effort. A system of registration and notification was set up across the Reich to ensure access to the patients whom the Nazis wished to examine. Numerous highly respected physicians, whose cooperation as expert evaluators had been gained on a voluntary basis, then decided life and death by filling in specially created forms. Their responses determined who was subsequently murdered.[6]

To guarantee secrecy, Brack and his colleagues in the KdF created a system of front organizations. This enabled their own office to disappear from official correspondence and at the same time bestowed a semblance of legality. One of these organizations, the Charitable Foundation for Institutional Care (*Gemeinnützige Stiftung für Anstaltspflege*), operated as the official employer of those involved, while the Reich Association for Sanatoriums and Asylums (*Reichsarbeitsgemeinschaft für Heil- und Pflegeanstalten*)—also known as RAG, from the first word of its German name—saw to the extensive correspondence between the central office in Berlin, various government agencies, expert evaluators, and the sanatoriums, asylums, and hospitals scattered throughout the Reich. Finally, the Charitable Ambulance Society (*Gemeinnützige Kranken-Transport GmbH*), Gekrat for short, was responsible for the transfer of the victims to the actual killing centers. The Reich Postal Service supplied Gekrat with buses. Operational headquarters, known as the "Central Office" (*Zentraldienststelle*), was set up at 4 Tiergartenstrasse. Over time, T4, an abbreviated form of this address, gained currency as shorthand for the murderous project.[7]

While the killing of children was usually done by administering luminal or morphine, it was not clear at first how to kill the adults. A query submitted to the Berlin-based Forensic Science Institute of the Security Police yielded the information that chemically pure carbon monoxide led to death within minutes, cost relatively little, and was available in large amounts. A first test in the Old Penitentiary in Brandenburg on the Havel delivered the crucial proof of feasibility in early January 1940. Subsequently, four killing centers were set up where the victims were murdered by introducing carbon monoxide into rooms that the perpetrators had specially remodeled as gas chambers. In addition to the test facility in Brandenburg, these were Grafeneck Castle in the Swabian Alps (Württemberg), Hartheim Castle near Linz (Austria), and Sonnenstein Castle in Pirna (Saxony).[8]

Officials from the KdF went about assembling the personnel for this unparalleled murder operation based on candidates' suitability and in some cases simply on their presence in the

organizers' private milieu. The director of the transport organization Gekrat was Reinhold Vorberg, one of Brack's cousins. Richard von Hegener, one of Brack's subordinates, was the brother-in-law of the president of the Reich Public Health Authority. Hans-Joachim Becker of the T4 economics department was a cousin of the wife of Herbert Linden, an official from the Reich Ministry of the Interior. Other key figures, such as the Kaufmann brothers, Fritz Schmiedel, Willy Schneider, Friedrich Lorent, and Friedrich Haus, were good acquaintances or friends of Brack.[9]

Personal connections aside, the T4 organizers also considered loyalty and ideological conviction relevant criteria for employment. Erich Bauer, the driver for the expert evaluators, was recruited through the SA in Berlin, where Dietrich Allers, a top T4 manager, had been his commanding officer. Kurt Meumann used his SA connections similarly to get a job as registrar at the "Euthanasia" Central Office in Berlin.[10]

Some of the KdF employees involved in the T4 operation liked to frequent the nightclub *Die Insel* after work. Franz Rum, one of the waiters, impressed a KdF staff member as trustworthy. Rum received a job offer and was soon employed in the Central Office as well.[11] In 1940, an acquaintance who worked at the Hartheim killing center told Arnold Oels, then unemployed, to report to the Berlin-based "foundation," where he was certain to have good prospects as a member of both the party and the SS. Oels, who promptly found a job in the personnel department and, years later, probably appeared several times over in Niemann's Berlin album, recalled in his postwar interrogation that such "applications" were more the exception: "As a rule, hiring took place only via recommendation and placement by higher party offices."[12]

Typist Edith Appel joined the murder program through her friend Ruth Eberl, the wife of T4 physician Irmfried Eberl, and was sworn to secrecy like all her colleagues. Nonetheless, she promptly told her parents about her new place of work. Upon hearing the attractive salary, her mother contacted her daughter's employer and persisted until she herself was hired as a secretary at the Brandenburg killing center.[13]

During the peak phase of Operation T4 (*Aktion T4*), in 1940–41, about five hundred persons from widely varying occupational backgrounds were involved in the implementation of this crime. They included the physicians working as expert evaluators or as medical directors in the killing centers, along with scores of male and female nurses. Besides such medical professionals, the program employed administrative experts, quite a number of secretaries, civil servants responsible for certifying deaths, and police officers acting as overseers, as well as drivers, photographers, gardeners, and cooks. Each had his or her specific field of expertise and worked to ensure that the murder program operated smoothly.

For the psychologically burdensome tasks, the T4 managers in the KdF sought out a special group. They entrusted the removal of the corpses from the gas chambers, the search for gold teeth and their extraction, and the cremation of the bodies to soldiers from the Waffen-SS, the military branch of the SS. The very motto of these soldiers—"My honor is loyalty"—suggested that one could expect special dedication to carrying out orders. For that purpose, numerous men deemed reliable based on their careers thus far in the Dachau or Buchenwald concentration camps or, like Johann Niemann, from Sachsenhausen, or in the ranks of the Waffen-SS were reassigned to the T4 program.[14]

In a postwar statement, Josef Oberhauser, one of the former concentration camp guards, recalled the early phase of experimentation in Grafeneck, which he experienced with Niemann, as well as the first vague instructions from the T4 physician in charge: "We were deployed for all kinds of work, but [our] main activity later [was as] burners [to cremate the bodies]. On the occasion of the first transport, Dr. Baumhard provided greater clarification: Unpleasant task—we have to try it out first."[15]

From these personnel, a group of genuine specialists in the killing of human beings developed over time. Niemann, too, must be considered among their number. Most were members of the Waffen-SS, who learned through daily practice how to design gas chambers for the greatest possible efficiency and what kind of ovens were best suited for cremating the bodies. These experts, together with Erwin Lambert, one of the bricklayers responsible for the actual structural changes, carried out the necessary installation work and alterations at each new T4 killing center.[16]

As a member of this special group, Niemann collected several photos from Grafeneck, Brandenburg, and Bernburg during his stint at these killing centers. Although some of these photographs originated in close proximity to the crime scenes, the images convey superficial impressions of rural idyll, comradery, and recreation, including a photo of Niemann's wife during a visit. The attendant subtext betrays the fact that this former concentration camp guard now assigned to T4 very much wished to see his new career stages represented as visible elements of his personal memory.[17]

The members of this heterogeneous group worked efficiently and amicably together as they identified, evaluated, transported, and killed their victims and then disposed of their bodies. However, the elaborate efforts to maintain secrecy soon proved futile. Over time, rumors about the terrible things happening at the T4 facilities began to circulate among the population. As a precautionary measure, officials closed the Grafeneck killing center at the end of 1940 and opened a new site a little later in Hadamar, northwest of Frankfurt am Main. Something similar took place with regard to the Brandenburg facility. Operations there were likewise suspended, and most of the personnel were moved to Bernburg (Anhalt), where they continued their work.[18]

Beyond that, other problems requiring solution emerged. The next of kin in several places began receiving death notices originating from the same facility, thus giving rise to further unwelcome rumors. In response, Friedrich Tillmann, an in-house "breakdown controller" at the Berlin Central Office, devised what he called "distribution departments." From that point on, every killing center used colored pins to mark the place of origin of each victim on a map. If a cluster emerged, then administrators sent death notices to family members from other locations and, if necessary, altered the dates of death. To better conceal the murderous system, the Central Office created "intermediary facilities" as well. Following secret evaluation, patients were transferred to these sites to create a cover story. After a few weeks, the Gekrat bus would arrive and take the patients to their death.[19]

Despite such refinements, the rumors persisted. In the city of Münster, the Catholic bishop Clemens Graf von Galen publicly criticized the state-sponsored program of murder in no uncertain terms during his Sunday sermon on August 3, 1941. The Nazi leadership responded with caution. In the war against the Soviet Union, which had just begun, this kind of criticism was most inopportune and entailed the risk of fomenting greater discontent. Therefore, Hitler personally decided that the "euthanasia" program in the Reich would ostensibly be terminated and, on August 24, instructed Brandt to inform those responsible in the KdF accordingly. By that point, more than seventy thousand people had been killed throughout the Reich over the previous nineteen months.[20]

In reality, the mass murders continued. From the spring of 1941, under the code name "14f13," physicians from the T4 program evaluated concentration camp inmates deemed "unworthy to live" and no longer able to work and had them murdered, usually in Bernburg, Sonnenstein, or Hartheim. These victims were often of Jewish origin. In addition, without any central coordination, institutionalized patients were systematically deprived of food and allowed to starve to death, or they were poisoned.[21]

Operation Reinhard in German-Occupied Poland

At the same time Hitler issued his instructions to discontinue the murder of institutionalized patients, his regime's genocidal crimes were escalating on the European level in the war of annihilation against the Soviet Union. A few weeks into the invasion, which began on June 22, 1941, the initial killing of selected Jewish men had broadened into unprecedented mass shootings that included women and children. By killing Jews regardless of age or gender in such large numbers, the perpetrators in the field were demonstrating their readiness to realize the "final solution of the Jewish question" in the most radical interpretation thinkable: as genocide.

Nazi propaganda had long threatened a solution first and foremost in terms of expulsion. In the occupied Soviet territories, the solution had now evolved into a campaign of mass murder. A growing number of SS and police units, along with their collaborators, were making the transition to the systematic shooting of entire Jewish communities. With that, the Holocaust in the Soviet Union, which would ultimately involve thousands of mass shooting operations, had become reality by late summer 1941.[22]

At about the same time, in what was a de facto continuation of Operation T4, task forces in the Soviet Union also began murdering patients from psychiatric institutions and those Roma who could be readily identified. Over the course of the war, the inclusion of these victim groups would produce tens of thousands of additional deaths on the Eastern Front.[23]

Subsequent to this dreadful escalation, another monstrous campaign of mass murder began to emerge on the eastern edge of the German-occupied Polish territories known as the General Government. Niemann would take part in this new killing program from the start. The operation would later receive the code name Operation Reinhard (*Aktion Reinhard*), in honor of Reinhard Heydrich, head of the Reich Security Main Office, who was killed by resistance fighters in Prague in June 1942.[24] As with the Holocaust in the Soviet Union, it is possible to trace how quickly German officials came to embrace the most radical concepts for a "final solution of the Jewish question," until then only a vague intention, and which ominous dynamics would shape this process.

Well into the summer of 1941, German planners and administrators in occupied Poland had discussed mass expulsion as the most suitable means for addressing the "Jewish question." However, the shootings in the Soviet Union then produced a shift in the perception threshold and considerations of feasibility. Based on the experience gained elsewhere, there no longer seemed to be any argument against killing Jews in the General Government in large numbers as well. In the German-annexed Polish territory farther to the west, known as the Warthegau, a killing center in the village of Chełmno (German: Kulmhof), not far from the city of Łódź, commenced operations using three mobile gas vans in December 1941.[25] At about the same time, construction of a similar camp was ramping up in the village of Bełżec, on the southeastern edge of the General Government's District Lublin. In March 1942, the mass murder of Jews from the Lublin and Galicia districts got under way there as well. In just a few months, the "final solution of the Jewish question" in the General Government had also been taken to the most radical extreme.[26]

In all, between March 1942 and November 1943, about 1.8 million Jews, as well as 50,000 Sinti and Roma, were murdered in the course of Operation Reinhard. Most of the victims perished in three specially constructed killing centers near the villages of Bełżec, Sobibór, and Treblinka. Right at the starting points of the deportation trains, the Nazis and their helpers shot tens of thousands of Jews who were sick or frail or put up resistance. Whenever a lack of transport capacity presented itself, the SS and police shot the Jews who could not fit on the trains.

When the last of the three killing centers suspended operations in the autumn of 1943, Operation Reinhard culminated in a concerted mass shooting operation lasting two days in early November. Organized under the cynical code name "Operation Harvest Festival" (Aktion Erntefest), SS and police task forces shot more than forty-three thousand people at the Majdanek concentration camp in Lublin and at forced labor camps in Poniatowa and Trawniki.[27] Only the coordinated efforts of highly diverse institutions and perpetrators made it possible to carry out such an enormous genocidal crime within two years. The following presentation examines the participants in this genocide and the contributions they made to its implementation.

Institutions and Personnel of Operation Reinhard

Within the General Government, it was Odilo Globocnik, the SS and police leader in District Lublin, who seized the decisive initiative at the regional level and thus assumed responsibility for radicalizing German policy toward Jews within his jurisdiction. A former regional party leader (Gauleiter) for the city of Vienna, Globocnik had lost his post in early 1939 owing to charges of corruption. With the German occupation of Poland, however, Himmler gave Globocnik a new lease on political life by appointing him the top SS leader in District Lublin and making him plenipotentiary for the development of German settlements in the East.[28]

Radical Nazis took it for granted that the "Germanization" of invaded countries was closely related to the removal of the Jewish population—no matter how it would eventually happen. As news of the escalation in mass shootings in Ukraine in the fall of 1941 made its way to Lublin, Globocnik began to frame his own suggestions for dealing with the Jewish minority in District Lublin. At a meeting with Globocnik and

Friedrich-Wilhelm Krüger, the higher SS and police leader for the General Government, on October 13, 1941, Himmler apparently approved the basic intent to proceed with the "final solution of the Jewish question" in District Lublin no longer in terms of expulsion but in terms of murder.[29] The three men appear to have also hastily included District Galicia in their deliberations. Fritz Katzmann, Globocnik's counterpart in Lwów (German: Lemberg; Ukrainian: Lviv), was alleging an urgent need for action in his region, because he thought too many Jews had survived the mass shootings carried out in the opening months of the invasion.[30]

Some months later, Himmler relieved Globocnik of his duties as plenipotentiary for German settlement, thus freeing up personnel so that the implementation of the new mass murder program could proceed with greater resolve. Globocnik assembled a command staff dedicated to the extermination of the Jews and appointed Hermann Höfle chief of staff. In March 1942, Globocnik and his men took up their work, operating first in the Lublin and Galicia districts.[31] During the ghetto liquidation operations, the SS and police leader was sometimes personally on-site. Over time, he and his men proved so devastatingly "successful" that what had originally begun as a regional plan was soon expanded to include other parts of the General Government and the administrative regions of Bialystok and Zichenau.

In most of the academic literature to date, scholars have therefore assigned Globocnik primary responsibility for Operation Reinhard. The fact that Globocnik, as the author of the final report for Himmler on Reinhard, had himself claimed responsibility for this campaign of mass murder in retrospect lends credence to this interpretation. To reinforce this argument, scholars also cite a letter to Himmler in which Viktor Brack mentioned relations between his office at the KdF and Globocnik. In the letter, Brack wrote, "On the instructions of Reichsleiter Bouhler, I long ago placed part of my men at the disposal of Brigadeführer Globocnik for the carrying out of his special assignment."[32]

This letter has provided the basis for numerous references to the KdF in the academic literature about Operation Reinhard, but the full extent of the office's involvement in the murder of Poland's Jews has remained strangely vague to this day. Numerous photos within the Niemann collection provide compelling evidence that the KdF did indeed play a pivotal role in Operation Reinhard. Images of Niemann and other perpetrators from the camps on a trip to Berlin show the visitors in the company of three KdF officials. All three of these officials—Blankenburg, Allers, and, presumably, Oels —were deeply involved in both T4 and Reinhard. The prints from this trip bear additional witness to the recognition and appreciation that the KdF bestowed on the Trawnikis, the auxiliary guards from the camps, who were nominally subordinate to Globocnik.

The series of photos taken at the funeral service for Niemann and the other SS men killed during the Jewish prisoner uprising on October 14, 1943, likewise illustrates the basic institutional jurisdiction and responsibility of the KdF. On this occasion, Blankenburg and Allers traveled to District Lublin for the sole purpose of attending the ceremony held at the military cemetery in Chełm. They can be seen in their SA uniforms standing at attention in front of the coffins, giving the "Hitler salute." By contrast, only Ernst Lerch, a comparatively less senior officer, was on hand to represent the office of the SS and police leader in District Lublin. In the aftermath of the funeral, Allers and Oels, acting on behalf of the KdF, also took special care of Niemann's widow and expressed their readiness to help her in dealings with the German bureaucracy.[33]

One of the key reasons for the participation of the KdF in the Holocaust in Poland and in all subsequent developments would have to be the fact that Globocnik himself, for all his radicalism, had no personnel at his disposal with any notable experience in mass murder on the scale envisaged. In this context, it seems telling that Josef Oberhauser, who was deployed at Belzec and elsewhere, recalled in a postwar statement that Globocnik did not want "to have all too much to do" with such procedures.[34] That serves as an indication of his need for know-how from elsewhere to carry out the murderous project.

Presumably through mediation on the part of Himmler, Globocnik was ultimately able to profit from the very group of technicians who had developed expertise in mass killing during the murder of institutionalized patients. Now this group was about to make a decisive contribution to implementing a new and much larger murder program. To meet Globocnik's need for experts in the killing of human beings, seemingly suitable actors were chosen from among the former T4 employees, who then set about devising a corresponding infrastructure, trying out killing methods in an experimental phase, and then ultimately implementing the systematic murder of Poland's Jews.[35]

By this time, the expertise of the KdF had long since reached a remarkable level of awareness among Nazi occupation authorities even beyond District Lublin. In October 1941, a civil administration functionary involved in the "Jewish question" in Riga asked Alfred Rosenberg's Reich Ministry for the Occupied Eastern Territories how he could proceed against the Jewish population in his jurisdiction in Latvia. The responsible ministry official replied tellingly that "Brack's auxiliary methods" had in the meantime come to represent the most effective approach. With this catchphrase, which was assumed to be known, the official euphemistically described the murder of "unworthy life" by means of gas and suggested that something similar could now be expected with regard to the Jewish population in the German-occupied East. Above all, however, the civil servant thereby emphasized the competence and responsibility of the KdF in this matter. The example serves to show how extensively even civil administration officials were privy to the technical details of the murder of institutionalized

patients. It also highlights how openly German officials, in their search for approaches, were communicating in the fall of 1941 about proven killing practices with regard to the "final solution of the Jewish question," which was evolving more and more concretely toward mass murder.[36]

An initial group of KdF killing experts assembled to meet Globocnik's personnel needs began arriving in Belzec in the autumn of 1941 to establish the first camp for what would become Operation Reinhard.[37] Under the command of Christian Wirth, a former Stuttgart police detective superintendent, all of these men except Wirth were SS soldiers who had worked at the T4 killing facilities, mainly in cremating the bodies, but also in operating the gas chambers. The knowledge they possessed was now in high demand in Lublin.

Oberhauser, one of the key perpetrators, described the transition from T4 to the Holocaust: "In October\November 1941, Schwarz, Niemann, and I were recalled by Berlin (Brack?) from Bernburg, in Berlin [we were] outfitted at the [SS]Operational Command Office [SS-Führungshauptamt], and then came to Lublin. The first batch consisted only of members of the Waffen-SS."[38] While Wirth would subsequently rise to become the organizational leader of Operation Reinhard, these SS soldiers soon came to fill important leadership positions.

The KdF, however, did not simply turn over these experts to Globocnik, as the aforementioned quotation from Brack's letter to Himmler suggests. Rather, the KdF, which was directly subordinate to Hitler, remained closely involved in the events that followed. For Brack, it was self-evident that, as head of the KdF's Main Office II in Berlin, he should continue to view the men in Poland as "his" personnel. In early January 1942, for example, he urged the SS Race and Settlement Main Office to expedite the paperwork related to the marriage of "SS-Oberscharführer Gottfried Schwarz, who is working with me on a special mission."[39]

Under Wirth's supervision, Schwarz, Niemann, and Ober-hauser, as well as Fritz Jirmann and Lorenz Hackenholt, dedicated themselves to the construction of the new camp in Belzec. In early 1942, another contingent of T4 men assigned by the KdF arrived. As the weeks wore on, Wirth's team was able to begin testing. By about mid-March, the future killing site was operable on a provisional basis, and the German personnel had received reinforcements in the form of fifty Trawnikis, who had been transferred to the camp to serve as additional guards.

On March 17, the first deportation trains from Lublin and Lemberg arrived. Their passengers were murdered in the Belzec gas chambers that same day. Over the next four weeks, mass murder became dreadful routine, as thousands of Jews from the districts of Lublin and Galicia were killed at this location on an almost daily basis.[40]

At the outset, it appears that a division of expertise and areas of responsibility between the perpetrators in Belzec and Lublin had not been defined. However, after a few weeks on the job, Wirth's murderous innovators made it emphatically clear that whatever else happened at the Belzec camp, the KdF would be directly involved. After April 17, 1942, Wirth and his men left Belzec for Berlin to submit their report, allow their superiors to deliberate, and receive new orders. In doing so, they clearly demonstrated that they felt no obligation to Globocnik in Lublin, but rather to the KdF in Berlin, and that it was from the latter that they awaited further instructions.[41]

Owing to the massive radicalization of Jewish policy at the highest level, far-reaching decisions regarding further practical procedures remained pending. Sometime between the end of November and early December 1941, Hitler must have made a policy decision on the murder of European Jewry. On December 14, Himmler, Bouhler as the head of the KdF, and Alfred Rosenberg, the Reich minister for the occupied eastern territories, appear to have met with Hitler for lunch to discuss the consequences of this policy shift and to coordinate with one another.[42]

The Wannsee Conference on January 20, 1942, represented a further important moment. It was there, under Heydrich's chairmanship, that procedural matters were communicated to ranking civil servants from the participating ministries and occupation authorities. With that, all the regional solutions sought by various authorities were merged at once into a large-scale murderous project for all of Europe. The regional approaches to date were in no way superfluous. The first phase of mass murder, just concluded in Belzec, and the Sobibor camp, then under construction, seem to have been adapted by officials in Berlin as elements of an approach suitable for use throughout the entire General Government and perhaps beyond.

Globocnik must have been informed in the spring of 1942 of the plans to expand the murder operations. The departure of the experts from Belzec had caught him by complete surprise, however, as Oberhauser later testified. Globocnik immediately left for Berlin to clarify the delineation of powers with the KdF. He now faced yet another need for KdF personnel: during a visit to Warsaw on April 17, Himmler had decided in the presence of Globocnik and Arpad Wigand, the SS and police leader for District Warsaw, to create an additional killing center, a site for the murder of the Jews living in the former Polish capital. It was on this occasion that the need for a third camp was formulated for the first time. That camp would in fact be built close to the village of Treblinka a few months later.[43]

As Victor Brack's wife Thea recalled after the war, Globocnik had showed up unannounced in Berlin on April 19, the day before Hitler's birthday, and asked her husband to arrange a meeting with Bouhler at short notice.[44] Within the framework of the arrangements made at this time, Bouhler and Globocnik seem to have reached a consensus as to their future spheres of activity given the expansion of the Holocaust into a European

dimension. In doing so, they settled the matter of their jurisdictions in the General Government as well.

In the wake of this agreement, Brack personally traveled to
Lublin and, in the company of Globocnik, visited Belzec, where
only a few Trawnikis remained to guard the otherwise abandoned killing site. A few days later, in May 1942, Wirth, Niemann, and other SS perpetrators reappeared at the camp and
in the weeks that followed set about enlarging its killing capacity. With the start of gassing operations at the camp in Sobibor
and the start of construction in Treblinka, the extermination
program began to assume considerably new dimensions.[45] The
regional solution originally considered for the districts Lublin
and Galicia had escalated into a murder program for the entire
General Government. Starting in June 1942, this could clearly
be construed from the points of departure of the deportation
trains as well.[46]

Thus, the extermination project that is today perceived historically as Operation Reinhard began to emerge only gradually with the completion of all three killing centers, the inclusion of additional districts of the General Government, and
then the arrival of numerous deportation trains from all of
Europe.[47] Aside from the members of the Waffen-SS who were
already stationed in Belzec, the KdF briefed at least 112 other
T4 perpetrators and gradually transferred them to Poland by
the summer of 1942. Upon arrival, they were outfitted in SS
uniforms to boost their authority within the camps and assigned the ranks of SS noncommissioned officers. However, all
remained nominal employees of the KdF, which also continued
to pay their salaries.[48]

This circle of persons, with expertise gained in carrying out
mass murder in the Reich, provided the decisive transfer of
knowledge that Globocnik and his men could not themselves
guarantee in occupied Poland. Especially in the early phase of
experimentation, officials from Berlin intervened as required

and ensured, for example, that Helmut Kallmeyer, the KdF's
in-house chemist, traveled to District Lublin to measure carbon monoxide levels and confirm beyond a doubt that the first
gas chambers were lethal. If required, he could make subtle
adjustments in the settings of the gasoline-fueled engine right
away.[49]

Overall, a division of competences based on each side's expertise and abilities began to take shape, an arrangement that
would remain in effect for the duration of Operation Reinhard.
Globocnik and his Lublin-based staff under Hermann Höfle
organized the deportations, first in the immediate vicinity and
over time in the entire General Government as well as the districts Bialystok and Zichenau, and in the process ordered numerous mass shootings at the points of origin. The KdF and its
personnel for their part handled the killing within the confines
of the killing centers in Belzec, Sobibor, and Treblinka, camps
that had been set up solely for that purpose.[50]

In postwar interrogations, several key perpetrators directly
addressed this division of tasks. Karl Streibel, who ran the
Trawniki training camp within Globocnik's jurisdiction, recalled Höfle explaining to him that "Wirth was entrusted with
this assignment and was instructed directly from Berlin."[51]
Later, Streibel himself testified about this: "Operation Reinhard
was probably assigned to Globocnik. But it was said that these
people were supposed to receive their orders from Berlin."[52] On
the matter of his own chief and his authority, he stated with
certainty that "Globocnik was not Wirth's superior with regard
to the future Operation Reinhard, rather in this respect Wirth
was directly subordinate to Berlin." And he added, the auton-
omy of the men from the KdF was no secret on-site: "In Lublin,
it was generally known that the Wirth Office, along with the
members of the killing centers, constituted their own office,
which liaised with the SSPF [Globocnik] only to the extent that
the Wirth Office was located in the area of the SSPF."[53] Georg

Michalsen, an SS man on Globocnik's staff who was deeply involved in the Holocaust, characterized the arrangement similarly: "I believe that this office was not subordinate to the SS and police leader in Lublin, but had a special official channel to the top."[54] Regarding the division of competences, he testified further: "As far as I remember, in those days, by 'Operation Reinhard' we understood Wirth's office with the three camps. [...] In our case, we were subordinate to Globocnik. In the case of Wirth and his people, there was the additional subordination to the KdF."[55]

The fact that Globocnik did not delegate a single one of his own SS men to the killing centers also indicates that Belzec, Sobibor, and Treblinka were the area of responsibility of the KdF. Had his general jurisdiction extended to the three camps, the power-conscious Nazi would have demonstrated this by installing his own men in key positions on-site. Instead, Globocnik became active only when men from the KdF became available for other assignments, as occurred after the closing of Belzec. Only then was he able to redeploy the proven experts to forced labor camps within his own realm of influence.[56]

The SS and police leader in Lublin also seems to have basically accepted the jurisdiction of the KdF over the Reinhard camps, because the operation of his own office ultimately profited from this division of competences. The arrangement served to relieve his staff of the considerable duties that administration of the camps would have entailed. Globocnik in turn expressed his gratitude for this by placing the Trawnikis at the disposal of the KdF as an auxiliary force.

By the end of July 1942, when Treblinka was also in operation and the division of jurisdictions between Berlin and Lublin had achieved routine efficiency, Wirth left his post as commandant at the Belzec camp and assumed responsibility for all three of the Reinhard killing centers. His new office, located in Lublin, operated under the designation "Inspector of the SS Special Units Operation Reinhard" (*Inspekteur der SS-Sonderkommandos Einsatz Reinhard*). This had the advantage that the KdF no longer had to intervene extensively in organizational questions in the distant General Government.[57]

When Irmfried Eberl, commandant at the new camp in Treblinka, later proved incapable of efficiently organizing the gassing of the people arriving on the numerous deportation trains, Globocnik appeared on the scene once again. Confronted with news of the chaos and ghastly conditions on-site in Treblinka, Globocnik saw that his primary interest—ensuring the smoothest possible liquidation of the Warsaw Ghetto—was suddenly in serious jeopardy. Thus, Globocnik and Wirth promptly drove to the site and quickly reorganized the camp to ensure that Treblinka became capable of functioning as the killing site for Warsaw's Jewish community. Along with additional personnel decisions, Eberl was relieved of his command, and a new commandant was put in place in the person of Franz Stangl from Sobibor.[58]

Even after Wirth had settled into his new office, Werner Blankenburg, Dietrich Allers, and other officials from the KdF regularly traveled to Lublin. Their visits to the individual Reinhard camps provide supplementary evidence for the general jurisdiction of the Berlin central office as well as the cooperation with Globocnik in Lublin.[59] Moreover, couriers shuttled back and forth between Berlin, Lublin, and the killing centers in order to bring the men on-site their salaries, to deliver official mail, and—at least in the case of Belzec—to pick up stolen valuables on a grand scale.

How command authority between Globocnik's office and the camps run by Lublin-based Wirth under the KdF's orders was regulated in detail can no longer be reconstructed, owing to the absence of documents and a lack of unambiguous depositions. In addition, no evidence exists as to how the KdF concretely operated with respect to Operation Reinhard and what kind of signals its officials gave, radicalizing or otherwise. But it is this very lack of source material that also ultimately makes the decisive fact seem so obvious: both offices, Globocnik's and Bouhler's, worked together in a spirit of mutual agreement and encountered little friction in carrying out the Holocaust in Poland.

Beyond the distribution of competences between Lublin and the KdF in Berlin, it was frequently Heinrich Himmler himself who guided the implementation of the genocide. He took note of recommendations, coordinated their realization, formulated decisive instructions on his own, brought together responsible entities, and guaranteed the necessary transfer of knowledge where required.

Himmler inspected Sobibor twice, on July 19, 1942, and on February 12, 1943. On the occasion of at least the second visit, he ordered a demonstration of the operation of the gas chambers. During his visits, he also made concrete recommendations. For example, it was apparently Himmler who proposed that women's hair be cut off and collected prior to their murder so it could be used for military production in the wartime economy. After his second visit, Jewish women were no longer allowed to cook for the camp's German personnel for reasons of security. Impressed by the organization of the killing process in February 1943, Himmler promoted several of the German perpetrators for their "outstanding" services in the killing centers. Niemann was among those who profited from this round of promotions, becoming an SS-Untersturmführer and thus entering the ranks of the officer corps.[60]

As the very code name Operation Reinhard suggests, the Reich Security Main Office (RSHA) also ranked among the most important institutions involved in the murder of Polish Jewry. Headed by Reinhard Heydrich until his assassination in the spring of 1942, the RSHA served as the central office for the state's political and criminal investigative police, known jointly as the Security Police, and the Nazi party's intelligence service, the Security Service (SD).

The Forensic Science Institute of the Security Police, a highly qualified professional facility based in Berlin, contributed its own expertise and specially trained experts to both the T4 program and Operation Reinhard. In the run-up to the "euthanasia" killings in Germany, Dr. Albert Widmann, a chemist at the institute, provided the basic method of killing by recommending chemically pure carbon monoxide. In the course of experiments involving carbon monoxide from the exhaust of a truck's gasoline engine instead of chemically pure carbon monoxide from steel cylinders, Widmann murdered dozens of psychiatric patients in Mogilev, Belorussia, in the late summer of 1941.[61] In doing so, he proved the practicability of the method that would soon be applied in all three Reinhard camps some months later. By some means, information about the effectiveness of Widmann's murderous experiments must have reached the T4 personnel in Belzec within weeks, as their own early experiments with the exhaust fumes from gasoline motors suggest.[62]

In addition to technical support, the RSHA facilitated Operation Reinhard through Security Police and SD offices in the General Government. As a rule, these offices participated in the deportation of Jews from the ghettos to the killing centers and, as required, assisted in the mass shootings of Jews on-site. Whether originating from within the Reich or elsewhere in occupied Europe, the trains for the deportations were provided as a result of coordination between Adolf Eichmann's section IV B 4 at the RSHA and other government agencies.[63]

This in turn points to the Reichsbahn, the German rail service, which made the trains available for the deportations to the Reinhard camps. For each deportation, the Reichsbahn submitted to the SS an invoice for a third-class one-way ticket per adult person. Acting at the behest of Eichmann or one of his subordinates, the Reichsbahn directed deportation trains from the Reich or other occupied countries most frequently to Sobibor. In the General Government, the "General Directorate of Eastern Railroads," founded after the takeover of the Polish railroads, ensured that in the middle of a war—despite the need for supplies and reinforcements on the Eastern Front— locomotives and railway cars, along with their engineers and firemen, stood at the ready for transports to the killing centers, sometimes even more than once a day.[64]

Beyond major German government agencies such as the RSHA and the Reichsbahn, the civil administration in the General Government played a key role in registering the Jewish communities, plundering their belongings and financial resources, and disenfranchising them by means of innumerable antisemitic regulations. Officials from the civil administration established a system of slave labor that was both comprehensive and dangerous. Often acting entirely of their own accord, these administrators repeatedly demanded their area of influence receive preferential treatment in being made "free of Jews." In doing so, they, too, made a significant contribution to the radicalization of Nazi Jewish policy.

With the exception of a few ghettos established early on under German occupation, the civil administration was also decisive in ghettoizing communities, sometimes shortly before their demise. This was an important precondition for ultimately forcing the Jews to the freight trains headed for the killing centers. To save time during such operations, Jews who put up resistance as well as those who could not walk on their own were shot on the spot and hastily buried.[65]

Faced with a persistent shortage of manpower, the Germans also drew on local institutions such as the auxiliary police. Local auxiliary police forces that facilitated the Holocaust were notorious. As of early 1943, the Polish police, known as the "blue police" due to their uniform, had a strength of more than ten thousand men, most of whom had served in the Polish police before the war. Faced with this and so many other threats, the Jewish minority could not expect much help and support from the Christian Poles around them, save for comparatively few instances. In a society traumatized by the German occupation and steeped in its own various and persistent forms of antisemitism, gestures of humanity were rare. Despite a dominant passivity, some among the Christian population did dare to rescue Jews. More common, however, were those locals who betrayed hidden Jews or acted as "Jew hunters"—fields of endeavor for which the occupation authorities provided financial reward.[66]

The German perpetrators also made use of an additional force of about 5,000 auxiliary guards, who were referred to by the location of their training camp in the village of Trawniki. The Germans distributed the Trawnikis to all three of the Reinhard camps in contingents roughly equal to company strength, with 120–150 men. Sometimes, they assisted in ghetto liquidations. These guards feature in numerous photos within the Niemann collection. As already noted, they represent a revealing link between Globocnik's areas of competence and the everyday work routine of the personnel from the KdF in Belzec, Sobibor, and Treblinka.[67]

And when a shortage of SS, police, or barracked Waffen-SS personnel presented itself in occupied Poland, even rather innocuous-sounding institutions could be counted on to stand in. Local foresters kept lookout for Jewish refugees in the woods, and municipal firefighters also took part in the murders.

Finally, a major characteristic of the Holocaust was the diverse and cruel ways by which German officialdom integrated the Jews into their own destruction. Jews who lived in the vicinity of a village chosen for the location of an killing center had to work as forced laborers and help with the camps' construction—only to be killed as the first victims when their work was done. Healthy Jews, usually young people, were chosen from among the deportees and subsequently put to work at the killing centers sorting the murdered victims' belongings, burying and later burning the corpses, and providing whatever other assistance the SS required so that the various stages of the killing process followed one another as smoothly as possible.

The mass murder that took place during Operation Reinhard was also accompanied by a gigantic campaign of plunder.

Before their death, the Germans and Trawnikis deprived the Jews of all the remaining belongings they had brought along on their final journey. Back in the victims' hometowns, the occupation authorities confiscated the property and possessions left behind. In the killing centers, the Jews' belongings—currency, jewelry and any other valuables, clothing, as well as whatever miscellaneous everyday objects had been seized—were then sorted and temporarily stored in warehouses. While the clothing came to benefit the needy within the Nazis' "people's community" (*Volksgemeinschaft*), the valuables were officially paid to the Reichsbank.

In a final report submitted to Himmler in December 1943, Globocnik listed in meticulous fashion all of the assets and goods seized and then provided an estimate of the financial proceeds totaling 178 million Reichsmark.[68] The actual scale of plunder should have been significantly higher for at least two reasons. For one, enormous quantities of valuables were diverted to Berlin from Belzec until the end of the mass murder operations there in November 1942. The aforementioned courier who delivered salaries to Belzec every Wednesday, departed for Berlin with suitcases and crates full of money and gold in tow. For another, despite whatever official bookkeeping existed, the perpetrators at every level of the hierarchy within Operation Reinhard simply pocketed what they could in almost unimaginable quantities. Niemann also participated in this on a large scale, as becomes evident upon examination of family bank statements.[69]

Rumors of the rampant corruption in the General Government soon made the rounds on the streets of German cities. Fittingly, the abbreviation introduced for this part of occupied Poland, GG, came to be used ironically as shorthand for *Gangstergau*, the gangsters' district.[70] Even more revealing is the fact that such anecdotes regarding material enrichment found their way into public discourse, while the underlying genocidal crime behind these ill-gotten gains remained conspicuously absent from public memory.

Freedom of Action

This wide-ranging organizational framework of diverse institutions shows how second- and third-tier actors made substantial contributions to initiating and implementing the Holocaust. By drawing on a complex division of competences and interlocking jurisdictions, these institutions enabled the murder of 1.8 million people in just over twenty months.

It was not only Hitler's imagination, the experience of the KdF, Himmler's radicalism, or the determination of SS officers such as Globocnik that was crucial to making this happen. It was the additional initiatives enabled by the freedom of action that the system had systematically bestowed on lower-ranking officials. Only this created the kind of scenarios in which adequate approaches were sought and found so as to realize something that had never been done before.

Through radical pronouncements and statements of approval in discussions at the highest level of party and state, Hitler created the framework for individual freedom of action. For his part, Himmler, as leader of the SS and chief of the German police, lent encouragement to his subordinates involved in the killing and, as communicator and controller, brought together the necessary expertise, as well as the institutions that seemed most appropriate.[71]

But only on the ground in Belzec could men such as Wirth or Niemann assess what was needed to make mass murder a reality. In the course of the first early experiments with a mobile gas van, these murderous innovators recognized that millions of people could not be murdered in the time allotted, given the limited capacity of vans. They constructed a gas chamber that was comparable in its mode of operation to the T4 killing facilities. From the start, capacity here was laid out on a larger scale. The earliest model seems to have relied on pure carbon monoxide in steel cylinders, which Gottfried Schwarz was able to obtain only after considerable effort in occupied Lwów. Complicating this approach further was the fact that such cylinders had a limited shelf-life.[72] As a consequence, a large-displacement gasoline engine was procured and the operating procedure for introducing carbon-monoxide fumes into the gas chamber was significantly altered yet again.[73] Then, after several weeks of lethal practice claiming tens of thousands of victims, the practitioners of mass murder determined that the dimensions of the three gas chambers in existence were still inadequate. For this reason, the ones in Belzec were torn down and built anew with larger dimensions, while the gas chambers under construction at Sobibor were built on a larger scale from the start. And even these modern constructions, after several devastating months, failed to meet the actual need. Accordingly, the capacity in Sobibor was doubled once more.

The killing centers' design features, which were constantly subject to further development based on ever-accumulating experience, reached their culmination in Treblinka, the third camp. It, too, had been expanded during construction and, measured solely by the number of its victims, ultimately proved to be Nazi Germany's most efficient killing center. In one year, the Germans murdered almost one million people at this location.

These developmental processes and operating procedures were essential for realizing the Holocaust. They extend far beyond any interpretation of a classic governing principle that relies primarily on command and obedience, on planning and implementation. In the fall of 1941, the Nazi leadership around Hitler had decided in principle to murder the Jews of Europe, but at the time it was not at all clear how it could be realized in practical terms, and whether subordinates would be willing to implement it.

But Wirth and others who had already proven themselves in committing crimes on behalf of the regime, men such as Niemann, found approaches for realizing such a gigantic program of mass murder. Only through their personal initiative and creativity, along with their readiness to apply their expertise in killing on a daily basis, to develop and refine their knowledge,

did it gradually become apparent that the Third Reich would be able to carry out the "final solution of the Jewish question" in the sense of murdering millions of people.

The private photos now available in the Niemann collection, together with the personal letters and rare official documents supplementing them, provide revealing clues about the spirit of mutual agreement and self-confidence the perpetrators demonstrated as they carried out this German extermination policy. Such actors were unmistakably shaped by an awareness that they were not simply following orders, but were acting on behalf of Nazi Germany at a crucial moment to implement radical policies, gather new findings, and apply their creativity and initiative to make a theoretical intent to commit mass murder a terrible reality. In doing so, individuals such as Niemann profited from an astonishing degree of power and, in the middle of a world war no less, a remarkable array of privileges, which they showcased in their photographs. Alongside ideological convictions and professional ambition, that power and privilege surely provided a strong additional motive for the inhumane actions of these men.[74]

Notes

1. This point is made convincingly by Kershaw, *Hitler*, v. 1, pp. 665–744. For a novel approach to Hitler's personality and rule, see Pyta, *Hitler*; on the war in Poland, see the contributions in Mallmann and Musial, *Genesis*; on the context, see Reemtsma, *Vertrauen*.

2. Angrick, *Experiment*; Mallmann, "Türöffner"; Cüppers, *Wegbereiter*, pp. 175–186; idem, *Rauff*, pp. 111–124.

3. For an overview, Klee, "*Euthanasie*," pp. 15–28; Friedlander, *Weg*, pp. 27–40.

4. Ibid., pp. 65–62; Klee, "*Euthanasie*," pp. 36–37, 61–74; Hinz-Wessels, *Tiergartenstrasse*, pp. 60–62.

5. In detail, Beddies and Hübener, *Kinder*; Benzenhöfer, "*Kinderfachabteilungen*." The findings here are based in part on unreliable postwar statements; see the critical analysis regarding the first murder by Benzenhöfer, *Fall Leipzig*.

6. Klee, "*Euthanasie*," pp. 82–103.

7. See Friedlander, *Weg*, pp. 119–144; on the designation, Hinz-Wessels, *Tiergartenstrasse*, pp. 72–74.

8. Friedlander, *Weg*, pp. 152–163; Ley and Hinz-Wessels, *Euthanasie-Anstalt*, pp. 18–22, 62–67.

9. Friedlander, *Weg*, p. 313; on the responsibility of those named, ibid.; in addition, Klee, "*Euthanasie*," pp. 166–172.

10. Interrogation of Erich Bauer, January 9, 1962, HHW, 631a/1489.

11. Interrogation of Erich Bauer, December 7, 1962, LNW, Q 234/4286; interrogation of Kurt Meumann, July 3, 1962, LNW, Q 234/4452; interrogation of Franz Rum, November 23, 1961, LNW, Q 234/4267. On the selection of personnel, see interrogation of Arnold Oels, May 17, 1962, BArch, B 162/508.

12. Interrogation of Arnold Oels, April 24, 1961, ibid.

13. Interrogation of Edith Appel, October 13, 1961, BArch, B 162/4428.

14. On personnel, see Friedlander, *Weg*, pp. 172–175, as well as the chapter on Niemann's biography in this volume.

15. Interrogation of Josef Oberhauser, January 10, 1968, HHW, 631a/1649.

16. See the chapter on Niemann's biography in this volume; interrogation of Erwin Lambert, October 2, 1962, BArch, B 162/4432; interrogation of Josef Oberhauser, February 26, 1960, BArch, B 162/3167.

17. See the photos in Photos from the Niemann Collection, from the Period of Operation T4.

18. Klee, "*Euthanasie*," pp. 289–292; Friedlander, *Weg*, pp. 161–163.

19. Greve, *Vernichtung*, pp. 47–49.

20. Hinz-Wessels, *Tiergartenstrasse*, pp. 92–95; Friedlander, *Weg*, pp. 191–194. On economic motives, which can also be verified during *Aktion Reinhard,* see Rauh, *Selektionskriterien*; Hohendorf, *Selektion.*

21. Klee, "*Euthanasie*," pp. 345–355, 379–389, 429–441.

22. On the origins, Mallmann, *Türöffner*; idem, *Sprung*, pp. 239–264; Cüppers, *Wegbereiter*, pp. 175–186; Matthäus, "*Operation Barbarossa.*"

23. On the "euthanasia" murders in the Soviet Union, see Klee, "*Euthanasie*," pp. 367–370; on Roma, Fings, *Sinti und Roma*, pp. 388–398; Holler, *Völkermord.*

24. In the summer of 1942, the code name "Einsatz [Operation] Reinhard" began appearing in documents, along with variations using Reinhardt or Reinhart, see message SS-Sonderkommando Sobibor, July 1, 1943, FSB, K-779 (Trawniki); telegram Höfle to Heim, Jan. 11, 1943, PRO Kew, HW 16/23, decode GPDD 355a. By 1943, the term *Aktion Reinhard* had established itself, see SSPF Lublin to Pers. Stab RFSS,

March 3, 1943, BArch, NS 19/2234. The claim that this operation was named for Fritz Reinhardt, the top civil servant (state secretary) within the Ministry of Finance, seems by contrast unconvincing.

25. On Chelmno, Krakowski, *Todeslager*; Klein, "Kulmhof/Chelmno." SS officer Herbert Lange, the first commandant at Kulmhof, had already overseen the murder of thousands of patients in the large region as part of the "euthanasia" operation, using, inter alia, one of the first gassing vans, a vehicle that relied on chemically pure carbon monoxide.

26. On the beginning of construction in Belzec, see interrogation of Eustachy Ukraiński, October 11, 1945, BArch, B 162/43904 (LG Bonn 28 KLs 8/10), Bd. Personenakte 3; Kuwałek, *Vernichtungslager*, pp. 51–61. On later events, see this book's chapter on Niemann's biography.

27. For a groundbreaking study, Arad, *Belzec*; for an overview, Lehnstaedt, *Kern*; as well as the contributions in Lehnstaedt and Traba, "*Aktion Reinhardt*"; on Harvest Festival, Grabitz and Scheffler, *Spuren*; Klemp, "*Aktion Erntefest.*"

28. On Globocnik, Sachslehner, *Millionen*; Rieger, *Creator.*

29. *Dienstkalender Himmlers 1941/42*, entry for October 13, 1941, p. 233.

30. See Bodek and Sandkühler, *Katzmann-Bericht.*

31. Perz, *Österreicher*, pp. 61–62.

32. Brack to Himmler, June 23, 1942, BArch, NS 19/1583.

33. See figures 8.3–8.33, and 9.1–9.12; the letter from Allers to Henriette Niemann reproduced in this volume as appendix 2, figure 2.

34. Interrogation of Josef Oberhauser in the main trial proceedings, June 12, 1973, HHW, 36346/12.

35. Rückerl, *NS-Vernichtungslager*, pp. 72–73, Friedlander, *Weg*, pp. 468–471, and Klee, "*Euthanasie*," pp. 374–377, pointed out the continuities in personnel between T4 and Reinhard, albeit without analyzing the role of the Chancellery of the Führer more closely.

36. Draft, Rassereferent RMbO (Erhard Wetzel) to RKO (Hinrich Lohse), October 25, 1941, BArch, All. Proz. 1/NO-365.

37. See the chapter on Niemann's biography in this volume.

38. Interrogation of Josef Oberhauser, January 10, 1968, HHW, 631a/1649.

39. Brack to Rasse- und Siedlungshauptamt, January 5, 1942, BArch, RS personnel file for Gottfried Schwarz.

40. See the contributions about Niemann and the Belzec killing center in this volume; also Sandkühler, "Trawniki-Männer," pp. 182–184; Kuwałek, *Vernichtungslager*, pp. 129–147.

41. Interrogation of Josef Oberhauser, April 20, 1960, LNW, Q 234/3167; interrogation of Josef Oberhauser, December 12, 1962, LNW, Q 234/3172; in detail also the main trial proceedings, June 12, 1973, HHW, 36346/12. Niemann and Barbl did not travel to Berlin but took care of procuring a motor and other elements for the gas chambers in Sobibor and installing them; see the contributions on Niemann's biography and the construction of Sobibor in this volume.

42. See *Dienstkalender Himmlers 1941/42*, entry for December 14, 1941, p. 290. On the significance and participants of the Wannsee Conference and Hitler's decision, see Roseman, *Wannsee-Konferenz*; Klein, "*Wannsee-Konferenz*"; in addition, the contributions in Kampe and Klein, *Wannsee-Konferenz*. For a diverging interpretation of Hitler's decision see Longerich, *Hitler*, pp. 826–637.

43. Interrogation of Josef Oberhauser, June 12, 1973, HHW, 36346/12; *Dienstkalender Himmlers 1941/42*, entry for April 17, 1942, pp. 400–401.

44. Interrogation of Thea Brack, June 7, 1947, Subsequent Nuremberg Trial 1 (Doctors' Trial), Brack vol. 4, Doc. 57.

45. Interrogation of Josef Oberhauser, June 12 and 19, 1973, HHW, 36346/12.

46. After the expansion of the gas chambers at Belzec, the first deportation trains from District Cracow arrived in early June. The passengers of two deportation trains from the Theresienstadt ghetto were murdered at Sobibor on June 15 and 16, see Sandkühler, "Trawniki-Männer," p. 180; https://deportation.yadvashem.org/index.html, February 2, 2022.

47. Musial, "Ursprünge," pp. 74–61, argues by contrast that Operation Reinhard was geared from the outset to the murder of the Jewish population of the entire General Government; for a general view of the course of events in the General Government see Arad, *Belzec*, pp. 125–153.

48. Interrogation of Arnold Oels, December 14, 1962, BArch, B 162/508; on the group of persons, Berger, *Experten*, which is both exhaustive and well-argued.

49. Although West German justice officials carried out an investigation into the activities of the chemist Dr. Helmut Kallmeyer, the case was closed without indictment; see Einstellungsverfügung Staw. Kiel, December 15, 1961, BArch, B 162/2209.

50. Berger, *Experten*, p. 85, likewise characterizes the relationship between Globocnik and the Chancellery of the Führer as "division of labor"; most recently, Hembera, *Rolle*, pp. 38–40.

51. Interrogation of Karl Streibel, November 26, 1962, BArch, B 162/43904—LG Bonn 28 KLs 8/10, Bd. Personenakte 3.

52. Ibid., June 13, 1963, BArch, B 162/2211.

53. Ibid., November 26, 1962, BArch, B 162/43904—LG Bonn 28 KLs 8/10, Bd. Personenakte 3.

54. Interrogation of Georg Michalsen, January 25, 1961, ibid., Bd. Personenakte 2.

55. Ibid., June 7, 1963, BArch, B 162/2211.

56. Among the men who had worked at Belzec, Gottlieb Hering, Hans Girtzig, Heinrich Gley, Max Gringers, Walther Kloss, Karl Schluch, and Hans Zänker were transferred to the forced labor camp in Poniatowa. Gottfried Schwarz, Robert Jührs, and Ernst Zierke ended up in Dorohucza, while Friedrich Tauscher and Reinhold Feix were redeployed to Budzyn; see Berger, *Experten*, pp. 403–415.

57. Message SS-Sonderkommando Sobibor, July 1, 1943, FSB, K-779 (Trawniki).

58. Judgement LG Düsseldorf, September 3, 1965, JuNSV, vol. XXII, p. 49; see Sereny, *Abgrund*, pp. 165–173; Berger, *Experten*, pp. 121–122.

59. Interrogation of Kurt Franz, December 3, 1959, BArch, B 162/3165; interrogation of Erich Bauer, December 7, 1962, LNW, Q 234/4286.

60. See *Dienstkalender Himmlers 1941/42*, entries for July 19, 1942, p. 496; also statement of Eda Lichtmann, March 3, 1964, LNW, Q 234/4569; statement of Moshe Bachir, December 14, 1965, LNW, Q 234/4464. On the second visit, on February 12, 1943, see ibid., and December 20, 1965, ibid.; statement of Chaim Engel, May 16, 1950, LNW, Q 234/4469.

61. See Cüppers, *Rauff*, pp. 114–116. In this context, the case of Dr. August Becker is instructive. In 1940, Becker transferred from the SD to T4. There, he conferred regularly with Brack on technical issues, procured carbon monoxide, and delivered it to the killing sites. Upon returning to the Reich Security Main Office one year later, he inspected the use of gassing vans on behalf of Walther Rauff, the head of the technical affairs division, and others (ibid., pp. 113–114, 139–141).

62. Interrogation of Josef Oberhauser, December 12, 1960, LNW, Q 234/3172; main trial proceedings, June 19, 1973, HHW, 36346/12; interrogation of Anna Fuchs, March 28, 1966, NIOD, 804 INV/47.

63. Schelvis, *Vernichtungslager*, pp. 63–65, 237.

64. On the role of the Reichsbahn, see Gottwaldt and Schulle, "*Judendeportationen*"; Gottwaldt, *Reichsbahn*.

65. On the responsibility of the civil administration, Pohl, *Judenverfolgung*, pp. 75–63; Roth, *Herrenmenschen*, pp. 175–234.

66. See Grabowski, *Hunt*; on the inner-Polish debate, Kowitz-Harms, *Shoah*, pp. 80–120.

67. Regarding various designations, those in circulation included *czarni*, "black ones" (due to the color of the uniforms), *Hiwis* (for *Hilfswillige,* "volunteer helpers"), and *Askaris* (for the auxiliaries in the Wilhelmine colony of German East Africa); see the chapter on the Trawnikis in this volume.

68. Abschlussbericht Aktion "Reinhardt," Stand 15.12.1943, BArch, NS 19/2234.

69. Survivors frequently pointed to this, e.g., statement of Moshe Bachir, December 12, 1965, LNW, Q 234/4464; statement of Alexander Petscherski, July 17, 1974, LNW, Q 234/4478. See also the chapter on Henriette Niemann in this book.

70. Bajohr, *Parvenüs*, p. 75.

71. For a completely new look at Hitler's personality and rule, Pyta, *Hitler*; also an essential study, Kershaw, *Hitler*. On Himmler see Longerich, *Himmler*.

72. Interrogation of Josef Oberhauser, December 12, 1960, LNW, Q 234/3172; main trial proceedings, June 19, 1973, HHW, 36346/12; interrogation of Anna Fuchs, March 28, 1966, NIOD, 804 INV/47.

73. Ibid.; interrogation of Kurt Franz, September 15, 1961, HHW, 461-36346/104.

74. On the motives of perpetrators, see Cüppers, "Täter," pp. 423–425.

5

Belzec

The First Operation Reinhard Killing Center

FLORIAN ROSS AND STEFFEN HÄNSCHEN

In 1941, approximately two million Jews lived in the so-called General Government. In 1942, over the course of ten months, around 450,000 of them fell victim to the systematic killings in the Belzec killing center.[1] The number of Sinti and Roma murdered there is not known.[2]

After the German occupation of Poland in September 1939, the Jewish population was forced out of public life in short order and deprived of its livelihoods. Jews were increasingly dependent on the supply of foodstuffs provided by the German civil administration.[3] In the ghettos, the occupiers created an abysmal housing and food situation, which they promptly exploited to offer new, severe criticism with antisemitic implications. Now, they said, "epidemic plagues" might break out.[4] Moreover, the Jews were depicted as an economic and social burden, but a radical, final "solution to the Jewish question" was still linked with the intention to expel the Jewish population from the General Government. The initial military successes during the invasion of the Soviet Union in the summer of 1941 appeared to offer the prospect of such an expulsion. But after the blitzkrieg had slowed and the German advance was stopped, the plan to force the Jews to leave the General Government and go "to the East" proved no longer feasible.

In 1941, the decision to murder the Jewish population gained acceptance within the Nazi regime and among its governors in occupied Eastern Europe. In the Soviet Union, beginning in the late summer of 1941, the death squads expanded their mass murder actions from Jewish men to women and children. In the Warthegau, a search for a killing site for Jews from the region began in July 1941. The location chosen was Chełmno/Kulmhof. From December 8, 1941, Jews were murdered there in so-called gas vans.

In this situation, when hundreds of thousands of Jews living in the occupied territories of the Soviet Union were being murdered behind the German front line, and German technicians were occupied with experiments to identify the most efficient method of killing, Reichsführer-SS Heinrich Himmler tasked the SS and police leader (SSPF) of District Lublin, Odilo Globocnik, in the fall of 1941 with the creation of a killing center in the region. The location selected was Bełżec. No written directive to establish Belzec, the first of the Operation Reinhard (*Aktion Reinhard*) camps, or documents regarding its building have survived, and therefore the origins of the killing center can be reconstructed only sketchily.[5]

Start-Up Phase

The decisive factor in the choice of the site was the easy accessibility of Bełżec. Centrally located between the districts of Lublin, Galicia, and Cracow with their roughly one million Jews, the town was connected to the railroad network leading to Cracow, Lublin, and Lwów. From the railroad station, a siding used by the forestry industry ran one thousand feet (300 m) southeast to an unloading ramp that could be incorporated into the structure of the killing center. The Germans were already familiar with the area around Bełżec, because a network of labor camps with more than ten thousand forced laborers, mostly Jews and several hundred Sinti and Roma, had been located there from May to October 1940. Approximately three thousand of the forced laborers were housed in the town of Bełżec itself.[6] Hermann Höfle, who was deployed in spring 1942 as the coordinator of Operation Reinhard in Globocnik's SSPF office, had worked as camp commandant in Bełżec in 1940.[7]

In the fall of 1941, five members of the Waffen-SS met in Bełżec. Four of them, Josef Oberhauser, Gottfried Schwarz, Fritz Jirmann, and Johann Niemann, had already been jointly sworn in for their service in Operation T4 (*Aktion T4*) two years earlier, in October 1939, in the Chancellery of the Führer (*Kanzlei des Führers*, KdF) in Berlin. They all had participated from the outset in the "euthanasia" murders of T4. Their job, as so-called burners or stokers (*Brenner*), was to pull the dead bodies out of the gas chambers and burn them in the ovens of the crematorium. Lorenz Hackenholt, the fifth member of the group, also was ordered to Bełżec by the KdF. It was the responsibility of these men to guide the construction of the Belzec facility on the basis of the knowledge they had gained in the T4 program. At first glance, the five—a brewer, a painter, a mason, a farmer, and a common laborer—appear relatively unqualified to set up a killing center of this magnitude. However, this manageable group of "experts" had acquired their real credentials at the "euthanasia" killing centers in Grafeneck, Brandenburg, and Bernburg, where they had taken part in the murder of approximately 10,000 persons at each site.

In developing the Belzec killing center, the five Waffen-SS comrades could rely neither on knowledgeable superiors nor on structures already in existence. Instead, they had to be enterprising and proactive. The materials needed for building the camp were not allocated to them by authorities at a higher level; they had to source them independently. The Central Construction Office of the Waffen-SS in Lublin confined itself to appearing on site at irregular intervals to gather information about the progress of the work, and dispensing advice. To procure the necessary building supplies, Josef Oberhauser made intermittent visits to Lublin and Zamość during the initial phase.[8]

The camp was built on the outskirts of Bełżec, atop the densely forested Kozielsk Hill. To this end, the Germans first had to create the preconditions, clear the hill, and level the ground. After that, construction of the work and housing barracks for Trawnikis and Jewish prisoners, as well as the building of the gas chamber, began. From mid-November until the end of December 1941, approximately twenty to thirty conscripted but well-compensated craftsmen from Bełżec took part in the construction work.[9] The first group of Trawnikis, who came to Belzec from the training camp in the village of Trawniki in November 1941, were immediately called on to help with the project.[10] Similarly, from January 1942 around 150 Jews from neighboring Lubycza Królewska had to perform forced labor at the construction site.

One of the main tasks of the men in the German advance detail was to ascertain the most effective and also most economical method of killing. In the process, they initially were guided by their experiences in the "euthanasia" program. For several weeks they experimented with carbon monoxide from gas cylinders brought from Lwów. Next, there were "trial gassings" in both a mobile gas van and the newly built gas chamber, to which groups of Poles with mental and physical impairments fell victim. Finally, one method won out: those doomed to die, it was decided, would be murdered in a stationary gas chamber with exhaust fumes from a tank engine acquired expressly for this purpose. In February 1942, approximately fifty Jews were killed in a first trial gassing, which demonstrated the practicability of the results obtained during the preceding weeks.

During the almost five-month period of Belzec's construction, the SS men sought to organize the subsequent mass murder as smoothly as possible—from the arrival of the train at the Bełżec station, its routing to the camp, the herding of the Jews from the freight cars, the removal of their clothing, the path to the gas chamber, the murder, all the way to the burying of the corpses. The valuables, money, and clothing taken from the deportees were stored in separate spaces, for the subsequent benefit of the German population. By and large, these practices were adopted by the commandants of Sobibor and Treblinka, the killing centers of Operation Reinhard that were established later. In contrast to those two camps, however, Belzec's state of development is to be characterized as rather simple and basic.

The arrival of two death trains at the ramp in Belzec on March 17, 1942, can be termed the beginning of Operation Reinhard.[11] Jews from Lublin and Lwów were the first of the approximately seventy thousand persons who were murdered in the gas chambers of Belzec within a four-week period ending on April 16, 1942.

Modification of the Camp in the Spring of 1942

As early as mid-April, the murder operations in Belzec had reached the limits of their capacity. Too many corpses had been buried in the mass graves. After decomposition began, the remains forced their way through the surface of the soil and into the open. This attracted attention, in particular that of Franz Stangl, then serving as commandant of Sobibor, when he visited Belzec in the early summer of 1942: "I went there by car. [. . .] The smell. It was everywhere. Wirth wasn't in his office. I remember, they took me to him . . . he was standing on a hill, next to the pits . . . the pits . . . full . . . they were full. I can't tell you; not hundreds, thousands, thousands of corpses . . . oh God. [. . .] They had put too many corpses in it and putrefaction had progressed too fast, so that the liquid underneath had pushed the bodies on top up and over and the corpses had rolled down the hill."[12]

With the observance of a "pause in resettlement" from April 17 until mid-May 1942, the murder enterprise in Belzec came to a halt for the first time. In addition, there was a "transport suspension" from June 18 to July 8, 1942. The German railway in the General Government, the *Ostbahn*, was unable to provide any more trains and cars for the deportations, because the needs of the Wehrmacht summer offensive in the Soviet Union had higher priority. The Germans took advantage of the pause in resettlement and the ensuing suspension of the transports to reorganize the operations in Belzec and undertake appropriate building alterations. The measures served primarily to increase the killing capacity. How successful this optimization was from the German standpoint is shown by the body counts after the killing center reopened: in August 1942 alone, around 135,000 Jews were murdered in Belzec; at least one death train arrived daily.

During the modifications to the camp, the individual stations through which the victims had to pass were moved farther apart: the ramp where the Jews left the train, the barracks where they undressed, and finally the path they took to the gas chamber, which now was longer. The deportees now had to walk through a corridor that led uphill to the building with the gas chambers. Screens consisting of barbed wire interwoven with pine branches prevented them from seeing what was going on around them. In March 1942, the gas chambers had still been within direct sight of the arrival ramp. A few

Jews, taking advantage of the confusing situation when they got off the death trains, had hidden and later escaped from the grounds of the camp.

Following another change in procedure, it was no longer the Trawnikis who opened the doors of the railroad cars and forced the deportees out and onto the ramp. Instead, Jews, who had been selected from previous transports for inclusion in work detachments, were forced to take over these tasks. In addition, they had to clean the cars before they were locked and pulled out of the camp again by the locomotive.

During the renovation, two camp sections were created in Belzec. They were separated by barbed wire and branches and linked by an access point. The death trains arrived in Camp I, also known as the Lower Camp. At the single-track, later double-track, ramp, the Jews were forced to undress and hand over their valuables. The women's hair was cut off before they entered the passageway leading to the gas chambers. Trawnikis and their German superiors drove them in that direction, urging them on with loud shouts, rifle butts, sticks, and whips. In Camp II, the Upper Camp, the overseers pushed the frightened people into the chambers, into which exhaust gases were channeled. The three gas chambers, which had been located in wooden barracks near the ramp, were dismantled during the reconstruction and replaced with a massive stone building in the Upper Camp, with six gas chambers. Vasilij Podenok, a Trawniki, remembered quite well how the victims were herded into these rooms: "It must be emphasized that the whole process of exterminating people presented a very dreadful sight. The people were terrified, they went insane when faced with imminent death, screamed, ran frantically to and fro, said goodbye to one another, lost consciousness."[13] Then death by suffocation ensued. Jewish forced laborers dragged the corpses out of the chambers, searched them for valuables, broke out any gold teeth they found, and threw the bodies into huge pits.

Topography of the Camp

Besides the grounds of the camp, with a surface area of about 18.5 acres, the group around Niemann had commandeered additional buildings in the small town of Bełżec. In December 1941, the Germans set up their housing and administration zone in two adjoining houses dating from before the First World War. The two structures were approximately three-tenths of a mile from the extermination site.[14] A Trawniki stood at the entrance to the compound as a sentry. One of the houses, the so-called commandant's office or headquarters, contained a kitchen, a dining room that also served as a staff room, and the camp office, in addition to living quarters. In the kitchen, the sisters Zofia and Nadia Jarocki from Bełżec, both civilian employees, prepared the meals for the Germans.[15] The second house was used exclusively as living quarters.

The headquarters building was the place where work in the camp was organized at mealtimes. "Over dinner, Schwarz, Hering, and Jirmann discussed what was scheduled for the following day. If someone had to perform a particular function, that was announced to him at breakfast by one of the three men previously named," Heinrich Gley reported after the war.[16] Heinrich Unverhau also confirmed that the organization of work did not take place "by means of a formal duty roster, for example at a roll-call; rather, [it] was settled at the breakfast table or during the midday meal."[17]

The German housing and administration area also included a wooden barracks building in which, in addition to Germans, six to eight Jewish women had their lodgings. The women, who performed cleaning and kitchen duties, were required to speak and understand German.

In a second wooden building, Erwin Fichtner had his office. As the so-called accounting and pay NCO (*Rechnungsführer*), he was responsible for handling commercial transactions. The

Polish mechanic Kazimierz Czerniak said, "I went to the commandant's office of the Belzec camp every week to pick up the money for the work done for the camp."[18] Alojzy Berezowski went to Fichtner's office "in connection with the rent payment for the rail spur" that led into the camp.[19] Erwin Fichtner's duties also included recording the confiscated valuables of the murdered Jews and processing them for further transport to Lublin. The stolen goods, gathered and sorted, were delivered to the SS garrison administration headquarters in Lublin. The SS man Werner Dubois had laid out a large garden in the German housing and administration sector. Robert Jührs recalled that "vegetables were grown."[20]

Once the murder began in Belzec, individual Jews from outside came to the "commandant's office" to inquire about the whereabouts of their family members. They were forced into the gas chambers and killed.[21]

Individual German perpetrators were lodged outside of the German housing and administration sector, in the homes of Polish or Ukrainian families who lived on the other side of the road to Lublin and Lwów. The so-called Kessler Mill in the immediate vicinity also was used as living quarters.

Outside the actual killing center, the camp complex also included the buildings of a railroad yard, around two-tenths of a mile from the camp and directly next to the public railroad station. Here, in a locomotive shed, a Jewish forced labor detachment was required to search through, sort, and temporarily store the belongings of the murdered Jews. Prisoners had previously gathered together the few possessions left behind by the deportees on the ramp and in the barracks where they undressed. Their belongings were loaded into railway tippers and pushed to the locomotive shed. Over time, enormous piles of clothing built up inside and next to the building. At regular intervals the garments and other possessions of the Jews were taken to central warehouses in Lublin.[22] The camp metalworking shop and the generator set for the power supply were located in other buildings in the railroad yard.

In the center of the small town of Bełżec, the Germans used a water-pumping station as a laundry. The mason Eugeniusz Goch stated after the war, "At this time I was given the job of bricking in the kettles in the camp's washhouse. The clothes of the Jews who were murdered in the killing center were washed in this washhouse."[23] How long this washhouse was in operation and what had led the perpetrators to create it are puzzles we can no longer piece together.

Around three-tenths of a mile from the killing center lay the Bełżec railroad station. All the death trains stopped here. The ramp itself had space for approximately fifteen railroad cars. Longer trains were separated into two or three sections at the station. Then, under the watch of the German railway official Rudolf Göckel, the sections were pushed to the ramp. On days when as many as four trains arrived, it often took an entire day or more for the freight cars with the deportees to be moved into the camp. A few Jews managed to take advantage of the stop at the station to escape. Sofia Molenda, then thirteen years old, lived nearby with her parents. She recalled, "I often saw how the transports arrived in the evening and were not pushed into the camp until early the next morning. They stood on the siding all night long. Some of the imprisoned Jews tried to escape. They were killed in the process. Others begged and pleaded for food and water."[24] The Polish railroad worker Wiktor Skowronek testified after the war, "Once, in the summer of 1942, approximately thirty people, both men and women and of various ages, were shot after an overnight stay by such a transport in the station, when they jumped out of the cars in an attempt to save their lives."[25] The Bełżec railroad station was completely destroyed on July 7, 1944, in an air strike on an ammunition train.

The German Camp Staff

In March 1942, the German camp staff in Belzec consisted of about fourteen men. In June/July and September/October 1942, the number of personnel was increased to thirty-seven, although there were never more than about twenty on-site at the same time. With one exception, they all had come to Belzec from Operation T4. Anyone with a civilian occupation was given a short military training course and the rank of SS-Unterscharführer. The insignia of the SS did not appear on the collar badge, however.

The camp commandant from December 1941 to July 1942 was SS-Obersturmführer Christian Wirth, who subsequently was detailed to Lublin as inspector of the three Operation Reinhard killing centers. In August 1942, Detective Chief Inspector Gottlieb Hering assumed the position of camp commandant, which he held until shortly before the camp was closed. Like Wirth, Hering had belonged to the Stuttgart police force before his participation in the T4 program.

Only one member of the German camp staff had to stand trial after the war: Josef Oberhauser, who was part of the first group of SS men in Belzec. On January 21, 1965, after a main hearing lasting four days, the former SS-Oberscharführer was sentenced to a prison term of four years and six months. On January 30, 1964, the Fourth Criminal Chamber of the Munich I Regional Court (*Landgericht*) rejected the request to initiate a full trial of six other German perpetrators.[26] Following their statements, the court found, "The accused irrefutably acted in the knowledge that they were in an utterly hopeless dilemma and could do nothing other than obey the orders issued to them."[27]

In subsequent investigation proceedings against Werner Dubois for having been part of the Sobibor camp staff, new facts emerged, permitting the conclusion that dropping the Belzec proceedings against him was not justified. On June 9, 1971, the office of the public prosecutor in Munich again brought charges against him. Dubois was accused of having participated in the wicked and cruel murder of three hundred thousand persons in Belzec. Before proceedings against him could be opened, however, he died on October 22, 1971.

Trawnikis

As in the other Operation Reinhard camps, men from the SS training camp in Trawniki were deployed to guard the Jewish prisoners and the grounds of the camp in Belzec. In total, the Germans are alleged to have brought to Belzec as many as 344 Trawnikis between the beginning of construction and the closing of the killing center in 1943. As a general rule, however, the number of men stationed there at any one time never exceeded 70 to 120.[28] The first Trawnikis were summoned to Belzec on November 18, 1941, and divided into three groups. The first platoon guarded the camp and the Jewish laborers; the second was on standby for deployment along the route from the train station to the camp when a deportation train arrived. The third platoon prepared for the next shift.

For their German superiors, the Trawnikis were not reliable underlings, a fact that surely was due in part to the circumstances of their recruitment in POW camps with intolerable living conditions. Their lack of dependability became apparent in various ways, including their frequent and sometimes documented attempts to escape. In late 1941, shortly after the arrival of the first Trawnikis in Belzec, a guard evaded his duty and was shot.[29] On July 8, 1942, at least four Trawnikis were shot along with Jewish prisoners after their joint plans to escape were betrayed.[30] Escape attempts of this kind were recorded even after the termination of the systematic murder in Belzec. On March 3, 1943, five Trawnikis successfully made their way through to the partisans. Approximately ten guards were shot while on the run.[31] After they had been disarmed, around 50

Trawnikis were sent back to the training camp on March 26, 1943. The Germans considered them a security risk.[32] One day later, on March 27, seventy-five new guards arrived in Belzec, but only two weeks later, the Germans had lost confidence in them also. Seven Trawnikis were shot on April 10, 1943, and the remaining guards were sent back to their training camp. For the intervening period, until new men arrived from Trawniki, members of the German Order Police's Reserve Police Battalion 67, stationed in Zamość, were ordered to Belzec. For three days, beginning on April 11, 1943, the battalion secured the camp, which had already been closed. Some police officers later testified that they had had to execute thirteen additional Trawnikis.[33] Policeman Johannes Altenkamp from Essen confirmed the mutiny of the Trawnikis: "We had to stand sentry along the outer periphery of the camp. It was said that the guards (so-called Trawnikis) had mutinied."[34]

After the war, at least fifty-three Trawnikis who had worked in Belzec under German control were put on trial in the Soviet Union and convicted. At least seventeen of the defendants were sentenced to death and executed.[35]

The Trawniki Samuel Kunz, deployed in Belzec and well known to the West German justice system, was never convicted. On July 29, 1941, the twenty-year-old Red Army soldier was taken prisoner near Kiev and sent to a POW camp near Chełm. Kunz was of German descent, which was surely one reason why he was transferred to the SS training camp in Trawniki on September 1, 1941. Presumably he went to Belzec in November 1941 as one of the first guards, proved himself reliable in the Germans' view, and remained on-site until March 1943. When the Red Army moved closer, Kunz, as a member of SS Battalion Streibel,[36] took part in the westward retreat. In September 1944, while the war was still in progress, he applied for naturalization and was granted German citizenship.

After the war he lived near Bonn and, in 1965, was hired as a handyman by the Federal Ministry for Regional Planning and Urban Development. In July 1972, he was given civil-servant status, and he retired on September 1, 1981. In April 1961, the Munich public prosecutor's office had initiated investigation proceedings against Kunz. As his whereabouts could not be determined, the proceedings were dropped in August 1963. Further investigation of Kunz by the public prosecutor's office in Hamburg ended on July 31, 1968, without results. In July 2010, proceedings against him were opened. The public prosecutor's office in Dortmund charged him with having been an accessory to at least 430,000 murders in Belzec. On November 18, 2010, before the trial could begin, Samuel Kunz died at the age of 89.

Jewish Prisoners

The statements of Rudolf Reder, SS men, and Trawnikis suggest that, from August 1942, approximately five hundred Jewish prisoners performed forced labor in Belzec. This figure changed constantly, however, depending on the number of transports arriving and the size of the labor force required by the Germans. When more transports arrived, more workers were selected; then, when they were no longer needed, they were murdered.

When a death train arrived at the ramp, the Germans assigned individual Jews to forced labor. In the early period of the camp's existence, they were shot after a few days and replaced with newly arriving fellows in misery. In the early summer of 1942, the Germans changed their approach and set about creating a continuously operating "workforce." Now the forced laborers were assigned to permanent details, or detachments (*Kommandos*), although the new arrangement did not mean that the actions the overseers took against them were any less violent.[37]

From this point in time, contact was no longer permitted between the work details in the Lower Camp (Camp II) and the prisoners in the killing area of the Upper Camp (Camp I) who were forced to drag the dead out of the gas chambers, break out gold teeth, dig mass graves, and bury the bodies.[38] The prisoners in the Lower Camp were used for building barracks, chopping wood, and working in the camp kitchen, the tailors' workshop, and the shoemakers' detachment. In addition, they had to assist when the death trains arrived. One detachment supervised the completely exhausted Jews as they climbed and fell out of the railroad cars, helped them undress, and, as ordered, confiscated their luggage and clothing and took these items to the collection sites, where another Jewish work detachment sorted the belongings.

One can scarcely imagine the physical and mental agonies to which the Jewish forced laborers were subjected in the killing center. Rudolf Reder characterized the mental and emotional state of the group of prisoners: "I don't know how to describe the mood in which we lived, we doomed prisoners, or what we felt hearing those horrible pleas of the people being suffocated each day, and the cries of the children. Three times a day we saw thousands of people on the verge of losing their minds. And we were close to insanity. We moved from one day to the next without knowing how. We had not a moment of illusion. Each day we died a little along with entire transports of people who for a short moment still experienced the torment of illusion."[39]

The majority of the prisoners in Belzec were men. The share of women was presumably less than 10 percent. Estimates vary as to when the first Jewish women were deployed for work in Belzec and how many of them there were. People living in Bełżec reported that they had seen female prisoners as early as April 1942. The presence of women in Camp I is documented from October 1942 at the latest.[40] In total, there are said to have been no more than forty women selected at the ramp in Belzec.[41] In the town of Bełżec, a female Jewish dentist maintained a practice where SS men and Trawnikis were treated until the

closure of the camp. She worked for the German perpetrators without being directly integrated into the camp structure.[42]

In some cases, Jews could leave the camp under the watchful eye of Trawnikis. These prisoners were used to tear down barracks or procure foodstuffs in town. For example, a Jew named Herc regularly picked up bread for the camp in a bakery in the town.[43] Jewish women also worked sometimes in a laundry in the town of Bełżec. A Jew who supposedly was a banker paid the outstanding accounts of the Germans in the surrounding area.[44]

The Small Town of Bełżec and the Death Camp

At the beginning of the 1940s, Bełżec had a population of somewhat more than 1,800. As a result of their proximity to the camp and contacts with its personnel, the local inhabitants were directly confronted with the mass murder.

Robert Kuwałek identified a total of 179 death trains that stopped at the Bełżec station and waited there sometimes a day or a night to continue the journey to the camp. Maria Warzocha, twenty years old at the time, watched the trains from her parents' house and heard the background noise when the people were herded out of the train and into the gas chamber: "Often I peeped out the window from behind the curtain and counted the freight cars. I heard the people on the transports calling out, 'Water, water.' I remember the terrible, shrill screams of women, little children, and men, which you could hear after the cars had been unloaded. The screaming gradually increased and then transitioned into noise that could be heard all over Bełżec. After about 15 minutes, the noise died down completely."[45]

The events could not be concealed from Germans who were traveling through, either. The railroad yard in which a Jewish work detachment sorted the belongings of the murdered Jews was easily visible, located directly next to the track and the public train station. The German district farmer (*Kreisland-wirt*) with responsibility for the small town of Bełżec, Heinz Kettner, described a train journey past the camp: "This camp was surrounded by barbed wire and a high fence of greenery. It was also guarded by non-German volunteers [*Hiwis*]. Even though the foliage made it impossible to see inside, while passing by one could nevertheless see enormous heaps of clothing, at least twice as high as a house and being piled higher and higher by Jewish workers."[46] The Eastern Railway official Oskar Diegelmann passed through Bełżec on business trips and observed the work of the Jewish prisoners: "Behind the locomotive shed I saw mountains of garments of all kinds. There were also huge quantities of shoes, as well as jewelry and other valuables. [. . .] Clothing that no longer seemed wearable was doused with gasoline and burned."[47]

The Wehrmacht NCO Wilhelm Cornides received a special impression of the killing center and the local population's awareness of it. On August 31, 1942, he traveled through the town of Bełżec in a passenger train. The southern boundary of the camp extended almost to the tracks of the Lwów–Lublin–Warsaw route. In his diary entries, he wrote, "We went past the Belzec camp. Previously we passed through tall pine forests for a considerable time. When the woman called out, 'Now it's coming up,' we saw only a tall hedge of fir trees. A strong, sweetish odor was distinctly noticeable. 'They already stink,' the woman said. 'Oh, nonsense, that's the gas,' the railroad policeman laughed. In the meantime—we had traveled around 220 yards—the sweetish odor had turned into a pungent smell of burning. 'That's from the crematorium,' the policeman said. Shortly after that, the fence came to an end. We saw a guard-house with SS sentries in front of it."[48]

With knowledge of what was happening in the camp, the town's population maintained brisk trading relations with the Germans and the Trawnikis. A bakery in Bełżec produced 220 to 265 pounds of bread daily for the killing center. The flour for the bread and the wood for the oven were provided by the Germans. The bakery owner received 80 groschen for every 2.2 pounds (1 kilo) of bread. The branch of the agricultural and trading cooperative in Bełżec supplied the Germans with a variety of goods. Craftsmen from Bełżec and the surrounding area sold their services to the Germans. In addition to official dealings such as accommodating German perpetrators in villagers' homes, baking bread for the camp, and providing medical care, local residents also profited indirectly from trade. For example, in their free time, the Trawnikis frequented the shops and were welcome customers. "In the process, they paid sometimes with money, sometimes with watches. The guards had money and other precious objects from the camp."[49]

One popular gathering place for the Trawnikis was the Komadowski Bar in the center of Bełżec, which can be seen in Johann Niemann's photos. Doing business with the Trawnikis was often lucrative: "Anyway, all that interested me was my profit. I paid 60 zloty for a liter of vodka and sold it for 200 zloty. It often happened that I joined them in drinking the schnaps they bought from me."[50] The Trawnikis' money also lured "dealers" from out of town to Bełżec. In addition, prostitutes waited for the men on the grounds of the railroad station.

But besides the individuals who reaped profits from the proximity of the camp and cooperated with the perpetrators, there were also people who risked their lives to save Jews from death in the gas chamber. Three inhabitants of Bełżec were recognized by Yad Vashem as "Righteous Among the Nations." They had hidden Jewish women in the town during the German occupation.[51]

Public Murder

The location of the Belzec killing center was not such that the events could be concealed from the public eye; the systematic killing of Jews could not escape notice. Once the murders in

Belzec began, knowledge of the killing center spread throughout the region. Polish railroad workers and people living in neighboring houses watched freight trains full of human beings roll into the camp, but no one left the camp again. The Jewish communities from which people were transported to Belzec sought to learn where the deportees had been taken. Soon the first escapees turned up, people who had made it back to their hometowns. As soon as three weeks after the beginning of the mass murder in Belzec, the Polish physician Zygmunt Klukowski wrote in his diary entry for April 8, 1942, "We already know now with complete certainty that one train from Lublin and one from Lwów, each with twenty cars, come to Belzec every day. Here they make the Jews get out of the cars, herd them behind the barbed-wire fencing, kill them with electric current (or poison them with gas), and then burn the corpses. Even en route, people, especially railroad workers, are witness to dreadful scenes, as the Jews are already well aware why they are being taken there."[52]

From the summer of 1942, the existence of the Belzec killing center, at least in the region around Bełżec, was a "public secret," as the physician Dr. Janusz Peter from the neighboring town of Tomaszów Lubelski expressed it in his memoirs.[53] News of the existence of a death camp also spread beyond the region, however. For example, knowledge of the camp reached Warsaw as early as the beginning of April 1942. On April 5 or 6, 1942, a fugitive known as "Slamek" (Szlama),[54] who had escaped from the Kulmhof killing center, warned the underground archive Oneg Shabbat in the Warsaw Ghetto about the events in Belzec: "It kills *oyf aza oyfn* [Yiddish: in the same way] as in Chelmno, is my turn coming too? The *beys-oylem* [cemetery] is in Belzec."[55]

The Polish underground movement also reported on Belzec on a number of occasions. The mass murder was first put on record in April 1942 in the information bulletin of the Home Army (*Armia Krajowa*, AK).[56] In June 1942, a first detailed report on the camp was published.[57] In the fall of 1942, Jan Karski, the agent of leading circles in the Home Army and the representative office maintained in Poland by the Polish government in exile, brought materials concerning the murder of the Polish Jews to the Polish government in exile in London. Karski had traveled from Warsaw to District Lublin and elsewhere, and in his report he explicitly mentioned the Belzec camp. The mass murder thus became known internationally.[58]

Closing and Dismantling of the Camp

The last death trains came from Rawa Ruska and reached Belzec between December 7 and 11, 1942. However, trains continued to run through the town en route to Sobibor. The reasons for the closure of the Belzec killing center are not documented, and the reason for calling a halt to the killing in this place at this time cannot be conclusively determined. Robert Kuwałek named three possibilities: first, the majority of the Jews from Galicia had already been murdered by this point; second, there was no room for any more mass graves; and third, the plan to murder the approximately three hundred thousand Jews of Romania in Belzec was dropped.[59]

Starting in August 1942, corpses were already being burned on a smaller scale to erase the traces of the mass murder. For that purpose, Jewish prisoners were forced to open the mass graves with their bare hands. From November 1942, three months after Johann Niemann had left Belzec, bodies of the victims were retrieved from the mass graves and burned on large pyres. Lorenz Hackenholt brought a mechanical excavator from the Treblinka camp for this endeavor. A resident of Bełżec recalled, "Right after this work, Hackehhold [sic] smelled of dead bodies."[60] Others reported that for months, at least until mid-April, three or even as many as five pyres had burned round the clock.[61] Dark clouds of smoke, with a strong smell of putrefaction, wafted across the countryside. "This odor was so revolting," a local resident said, "that at the Bełżec train station, just two kilometers from the camp, you could breathe only through a handkerchief."[62] After the corpses were burned, the ashes were tipped back into the graves. Complete erasure of the traces was impossible, however. During archeological research performed on the grounds of the camp between 1997 and 1999, it was determined that not all the bodies had been disinterred.

When it was apparent that the so-called unearthing work was coming to an end, the perpetrators began to dismantle structures on the grounds of the killing center: buildings, guard towers, barbed-wire fencing, and barracks. All traces were to be erased. Tadeusz Dujanowicz, a senior forestry official, recalled that SS men from Belzec came to him in the head forestry office in Tomaszów Lubelski in the spring of 1943 and demanded young saplings to plant in soil that was not in use. They wanted spruce trees at least 3.3 feet (1 m) tall, and they asked for planting instructions. They declined the offer to involve an expert from the forestry office.[63] The spruce trees were densely planted on parts of the grounds of the Belzec killing site.

The Germans told the approximately three hundred Jewish prisoners[64] who performed demolition and forestation work until the end that they would soon be taken to a labor camp. On June 26, 1943, they were made to board a train. A journey into the unknown ensued. When the train headed toward Chełm, they realized that the Germans' promises had been lies.[65] Some tried to escape from the cars, and at least two men succeeded.[66] The arrival of the train in Sobibor impressed itself on the memory of the prisoners in the camp there. Although they themselves were locked in their barracks, they became aware that the new arrivals refused to get out of the cars and tried to attack the Germans. Sobibor survivor Thomas Blatt recalled, among other things, the arrival of the train. From their barracks, he

said, they had heard the shots that killed the new arrivals. From the contents of the slips of paper they found in the dead men's clothes later on, they could tell that the prisoners were from Belzec. According to the messages, the men had been told that they were being taken to Germany. There were tables in their railroad cars, and they had received provisions for three days: bread rations, vodka, and canned goods. In the event their slips of paper were found, they wrote, this would be proof that they had been deceived. "Don't trust the Germans," they cautioned the prisoners in Sobibor. They urged the Sobibor prisoners to exact revenge.[67] The messages of the prisoners from Belzec and their attack on the Germans strengthened the will to resist in Sobibor.

After the Germans had cleared the camp grounds and left Belzec, residents of Bełżec and the surrounding area set out for the site. Equipped with shovels and rakes, they rummaged through the grounds of the former killing center. As the mason Eugeniusz Goch said, they dug up the unguarded land in a search for gold and valuables.[68] It evidently took some time until the German authorities learned of this.

In September 1943, the SS man Heinrich Unverhau, who had been deployed in Belzec from June/July 1942 to June 1943, received instructions to go with Trawnikis from Sobibor to Belzec.[69] With the assistance of craftsmen from Bełżec, Unverhau had a residence and an outbuilding constructed on the former camp grounds, and had the land reforested. After the work was done, a German "commission" searched the terrain, looking for remnants that indicated the site's role as a killing center. Above all, all traces that offered proof of the extermination of the Jews were to be obliterated. Armbands, books, and identification papers were burned.[70] After the commission had released the site, an ethnic German Trawniki moved into the "farmhouse" and guarded the area. By July 1944, however, he was forced to leave his new home again. He fled from the advancing Red Army.

Flight and Survival

As during the "operations" in the ghettos and the journey in the death train, Jews also attempted to escape the massacres in Belzec. The history of resistance and escape attempts in the Belzec death camp is documented only in a few tiny puzzle pieces. A revolt like those in Treblinka and Sobibor, which would have given the prisoners a chance to escape and survive, did not occur in Belzec. In the accounts of Jewish survivors, however, there are repeated mentions of escapees who returned from Belzec to the ghettos and related what they had experienced. In late March 1942, two or three people went to the Jewish council (*Judenrat*) in Zamość and explained that they had been transported the previous day from Lublin to Belzec and seen the murders committed there. The survivor Nachman Schuman recalled that he met an escapee from Belzec who had managed, in February 1943, to get out of the camp in a freight car that was transporting the clothing of murdered Jews.[71]

Only rarely have the names and subsequent fates of the prisoners who escaped become known. There is documentation of some Belzec escapees, whose trace vanishes after they fled, however. On April 13, 1942, bright and early, thirteen-year-old Lejb Wolsztajn went to see the chairman of the Jewish council in Zamość. Along with his mother and seventeen-year-old sister, he was among the first Jews transported from Zamość to Belzec, on April 11, 1942. Here he was able to hide in a toilet pit and escape at night.[72] Edward Podgorski worked as a Jewish medical orderly in the Lublin ghetto. After the deportations from Lublin began, he had an opportunity to speak with a young man who had escaped from Belzec. He had managed to hide in a shed. Podgorski knew the man personally; his name was Schmierer, and he was the son of a furniture manufacturer. Schmierer reported that the people had to undress in Belzec and go into so-called shower rooms, which in reality were gas chambers. "The young man," Podgorski said, "related this to

our group, and we passed it on. Then everyone in the ghetto knew it."[73]

On March 20, 1942, 700 Jews were transported from Żółkiew to Belzec. The Jewish women refused to enter the gas chambers. Two women, Mina Astman and Małka Thalenfeld, took advantage of the resulting confusion to crouch in a refuse pit. At dark they fled from the camp and returned to Żółkiew a few days later.[74] Attempts to escape were made also by the last prisoners of Belzec. Sylko Herc reappeared in the small town of Bełżec after escaping from the train to Sobibor and told Edward Luczyński that he wanted to go to his family in Cracow.[75]

To this day there is verifiable information only on three men who successfully escaped from Belzec and survived the end of the war: Rudolf Reder, Chaim Hirszman, and Israel Spira.[76]

Israel Spira was born on November 12, 1889. He was the rabbi of Pruchnik and subsequently of Ustrzyki Dolne. With the onset of the Second World War, he moved to Lwów, where he soon had a large Hasidic following. In October 1942, he and his wife, Perel, were transported to Belzec. The number of days Israel Spira had to spend in the killing center is not part of the historical record. Together with two other Jews, he was designated to accompany a train carrying the clothing of murdered people to the Janowska Street forced labor camp in Lwów. Here, with the help of a Hasidic follower, he was able to disappear in the mass of forced laborers. One day at dusk, as Spira was marching back to the Janowska camp with his work detachment, he made his escape. Later he was recaptured and, in June 1943, deported to Bergen-Belsen—he possessed a South American passport. On April 13, 1945, he was liberated in a death train out in the open countryside. In 1946, he immigrated to the United States and lived in New York, where he died on October 30, 1989, at the age of almost one hundred. Israel Spira did not record anything in writing about his time in Belzec. What he said about his imprisonment in the Janowska camp apparently applied also to Belzec: "People often asked me to put the stories from Janowska together in a book. I said that I'm not writing any more books."[77]

Chaim Hirszman came from Janów Lubelski. On November 2, 1942, he, his wife Sara, and their one-and-one-half-year-old son Sewek were transported to Belzec. At the ramp, he was selected for forced labor in the camp. His wife and son were killed immediately. In Belzec, his tasks included burning the corpses of the victims and helping with the closure and dismantlement of the camp. Hirszman successfully escaped from the train taking the last members of the Sonderkommando from Belzec to Sobibor on June 26, 1943.

In March 1946, his second wife, Pola Hirszman, described her husband's escape. "My husband [. . .] made an arrangement with two buddies who were in the same freight car with him. They took up the boards from the floor of the car, and then decided by lot who would get to escape first. The lot fell to my husband. He squeezed through the opening, legs first, and then slid through the hole. He had to lie there until the train had passed, and even then he couldn't stand up right away, because the Germans were standing on the roofs of the cars with automatic weapons. The two buddies were supposed to escape right after my husband. They had agreed on a place to meet. My husband waited there, but the others didn't come, they probably had not managed to escape."[78] After his escape, Hirszman joined a communist partisan group. On March 19, 1946, he began to disclose his memories of the Belzec camp to the Jewish historical commission in Lublin. That evening he was shot in his apartment in circumstances that were never fully explained. Allegedly the perpetrators wanted to get possession of a weapon. Hirszman's fragmentary account was completed by his wife.[79]

Rudolf Reder was transported from Lwów to Belzec on August 16, 1942, and selected for forced labor. He was required to dig pits, drag the bodies of the murder victims out of the gas chambers, and hastily bury them in the pits. In his account

concerning Belzec, he wrote, "Our legs sank in the blood of our brothers, we were treading on mounds of corpses—that was the worst, the most horrible thing."[80]

In November 1942, Reder was able to escape when he was sent to Lwów with four SS men and one Trawniki to purchase sheet metal. The Trawniki Karol Trautwein, with whom he was sitting alone in a truck, had dozed off. Reder got out, ran away, and hid in the home of a former Polish domestic worker until the war ended. After the war, he married the woman who had saved his life, left Poland, and moved to Canada in 1951. Rudolf Reder died in Toronto on October 8, 1977. As early as 1946, the Central Jewish Historical Commission in Cracow published his account of the months he was forced to spend in Belzec. There are many descriptions of the death camp from the perspective of the German perpetrators, the Trawnikis, and, of course, Poles from Bełżec. But the account by Rudolf Reder is the only detailed documentation by a Jew who survived Belzec.

Belzec after 1944

After the Trawniki left behind on the grounds had fled before the arrival of the Red Army, inhabitants of Bełżec looted the "farmhouse." In addition, grave robbers gathered in the area of the former death camp. The deputy commandant of the citizens' militia in Bełżec, Mieczysław Niedużak, described it: "After the closure of the camp, the local population began digging up the grounds to find gold or valuables left behind by Jews. Individual corpses were exhumed, and sometimes mass graves, too, were opened. The bodies were in a state of complete decomposition. People searched for gold teeth in the mouths of the corpses. That explains why the camp terrain is heavily plowed up and consequently contaminated. At present one sees a great many human bones and ashes of burned corpses at the earth's surface, and one also finds women's hair and wigs.

People pulled the bodies of dead children out of the former latrine."[81]

The extent of the grave looting can be surmised from the fact that the deputy commandant had to admit that the local security authorities were unable to put an end to the goings-on: "After the Germans had fled Bełżec, the local militia tried hard to prevent the excavations on the camp grounds, but this was hard to achieve. As soon as one group had been driven away, the next one was right there."[82]

The commonplaceness of "hunting for treasure" on the former camp grounds was described by a local resident who was a schoolboy at the time: "In the following years it was completely normal and natural that, after school was out for the day, a great many of the students (not all) went in a group to the grounds of the former camp, where we started searching for valuable objects."[83] The valuables found at the former camp site were usually sold to dealers, who resold them to jewelers in Cracow and elsewhere.

An early judicial inquiry by Polish authorities into the mass murder in Belzec took place early on, in the years 1945–1946. The Lublin District Commission for Investigation of the German Crimes interrogated thirty-six persons—Polish railroad workers and people from Bełżec and the surrounding towns and villages. These interrogations are an important source of knowledge about the events in the death camp and the actions of the German perpetrators.[84]

In 1947, the Council for the Protection of Struggle and Martyrdom Sites (ROPWiM) officially took charge of the former death camp and assumed responsibility for its commemoration in Bełżec. This Polish state institution had responsibility for all the sites of German crimes in Poland. The efforts to set up memorials, however, focused at first on camps where Christian Poles, in addition to Jews, had been imprisoned, such as Majdanek and Auschwitz. For the grounds of the former Belzec

killing center, the authorities did not develop a plan during the first years after liberation; the site was largely abandoned. Not until 1949 did they have a small, unlocked crypt erected in the northern part of the camp area, in which skeletal remains of the victims found on the surface of the earth were gathered.[85] The fence installed in 1954, which was intended to protect the site, enclosed only three sides, however, and it was stolen within a short time. On the southwest side of the former camp, a railroad-line approach road was specially created for a sawmill that was built in the immediate vicinity during the 1950s. Heavy trucks now drove over the terrain and contributed to its devastation.

Not until the early 1960s did plans for establishing a memorial begin to take shape. It was opened on December 1, 1963, on a section of the grounds.[86] A museum presenting the history of the camp was not yet part of the overall concept, and the buildings used by the Germans outside of the camp proper, such as the train station, the locomotive shed, and the housing and administration sector, were not included in the project.

The central component of the memorial was a block of stone at the spot where the crypt had previously stood. At the foot of the block, a "metaphorical sculpture of two figures" was erected to represent "the suffering and the help of fellow men under tragic circumstances." The words inscribed on the stone block were, "In memory of the victims of Nazi terror who were murdered in the years 1941–1943."[87] No mention was made at this site of the fact that the overwhelming majority of the victims were Jews. Other components of the memorial were monumental concrete urns that stood atop the mass graves and were meant to symbolize eternal fire.

A plaque at the entrance provided the information that six hundred thousand Jews and around 1,500 Christian Poles were murdered in the camp.[88] From this point on, the care and supervision of the site were in the hands of the local forestry authorities. To ensure that the memorial site was guarded, and to make digging difficult, a forester's lodge was built nearby.[89] The opening of the memorial site received scant attention from the general public. Within a short time, the stone components deteriorated because they were not structurally sound. The memorial fell into disrepair, and the place continued to garner little attention.

In the mid-1990s planning began for the erection of a new memorial in Bełżec. The American Jewish Committee (AJC) and the Polish government cooperated in the implementation of the plans and shared the costs. The decisive initiative for the project came from Miles Lerman, a longstanding and highly energetic advocate for the creation of a new memorial site. Lerman, a native of Tomaszów Lubelski, had lost his entire family in Belzec.[90] On June 3, 2004, the memorial site was dedicated in its present form. It combines commemoration of the camp's victims with a museum, which is under the authority of the Majdanek State Museum in Lublin. The components of the architectural and sculptural work symbolize the suffering and death of the Jews. The primary goal of the composition was to create a symbolic cemetery protecting the thirty-three mass graves. From the opening in 2004 to December 2017, 456,581 persons visited the memorial site in Bełżec.[91]

In 2015, part of the housing and administration sector was turned over to the Majdanek State Museum.[92] This sector included the so-called commandant's office and an outbuilding that the Germans had ordered to be built in the summer of 1942. Other buildings from the camp era have thus far not been included in the memorial zone. Therefore, the second house located in the housing and administration area and used exclusively as living quarters is not part of the stretch of land placed at the disposal of the Majdanek Museum. In addition, the locomotive shed in the immediate vicinity of the memorial site and the laundry building occasionally used by the Germans have thus far not been designated as places connected with the history of the Belzec killing center.

Bełżec in the Niemann Photo Collection

Johann Niemann spent approximately nine months in Belzec, from the fall of 1941 until the summer of 1942. His store of photos contains four pictures from that time period. Two of these shots were taken in the winter of 1941–1942 on the grounds of the Germans' housing and administration sector (see figs. 5.2 and 5.3.).

Thus far, four photos of the grounds of the housing and administration area are known. One shot shows Germans standing sentry in front of the entrance to the area.[93] One photo supposedly shows Erich Fuchs during weapons training behind the commandant's office.[94]

Two other shots of the headquarters sector appear in the photo album of Dr. Janusz Peter, a physician and local historian from Tomaszów Lubelski. Visible in one picture is a group of ten perpetrators who have posed behind the headquarters building.[95] The second photo shows the yard of the housing and administration area with the office of the accounting and pay NCO and a part of the outbuilding. One person in the photo is identified in the album as "Unteroffizier [NCO] Pichner." The photo album of Dr. Janusz Peter is preserved in the Janusz Peter Regional Museum in Tomaszów Lubelski.[96]

The third photo in the inventory of the Niemann collection, which was taken in Bełżec, shows SS men on the road between the death camp and the German housing and administration sector. They are standing on the main road that crosses through the town of Bełżec and links the large cities of Warsaw and Lwów. In the fourth photograph, two Trawnikis are seen in the Komadowski Bar, located in Bełżec (see figs. 5.1 and 5.4).[97]

Notes

1. Until the 1990s, it was assumed that 600,000 persons had been murdered in Belzec. This number was based on calculations made in 1945/46 by the Lublin District Commission for the Investigation of German Crimes in Poland. Today, the Bełżec Memorial Site estimates the number of victims at approximately 450,000. This number roughly corresponds to that reported to the Reich Security Main Office in Berlin in January 1943 by Hermann Höfle, the official with responsibility for the deportation and murder of the Jews in the office of SS and Police Leader Odilo Globocnik in Lublin. For Belzec, Höfle estimated the number of persons deported to the camp by December 1942 at 434,508. On the so-called Höfle telegram see Witte and Tyas, "A New Document."

2. The Polish historian Robert Kuwałek mentions the deportation of Roma to Belzec from Kołomyja and Stanisławów in the spring of 1942 and from Borysław and Drohobycz in August 1942, but gives no numbers. See Kuwałek, *Belzec*, pp. 251–252.

3. See Musial, *Deutsche Zivilverwaltung*.

4. After the widespread outbreak of typhus in the General Government in 1940, the German authorities feared a new epidemic. See Browning, "Genocide and Public Health."

5. As a result, there were differing interpretations of the origin and purpose of the killing center. The question was whether, from the very outset, all the Jews of the General Government, indiscriminately, were to be murdered in Belzec, or the intake area of Belzec was to be limited to a specific region in the General Government and only those Jews who were ill, old, and unfit for work were to be killed. The Germans still drew such a distinction in the case of the first transports from the large cities of Lublin and Lwów in March 1942; only in the late summer of 1942 did they begin to transport Jewish communities in their entirety to the death camps. See Kuwałek, "Bełżec," in Benz and Distel, *Der Ort des Terrors*, vol. 8, p. 332.

6. On the labor camps in and around Belzec, see Silberklang, *Tears*, pp. 128–129.

7. Perz, "Warum Österreicher?" in Lehnstaedt and Traba, *"Aktion Reinhardt,"* p. 61.

8. There are speculations that a shortage of building supplies led to a delay in the building of Belzec and that the death camp actually was intended to be "operational" in December 1941, at the same time as Kulmhof.

9. Kuwałek, *Belzec*, p. 59.

10. On the origin and function of the Trawnikis see the chapter by Martin Cüppers in this volume.

11. It cannot be ruled out that a death train reached Belzec even earlier than March 17, 1942. See Pohl, *Nationalsozialistische Judenverfolgung*, p. 186.

12. Sereny, *Darkness*, p. 111 ff.

13. Interrogation of Vasilij Podenok, February 23, 1965, BArch B 162/43904 (LG Bonn 28 KLs 8/10), Bd. Personenakte 3.

14. The German customs office was housed in the buildings from 1939 to 1941.

15. Interrogation of Natyna Krystna, October 12, 1966, StAM 33033/34.

16. Interrogation of Heinrich Gley, May 2, 1963, ibid.

17. Interrogation of Heinrich Unverhau, May 6, 1963, ibid.

18. Interrogation of Kazimierz Czerniak, October 18, 1945, ibid.

19. Interrogation of Alojzy Berezowski, November 5, 1945, ibid.

20. Interrogation of Robert Jührs, October 11, 1961, StAM 33033/11.

21. Interrogation of Eugeniusz Goch, October 14, 1945, StAM 33033/34.

22. The items in the central storehouse for the clothing of those murdered in Operation Reinhard were taken to the Old Airfield camp in Lublin, where mostly Jewish female forced laborers searched through them, sorted them, and packed them up yet again. Medications, shoes, and other items went to various warehouses in Lublin. From there the things were sent deeper into the Reich or distributed to ethnic Germans resettled in the Zamość region. Individual trains with clothing from Belzec also found their way to the Jewish forced labor camp on Janowska Street in Lwów.

23. Interrogation of Eugeniusz Goch, October 14, 1945, StAM 33033/34.

24. Interrogation of Sofia Molenda, October 19, 1966, ibid.

25. Interrogation of Wiktor Skowronek, October 16, 1945, ibid.

26. The men were Ernst Zierke, Robert Jührs, Heinrich Unverhau, Kurt Franz, Erich Fuchs, and Werner Dubois. Three of them were convicted in later proceedings as a result of their crimes in Sobibor and Treblinka: Kurt Franz (Treblinka) was sentenced on September 3, 1965,

to life in prison, Erich Fuchs (Sobibor) on December 20, 1966, to four years in prison, Werner Dubois (Sobibor) on December 20, 1966, to a three-year prison term.

27. Refusal to open the main proceedings against Zierke, Jührs, Unverhau, Franz, Fuchs, Dubois, January 30, 1964, StAM 33033/34.

28. The Office of Special Investigations, a unit of the United States Department of Justice focused on prosecution of Nazi war criminals, identified 344 individuals. For different estimates see Pohl, "Trawniki-Männer," Sandkühler, "Trawniki-Männer," and the article by Martin Cüppers in this volume.

29. Pohl, "Trawniki-Männer," p. 286.

30. See Sandkühler, "Trawniki-Männer," p. 157.

31. Pohl, "Trawniki-Männer," p. 286.

32. Ibid., p. 287.

33. See final report on the termination of proceedings against members of Order Police Battalion 67, September 18, 1969, HHW 468-1373/149.

34. Interrogation of Johannes Altenkamp, January 17, 1968, LNW Q 234/7883.

35. Pohl, "Trawniki-Männer," p. 286.

36. SS-Sturmbannführer Karl Streibel was the commandant of the SS training and labor camp in Trawniki. In the Hamburg Regional Court, Streibel was accused of the murder or complicity in the murder of 400,000 Jews in Belzec, 200,000 in Sobibor, and 250,000 in Treblinka, as well as complicity in many thousands of murders during the so-called ghetto liquidations. On June 3, 1976, Streibel was acquitted. The court found credible his testimony that he had not known the purpose for which his men were trained or subsequently deployed.

37. The historical record does not contain an explanation for the creation of permanent work detachments. Possibly the Germans took the view that the detachments would work more effectively than the new arrivals, who needed a breaking-in period first. Perhaps they also preferred having specific contact persons with whom they found it easier to conduct their activities.

38. See Kuwałek, *Belzec*, p. 214. From the accounts of the survivors Chaim Hirszman and Rudolf Reder, however, we gather that this separation was not handled uniformly in Belzec, even from the summer of 1942.

39. Reder, "Bełżec," p. 141.

40. Sandkühler, "Trawniki-Männer," p. 214.

41. See Kuwałek, *Belzec*, pp. 212–213.

42. Interrogation of Maria Czachor, October 15, 1966, StAM 33033/34.

43. Herc told the woman who owned the bakery what was happening in the camp. See interrogation of Krystyna Natyna, October 12, 1966, StAM 33033/34; interrogation of Mieczysław Kudyba, ibid.

44. See Peter, "W Bełżcu," p. 194.

45. Interrogation of Maria Warzocha, October 13, 1966, StAM 33033/34.

46. Interrogation of Heinz Kettner, HHW 468-1373/25-26, fols. 1196–1197.

47. Interrogation of Oskar Diegelmann, December 12, 1961, StAM 33033/34.

48. *VEJ*, vol. 9, p. 399.

49. Interrogation of Andrzej Panasowiec, October 17, 1966, StAM 33033/3.

50. Interrogation of Edward Luczynski, October 13, 1966, StAM 33033/34.

51. Cecilia and Maciej Brogowski took four-year-old Irene Sznycer into their home in 1941. Passed off as the family's niece, she lived with them until the liberation in 1944. Julia Pępiak lived with her family in the center of town. Until the liberation, she hid a neighbor's daughter and her child in a barn. In 1968, Julia Pępiak commented, "When you shut the door in a Jew's face in those days, it meant sending him to a horrible death. I was not able to deny them help."

52. See Klukowski, *Tagebuch*, p. 337. Klukowski lived around forty-four miles from Bełżec, near Zamość.

53. Peter, "W Bełżcu," pp. 189 ff. The SS man Josef Oberhauser also used the term "public secret" when he was questioned about Belzec in West Germany at the beginning of the 1960s. Interrogation of Josef Oberhauser, December 4, 1961, StAM 33033/34.

54. "Slamek" Winer (Bajler) was transported to the Kulmhof (Chelmno) killing center on January 6, 1942. In late January 1942, he managed to escape. In February 1942, he gave a report on Kulmhof to the Oneg Shabbat archive in the Warsaw Ghetto. On April 12, 1942, Slamek was transported from Zamość to Belzec and murdered.

55. Sakowska, *Zweite Etappe*, pp. 190 ff.

56. "Mordowanie Żydów w Lubelszczyźnie" [The Murder of the Jews in the Lublin Area], in *Biuletyn Informacyjny of the Armia Krajowa*, April 16, 1942, no. 15.

57. The conclusion of the text read "We are dealing here with one of the most shocking German crimes." See "Obóz w Bełżcu" [The Camp in Bełżec], in Biuletyn Informacyjny, June 3, 1942, no. 22.

58. Karski published his report in book form in 1945. Here and in other postwar accounts, he claimed to have been inside the Belzec killing center. The description of the place, however, gave rise to doubts about this assertion (Karski, *Secret State*). On Jan Karski, see Libionka, *Zagłada Żydów*, p. 105.

59. An accord between the German Reich and Romania provided for the transport of 300,000 Jews to Belzec, beginning in December 1942. After the agreement became known, there was protest in Romania in the fall of 1942, and the Romanian government dropped the plan; see Kuwałek, *Belzec*, pp. 176 ff. On the three options see Kuwałek, *Belzec*, pp. 235–236.

60. Interrogation of Jan Głąb, February 19, 1946, StAM 33033/34.

61. Sandkühler, "Trawniki-Männer," p. 220.

62. Interrogation of Władisława Göbel, December 17, 1959, StAM 33033/34.

63. Interrogation of Tadeusz Dujanowicz, October 17, 1945, StAM 33033/34.

64. Sandkühler, "Trawniki-Männer," p. 214.

65. Report by Pola Hirszman, AŻIH, 301/1476. It is not evident from Pola Hirszman's account why the prisoners had realized while passing through Chełm that the Germans had lied.

66. The men were Chaim Hirszman and Sylco Herc.

67. Blatt, *Ashes*, pp. 113.

68. Interrogation of Eugeniusz Goch, October 14, 1945, StAM 33033/34.

69. Interrogation of Heinrich Unverhau, May 6, 1963, ibid.

70. Interrogation of Eugeniusz Goch, October 14, 1945, ibid.

71. Report by Nachman Schuman, AŻIH, 301/5316.

72. Interrogation of Mieczysław Garfinkiel, October 5, 1945, StAM 33033/34.

73. Statement by Edward Podgorski, July 30, 1974, HHW 468-1373/110, fols. 313–322.

74. See Taffet, "Juden von Żółkiew," p. 327. Taffet states that the two women took advantage of the Germans' "lack of experience."

75. Interrogation of Edward Luczynski, October 15, 1945, StAM 33033/34.

76. There may have been another escape from Belzec. However, as in the Spira case, the record contains only a single postwar statement made by the person in question, with no further confirmation: Sara Ritterband, née Salomea Helman, stated in Haifa on February 1, 1960, that she and her five-year-old daughter had been transported to the Belzec camp and assigned to work in the laundry. In addition, she said that when Belzec was closed, she and 20 to 30 other women were sent to the Trawniki forced labor camp and from there to Auschwitz and then to Bergen-Belsen. Information about Sara Ritterband's life history varies and is contradictory. The relocation of the 20 to 30 women to Trawniki is not confirmed by any other statements. See StAM 33033/34, fols. 563–566.

77. In the 1970s, Yaffa Eliach had her students conduct interviews with Holocaust survivors, including Israel Spira. Eliach published records of the conversations under the title *Hasidic Tales of the Holocaust*.

78. Report by Chaim and Pola Hirszman, March 19, 1946, AŻIH, 301/1476a, published in Libionka, *Obóz Zaglady*, pp. 93–99, here p. 98.

79. Ibid.

80. Reder, "Bełżec," p. 130.

81. Interrogation of Mieczysław Niedużak, October 17, 1945, AIPN Lu 1/15/105.

82. Interrogation of Mieczysław Niedużak, ibid. In the late 1950s, grave robbers were sentenced by a Lublin court. The sentences pronounced are not known, however (Dziuban, "(Re)politicising," p. 44).

83. Interview of Antoni Walentyn, February 27, 2004 APMM, section Bełżec, XXVI-3, report 16.

84. The interrogations were published in Polish in 2013: Libionka, *Obóz Zaglady*, pp. 112 ff.

85. ROPWiM report for 03/1948 to 12/1949, AROPWiM, Sign. 1/95.

86. The camp had been approximately 3.7 acres larger than the 1963 memorial area.

87. Polish: "Pamięci ofiar terroru hitlerowskiego, pomordowanych w latach 1942–1943."

88. On the plaque it was pointed out that the murdered Poles had helped Jews. Robert Kuwałek considers this assertion untenable. In his opinion, detailed information on the number of Christians murdered in Belzec is impossible to obtain because of the lack of documents (Kuwałek, *Belzec*, pp. 247 ff.). Polish: "W tym miejscu od lutego do grudnia

1942 r. istniał hitlerowski obóz zagłady, w którym poniosło męczeńską śmierć przeszło 600 000 Żydów z Polski i innych krajów Europy oraz 1500 Polaków za pomoc okazaną Żydom."

89. The plans called for a memorial room in the building, but the room never became a reality. See AROPWiM, Sign. 52/5, letter by ROP-WiM secretary-general, J. Pietrusiński, to the forest administration in Lublin, August 12, 1963; letter by Polish forestry minister, R. Gesing, to the ROPWiM president, J. Wieczorek, August 24, 1962, AROPWiM, Sign. 52/6.

90. In addition to his tireless efforts to establish an appropriate memorial at the former site of the Belzec death camp, Miles Lerman was very active in commemorating and teaching about the Holocaust in his new home, the USA. One of the founding members of the United States Holocaust Memorial Museum, Lerman helped shape the institution until his death in 2008.

91. Information based on annual reports of the Bełżec Memorial.

92. Since 2010 the house that served as the commandant's office has been unoccupied. In September 2013 the Bildungswerk Stanisław Hantz contacted the owner, the Polish State Railways (PKP), in an effort to buy the building and thus protect it from dereliction. Sale was possible only in the context of an auction. The PKP had chosen June 22, 2015, as the auction date. The value of the land with buildings was set at just under 33,000 euros. To forestall private investors, the Bildungswerk launched an international campaign for donations. As a result, the upcoming auction came to the public's attention, and protests arose. On June 7, the PKP canceled the auction and handed the site over to the Polish Ministry of Culture. In November 2015, it was placed at the disposal of the Majdanek Museum.

93. Josef Oberhauser, Fritz Jirmann, Kurt Franz. See photo in YVA - PC, Item ID 34547.

94. The same pile of wood also appears in a photo in the Niemann collection (see fig. 5.3).

95. Six perpetrators were identified in the Oberhauser proceedings: Lorenz Hackenholt, Ernst Zierke, Max Gringers, Fritz Tauscher, Arthur Dachsel, and Heinrich Barbl.

96. The photo album also contains four images produced on the grounds of the killing center and one shot of Trawnikis standing in front of the entrance to the camp. It is not known how the photos came to be part of the Peter album; presumably they are prints made in one of the three photo labs in existence in Tomaszów Lubelski during the German occupation.

97. A photo from the Komadowski Bar that must have been taken around the same time was already known. The similarity of the two photos is recognizable by the vase of asters on the table (photo in GFH, Registry Nr. 44597p).

Niemann's Photos from Belzec

Figure 5.1. SS men and Trawnikis in Bełżec in the spring of 1942. *Second from left*, presumably Christian Wirth, to his right, Johann Niemann and probably Kurt Franz. The photo presumably was taken on the road that still links the cities of Lwów (now Lviv) and Lublin today. The housing and administration sector shown in the following images was located there, while the actual death camp was approximately a quarter of a mile away.

Figure 5.2. Germans and Trawnikis in the housing and
administration area in the spring of 1942. *Left to right,*
Heinrich Barbl, Johann Niemann, and probably Kurt Franz.

Figure 5.3. Trawnikis during a shooting demonstration in the yard of the commandant's office being instructed by Niemann (*center*), in the spring of 1942. In the background, an additional building for quartering the camp personnel is visible. In the wooden shed between the quarters and the commandant's office, firewood was stored for a time. Later the shed was torn down.

Figure 5.4. Two Trawnikis in the Komadowski Bar in the town of
Bełżec, 1941–1942. Trawnikis pawned valuables that had belonged
to murdered Jews in exchange for alcohol, among other things.

6

The Sobibor Death Camp

STEFFEN HÄNSCHEN, ANNETT GERHARDT,
ANDREAS KAHRS, ANNE LEPPER,
AND MARTIN CÜPPERS

Sobibor was the second camp constructed for the plan known as Operation Reinhard (*Aktion Reinhard*). Its primary purpose, like that of Belzec and Treblinka, was to murder the Jewish population of Poland. Within fewer than eighteen months, between May 1942 and October 1943, German perpetrators killed approximately 185,000 Jews in Sobibor.[1] The victims, however, were not limited to the Jewish population of the General Government; they also included a great many Jews who had been deported to the Lublin District from places outside Poland. The largest group consisted of around 34,000 Jews from the Netherlands. Others came from Lithuania, Belarus, western Ukraine, France, Germany, Austria, the Czech Republic, and Slovakia. Comparison with the other two Operation Reinhard camps reveals that the largest number of non-Polish Jews died in the gas chambers of Sobibor.[2]

The Mass Murder

Most victims were brought to Sobibor by train. Smaller groups from the immediate vicinity came by horse and cart, in trucks, or on foot. As many as five thousand Jews were forced into each of the deportation trains. Without food and water, they sometimes had to spend several days in sealed freight cars.

After arrival at the public railroad station in Sobibór, the trains were split into parts; fifteen cars at most were shunted through the entrance gate into the camp; the rest were pushed onto a siding, where the people jammed together inside the cars had to await their turn.[3] Inside the camp, the deportees were forced out of the freight cars. They now found themselves at a place, created by the Germans, a place that existed for the sole purpose of killing them. The handling of the victims after their arrival varied in accordance with their place of origin. The Jews from occupied Poland were frequently aware that they were to be killed, as such knowledge had spread like wildfire in the region's ghettos after the first gassings in Belzec in March 1942. The deportations from their home towns already entailed the use of extreme violence. The Germans and their helpers forced the victims into freight cars amid shootings and beatings. Many died during the journey to Sobibor. Once they arrived, the Germans drove them into the gas chambers at lightning speed and with brutal force, to nip any resistance in the bud. The perpetrators were not always successful, however. On a number of occasions, deportees offered resistance when getting out of the freight cars and attacked individual members of the camp staff, who reacted with even greater violence.

Deportees from Western European countries, however, generally did not know what awaited them. At first, many were deceived by the Germans' reassurances that they were to be "resettled." Traveling in relative comfort in some cases, these people came to Poland in passenger coaches and were even allowed to take provisions along. Attractive, well-maintained houses—as shown in Niemann's photos—were then the first structures the deportees saw when they reached Sobibor. Initially, these staged settings hid the true function of the camp. Sometimes, the incoming deportees were required to write postcards to those back home, announcing their safe arrival. As an additional element of deception, an SS man gave a speech. Samuel Lerer, who looked after the Germans' horses in Camp II, recalled the following words of SS-Oberscharführer Hermann Michel: "Jews, you'll just undergo a disinfection process, and later we'll send you to Ukraine to work. Germany still needs you!"[4] Not infrequently, the frightened deportees applauded upon hearing these words.

After leaving the train, the deportees had to proceed to an assembly site. There the Germans, whenever necessary, selected individual Jews from the crowd of the doomed to perform incidental jobs. The feeble, ill, and elderly were taken via narrow-gauge field railway to specially dug pits near the gas chambers, where they were shot. All the others had to strip naked and hand in their valuables for "temporary safekeeping" at the "counter," a drop-off point designed to deceive them. Then, in large groups, they were hustled toward the gas chambers, with the women and children usually going first and the men left until the last. The SS men cynically used the term "tube" (*Schlauch*) for the narrow passageway leading to the gas chambers, which was enclosed on both sides by barbed wire interwoven with tree branches.[5] Esther Raab, who had been deported to Sobibor from Chełm, worked in the stables, directly adjacent to the tube, and thus became an eyewitness to the brutal methods of the camp staff: "Every day I could see how the SS men

and the Ukrainian guards drove the naked people into the gas chambers in a ferocious and brutish way, beating them with rifle butts and stabbing them with bayonets."[6]

The actual killing area was also separated by a fence to conceal it from the rest of the camp. The Jews did not see the building with the gas chambers until they had stepped through the last access gate. The survivor Dov Freiberg told how he managed to sneak a quick look into the part of the camp that otherwise was hermetically sealed off: "Only once, when the gate was opened, I saw a big pile of dead people. The building was made of masonry, on the front was a red Star of David decorated with green stuff, one window and iron doors, a flat roof, and on the roof a little window where an SS man used to sit."[7]

At the gas chambers, Germans and Trawnikis, with brutal violence, herded the people together and forced them into the dark rooms. As soon as the anguished cries became audible, a flock of geese, kept nearby for acoustic camouflage, became restless, and their honking mingled with the frightened shouts. Then a gasoline engine, set up directly next to the gas chambers, produced the carbon monoxide exhaust gases that were channeled through a pipeline system into the interior of the chambers. It took approximately twenty minutes for the victims to die a horrible death. Finally, Jewish labor detachments had to pull the bodies of the dead out of the gas chambers and hastily bury them in mass graves. In a later phase, the corpses were immediately burned on large pyres.

Origin and Topography

The death camp was situated directly opposite the Sobibór railroad station, around three miles from the eponymous village and from the Bug River. To this day, the railroad line links the small towns of Chełm and Włodawa. The Bug, which now forms part of the border between Poland and Belarus and between Poland and Ukraine, in those days marked the eastern border of

Figure 6.1. Aerial photograph taken by the Wehrmacht, May 28, 1944. The photo shows the grounds of Sobibor approximately seven months after the camp was closed. Above the railroad line, the buildings of the front camp and the area of the Erbhof can be seen. However, other buildings in Camp I, Camp II, and Camp III had already been dismantled, for the most part. NARA, GX 8102.

the General Government, dividing it from the Reich Commissariat Ukraine, which was also occupied by Nazi Germany. The region was sparsely populated, and forests and marshes characterized the landscape in this part of what now is eastern Poland.

There are indications that Sobibór had already come to the Germans' attention when they were searching for a site for the first planned killing center of what later became Operation Reinhard. As early as the late fall of 1941, Polish railroad workers observed SS officers inspecting the grounds of a forest warden's office across from the railroad station and making measurements.[8] Construction, however, did not actually begin before the end of February 1942, when it was decided to build a second camp, in addition to Belzec, for the murder of the Jewish population. The first work was overseen by Hauptsturmführer Richard Thomalla from the SS Central Construction Management Office (*SS-Zentralbauleitung*) in Zamość.[9] Already in existence in the area chosen were a forester's house built before the war, with corresponding barns, an office of the postal service, and a wooden chapel. These buildings were now incorporated into the camp. For its further development, Jewish forced laborers from surrounding ghettos and labor camps served as a workforce. Afterward, they were among the first victims of the death camp.

During this phase, Johann Niemann came to Sobibor for the first time. In mid-April 1942 he had been detailed from Belzec for the construction of the actual killing facilities. Together with the SS man Erich Fuchs, he procured the engine, which was set up next to the gas chamber. After that, he went back to Belzec for the next four months.[10] Additionally, in early April 1942, twenty other men from the Operation T4 (*Aktion T4*) killing centers in the Reich were assigned to duty in the new camp. Franz Stangl, an Oberleutnant who had previously been deployed with the urban police (*Schutzpolizei*) in Linz, was appointed commandant.[11]

In early May 1942, just under two months after the beginning of the mass killings in Belzec, the Germans launched a killing operation in Sobibor as well. During this early phase, the camp was still equipped in a rather makeshift fashion. Dov Freiberg recalled that "all the facilities were somewhat primitive" when he was deported to Sobibor in May 1942.[12] Only a few additional barracks and houses had come into existence on the grounds by this time. In the months that followed, the camp was steadily expanded. The Niemann photos clearly reflect these different stages in the construction process. One such example is the building with recreation and common rooms for the German perpetrators, which they called the "staff club" ("*Kasino*"). The "old" staff club, in which Johann Niemann also had his quarters, was built in June 1942 and can be seen in several prints. The "new" staff club, at another location in the front compound, appears in one photo taken during the construction process and in another after the renovation was complete.

In the summer of 1942, Operation Reinhard was in high gear. The "big operation" in Lwów (Lemberg), the third-largest Jewish ghetto in the German region of occupation, had just concluded with the mass deportations to Belzec. In August 1942 alone, the Germans had deported almost fifty thousand persons from there and murdered them in Belzec.[13] Since July 1942, thousands of Jews from Warsaw had been arriving in Treblinka daily, and the sheer volume of victims led to a temporary halt in the systematic murder there. At the same time, the Germans decided that the capacity of the gas chambers in Sobibor also was too small. Moreover, there were unforeseen logistical problems. Rail traffic between Lublin and Włodawa had to be suspended at the end of June 1942, because the roadbed of the railroad line had sunk under the weight of the large numbers of transports and had to be restabilized. Thus Sobibor, originally planned as the second destination for the deportations from the Warsaw Ghetto, was out of the picture.[14]

Various redeployments between the Belzec, Treblinka, and Sobibor camps were part of an effort to restructure the camp operations and organize the killing process "more efficiently." To that end, Franz Stangl was transferred from Sobibor to Treblinka in September 1942 to serve as commandant there. Niemann, in turn, was moved from Belzec to Sobibor because of his experience and expertise in killing.[15] The new commandant of the Sobibor camp was the former police official Franz Reichleitner, who, like his predecessor Stangl, had previously been deployed in the Hartheim "euthanasia" center. Simultaneously with the personnel changes, the killing capacities in Treblinka and Sobibor were expanded in the late summer of 1942. Larger gas chambers were now built in these camps too, as in Belzec at an earlier date. In Sobibor, the German perpetrators took advantage of the three-month shutdown of the railroad line to accomplish this work. Furthermore, the expansion brought in its wake a fresh influx of additional German guard personnel, which meant that yet another group from Operation T4 was assigned to Poland.

Three months later, in October 1942, once the work on the railroad line had been finished, the second phase of the systematic murder in Sobibor commenced. At that time, many of the ghettos still extant in the Lublin District were liquidated, and all the Jews remaining there were murdered. While the Germans discontinued the killing operations in Belzec at the end of 1942, additional groups of victims were included in the murders in Sobibor. Besides the transports from the General Government, deportation trains from France and the Netherlands also began arriving as of early March 1943.

Structure of the Camp

Over the course of eighteen months, five sections, or compounds, were created in the Sobibor camp: the so-called front camp (*Vorlager*) as well as camps I through IV. There was no exact, predetermined plan for the development of the site. Instead, the men detailed from Operation T4 had to improvise in many respects. The Central Construction Management Office of the SS in Lublin supplied them with only part of the requisite construction materials; they acquired the remainder on their own initiative. For this purpose, the camp SS ordered several houses in the villages of the surrounding area to be torn down—houses formerly occupied by Jewish families—and requested additional materials from the lumber mills and brickyards in the area. The SS also required Jewish communities, such as the one in nearby Włodawa, to furnish construction materials.

To obscure the view from outside, a barbed wire fence approximately 10 feet high was put up around the camp and in some places inside the camp area as well. A Jewish work detachment was required to weave pine branches into the barbed wire. This "green fence," which came to symbolize the Operation Reinhard camps because of its recurrence in many descriptions given by survivors,[16] is visible in several of Niemann's photos. Several guard towers and a path for patrols, running inside the double-row fencing, were among the security measures for the camp. In addition, in the spring of 1943, the camp staff laid a minefield outside the fence to protect against partisans and to prevent escape by the Jewish prisoners.

The **front camp** served mainly as living quarters and as a common area for Germans and Trawnikis. Over time, seventeen buildings came into existence.[17] During major reconstruction work in the spring of 1943, the paths in this part of the camp were relocated, embellished with low fences made of birch boughs, and beautified with bordering flowerbeds. Such details were already familiar, particularly to the SS soldiers who, like Niemann, had been trained in the concentration camps. The work done by Jewish prisoners made the front camp into an idyllic compound with small, white-plastered houses. The Germans obviously wanted to make this part of the camp as pleasant as possible, as a contrast to the limited possibilities prevailing in wartime. Guests were received there, and the facilities included a staff club, a bowling alley, a kitchen, and a washhouse. A Jewish dentist was required to provide medical care to the German camp staff. The special atmosphere of the front camp left a lasting impression on the deportees. This area of the camp was the first thing they caught sight of. The Jewish survivor Eda Lichtman described her arrival in Sobibor: "Nobody wanted to believe that this is a place where people are exterminated."[18] North of the German section of the camp were the housing barracks of the Trawnikis.

In **Camp I**, which adjoined the front compound to the west, were housing barracks for the Jewish prisoners as well as various workshops, including worksites for tailors, cobblers, leatherworkers, woodworkers, metalworkers, and painters. A bakery and a laundry were located between Camp I and Camp II. During the final construction phase, beginning in the summer of 1943, the area was expanded once again to build accommodations for the Jewish prisoners. From late September, Red Army prisoners of war also were used for this purpose, men who had shortly before been selected for work from a transport that had originated in Minsk.[19]

Camp II and the so-called hereditary farm (Erbhof) formed another section of the camp, into which the Germans incorporated buildings that had been erected before the war. Before the arrival of the SS, the administrative office of the local forestry authorities, as well as various annexes, had been located here. After the takeover of the premises, the SS used the forester's lodge as its administration center. Among other things, the stolen valuables and foreign currency were stored here.[20] In addition, the building served as living quarters for the so-called head cashier and other SS men, and it also contained another common room.[21] According to reports, Germans occasionally

Front Camp

1	Guardhouse
2	Dentist/Trawnikis' arrest cell
3	New staff club
4	Garage/barber for the camp SS
5	Washroom for the camp SS
6	Laundry
7	Old staff club, including living quarters of Stangl and Niemann
8	"Swallows' Nest," including living quarters of Gomerski, Wagner, and Frenzel
9	Storeroom and ironing room for the camp SS
10	Trawnikis' living quarters
11	Former postal building (still in existence)
12	Ammunition depot
13–15	Trawnikis' living quarters
16	Trawnikis' clubhouse
17	Living quarters for Trawniki platoon leaders
18	Guard tower

Camp I

1	Possibly workshop or latrine
2–4	Workshops
5	Bakery
6	Cobblers' workshop for Trawnikis
7	Workshop
8	Women's barracks
9	Kitchen for Camp I
10–11	Men's barracks
12	Painters' workshop

Camp II

1	Former forester's house
2–3	Storerooms for food
4	Pigsty
5	Horse stable
6	Barn
7	Utility building
8	Shoe storeroom
9	Fire detection tower
10–15	Sorting barracks
16	Drop-off site for hand baggage
17	Hair-cutting barracks
18	Undressing area
19	"Counter" at the entrance to the "tube"

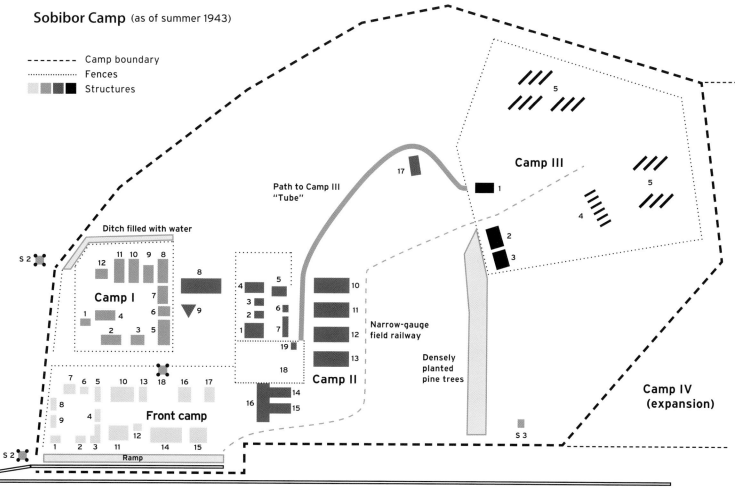

Sobibor Camp (as of summer 1943)

- - - - - Camp boundary
··········· Fences
▨▨▨■ Structures

Camp III

Path to Camp III "Tube"

Ditch filled with water

S 2

Camp I

8

9

Camp II

Narrow-gauge field railway

Densely planted pine trees

Camp IV (expansion)

Front camp

Ramp

S 2

S 3

S 1

Railroad line

Camp III

1 Building with the gas chambers
2 Housing barracks for Jewish Sonderkommando, Camp III
3 Kitchen for Camp III
4 Burning of corpses
5 Area of mass graves

Other Structures

S1 Railroad station building
S2 Guard towers
S3 Chapel from the prewar period (site of shootings)

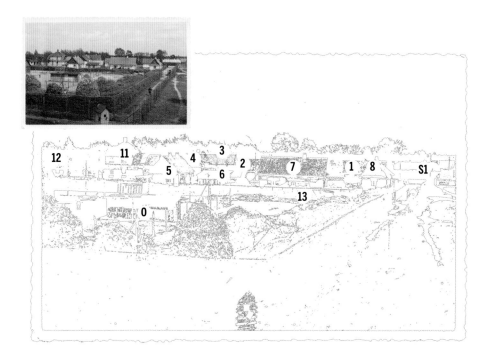

Figure 6.2. Camp I and Front Camp

1	Guardhouse
2	Dentist/Trawnikis' arrest cell
3	New staff club
4	Garage/barber for camp SS
5	Washroom for camp SS
6	Laundry
7	Old staff club, including living quarters of Stangl and Niemann
8	"Swallows' Nest," including living quarters of Gomerski, Wagner, Frenzel
11	Old postal building (still in existence)
12	Ammunition depot
13	Stack of boards, presumably remnants of the roofing at the former assembly site
0	Possibly workshop or toilets
S1	Railroad station building

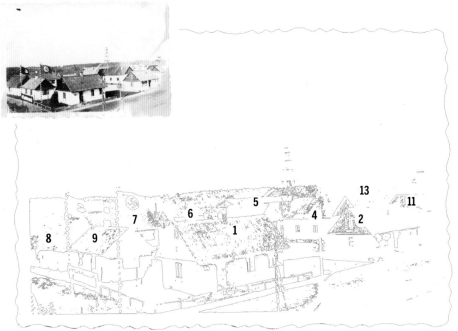

Figure 6.3. Front Camp

1	Guardhouse
2	Dentist/Trawnikis' arrest cell
4	Garage/barber for camp SS
5	Washroom for camp SS
6	Laundry
7	Old staff club, including living quarters of Stangl and Niemann
8	"Swallows' Nest," including living quarters of Gomerski, Wagner, Frenzel
9	Storeroom and ironing room of camp SS
11	Old postal building (still in existence)
13	Living quarters of Trawnikis

used the building also to house Jewish women, whom they sexually exploited and abused.[22]

Over time, the forester's house and the adjacent barns were separated from the rest of the camp with a wooden fence. The result was an enclosed area called the "Erbhof."[23] The term was a reference to the Nazis' "blood and soil" ideology. After the proclamation of the law implementing hereditary farms (*Reichserbhofgesetz*) on September 29, 1933, the only farmer allowed to own a hereditary farm was one who could prove that he was of "German or tribally similar blood" by presenting documentation of his ancestry. The establishment of a "hereditary farm" in Sobibor contributed to the deception of the deportees. In addition, in the midst of the death camp, it was a cynical expression of the claim the German perpetrators asserted with regard to occupied Poland.[24] During his time as a guard in the Esterwegen concentration camp, Niemann had already been presented with the prospect of a hereditary farm to supplement his meager pay.[25] In Sobibor, the Erbhof was used primarily for the self-supply of the camp staff. Presumably under the guidance of the former farmer and T4 man Rudolf Beckmann, chickens, pigs, and a great many geese were kept, and beds for flowers and vegetables were laid out.[26] In addition, three or four horses were stabled there, and a rabbit-breeding operation was introduced. All the work had to be done by Jewish prisoners, who at the same time were strictly forbidden from helping themselves to the food. As is clearly evident in Niemann's photos, horses were also a status symbol in Sobibor, while dogs were employed against the prisoners as weapons and additional instruments of repression.

In the early days, the deportees, once out of the train, were led around the German housing area, the front compound, to a roof-covered assembly site at the southern end of the camp. From there the camp staff took the Jews in groups to a different site, where they were forced to undress. Finally, they were forcibly herded toward the gas chambers. People who were no longer strong enough to negotiate this path on their own were put into wagons and driven to a small wooden chapel built before the war. There they were shot beside a pit.[27] With the development of the Erbhof and the erection of the wooden fence, this course of events changed, beginning in the summer of 1942. From then on, the undressing and robbing of the deportees took place in a sandy area directly in front of the lockable gates to the yard. The pathway to the gas chambers led from here straight to the north, past the Erbhof. From February 1943, the women on this path were forced to make an additional stop in barracks where Jewish prisoners were required to cut their hair.[28] Again, those who could not walk were taken by means of a narrow-gauge railway from the ramp into Camp III, where they were shot. The railway was also used to transport heavy pieces of baggage as well as the corpses of deportees who had already died inside the deportation train. In the Camp II compound, over time, at least three large barracks were built, in which the plundered belongings of the victims were examined and stored. Here, Jewish prisoners had to search the clothing and baggage for articles of value, sort everything, and pack the items up in bundles for further transport. Freight cars carrying the processed goods made regular trips to large warehouses in Lublin.

Located in **Camp III** were not only the gas chambers but also the mass graves for the murder victims and the area that was later used for the pits where corpses were burned. The members of the Jewish special work detail, the Sonderkommando, were required to live there, completely isolated and housed in their own separate barracks. The workers in the killing area were almost exclusively Jewish men; infrequently, women were deployed in the separate kitchen. Owing to its exceptional isolation, almost nothing is known about Camp III to this day, and it is probable that none of the prisoners deployed there survived.

The Jewish prisoners working in the Sonderkommando were in nothing less than a nightmarish situation. They were directly involved in the killing process and entrusted with a terrible task. After the gassing, they had to drag the entangled bodies of the dead out of the gas chambers, search them for valuables, and pry out any gold teeth. Then the corpses were hastily buried and later burned. In addition to the physical and mental strain, these workers were isolated from the Jewish prisoners in the other parts of the camp, and they felt the harsh pinch of hunger, as they were not adequately fed by the Germans. The area where they lived and worked was surrounded with extra fencing, and they were forbidden, under penalty of death, from leaving it or making contact with the other prisoners. Abraham Margulies, himself housed in Camp I, was working near the fence around Camp III one day and saw one of the Jews deployed there. A brief conversation developed, during which the man said, as if delirious, "Today I burned my father."[29]

When the murders began, the Germans ordered several mass graves to be dug, interspersed throughout all of Camp III. They measured as large as 65 feet × 230 feet. In the heat of summer 1942, an unbearable stench from the burial pits soon spread in the vicinity of the camp, and the drinking water was in danger of being contaminated. That led the Germans to bring an excavator into the camp in the fall of 1942, in order to exhume the buried corpses so that they could be burned. For this purpose, Jewish prisoners had to place railroad rails on top of each other to form a large grate, onto which they next stacked up alternating layers of wood and half-decayed corpses. The pyramid-shaped pile was doused with oil and set on fire. The flames of these pyres blazed many feet high and were visible far beyond the boundaries of the camp.[30] Sobibor was the first Operation Reinhard camp in which the murder victims were burned in this manner. Only after sufficient experience had been gained did the SS man Herbert Floß go to the other two sites to organize and supervise the burning of corpses there according to the same model.[31]

By the fall of 1942, Camp III was remodeled and the capacity of the killing facilities was substantially enlarged. There were initially three gas chambers, but now, as part of the expansion, a new building with eight gas chambers, each approximately 172 square feet in size, was constructed.[32] According to the statements of German perpetrators, between 70 and 150 persons could be jammed into each of these chambers. Steel doors, which at first were built into the back walls of the chambers, proved unsuitable when it came to pulling out the dead bodies. As a result, the Germans had the walls broken open so that large, swing-up wooden doors could be installed.

On July 5, 1943, the Reich Security Main Office in Berlin ordered Sobibor to be converted into a "concentration camp." Munitions captured in the war were henceforth to be sorted and reconditioned on site. The SS Economic and Administrative Main Office (*SS-Wirtschafts- und Verwaltungshauptamt*), which was in charge of all concentration camps, objected, in concert with Lublin SS and Police Leader Odilo Globocnik, on the grounds that formal reorganization as a labor camp was superfluous. Nonetheless, the reconditioning of captured munitions bestowed on Sobibor—in comparison with Belzec, Treblinka, and Sobibor's previous function—an unusual additional responsibility, which caused the camp to be enlarged one last time. The expansion resulted in the building of Camp IV, bringing Sobibor in the summer of 1943 to its largest dimensions ever, at a size of approximately 1,300 × 3,280 feet.[33] It was thus around four times the size of Belzec. The project never progressed beyond the first stage of construction, however, because the uprising of October 14, 1943, rendered all expansion plans moot. Subsequently, it was quickly decided instead to close Sobibor, as the last of the three Operation Reinhard camps, once and for all.

The Jewish Prisoners

In the initial period, the Jews who were forced to play a part in the killing process were also killed each time, once the deportees from the transport in question had been murdered and quickly buried in the pits. As time passed, however, the Germans set up permanent labor detachments in order to organize the murder process more efficiently. Now, Jews deported to Sobibor were selected from the arriving transports by the SS men, in an effort to maintain camp operations by means of forced labor on an ongoing basis. In addition, from the spring of 1943, the Germans selected smaller groups of deportees for distribution to Jewish forced-labor camps in the region. At the end of the camp's existence in October 1943, at least 650 men and women had to perform forced labor in Sobibor.[34] The Jewish men and few Jewish women who were deployed at the gas chambers in Camp III and completely isolated from the other sections of the camp, however, continued to be routinely murdered, in order to eliminate witnesses to the crimes and minimize the risk of resistance.

For the purpose of better control, the prisoners were arranged in a strict hierarchy—there were privileged supervisors, known as *Kapos*, as well as an *Oberkapo*. They passed on the instructions of the Germans and pushed the Jewish prisoners to do hard labor. Arkadij Wajspapier was deported from Minsk to Sobibor in the second half of September 1943. Later, he described the daily routine in Sobibor: "Early in the morning we were waked by the Elders of the prisoners, 'Kapo' is what they were called. After that was breakfast, which consisted of 150 grams [5.3 ounces] of coarse bread and one cup of cooking water or coffee. Then [after the roll-call] they sent us off to work. At midday there was a soup, which we called dishwater ['*Plörre*'], and no bread. After we had slugged down this dishwater, we worked until nightfall. Then they herded us into Camp I and gave us supper: 100 grams [3.5 ounces] of coarse bread and a cup of cooking water. After supper the prisoners were lined up by the Kapos [. . .] for inspection, after the end of which we went to the barracks to sleep. We slept on the bare boards of the plank beds. There were no bed linens at all."[35]

Surviving at Death's Door

The Jewish prisoners selected for labor found themselves, after their arrival, in a reality that they were completely unable to comprehend. Sobibor was the traumatic culmination of years of marginalization, deprivation of rights, and brutal persecution. In the camp too, these prisoners were faced with violence and mortal danger. Yet at rare moments wrested from the reality of the camp, inmates struggled for their humanity and their personhood, escaped from the horror, and sought diversion in outward exuberance to gain a bit of the strength and courage needed to endure their existence. Thomas Blatt, then sixteen years old, was deported to Sobibor from the Izbica ghetto on April 28, 1943. After the SS men had selected him for labor, he walked, wide-eyed and incredulous, through the area where the Jewish prisoners lived and worked. Looking back, he recalled, "From somewhere, music could be heard. We followed it all the way to the area at the back, behind a tailors' workshop. Here, at this godforsaken spot, there was a little band, and a couple was doing the tango! The two were wonderful dancers, their movements were perfectly in sync with one another. Jozek told me that they were Dutch ballet dancers from The Hague. We moved on. Here and there, Jews were standing around in little groups or in couples. I turned to my friend: 'Jozek, what's going on here? How can they laugh, dance, make small talk, and think of women? Look around you … barbed wire here and there on every side. We will never get out of here. How is this possible?'"[36]

In fact, some prisoners spoke of "privileges" in the shadow of the ongoing murders, such as the opportunity to move about relatively freely in the section of the camp that had been assigned to the Jews. Male visitors in the women's barracks were part of everyday life, and even love affairs blossomed under the Germans' eyes. Eda Lichtman from Jarosław described the living conditions in the camp: "Our situation was quite good. We had as much to eat as we wanted, from what was taken away from the Jews. In the daytime we could meet up with the men who worked in the storerooms and workshops. We had permission to go into the room where the Jews' clothing was and pick out whatever we wanted. Sometimes the men found gold among the garments, and in exchange they got food from the Ukrainians who guarded us."[37]

The individual situation of the Jewish prisoners was in large measure dependent on chance and caprice. As Eda Lichtman's narrative makes clear, only those who had access to the deportees' baggage—for example, as a result of working in the sorting detail or during the arrival of the transports—could ensure that they were supplied with food, clothing, and other necessities, all taken from the belongings of the murdered Jews. The woodworker Kalmen Wewryk from Chełm spoke of forced laborers who were deployed at the ramp when the deportees were forced out of the freight cars: "The railroad station detail came into our barracks for a night and kept us awake all night. They were so cheerful, they were in very good spirits. They believed they had cheated death—it was destined only for others. They were in such an excellent mood because their bellies were full. They had had a feast, and their pockets were full, too—of cookies, salami, and even whiskey. They got these treats from the incoming Jews whom they had unloaded from a train."[38]

In addition to the hard labor, the Jewish prisoners in the camp were constantly subjected to brutal abuse. In their accounts, survivors never once failed to describe such acts of violence on the part of Germans or Trawniki guards. From the perpetrators' standpoint, there was hardly any reason to go easy on those selected for forced labor. The efficiency of the systematic murder process was the primary concern, and the life of the prisoners counted for nothing. Only "labor prisoners" with special qualifications, such as those who processed the deportees' gold and valuables, received better treatment. Otherwise, "replacements" for the Jewish men and women who did forced labor were available in every newly arriving transport, and any suspicion, however slight, of an effort at resistance was sufficient grounds for murder. Even the tiniest lapse or breach was punished with a minimum of twenty-five blows with a club; other perceived offenses earned far more drastic punishments. The transgressions included simply standing around without working, as well as being in possession of food. Illnesses and the consequent impairment of working power signified extreme danger to the prisoners' lives. Regina Zielinski, a native of nearby Siedliszcze, reported after the war, "We were very afraid of being sick and unable to work anymore, because we knew that the sick people were taken to a so-called third camp, which meant extermination. [. . .] Physical abuse in the camp was very common. Above all, prisoners were beaten by the SS when, in their opinion, the work was going at too slow a pace."[39] One major strategy for survival was to avoid catching the eye of members of the camp staff, because attracting attention entailed the threat of arbitrary abuse.

It was excruciatingly difficult for the prisoners to have to live in close proximity to the mass murder and contribute to it through their labor. Not infrequently, when sorting the victims' possessions, they found articles of clothing belonging to their closest relatives. The fiery glow of the burning mounds of corpses was visible everywhere on the grounds, and, depending on the wind direction, a ghastly stench of burned flesh and hair spread through the surrounding area. The air people breathed, the food they ate, and the clothing they wore all seemed to have been contaminated by death. Whenever a new deportation transport arrived at the camp's ramp, everyone could see the victims being driven toward the gas chambers; everyone heard the cries that rang out across the camp grounds, followed by a ghostly silence.

Some prisoners, unable to endure the apocalyptic daily routine, viewed suicide as the only way to escape from the hopeless situation. Others tried to adjust to things somehow and to suppress the unbearable as far as possible. The thought of escaping was ever-present, though putting it into practice was extremely dangerous, because failure meant not only one's own death but also, as a deterrent, collective punishment of one's fellow sufferers. Three sizeable attempts to escape are known to have been punished with mass shootings of prisoners who stayed behind. First, several Jewish workers from the forest detachment had escaped; a second escape attempt, by Dutch prisoners, was betrayed in advance. Various survivors also spoke of a third attempted mass escape: in the summer of 1943, members of the Sonderkommando in the killing area of Camp III dug a tunnel to freedom from their barracks building. Shortly before the work was completed, however, the plan was betrayed, and the prisoners were murdered at once.[40]

From the summer of 1943, there was a marked decrease in the number of deportation trains to Sobibor. That development also led to a shortage of food in the camp. Hunger was the result, especially among those prisoners who were not deployed directly at the ramp to process the few transports that were still arriving. As a member of the woodworkers' detachment, Kalmen Wewryk was also affected by it: "Once I saw four of these Jews from the train station detachment sitting together and eating sandwiches, cake, and other things. I was terribly hungry, so I begged them, 'Please, comrades, give me a piece of bread, or even just half of one.' In reply they said, 'Go to hell.'

They refused, and on top of that showered me with a storm of the worst abuse."[41]

Most of those selected for labor in Sobibor were young men. Women were distinctly in the minority in the death camp; there were approximately 150 of them in the summer of 1943. The sexes were housed in different barracks in Camp I but could make contact with each other. Women had to sort the belongings of the victims, but they also were deployed in the sewing room and as servants or cooks and cleaners in the housing compound of the camp staff. When a typhus epidemic broke out in the summer of 1942, the Germans set up a laundry for the prisoners, in which three women worked. The Dutch Jew Selma Wijnberg, twenty-one years old at the time, was selected for labor on April 6, 1943, along with two other women, after her arrival in Sobibor. From then on, her job in the camp was to sort the clothes of the murder victims. Later, in an interview, she remembered those days: "We had to sort clothing. We had to [separate] it into top quality and inferior quality; and we were supposed to pay attention to what was in the pockets, had to take it out. And we had to empty the backpacks. You know, I didn't know what I was doing. I had—and I remember it clearly—I had no idea [. . .] that this came from the people who had come here. [. . .] I remember that the clothes of the nice older man were there too, the man with the five children. [. . .] At five o'clock we went to roll-call and were taken to Camp I, where we slept. And we went into Camp I, we had to dance for the Germans. [. . .] And at the same time the fire was blazing and you could smell it, [. . .] the bones and the hair [. . .]—all over the camp. It was very, very massive. And we had to dance. The Germans stood there, they laughed and were having fun. [. . .] [A] few Jews had instruments, and they played music. There was an order that we were supposed to dance."[42]

The female prisoners in the camp were in a special situation. Less likely to face beatings or imminent deadly violence, they were nonetheless constantly at risk of being sexually assaulted. Time after time, rapes were committed by Trawnikis and Germans.[43] Eda Lichtman later testified that she heard the violence of the members of the guard force toward women at close range: "Back then we heard the screaming and sobbing of the girls."[44] There were at least sixty survivors of Sobibor, and seven of them were women.[45] Their statements in the trials of the German perpetrators suggest what they had to go through in the camp and what coexistence had been like. Vividly, they described how the prisoners attempted to come to terms with everyday life in the camp and develop psychological coping mechanisms. Essential to their survival were strategies of repression as well as a deadening of inner feelings about the permanent confrontation with violence and death. Regina Zielinski testified, "We lived in the camp not like human beings, but more like robots, from day to day. Among the prisoners, not all of the numerous abuses committed against our fellow inmates were discussed every time. For example, it was possible for a baby to be slammed headfirst against the side of a freight car by a guard, and killed in this way, without such an event necessarily being the topic of the private conversations among fellow prisoners."[46]

The Guards

Approximately 120 men from the T4 program, who had played a part in the murders of institutionalized patients in the territory of the Reich, were transferred over time to occupied Poland and deployed in the three Operation Reinhard camps.[47] In Sobibor, during the eighteen months of its existence, there were slightly more than fifty of these men in total. They routinely visited their families in the territory of the Reich or were able to spend their leave on the Attersee in Austria, in a rest and recreation facility operated by the T4 organization. Presumably, there were never more than twenty-five Germans present in Sobibor at the same time. Their brutal treatment of Jews was not limited to the confines of the camp. According to reports, they also played a role in at least one incident in nearby Włodawa, when the Jewish inhabitants were deported to Sobibor.[48] The German camp SS delegated the guarding of the camp and the supervision of individual labor detachments to approximately 120 Trawnikis. These auxiliaries were deployed in every section of the camp; they patrolled the area along the camp fence, manned the guard towers, guarded the Jewish prisoners, and provided additional security for the entire killing process when the deportation trains arrived.

Although there was often no strict separation in the range of duties of the German perpetrators on site, specializations and areas of responsibility did develop over time. Among the perpetrators whom survivors recalled especially vividly was the "preacher," Hermann Michel, who made a cynical speech to the deportees before they were murdered, and lied to them about alleged future work deployments. Also frequently mentioned was the "treasurer," Hans Schütt, who likewise was on hand for the purpose of outrageous deception. Sitting in a bogus cashier's booth in close proximity to the assembly site, he took possession of the valuables of the Jewish deportees before their walk into the gas chambers. The Austrian Gustav Wagner, who, as the temporary "camp sergeant," was also responsible for the Jewish prisoners and terrorized them ceaselessly, turns up in almost every report, described as a brutal, greatly feared, and cold-blooded perpetrator. The rather reserved and diffident impression made by Wagner in the Niemann photos is surprising in view of the numerous and consistent statements about his dreadful presence in the camp and the countless assaults and individual murders for which he was personally responsible. Almost as feared as Wagner, and frequently given particular mention in survivors' statements, were Erich Bauer, who operated the engine of the gas chamber, and Karl Frenzel, who served under Wagner and supervised the Jewish prisoners and the railroad station detail. Johann Niemann was in charge of the killing section in Camp III. In addition, he trained Trawniki subunits, and on occasion, he evidently delivered the speech designed to deceive the deportees.[49] His status as deputy camp commandant is clearly communicated in a number of his photos. Both posed scenes and casual snapshots from the everyday life of the camp shed light on Niemann's official authority in dealing with his German subordinates and the Trawnikis. His bearing seems to change in accordance with his promotions to higher SS ranks, and his appearance and manner reflect an increasing awareness that he exercised power and belonged to an elite.

Apart from Niemann and a few others, the Germans deployed in the General Government did not come from a background of military hierarchical relationships. The majority had completed training in a skilled trade. Upon deployment in the Operation Reinhard camps, they quickly experienced an enormous increase in individual power. In their implementation of the mass murder and their treatment of the Jewish prisoners, the Germans enjoyed considerable latitude and could mistreat their victims almost at will and exploit them in all kinds of ways. In the process, existing rules could be interpreted according to the perpetrators' own notions. Thus, a system based on violence and lethal hierarchies arose in the camp. In this system, some Germans were conspicuous by their severe brutality, while others preferred to operate in the background. For the rest of their lives, the Jewish survivors never managed to shake off the memory of the Germans' behavior. Esther Raab described it in 1963: "I still have terrible memories of the former members of the camp staff. Although more than 20 years have gone by in the meantime, I am able to testify about the behavior of the accused because I cannot forget the dreadful experiences. Even today, I sometimes dream about Sobibor, fearful that Wagner or Frenzel might kill me."[50]

Although it was officially prohibited and noncompliance was subject to harsh punishment, many perpetrators took advantage of the lack of oversight to enrich themselves. The murder of the Jewish population could signify an extremely lucrative business for each individual German, and not only because of the special bonus of eighteen Reichsmarks which they received for each day spent in the death camp. Many deportees had some of their possessions with them upon arrival. The camp staff had instructions to collect these goods, have them sorted, and send them to Lublin for further disposition. Valuables and money were stored separately and also forwarded separately to the garrison administration of the SS in Lublin, where the stolen items were processed by a special Jewish labor detachment. The robbery was extremely profitable, and not only for the National Socialist state. The German perpetrators on-site also profited and enriched themselves almost at will. The Trawnikis, too, helped themselves on numerous occasions and used valuable items from the belongings of the victims as barter objects in the area surrounding the camp. In addition, the Germans had the Jewish prisoners who were deployed as craftsmen make articles of all kinds for them. In mid-December 1942, eight women and girls were selected to knit winter stockings and sweaters for the camp SS. They were housed in a separate room to protect the knitting materials from infestation by vermin. The wool came from the baggage of the deportees.[51] Wives and families also profited from the robbery. Jewish survivors reported that the SS men regularly had parcels made up, containing valuables, jewelry, clothing, and toys, which they sent to their families in the territory of the Reich or took home when they went on leave.[52]

The Death Camp and the Outside World

At the Sobibór railroad station, a passenger train passed through four times a day on the line connecting Chełm and Włodawa. That fact alone made the station a public place. Civilian travelers from the surrounding area waited for their train, and there was a waiting room in the station building. In the same building, the Pole Irena Sójka ran a restaurant, in which both Trawnikis and SS men customarily drank and partied after they went off duty. Aurelia Jaworska, also a Pole, regularly took the train to her place of work. One day she went into the dining area in the station building, where guards from the death camp were sitting. Pointedly exaggerating individual details in her notes, she recalled her impressions: "I have to buy cigarettes. The door to the dining area is closed. Behind the door, lively conversations in German and in Russian are audible. After a brief hesitation, I go into the restaurant, and at the door I can already see that my entrance caused general amazement—obviously the local eatery, according to unwritten rule, is meant only for the local potentates. What strikes me above all is the unusually richly laid table, on which incredible numbers of bottles with foreign labels stand, and the abundance of food, which contrasts with the otherwise poor furnishings. Seated at the tables are men, every one of them unbelievably tall, who wear German uniforms and leather jackets, and the small details of their clothing are evidence of great wealth. They speak Russian and German in alternation. Clearly inebriated, they are enjoying themselves and telling stories from their families. A huge balalaika player has an unusually valuable ring on one finger."[53]

The camp gate, with the marking "SS-Sonderkommando," is also visible in two of Niemann's photos. It was directly opposite the railroad station building. The platforms at which passenger trains stopped and travelers got on and off every day were located at the same place where the deportation trains stood until they were shunted into the death camp. Jammed together in the freight cars, the deportees had to endure the wait, in some cases next to the dead bodies of their family members. They called for help and begged for water. Jews who had escaped from the cars were frequently shot along the railroad line by the escort details for the trains, and local residents were then tasked with taking the corpses away. Paul Winkler, a citizen of the Reich, lived near Sobibor in the town of Włodawa, and in his interrogation, he made it clear that all the Germans in the area were aware of the existence and the function of the death camp: "That there was an extermination camp in Sobibor was definitely known to me and to everyone else in the town of Włodawa. Whenever you went by train from Cholm to Włodawa, you could see the transports of Jews, thousands and tens of thousands, going to Sobibor. At night, from Włodawa you saw the fiery glow from Sobibor, and besides you noticed a peculiar odor. It was known that the Jews were exterminated there."[54]

Even the camp grounds of Sobibor were not an area completely isolated from the outside world. The front camp served as a reception area for guests, as the example of the customs official in Niemann's photos so impressively attests (see figs. 6.26–6.29). Some came from nearby localities, others, like the couriers from the Chancellery of the Führer in Berlin, from the German Reich.[55] And yet, the function of the death camp must have been beyond question for all of them. Hospitality was provided to the Germans by several Polish and Ukrainian women working in the camp, civilians who had volunteered for this job.[56]

The deadly purpose of the camp was clearly perceptible in the region. Almost daily, shots could be heard from there. When the corpses putrefied in the summer of 1942 and, beginning in the fall, the bodies were burned on pyres, a dreadful stench settled over the entire surrounding area. Depending on the wind direction, it could still be detected in Włodawa, around six miles away. Railroad workers could see small children, sick people, and elderly Jews being taken to the pit near the chapel, located close to the camp fence, where they were shot. In some places, local residents even had a view into the interior of the camp, as the son of the stationmaster reported: "For the people who worked at the station, the gas chamber was partially visible. It could be seen from the attic of the station building. I myself saw the gas chamber in this way."[57]

The arrival and subsequent murder of tens of thousands of human beings also brought, if nothing else, unforeseen riches into the rural area around Sobibor. Polish railroad workers, in unguarded moments, could steal all kinds of things from the parked freight cars filled with clothing and portable belongings.[58] In addition, Trawnikis regularly carried valuables, money, and gold out of the death camp and sold or swapped the things in surrounding villages, especially in exchange for alcohol and food, or used them to pay prostitutes.[59] It was not only the Trawnikis, however, who made acquaintances in the area. Members of the German guard force also maintained various social relationships. Józef Maliński, a Polish employee of the senior forestry office in Sobibór, had close contact with the commandant of the death camp, Franz Reichleitner, who regularly ordered wood for burning the corpses. When the forestry office dedicated a new building in Sobibór, German SS men from the camp were also invited, as if a matter of course.[60] A married couple named Sójka became more closely acquainted with Trawnikis and several members of the German guard force. While Irena Sójka ran the restaurant in the Sobibór railroad station, her husband, Czesław Sójka, worked as a train dispatcher for the Polish railway. As immediate neighbors, they knew exactly what was happening inside the camp and heard stories about how the Jews were murdered. After the war they could recall not only the names but also character traits of individual perpetrators.[61] Individual Polish residents of Sobibór allowed the German SS men from the death camp to share in their private lives as well. For example, the aforementioned forestry employee Józef Maliński invited several members of the German camp SS to the baptism of his child.[62]

The Sobibor Photos in the Niemann Collection

In Niemann's collection, sixty-two photographs with forty-nine different subjects can be assigned to Sobibor.[63] The prints were not part of the two photo albums that have survived; rather, they were stored separately as single pictures. Admittedly, the images provide only a very selective impression of the place where they originated; nonetheless, the Niemann photos make Sobibor now the visually best-documented of the Operation Reinhard camps.

In terms of content, three types of subjects are dominant: twenty-nine photos show scenes from the off-duty life of the Germans in the camp section where they were quartered. Trawnikis can be seen in ten pictures. Niemann, as the SS man in charge of the auxiliaries in Sobibor, evidently included the photos in the collection as documentation of "his" men. Finally, a considerable number of photographs offer glimpses of the camp's topography and various construction phases for several camp sections. On the basis of the phases documented in the photos and with the help of other surviving sources, the time when the pictures were taken can be narrowed down to a period of presumably less than twelve months, between the early fall of 1942 and the summer of 1943. That roughly corresponds to the time of Niemann's presence in Sobibor. The two overview photos of the front camp and Camp I, as well as the photo of the entrance gate described by survivors (see figs. 6.4–6.6) are of extraordinary significance. Nine other pictures show the Erbhof, or hereditary farm, and the camp's own agricultural operation—an area that presumably was especially important to Niemann because of his background and his documented liking for horses.

Matching formats, identically cut edges in some cases, and, not least, the consistency of the prints' content make it possible to identify different series of images. The numbers penciled on the back of numerous photos are a further indication that prints were being passed around and given to several SS men as mementos. The thirteen existing duplicates among Niemann's photos of Sobibor attest to the fact that the Germans, in some cases, ordered several prints of each subject for their own purposes. In the final analysis, for large parts of the Niemann collection, it remains unclear who was taking the photographs in

Sobibor. Nonetheless, there are approaches to an explanation. Niemann himself obviously did not own a camera. He can be seen in many of the photos, which likewise makes him seem implausible as the photographer of other scenes. The varying quality of the images, too, suggests that there are likely to have been different photographers. Niemann's SS comrade Herbert Floß may also have acted as an amateur photographer in Sobibor, as he did during the trip to Berlin. In addition, it stands to reason that, among others, those members of the camp staff who were professional photographers and had been deployed in this function earlier also, at the T4 killing centers, took some of the photos. In Sobibor, that included the brothers Franz and Josef Wolf as well as Thomas Steffel. Using the example of a series taken in the front camp, a possible context for the origin of the photos also becomes clear: in two photos, the T4 photographer Franz Wolf can be seen playing chess on the terrace of the new staff club, while he does not appear in other photos from the same series. Quite possibly he took some of the photographs himself, and simply handed his camera to a comrade for two shots (see figs. 6.20–6.23).

Niemann is at the center of a great many scenes. Some pictures show him in an especially contrived pose or at unprotected places, which suggests that such photos were taken at his request. One that particularly stands out is a staged picture of Niemann on horseback on the ramp at Sobibor, for which the photographer, standing on the train track, shot him from an extremely low angle. The choice of precisely this spot as the scene of a heroic-seeming self-dramatization sheds an indicative light on Niemann's character. It is probably no coincidence that this print is among the few photos of his produced in postcard format and thus considerably larger than the 35 mm format that was otherwise standard.[64]

At first glance, mass murder and daily violence in Sobibor make no appearance in the photo collection. A closer look at the subjects, however, offers glimpses of the infrastructure of the Operation Reinhard camp: discernible in two photos, to the left of the old staff club in the front camp, is the thatched roof of a shelter in Camp I, beneath which the deportees had to assemble in the early stage of the death camp's existence before the women, children, and men were herded in succession to the undressing site and then to the gas chambers (see figs. 6.11 and 6.13). In front of the large wooden gate through which the photographer shot the horse stable of the Erbhof, the trampled sand at the assembly site is apparent. At precisely that spot, tens of thousands of deportees had to undress before being forced to go through the tube to their death (see fig. 6.34). Finally, in the background of the picture, which actually shows Trawnikis taking a break after drill, one can see the gable of the hair-cutting barracks, which had a direct connection to the tube. At right, in Camp III behind the "green fence," what is probably the roof of the gas-chamber building can be made out. In two other photos, the gripper arm of an excavator is visible behind the roofs of barracks in Camp I. From the late summer of 1942, this equipment was used to remove the corpses from the overflowing mass graves so that they could be burned on pyres (see figs. 6.5, 6.7, 6.46) Despite the photographers' selective scenes with their intentional omissions, and the additional selection made by the owner so that things would seem harmless, the Niemann photos nonetheless offer unique glimpses of the Sobibor death camp.

Notes

1. The exact number can never be determined, because the perpetrators' records are missing. The only official victim count provided by the Germans was transmitted from Lublin to Berlin by the Operation Reinhard staff on January 11, 1943. The radio message contained the information that as of the end of December 1942, 101,370 Jews had been murdered in Sobibor. Cf. Witte/Tyas, "A New Document," p. 469. Robert Kuwałek estimated in 2014 that the number of victims was between 170,618 and 183,588 (Kuwałek, "Nowe ustalenia," p. 60). Jules Schelvis

arrived at slightly lower numbers in 2007. He assumed that around 170,000 Jews were murdered in Sobibor (Schelvis, *Sobibór*, p. 198).

2. Kuwałek, "Nowe ustalenia," p. 60, specifies the victims' origins as follows: General Government, Lublin District: 71,218–81,038; Galicia District: 13,000–15,400; Cracow District: 1,300; German Reich (incl. Austria): 7,500; Slovakia: 24,000; Czech Republic: 6,600; Netherlands: 34,000; France: 4,000; Reich Commissariat Ostland: 8,050–8,750; District (*Bezirk*) Białystok: 1,000. In Treblinka the number of foreign Jewish victims was approximately 37,000.

3. Interrogation of Jan Piwoński, April 22, 1975, LNW, Q 234/4478; interrogation of Zygmunt Bialucha, May 11, 1984, LNW, Q234/4397; interrogation of Józef Maliński, August 23, 1984, LNW, Q 234/4409; statement of Kurt Thomas, February 15, 1966, LNW, Q 234/4481; see interview with Jan Piwoński in the film *Shoah,* by Claude Lanzmann; USHMMA Claude Lanzmann Shoah Collection Acc 1996.166.1 (https://collections.ushmm.org/search/catalog/irn539109#?rsc=138101&cv=0, February 10, 2022).

4. Report of Samuel Lerer, Warsaw, 1945, LAV NRW Q234/4572. Survivors also named Johann Niemann and Bruno Weis among those who made speeches to the deportees.

5. Interrogation of Hubert Gomerski, December 9, 1965, LNW, Q 234/4420 One survivor, Thomas Blatt, also referred to the path as the "road to Heaven" (*Himmelfahrtsweg*), Blatt, *Schatten*. p. 1011

6. Statement of Esther Raab, September 17, 1949, LNW, Q 234/4569. By "Ukrainian guards," Raab meant the Trawnikis, who were not always Ukrainians but frequently were perceived as such by Jews and the Polish population.

7. Statement of Dov Freiberg, July 25, 1945, LNW, Q 234/4573.

8. Interrogation of Jan Piwoński, April 29, 1975, NIOD 804/22.

9. See, among other interrogations, those of Józef Maliński, March 24, 1977; LNW, Q 234/4476; and Franciszek Parkola, May 5, 1967, NIOD 804/22.

10. Interrogation of Erich Fuchs, September 19, 1963, LNW, Q 234/4292.

11. See, among others, the interrogations of Hans Schütt, June 7, 1961, LNW, Q 234/4263; Kurt Bolender, June 5, 1961, LNW, Q234/4264; and Alfred Ittner, November 28, 1963, LNW, Q 234/4296.

12. Statement of Dov Freiberg, July 25, 1945, LNW, Q 234/4470.

13. In total, more than 130,000 Jews were killed in Belzec in the month of August. See Kuwałek, *Belzec*, p. 244.

14. Ganzenmüller to Wolff, July 28, 1942, BArch, NS 19/2655. In this document, Sobibor is unambiguously mentioned as the originally intended second destination for deportations from Warsaw.

15. Interrogation of Kurt Bolender, October 2, 1963, LNW, Q 234/4293.

16. See the report by the Treblinka survivor Richard Glazar, *Trap*.

17. Contrary to the widespread assumption, the commandants' living quarters were not in the former postal building (Front Camp, 11), but rather in the old staff club (Front Camp, 7).

18. Report by Eda Lichtman, undated, YVA O.33 File Number 14.

19. Conversation of Anne Lepper with Simeon Rozenfeld, November 23, 2017.

20. See, among other statements, that of Erich Bauer, December 10, 1962. LNW, Q 234/4226. The former postal building in the front camp, contrary to common belief, did not serve as an administration building; rather, it was used as accommodations for the camp SS.

21. Interrogation of Alfred Ittner, July 17, 1962, LNW, Q 234/4275; Schelvis, *Sobibór*, p. 82. Other inhabitants of the forester's lodge included Heinrich Unverhau, Arthur Dachsel, and Rudolf Beckmann, see interrogation of Heinrich Unverhau, September 14, 1961, LNW, Q 234/4266.

22. Interrogation of Erich Bauer, October 6, 1965, LNW, Q 234/4416.

23. The expansion of the forester's house area to create the "small farm" (*Kleinwirtschaft*) is attributed to Johann Niemann's initiative (Berger, *Experten*, p. 161).

24. Under National Socialism, the land-tenure and farming structure in the agricultural sector was regulated by the Reich Hereditary Farm Law (*Reichserbhofgesetz*), which defined "land ownership [. . .] as the exclusive right of the 'German-Aryan' members of society." See Münkel, "Bäuerliche Interessen", p. 550. The idea of the "hereditary farm" supported and encouraged the independent and *völkisch* community of small farmers and made it essentially impossible to transfer ownership of the land or to subdivide it. For further details: Münkel, *Nationalsozialistische Agrarpolitik*, p. 112.

25. An unmarried guard in Esterwegen earned 96 Reichsmarks per month. This meager wage was supposed to be made more attractive by the prospect of a farm, and therefore the guards were to be be given preference regarding the newly created settler homesteads. See Faulenbach/Kaltofen, *Hölle*, p. 146. The promise of a hereditary farm might also have been linked with land reclamation in the marshes.

26. Kurt Thomas (Ticho), a native of Czechoslovakia, recalled that the SS had "a pig farm in the area of the camp, which, unlike our own barracks, was kept immaculately clean. It was set up on the so-called hereditary farm, and it consisted of little wooden houses that were built side by side, so that all together they came across as a big complex." Report of Kurt Thomas to the World Jewish Congress, December 3, 1961, LNW, Q 234/4270.

27. Before the war, mass was held in the wooden chapel for the population of the surrounding villages. After the death camp was built, the chapel was no longer accessible to the locals because it was located on the camp grounds.

28. This was probably ordered after Heinrich Himmler's second visit to the camp. See interrogation of Hubert Gomerski, December 2, 1965 LNW, Q 234/4420; statement of Dov Freiberg, December 21, 1965, LNW, Q 234/4419; interview of Esther Raab, February 18, 1992, USHMMA, RG-50.042.0023.

29. Statement of Abraham Margulies, November 18, 1965, LNW, Q 234/4476.

30. Interrogations of Kurt Bolender, October 2, 1963, LNW, Q234/4293; Franz Hödl, April 18, 1963, LNW, Q234/4289; Erich Bauer, December 12, 1963, LNW, Q234/4465; and Hubert Gomerski, February 24, 1964, LNW, Q234/4297; see also Schelvis, *Sobibór*, pp. 109–111; Berger, *Experten*, p. 197.

31. See Vojta, "'Inferno.'"

32. Interrogation of Erwin Lambert, October 2, 1962, LNW, Q 234/4278.

33. See the correspondence between different SS offices, July 1943, ITS, 1.2.7.07 Generalgouvernement/NO/482.

34. Jules Schelvis stated that of this total in October 1943, 50 prisoners were in Camp III and 60 in Camp IV and therefore could not take part in the uprising (Schelvis, *Sobibór*, p. 197).

35. Statement of Arkadij Wajspapier, December 10, 1975, LNW, Q 234/4582.

36. Blatt, *Ashes*, pp. 96.

37. Statement of Eda Lichtman, December 29, 1960, LNW, Q 234/4569.

38. Wewryk, *To Sobibór*, p. 58.

39. Statement of Regina Zielinski, December 10, 1974, LNW, Q 234/4570.

40. Statement of Dov Freiberg, July 25, 1945, LNW, Q 234/4573; statement of Moshe Bachir, December 16, 1965, LNW, Q 234/8229; conversation with Eda and Itzaak Lichtman, Symcha Bialowicz, Abraham Margulies, Jakub Biskubicz in September 1963, LNW, Q 234/4570. See also the chapter in this volume on the revolt in Sobibor.

41. Wewryk, *To Sobibór*, p. 61.

42. Interview with Selma Wijnberg (later Engel), July 16, 1990, USHMMA, RG-50.030*0067, time: 01:44:00.

43. Sometimes, German perpetrators forced Jewish women in their common area to provide sexual services. See interrogation of Erich Bauer, October 6, 1965, LNW, Q 234/4416.

44. Statement of Eda Lichtman, October 26, 1983, LNW, Q 234/4392.

45. The exact number of survivors is still difficult to determine. The overview given by Schelvis, *Sobibór*, pp. 273–275, with a total of 47 persons, appears incomplete. A list from the investigation proceedings against Frenzel enumerates additional survivors who were unwilling to testify or had died in the meantime; on this basis, as many as 70 potential survivors of the camp have been named. Bem, *Sobibor*, p. 298, names 93 names, with reservations.

46. Statement of Regina Zielinski, February 27, 1978, LNW, Q 234/8234. Abraham Margulies used similar words: "We were hard, turned into stone, we no longer seemed to have anything human in us, as if we were merely tragic figures who, like automatons, did dirty jobs." Statement of Abraham Margulies in September 1963, LNW, Q 234/3470.

47. According to Sara Berger, 121 members of T4 were transferred to the Operation Reinhard Camps (Berger, *Experten*, p. 14).

48. Statement of Lia Pnina Knopmacher, trial of Karl Richard Josef Streibel et al. for participation in National Socialist crimes of violence committed during 1942–1944 by members of the SS training camp at Trawniki, in particular the killing of Jews in killing centers and in the Trawniki forced labor camp, involvement in the liquidation of the Warsaw Ghetto and a number of ghettos in the Lublin District by means of individual and mass shootings or deportations to killing centers, and participation in the suppression of the Warsaw Ghetto Uprising (Staatsanwaltschaft Hamburg 147 Js 43/69), Staw Hamburg 213-12_0039/5, fols. 2519–2521; interrogation of Jan Krzowski, February 28, 1966, LNW, Q 234/4310.

49. Statement of Abraham Kohn, January 18, 1977, NIOD, 804/16.

50. Statement of Esther Raab, May 8, 1963, LNW, Q 234/4289.

51. Statement of Regina Zielinski, February 27, 1978, LNW, Q 234/8234; also Berger, *Experten*, p. 160.

52. On the enrichment of the Germans in Sobibor and the parcels sent to the German Reich, see, among others, interrogation of Franz Wolf, April 6, 1981, LNW, Q 234/4415; record of the house search concerning the wife of Walter Nowak in Böhm, "'Karrieren,'" p. 141; Eda Lichtman, March 3, 1964, LNW, Q234/4569.

53. Report of Aurelia Jaworska, ŻIH, 302/119.

54. Interrogation of Paul Winkler in the trial of Richard Nitschke (SS-Untersturmführer in the Włodawa ghetto), LNW, Q 234/4523. Cholm was the German name for the town of Chełm.

55. Werner Mauersberger, a driver for the T4 program, brought two high-ranking officials from Berlin to Sobibor and spent two days in the camp. During his stay, he met the guard Werner Becker, whom he knew from the T4 killing center at Pirna-Sonnenstein. See interrogations of Werner Mauersberger, undated, and Werner Becker, undated, BStU Berlin, MfS HA IX/23408.

56. Józef Maliński, who worked for the forestry office in Sobibór, remembered that the daughters of the Polish stationmaster and the senior forestry official cooked for the Germans in the death camp. He was also able to provide their names (interrogations of Józef Maliński, August 23 and 28, 1984, LNW, Q 234/4409; Józef Maliński, March 24, 1977, LNW, Q 234/4476). Two other local residents of Sobibor confirmed this (see interrogations of Nadzieja Czop, December 13, 1978, LNW, Q 234/4583; Mieczysław Jańkowski, July 2, 1965, LNW, Q 234/4310). In addition, there are indications that Ukrainian women also were employed in the camp in 1943.

57. Interrogation of Jan Piwoński Jr., May 10, 1984, LNW, Q 234/4396.

58. Interrogation of Franciszek Parkola, May 5, 1967, NIOD 804/22.

59. Interrogations of Franciszek Petlak; ŻIH (Chełm), October 31, 1945, LNW, Q 234/4400; Józef Maliński, August 28, 1984, LNW, Q 234/4409, and Józef Maliński, March 24, 1977, LNW, Q 234/4476.

60. Interrogation of Józef Maliński, August 23 and 28, 1984, LNW, Q 234/4409.

61. See interrogations of Irena Sójka, July 8, 1967, KARTA, PL_1001_KLS_03_1_8, Ko. Kpp 91/67; Czesław Sójka, July 8, 1967, KARTA, PL_1001_KLS_03_1_7, Ko. Kpp 91/67.

62. Interrogation of Józef Maliński, August 28, 1984, LNW, Q 234/4409.

63. Thirteen photos show scenes in duplicate or triplicate.

64. In addition to the scene described, shown in figure 6.33, the photos on in figures 6.6, 6.38, and 6.40 are also in postcard format.

Niemann's Photos from Sobibor

Figure 6.4. The camp gate at Sobibor in the spring of 1943. Through this gate, Jews from the region were forcibly brought into the death camp on foot, by truck, or in horse-drawn carts. The railroad track led into the grounds through a separate entrance to the right of the gate. Clearly discernible are the pine branches woven into the camp fence to block the view from outside. Mordechaj Goldfarb recalled on January 29, 1962: "'Sonderkommando Sobibor,' that's what was written in white letters on a black sign, and there were black flags waving on both sides of it."

Figure 6.5. View of the front camp from the guard tower at the camp entrance, spring 1943. The German camp staff lived in this section. Identifiable in the background are rooftops in Camp I and the gripping arm of the excavator that was used in Camp III, beginning in the fall of 1942, to remove corpses from the mass graves so that they could be burned.

Figure 6.6. Camp I and the front camp in the background, as seen from a guard tower in the early summer of 1943. Jewish forced laborers can be seen next to the barracks building at the left edge of the image and in the foreground, between the stacks of firewood. On the right, in the corridor between the camp fences, two Trawnikis are on patrol. At the far end of the fencing, the light-colored roof of the railroad station building is visible. In the vacant area between Camp I and the camp fence at right, a wooden canopy was in existence during an earlier construction phase; under it, the deportees were forced to assemble. Generally, the men had to wait there while the women and children were herded between the front camp and Camp I into the gas chambers. Presumably the piled-up construction materials that can be seen at the center of the image are remnants of this wooden structure.

Figure 6.7. Looking toward Camp I and Camp II from the front camp, spring 1943. At left, next to the tall fire-detection tower from the prewar period, was the camp bakery. Sticking out above its roof is the arm of the excavator, with which the corpses were lifted out of the mass graves. The barracks, later renovated, at the right edge of the image served as living quarters for Trawnikis. From the guard tower at left, they kept a close watch on the deportees on the way to the gas chambers. As in two other photos from this series, foreign matter is visible on the camera lens in the upper left corner (see figs. 6.5 and 6.52).

Figure 6.8. The front camp in the spring of 1943. The building at left, known as the staff club (Front Camp, 7), also contained Niemann's living quarters. Visible between the staff club and the laundry on the right is the access to a cellar storeroom, still in existence today. The buildings were constructed by forced laborers at the death camp, who began the project by tearing down vacant houses in the vicinity, formerly the homes of Jewish families. During the construction process, the workers were continually mistreated. Mordechaj Goldfarb testified about the abuse on November 22, 1965: "Near the staff club there were 2 wells. Once I was thrown into one of these wells, which was not far from the staff club. Wagner had beaten me."

Figure 6.9. The old staff club after the renovation work, summer 1943. The building served as a dining room for the Germans and as accommodations for the camp commandant. Niemann also lived there. Only a few Jewish prisoners had access to the Germans' quarters, where they did repair work, shined shoes, or acted as personal servants of the camp SS. Jewish women were required to wash their clothes, sew, and clean the living areas.

Figure 6.10. The new staff club building (Front Camp, 3), completed in the summer of 1943. It was larger than the previous dining room, and it offered a sheltered terrace, created by the structure's L-shape. The Germans named the staff club "The Merry Flea" ("*Zum lustigen Floh*"). The furniture on the terrace was made by Jewish prisoners; the dishes and flatware came from the belongings of the murder victims. Among the eye-catching details are the perimeter surrounds made of birch branches and the stone wall with glass lamps for lighting in the evening. Eda Lichtman, who later immigrated to Israel, recalled her first impressions: "When you came into the camp, it gave the impression of being a resort. Tastefully built detached houses with their own grounds, a staff club, gardens, gravel-covered pathways, lawns, flower beds, and paths bordered with roses and sunflowers served as meticulous camouflage and hid from newcomers the fact that the death factory was there." (Translated from German).

Figure 6.11. Niemann on horseback (*left*) in the winter of 1942/43, in front of the old staff club. Also on horseback, probably SS-Oberscharführer Beckmann, standing at left, with presumably SS-Oberscharführer Karl Frenzel, next to him, holding a whip, SS-Oberscharführer Erich Bauer.

Figure 6.12. Niemann (*center*) in front of the old staff club, spring 1943. The former T4 driver Karl Richter worked as the kitchen manager. Johanna Koch, a Jewish woman born in Mainz, also worked there temporarily, before the Germans, fearing they might be poisoned, quit using Jews to help in the kitchen and killed these workers.

Figure 6.13. Group shot with Niemann (*third from left*) in front of the old staff club, spring 1943. In the foreground is the well; to the left and right behind the staff club, the roofing of the first assembly area for the deportees, next to Camp I, can be seen.

Figure 6.14. Niemann, with the rank of SS-Hauptscharführer,
in front of the old staff club, spring 1943.

Figure 6.15. Niemann (*center*) as an SS-Hauptscharführer with other
SS-NCOs in the old staff club, spring 1943. Seated at far left, probably
SS-Unterscharführer Franz Hödl; on the table is a hyacinth in bloom,
which makes it possible to give an approximate date for the photo.
On the wall behind the group of men hangs a portrait of Hitler. The
Jewish painter Moniek had been forced to paint such a subject for this
common room. Paintings done by prisoners were also popular gifts
for Germans to take to their families in the territory of the Reich.

Figure 6.16. Studio photograph of Niemann (*left*) as an SS-Hauptscharführer with SS-Scharführer Franz Hödl, between September 1942 and June 1943.

Figure 6.17. Niemann (*left*) next to SS-Oberscharführer Gustav Wagner on the terrace of the new staff club, early summer 1943. The construction work on the building was obviously not yet completed; a window is still missing at right. Niemann is wearing a copy of a full-dress uniform that was no longer official at the time; individual SS men nonetheless ordered Jewish prisoners to make copies. On the sleeves of his uniform tunic, Wagner wears the double stripes of the sergeant responsible for maintaining order in the camp. In Sobibor, he was especially feared among the Jewish prisoners for his brutality and unpredictability.

Figure 6.18. Members of the camp SS in the early summer of 1943 on the terrace of the new staff club. *Left to right*, Hubert Gomerski and Erich Schulze, both with the rank of SS-Scharführer, SS-Oberscharführer Gustav Wagner, Niemann, and an unidentified individual.

Figure 6.19. Niemann in civilian clothing in a horse-drawn cart in the front camp, early summer 1943. Around him, other members of the camp SS.

Figure 6.20. With an accordion, presumably SS-Unterscharführer Fritz Konrad, early summer 1943. On the building behind him (front camp, 5) is the sign "Crapper" ("*Abprotzstelle*"), made by Jewish forced laborers to point the way to the toilets. A photo previously known, allegedly showing this Sobibor perpetrator, undoubtedly shows a different member of the Waffen-SS with the same name.

Figure 6.21. Front camp, early summer of 1943. In the background, at right, the new staff club. Standing (*left to right*), all with the rank of SS-Unterscharführer, Rudolf Kamm and Willi Wendland; with the accordion, Heinrich Unverhau; presumably Fritz Konrad; and Johann Klier. Unverhau, transferred from Belzec to Sobibor only a short time before, was a trained musician and oversaw Jewish prisoners in the sorting barracks and in the forest detachment.

Figure 6.22. On the terrace of the new staff club, early summer 1943. With the violin, Heinrich Unverhau, Rudolf Kamm, presumably Fritz Konrad, as well as Willi Wendland and Johann Klier (*from left to right*). Frequently Jewish men and women also had to play instruments and dance, by order of the Germans.

Figure 6.23. Willi Wendland (*left*) and Franz Wolf playing chess in front of the new staff club, early summer 1943. Franz Wolf, together with his brother Josef, came to Sobibor in the spring of 1943. Both had been deployed as photographers with the T4 program.

Figure 6.24. Front camp, summer 1943. This photo and the eight that follow form a series of images documenting a sociable afternoon on the terrace of the new staff club. Niemann (in three-quarter view) with three other uniformed men. Comparison with Figure 6.17 reveals that shutters and flowerboxes have been attached to the building in the meantime.

Figure 6.25. On the terrace of the new staff club. *Left to right*, probably SS-Scharführer Erich Schulze; leaning forward, an unidentified person; seated, SS-Oberscharführer Erich Bauer; turned away from the camera, the camp commandant; SS-Hauptsturmführer Franz Reichleitner; half-concealed, Niemann; at the right edge of the image, seated, SS-Unterscharführer Dachsel.

Figure 6.26. Dachsel, Niemann, Reichleitner, and, seated and concealed from the camera, Bauer (*from left to right*). Standing in the foreground is a uniformed secretary of the Customs Border Guards (*Zollgrenzschutz*). This organization, under the authority of the Reich Ministry of Finance, played a part in guarding the borders and in Nazi occupation policy. One of the stations on the Bug River was only five miles from the death camp, in the village of Zbereże. The photo implies that Sobibor was a semipublic place, where the guards showed their guests hospitality. The survivor Esther Raab reported that a guest room also existed on the camp grounds.

Figure 6.27. Germans looking at photo prints. *Left to right*, Niemann; Reichleitner; Bauer, seated; in the background, presumably Erich Schulze; in front, the Customs Border Guards official. *At right*, standing in the door frame, are two civilian women who worked in the kitchen of the staff club. According to the statements of local residents, at times the kitchen workers were Polish women whose fathers were in contact with the camp SS. In 1943, Ukrainian women also are said to have worked for the Germans.

Figure 6.28. Dachsel, Reichleitner, Niemann, probably Schulze, Bauer, the two kitchen workers, and the Customs Border Guards official (*from left to right*). On the table, valuable crystal glasses are discernible to some extent, probably from the belongings of the murdered Jews. Alcohol played a major role in the everyday life of the German perpetrators.

Figure 6.29. Dachsel, presumably Schulze, Niemann, Reichleitner, the Customs Border Guards secretary, and, half-concealed, Bauer (*from left to right*). How safe and secure the Germans felt in Sobibor is indicated in the photo series also by the fact that they were not openly carrying firearms.

Figure 6.30. Dachsel; concealed from view, probably Schulze; Niemann; Reichleitner; and Bauer (*from left to right*). Arthur Dachsel was one of the oldest men deployed in the death camps of Operation Reinhard. Born in 1890, he came to Sobibor from Belzec in the early summer of 1943, and was responsible for supervising the Jewish prisoners used for labor in Camp IV.

Figure 6.31. Reichleitner, conspicuously familiar with one of the women; next to him,
Bauer; at the edge of the shot, Niemann (*from left to right*). Reichleitner had been camp
commandant since September 1942. Jewish survivors mention him only in passing,
because he obviously was seldom in evidence in the everyday life of the camp.

Figure 6.32. Bauer (*center*), who referred to himself after 1945 as the "Gas Master [*Gasmeister*] of Sobibor," with the kitchen worker. *Left*, Reichleitner; in the background, Schulze; *at right*, Niemann.

Figure 6.33. Staged shot of Niemann on horseback in the summer of 1943. In the background, a barracks building in which Trawnikis lived (Front Camp, 14). Discernible at the lower edge of the image is the wood-encased border of the ramp in Sobibor at which the deportation trains arrived. For this scene, the photographer climbed down onto the roadbed, the groundwork onto which the railroad tracks were laid. The print was exposed in mirror-reverse.

Figure 6.34. Sobibor, Camp II. This photo and the three that follow were taken in the summer of 1943 in the so-called Erbhof, with its stables and barns. Niemann stands at the center of the image. At the well, a Jewish woman prisoner is drawing water; at right, another Jewish forced laborer stands in front of the barn. Jews in Sobibor did not wear striped prisoner's garb as in the concentration camps; instead, they were given articles of clothing in the storehouse, garments that had belonged to the murder victims. The board fence and the gate in the foreground separated the yard from the sandy forecourt, where the deportees had to assemble and undress before they were forced into the gas chambers. Often they buried jewelry and other valuables in the sand to keep their possessions from falling into the Germans' hands. Moshe Bachir had to work in this area. On December 14, 1965, he recalled that "The people [had to] go through the tube. As soon as they were gone, we had to rake the sand to find any hidden money or gold."

Figure 6.35. Niemann (*right*) in front of the barn in conversation with a Jewish prisoner. In the white building on the left, there was a horse stable; two carved horse's heads were mounted on the dormer above the entrance. Easily recognizable in the top third of the image is the elaborate wooden sign with the word "Erbhof." Jewish craftsmen in Sobibor were required to make such signs and guideposts for the Germans.

Figure 6.36. Niemann (*left*) with SS-Unterscharführer Adolf Müller in front of the well in the Erbhof, summer 1943. Atop the roof over the well, there was a dovecote.

Figure 6.37. Niemann (*left*) with Müller at the same spot. Easily visible is Niemann's whip, the Germans' instrument of repression and symbol of power.

Figure 6.38. Niemann (*left*), with the rank of SS-Hauptscharführer, with an unidentified SS-Unterscharführer and presumably SS-Oberscharführer Rudolf Beckmann *(right)* in the Erbhof, spring 1943. Standing in front of the pigsty, they hold piglets, which were raised to supply the camp staff. Jewish prisoners were responsible for agricultural work. They were harshly punished or even murdered by the Germans if animals fell sick or died. Kurt Thomas recalled on December 3, 1961: "The SS had a pig farm in the area of the camp, which, in contrast to our own barracks, was kept spotlessly clean."

Figure 6.39. Camp II, summer 1943. SS-Unterscharführer Willi Wendland (*left*) and Rudolf Kamm on the grounds of the Erbhof, summer 1943. The geese were frequently mentioned by Jewish survivors and by locals who lived nearby. In his documentary *Shoah*, filmmaker Claude Lanzmann used cackling geese, running in a circle, to create an iconographic image of the history of Sobibor. Mordechai Goldfarb recalled on January 29, 1962: "When transports arrived, the geese were let out. Then their clamor mixed with the cries of the people."

Figure 6.40. In front of one of the sorting barracks in Camp II, summer 1943. *Left to right*, an unidentified SS-Unterscharführer, Niemann, an unidentified SS-Oberscharführer, SS-Untersturmführer Paul Rost. Niemann is holding Hans, the horse he often rode through the death camp.

Figure 6.41. Camp II in the spring of 1943. Niemann on his horse, probably in front of one of the sorting barracks, which were located near the ramp. In the barracks, Jewish prisoners had to sort and pack the belongings of the murdered Jews before sending the items to the Operation Reinhard warehouses in Lublin for further disposition.

Figure 6.42. Front camp, summer 1943. Niemann and an unidentified SS-Unterscharführer with shepherd dogs. Often the camp SS set the animals on Jewish prisoners. When deportation trains arrived, dogs spread fear among the Jews. Visible in the background of the photo, on the left, are the barracks where the Trawniki NCOs were quartered, as well as the gable of the forestry building. Discernible between them is the wooden fence that surrounded the undressing site for the deportees in Camp II.

Figure 6.43. SS-Unterscharführer Rudolf Kamm with a shepherd dog on the camp grounds in the summer of 1943.

Figure 6.44. A Trawniki platoon in an open space in the area of Camp I, probably in March 1943. Visible in the background are, *left*, the fire-detection tower from the prewar period and, *right*, the former forestry building, which was on the grounds of the Erbhof and served as quarters for some Germans from the camp SS and as an administration building. In a separate room, the victims' gold, jewelry, and cash were kept.

Figure 6.45. Probably the same Trawniki platoon, at the parade ground between Camp II and Camp III, in the spring of 1943. The second guard from left in the back row has been inconclusively identified by German forensics experts as being Ivan Demjanjuk. Together with 82 other Trawnikis, he was transferred to Sobibor on March 26, 1943. In this staged group photo, the insignia of the guards are easily recognizable. While epaulets without stripes denote low-ranking guards, one, two, and three stripes, in ascending order, designate the ranks of Oberwachmann, Gruppenwachmann, and Zugwachmann. Niemann had general responsibility for the duty roster of the Trawnikis in Sobibor. His subordinate Mikhail Razgonayev later claimed in court that Niemann personally had ordered him to shoot Jews in poor health at the edge of a pit.

Figure 6.46. The same Trawniki unit in the spring of 1943, at the parade ground in front of Camp III. The person lying in front, at the center, has been inconclusively identified by German forensics experts as being Ivan Demjanjuk; standing, on either side, are the two Gruppenwachmänner, and in the center is the Zugwachmann. Visible in the background are the roofs of two buildings that are part of the killing area. At the left edge of the image, one can see the gable of the barracks in which Jewish women were forced to have their hair cut before they were murdered. The second roof, to the right of the hair-cutting barracks, with a tall chimney-like structure, is part of the building containing the gas chambers.

Figure 6.47. SS-Oberscharführer Siegfried Graetschus (*second from right*) in the spring of 1943 with four Trawnikis, presumably also at the parade ground between Camp II and Camp III. With a similar career background as an SS-soldier and in the T4 program, Graetschus, like Niemann, was responsible for the further training of individual platoons of the Trawnikis stationed in Sobibor. The Zugwachmann on the right, the Gruppenwachmann, and the two Oberwachmänner on the left are also shown in the two previous photos.

Figure 6.48. Niemann (*center*), with the rank of SS-Hauptscharführer, between two Zugwachmänner in front of one of the barracks used to house Trawnikis, spring 1943. *Right*, with an adjutant's cord on his uniform tunic, most probably Alexander Kaiser. In Italy in 1944, the Soviet German still kept up a correspondence with his sweetheart, who lived in the Sobibór region.

Figure 6.49. Trawnikis at the same spot; in front, on the right, is Kaiser. As a joke, someone inside the barracks held an alarm clock up to the window.

Figure 6.50. SS-Scharführer Paul Groth (*center*) and Trawnikis
in the spring of 1943 in front of the elaborately carved sign
"Crapper [*Abprotzstelle*]" which points the way to the toilets.

Figure 6.51. Three Zugwachmänner and four Gruppenwachmänner in the spring of 1943, next to the guards' building in the entrance area of the front camp. The group represents a large part of the Trawniki NCOs stationed in Sobibor at that time.

Figure 6.52. A group of Trawnikis, busy with fenceposts, in the spring of 1943. The print has on the top left the same flaw in the image as figures 6.5 and 6.7.

Figure 6.53. Eight Trawnikis in a marching formation, spring 1943.

7

The Trawnikis

Auxiliaries to the Holocaust

MARTIN CÜPPERS

In the course of his administrative duties on July 1, 1943, SS-Untersturmführer Johann Niemann, deputy commandant of the Sobibor killing center, wrote a succinct report to his superior in Lublin. The report's recipient was Christian Wirth, the inspector for Operation Reinhard (*Aktion Reinhard*), Nazi Germany's campaign for murdering the Jews of Poland. Niemann was informing Wirth of the desertion of two so-called Trawnikis, auxiliary guards recruited primarily from the ranks of Soviet prisoners of war (POWs). The two men in question were Wachmann Ivan Kakarash, a twenty-three-year-old from southern Ukraine, and Wachmann Konstantin Dimida, also twenty-three, who had been born in Belorussia.[1] Both had slipped away the previous night, leaving their official identity cards but taking their rifles and ammunition. Niemann's report is one of the very few documents from Sobibor known to have survived the war.[2] While Niemann's report emphasizes his personal responsibility for the non-German guards at the camp, the desertion was hardly an isolated incident. The German police and SS had often had cause to report similar instances.

A platoon of the German rural police (*Gendarmerie*) from Chelm (Polish: Chełm), not far from Sobibor, reported that, in the early morning hours of December 26, 1942, the Trawnikis Viktor Kisilev and Vasyl Tsisher had gone absent without leave "from the Sobibor camp, taking two Russ. rifles and a sizeable amount of munitions." The two had even helped five Jews to escape. Four of the five otherwise doomed Jews appear to have made good their effort, at least for the time being. But early on the morning of January 1, 1943, Polish police, acting on a tip, shot and killed the two fugitive guards along with Pesia Liberman, a native of Chelm, who had just turned 16.[3]

Although this incident appears to show Jews and Trawnikis united in a common struggle to flee the Nazis, many Treblinka and Sobibor survivors remember the auxiliaries at the Operation Reinhard camps in a completely different light. Moshe Bachir, for example, insisted that the Trawnikis at Sobibor behaved "often worse than the Germans."[4] Other reports by Sobibor survivors, as well as similar accounts by survivors of Treblinka, illustrate how these auxiliaries ensured that the death camps functioned as intended by carrying out orders and committing endless atrocities and individual acts of murder. The range of options available to the Trawnikis at the Operation Reinhard camps lay between two extremes: dereliction of duty, as manifested by desertion, on the one hand, and the utmost readiness to commit violence and kill, as described by survivors, on the other.

The academic literature on this topic to date has examined both the diversity of the perpetrator group and the perpetrators' joint responsibility for the mass killings. In a multifaceted and richly documented essay, Peter Black, the world's leading expert on the Trawnikis, terms them the "front line troops" of Operation Reinhard.[5] David Rich, an official at the US Department of Justice who for many years investigated former Trawnikis living in the United States, characterizes these men in much the same way, as "foot soldiers" in the implementation of genocidal crimes.[6] In her 2015 doctoral thesis, Angelika Benz emphasizes the heterogeneity of the Trawniki group as well as the fact that these men largely were without rights, a state of affairs that in her view should lead to closer examination of previous generalizations.[7]

The Niemann collection includes a sizeable number of photographs depicting several dozen different Trawnikis. These images provide impressive documentation for the close working relationship between the SS man and his foreign subordinates, first at Belzec, and then at Sobibor. The photographs of a trip to Berlin reveal most vividly the Germans' special appreciation for a small group of particularly "deserving" members of this auxiliary force. With this in mind, it is necessary to address the questions that have gone largely unanswered to date: How many Trawnikis, with their distinct biographical backgrounds, served in the Operation Reinhard camps, and what was the scope of action they encountered there, in particular, in those places where Niemann commanded them?[8]

Soviet Prisoners of War Become Trawnikis

In the very first weeks after the attack on the Soviet Union in late June 1941, the German occupiers began to fall back on ever-larger numbers of indigenous men to help control the enormous territories just conquered. Toward the end of July 1941, Heinrich Himmler, the head of the SS and chief of the German police, instructed Odilo Globocnik, the SS and police leader in District Lublin and plenipotentiary for the planned SS bases in the East, to recruit captured Red Army soldiers "who appear especially trustworthy and are therefore suitable for deployment in the reconstruction of the occupied territories."[9]

In the weeks that followed, SS officials swarmed out to the prisoner of war camps and began assessing POWs based on appearance and health. Those deemed suitable were frequently taken along immediately. Globocnik's recruiters accommodated their future auxiliaries in a camp in the small town of Trawniki—the source of their later name—about twenty miles southeast of Lublin. German clerks recorded basic biographical details on special personnel forms. To facilitate recognition, passport photos were taken: one was attached to the forms kept on file, and another was fixed to the identity cards issued to the recruits. The men signed a personal statement officially swearing them into service and then received used Soviet, Polish, or even Belgian army uniforms, which, in many cases, had been dyed black.

During a subsequent training program sometimes lasting several months, the recruits learned basic German phrases, mastered the rudiments of military drill and guard duty, and received further instruction in the use of firearms.[10] Their training also included ideological indoctrination. As one former Trawniki put it, a "political orientation in a pro-fascist direction" took place. In the course of these lessons, German instructors also conveyed antisemitic and anti-Roma and Sinti content.[11]

The force that emerged starting in autumn 1941 was referred to by various names. In some cases, Germans called the men simply *Hiwis*, an abbreviation of *Hilfswillige* (literally, willing helpers). Others referred to them as *Askaris*, thereby recalling the auxiliary troops in Germany's African colonies during the Wilhelmine era. The Poles called them either "Ukrainians," a sweeping generalization, or *czarni*, the "black ones," owing to the most common color of their uniforms. The most widespread term for this force borrowed from the name of the town where its members were trained: "Trawnikis" or "Trawniki men."[12]

In 2013, Peter Black published an analysis of 800 personnel forms, available personnel rosters, and numerous postwar statements that creates a better overview of this auxiliary force. Most of the men were indeed former Red Army soldiers. Over half of the group studied were between nineteen and twenty-four years of age at the time of their recruitment. A sizeable 44.8 percent were Ukrainians, while 27 percent were Russians and 15 percent were ethnic Germans from the Soviet Union.[13] The range of known serial numbers, which were issued consecutively, suggests that more than five thousand men served as Trawnikis between 1941 and 1943. The circumstances of their recruitment varied significantly over the years.

The first wave of recruitment, during the summer of 1941, targeted Soviet Germans, frequently men from the Volga region, who would later attain positions of authority. Starting that autumn and lasting until the spring of 1942, recruits tended to be captured Red Army soldiers of Ukrainian or Russian origin. To ensure the greatest ideological distance from the Soviet Union, the Germans tried to give preference to certain ethnic minorities who had suffered exceptionally under Stalin's rule. But it was precisely during this recruitment phase that Soviet POWs found themselves confronted by the consequences of the Wehrmacht's Hunger Policy, which was partially responsible for the deaths of 3.3 million Red Army soldiers over the course of the war.[14]

Grigorii Kniga, a former Trawniki at Belzec, described the situation vividly after the war: "Conditions in these camps were terrible. Death was mowing people down. Starvation, cold, exhausting labor, and atrocities on the part of the guards drove the men to despair. Every one of us was expecting death."[15] Given the shockingly high death rate, pure survival instinct,

rather than any calculated choice to volunteer, was often a decisive factor in recruitment. In retrospect, this motive was also regularly mentioned and sometimes regretted.

During questioning by the Soviet authorities in 1974, Prokofii Buzinnyi, a former Trawniki at Sobibor, described how he had ended up as a German POW and had "faintheartedly" agreed to recruiters' appeals.[16] Jakob Engelhardt, an ethnic German who had been platoon leader of the first Trawnikis at the Sobibor construction site and observed the testing of the gas chambers, also described how hunger and disease in the POW camp drove him to accept employment with the Germans near the end of 1941.[17] In a similar vein, Aleksandr Semigodov, deployed in Belzec, explained that he "despondently" agreed to enlist so that he would not starve to death.[18]

Later recruits experienced very different conditions in the POW camps, which in turn suggests that different motives were in play. The approximately 1,250 Red Army POWs who arrived at Trawniki during the summer of 1942 no longer faced starvation to the same extent as in 1941. By mid-1942, the Germans were trying to keep prisoners alive for use as forced laborers for the wartime economy. Thus, POWs faced a choice between Globocnik's recruiters and representatives of the general plenipotentiary for labor deployment.

Starting in the fall of 1942, the SS and police no longer recruited soldiers from the POW camps, opting instead for young men from the civilian population, first and foremost from the districts of Lublin and Galicia.[19] In this final phase of recruitment, the choice to serve was most likely to have been voluntarily made rather than motivated by duress or coercion.

Knowledge of what went on at Belzec and Sobibor was widespread, especially among local civilians. At least seventy-six Trawnikis who served at Sobibor during its last months of gassing operations or during dismantling came from towns such as Chełm, Zamość, and Hrubieszów, that is, from the immediate vicinity of the death camps in District Lublin.[20]

This suggests that young men, fully aware of what was happening at these camps, enlisted to serve with the Germans in spite of or precisely because of the genocidal crimes taking place there. As members of the Ukrainian minority, some may have enlisted in the hope of getting to safety in the face of the advancing Red Army; alternatively, they may have been acting out of ideological conviction. Others may have volunteered in the hope of coming into possession of the victims' valuables, as many other guards had done before them.

The Trawnikis of Operation Reinhard

From the outset, the Trawnikis contributed to Operation Reinhard as an important contingent of personnel, both during the liquidation operations in the ghettos and at the killing centers where the deportation trains came to a halt. They also served as guards at various forced labor camps in District Lublin.[21]

The Germans chose noncommissioned officers (NCOs) for service at the Operation Reinhard camps on the basis of reliability or affinity for Nazism, but it was pure chance as to which Trawnikis from the rank and file ended up at one of these killing centers. Trained contingents varying in size from a squad of about ten men up to several platoons of roughly thirty men each rotated in and out of the three camps according to each commandant's needs. At the end of 1941, a first squad of fifteen Trawnikis deployed to Belzec to secure the construction site. Before the murder operations got under way there in the spring, the Germans swapped out this squad for a larger contingent of one hundred men. From that point on, Trawnikis provided the auxiliaries for Belzec, supporting the SS personnel in tasks ranging from forcing the Jews from the deportation trains, to terrorizing the victims during their final walk to the gas chambers, to overseeing the Jewish slave laborers compelled to hastily bury the corpses.

In postwar statements, a few of the former Trawnikis, sometimes using similar words, described the devastating routine that settled in over time. One of those interrogated portrayed the implementation of the Holocaust as a "kind of habitual activity" that constituted "a monotonous occupation," while another claimed that the process of mass murder amounted to "a procedure that belonged to daily life and therefore no longer had any special significance."[22] In the months that followed, auxiliary guards at Sobibor and Treblinka assumed the same array of tasks and duties developed at the model killing center of Belzec.[23] For their assistance in the Holocaust, they received a salary in Polish złoty from their training camp.[24]

The Ukrainians or Russians recruited from the Red Army POWs in 1941, as well as the young Poles and Ukrainians from the region of Lublin who signed on toward the end of Operation Reinhard, primarily held the two lowest ranks: Wachmann and Oberwachmann. By contrast, men of ethnic German origin, mostly from the Soviet Union or, far less common, Poland, held the higher ranks: Gruppenwachmann, Zugwachmann, and Oberzugwachmann, a rank introduced only in May 1943. Among these NCOs with greater command authority and responsibility, the number of Ukrainians, Russians, and Balts was comparatively small.[25] Although the NCOs could face assignments that did not necessarily reflect their rank, Gruppenwachmänner as a rule led a squad of at least ten guards, while Zugwachmänner commanded a platoon of two to three squads, or twenty to forty men.[26] For the German personnel, this kind of gradation in the ranks largely eliminated difficulties in communicating with the overwhelmingly non-German-speaking auxiliaries. Since the Soviet Germans in NCO positions tended to know German, they functioned as intermediaries, passing on instructions from the SS personnel to their subordinates, who as a rule had mastered only a limited range of German words and phrases.[27]

Analogous to the mass murder procedures in the death camps, which were developed by means of trial and error and continually evolved, the need for Trawnikis also progressed. If at first they had to escort the Jews through the various stages leading to extermination, the general need for guards in the Operation Reinhard camps steadily grew in accordance with the boost in efficiency achieved by the establishment of Jewish forced labor details. Starting in early 1943, the growth in partisan activity in District Lublin also required additional personnel. Thus, amid the ongoing extermination operations, it was simultaneously necessary to build living quarters and mess halls for the auxiliaries, who kept arriving in ever larger contingents and expanding their presence on-site.

The number of Trawnikis who served at Belzec, Sobibor, and Treblinka apparently varied quite significantly from one site to the next. Structural differences between the camps and the length of time each location existed help explain these differences. Analysis of the available, but incomplete, personnel records provides some valuable clues.[28] At least 322 Trawnikis deployed to Belzec at some point in their career with the Germans.[29] By contrast, considerably more of these guards—393 in all—served at Sobibor, while 168 Trawnikis worked at Treblinka. In considering these numbers, however, one must keep in mind that scores of Trawnikis never experienced the mass murder operations, since their transfer took place only during the dismantling process, after the killings in the gas chambers had already ceased.

Therefore, comparison of more significant "core time periods" when the gas chambers were in operation at each Operation Reinhard camp yields a different picture. Between March and December 1942, 179 Trawnikis deployed to Belzec, while 353 men from this force rotated in and out of Sobibor between April 1942 and October 1943, close to twice as many as were posted to the first killing center. By contrast, from July 1942 to August 1943, sources indicate the presence of only the aforementioned 168 auxiliaries at Treblinka.

Instead of simply adding the numbers to get an approximate total for the Trawnikis who were present during the period of murder operations at the Operation Reinhard camps, one must also keep in mind that, over time, many of these men were stationed at more than one of these sites. At least twelve Trawnikis who worked at Belzec while the gas chambers were in operation later transferred to Treblinka, while thirty-four moved on to Sobibor. At Treblinka, nineteen of the guards had demonstrably served beforehand at Sobibor. Of the sixty-two Trawnikis posted to more than one death camp, forty-four gained their first experience at Belzec, suggesting that this facility was an important testing ground for the use of the Trawnikis. From there, those who had proven themselves could be sent elsewhere.

This seems to have been the case above all with regard to the NCOs, who started at Belzec and then often moved on to apply their new skills at other camps if they had "distinguished" themselves in the eyes of the SS. It is possible to verify this career progression with regard to the Zugwachmänner Arnold Dalke, Alexander Kaiser, Richard Klatt, Boris Rogosa, Franz Bienemann, and Emanuel Schulz. These men remained etched upon the memory of Jewish survivors, and some appear in photos from the Niemann collection. Bienemann and Schulz even served at all three Operation Reinhard camps. Based on the available documents, at least 638 Trawnikis transferred in and out of the killing centers while the gas chambers were active.[30]

In spring 1942, during the early phase of the mass murder operations, German training instructors from the Trawniki training camp were also sent to the Operation Reinhard camps. Reinhold Feix accompanied his men to Belzec, while Herbert Schäfer went to Sobibor. Erich Lachmann—an NCO from the German Order Police (Ordnungspolizei), which, like the SS, was commanded by Himmler—then succeeded Schäfer in June 1942. When Lachmann proved to be unreliable, he was sent back to the training installation. This coincided with Niemann's arrival at Sobibor that same summer, at the latest.[31]

At Belzec, over time, Gottfried Schwarz seems to have become responsible for the auxiliaries and assigned them their duties. Fritz Jirmann and, by all appearances, Johann Niemann were entrusted with providing the guards further training, which the Operation Reinhard camps' SS personnel considered necessary in light of the brief nature of their instruction until then. After Jirmann's death, Werner Dubois filled in as a substitute. While at Belzec, Kurt Franz was likewise entrusted with this assignment until his transfer to Treblinka.[32]

All four of the photos in the Niemann collection that are related to Belzec depict Trawnikis and reflect both their close working relationship with the Germans as well as the training that the SS men aimed to complete. The photo taken behind the commandant's office at Belzec shows Niemann and several of his auxiliaries simulating target practice (see figs. 5.1–5.3).

The other two killing sites soon adopted the working model for handling the guards that had taken shape at Belzec. After accumulating several months of experience with these men, the deputy commandants were given responsibility for the Trawnikis: Johann Niemann at Sobibor, Gottfried Schwarz at Belzec, and Kurt Franz at Treblinka. It was no coincidence that all three belonged to the Waffen-SS. Their professional military training gave cause to believe that they would be especially qualified to command the Trawnikis. For the same reason, this group was entrusted with the further military training of individual platoons. After all, it certainly seemed that Waffen-SS soldiers ought to be best suited to guarantee the further military training that the auxiliaries needed. Accordingly, Niemann not only commanded all the Trawnikis at Sobibor but

also regularly assigned Trawnikis their various duties for mass murder operations prior to the arrival of deportation trains.

As he had previously done at Belzec, Niemann also appears to have taken over the training of a particular platoon of Trawnikis, probably the 3rd. In addition, he commanded the guards who were detailed to Camp III, the area with Sobibor's gas chambers.[33] Alongside Niemann, Siegfried Graetschus was responsible for the military training of the 1st Platoon, and Herbert Floss for that of the 2nd Platoon. After Floss transferred out of Sobibor, Kurt Bolender took over, with Hubert Gomerski later acting as an occasional substitute.[34]

The Germans who oversaw the auxiliaries in the Reinhard camps maintained the strict disciplinary regime established at the Trawniki training center. Niemann and his counterparts at Belzec and Treblinka seemed well suited to this task, given their socialization in the concentration camp guard school of atrocious violence. Surviving documents and statements by former Trawnikis suggest that for them everyday life entailed severe punishment for any and every infraction of regulations.[35]

During the early period of Sobibor's existence, the aforementioned NCO Jakob Engelhardt, acting contrary to orders, allowed some of his men to leave the confines of the camp. One of the Germans learned of Engelhardt's lapse and reported it. As punishment, all the Trawnikis had to stand at attention for an hour and a half.[36] In another instance, two auxiliary guards from Sobibor deserted but ultimately returned after some time. Nonetheless, the head of the camp's SS personnel had both men shot.[37] Contrary to orders, Petr Tadich also abandoned his post at Treblinka in May 1943 to meet his girlfriend and give her some valuables stolen from murdered Jews. Along the way, he got involved in a shoot-out with Poles, thus ensuring that his wrongdoing came to light. Deputy Commandant Kurt Franz himself is said to have shot Tadich.[38]

Heinrich Unverhau experienced the rare instance when the fundamental hierarchical relationship was reversed. Before his transfer to Belzec in the early summer of 1942, Unverhau had already served in the T4 killing centers Grafeneck and Hadamar. By 1943, he was one of the SS personnel at Sobibor, where he sometimes played violin and accordion while off duty. While still stationed at Belzec, Unverhau had to be hospitalized off-site due to complications arising from a case of typhus. His superiors apparently began to worry that in delirium he could betray secrets related to his daily work routine. This resulted in an unusual scenario, which he recalled in court in 1965: "During my entire stay at the hospital, I was accompanied by a German-speaking member of the Ukrainian guards, who did not let me out of his sight even during the operation."[39]

Repercussions of this disciplinary system bred suspicion toward the Germans and became all too apparent in the events surrounding the death of Fritz Jirmann. During the dismantling of Belzec in March 1943, Jirmann intended to kill two Trawnikis single-handedly in the detention bunker. When the two, sensing danger, fought back, Jirmann withdrew and retreated into the shadows. Heinrich Gley, who was posted outside the detention area to secure the perimeter, took Jirmann for a fleeing Trawniki. He fired on his comrade in error and in doing so killed him.[40]

Beyond the system of discipline, the Germans, at the Operation Reinhard camps and wherever else National Socialist extermination policies were implemented, cultivated an effective system of incentives in order to motivate subordinates to participate in the crimes. Accordingly, those Trawnikis who distinguished themselves in their daily work routine and demonstrated particular cruelty vis-à-vis their victims were rewarded. For shootings of Jews who were weak or ill, frequently conducted in the notorious "hospital" (*Lazarett*), the Germans

tended to call on precisely those security guards who showed initiative. This guaranteed that such murders took place without incident for the most part.[41]

Trawnikis at Belzec and Sobibor

Similar to the previous developments in Belzec, a squad of twelve auxiliaries led by Zugwachmann Jakob Engelhardt reported to Sobibor while it was under construction in early 1942.[42] When mass killing got under way there in April, a considerably larger contingent of at least thirty men replaced the first squad, whose members returned to Trawniki. Arnold Dalke was one of the leading NCOs among the replacements.[43]

After the summer of 1942 and Niemann's transfer to Sobibor, there were three platoons of Trawnikis under the command of the Zugwachmänner Kaiser, Maurer, and Bienemann. Niemann assigned these men and their platoons to guard duty for 24-hour shifts on a rotating basis. Of the other two platoons, one was on standby and the other off duty. Whichever was available, Niemann deployed it to oversee the arrival of deportation trains at the ramp, supervise the undressing of the victims, and escort the Jews on their final journey to the gas chambers in Camp III. At each stage, many of the Trawnikis beat the Jews relentlessly, stole whatever they could, and committed numerous individual acts of murder.[44] This process culminated in the killing area, where Trawnikis forced the victims into the gas chambers, brutally quashed all forms of resistance, and operated the gasoline engine that produced the deadly exhaust.

Finally, as already mentioned, the auxiliaries were also regularly detailed to the area cynically called the "hospital." Initially located at an old chapel outside Camp III, then moved into the actual killing area not far from the gas chambers, the "hospital" was where specially chosen guards killed the elderly and others who were sick and unable to walk unaided to the gas chambers. These people were transported in wagons to the pits and quickly shot. Later, the Germans built a special narrow-gauge railroad and used dump cars to the same end.[45] Thus, Trawnikis served throughout the relevant sections of Sobibor. The same was true for Belzec and Treblinka.

As the auxiliary guards at Sobibor were swapped out more than once, the total number of Trawnikis deployed there appears to have grown steadily until the autumn of 1943. On March 26, 1943, eighty-four Trawnikis arrived at Sobibor as replacements and reinforcements. It was on this day that Ivan (John) Demjanjuk, serial number 1393, also transferred to Sobibor. In a case of mistaken identity, Demjanjuk would later stand trial in Israel, where he was accused of having been "Ivan the Terrible," a notoriously cruel guard who worked the gas chambers at Treblinka; Demjanjuk was at first condemned to death but then later acquitted when new evidence emerged. Years later, he would again face trial in a Munich court for having served as a guard at Sobibor, which sentenced him to prison. He died before the sentence became legally binding.[46] Analysis by German forensics experts of photos from the Niemann collection support an inconclusive identification of Ivan Demjanjuk, who in the recent past gained prominence as a result of the various efforts to prosecute him (see figs. 6.45–6.46).

In response to the Treblinka uprising on August 2, 1943, the Germans rushed 17 men from Trawniki to Sobibor as reinforcements that same day. Demjanjuk's contingent withdrew after about six months, and on September 16, one hundred new auxiliaries reported to Sobibor.[47] Months after the Jewish uprising and the end of the killing operations at Sobibor, a final transfer occurred on March 30, 1944, when another twenty Trawnikis arrived to secure the site during dismantling.[48]

Niemann's photo collection offers vivid evidence of his close working relationship with the Trawnikis. In all, these guards feature in eighty-four prints. The four photos from Belzec show different men and convey a certain impression of the everyday work routine. In the two photos taken near the camp, SS personnel appear together with Trawnikis. The third photo depicts Niemann and some of his men simulating target practice behind the commandant's office, while in the fourth photo, two guards pose for the camera in a room furnished as a bar for the Trawnikis (see figs. 5.1–5.4).

Niemann's photographs from Sobibor are significantly more extensive. Black-clad men marching in formation and working in and around the camp area appear in two prints. Three photos show the same platoon of twenty-two Trawnikis, one inconclusively identified by German forensics experts as Ivan Demjanjuk, during drills between camps II and III. In addition, the unit's NCOs were photographed together with Siegfried Graetschus in the same area. A fifth photo taken in the snow close to the fire watchtower most likely portrays the same platoon as well, at an earlier time (see figs. 6.44–6.47 and 6.52–6.53). The accumulation of prints related to this platoon suggests that Niemann interacted closely with it in the course of his official duties. At Sobibor, it may be that Niemann, like Graetschus, was responsible for the military training of this formation in addition to assigning the guards their duties. Aside from such photos with this platoon, a photograph of the entrance to the front camp at Sobibor shows three Zugwachmänner and four Gruppenwachmänner, who probably made up a significant share of the Trawnikis' leadership on site in the spring of 1943, when the picture was made.

Two photos feature one of the most important guards at Sobibor. His uniform tunic includes the cord of an adjutant (see figs. 6.48 and 6.49). The person in question is Alexander Kaiser, whom survivors mentioned several times as a leading Trawniki. Beyond their memoirs and depositions, very little reliable information about this man appears to have survived to this day. He may have been born in 1919 or 1920 in the traditional area of Volga-German settlement, a region that now lies for the most part in Saratov Oblast. More than twenty years later, as a captured Red Army soldier, Kaiser let himself be recruited by the Nazis for guard duties in September 1941 and came to Trawniki. There, he quickly attained an NCO rank, not least of all because of his knowledge of German.

Having apparently proven himself during his first mission in the Lublin ghetto in March 1942, Kaiser arrived shortly thereafter at Belzec, where he reportedly committed numerous individual murders. Later that same year, he was posted to Sobibor. Rising over time to the rank of Zugwachmann, Kaiser held one of the top leadership positions among the Trawnikis. After the Jewish uprising at Sobibor, he transferred to Italy like so many of the other Operation Reinhard perpetrators. A photo taken there shows him in the uniform of an SS-Oberscharführer, suggesting that he had by then become a citizen of the German Reich, owing to his ethnic German origins. He seems to have survived the war, but his trail eventually went cold. Leads to the effect that he was living in Tajikistan as of 1970 were never substantiated. Alexander Kaiser apparently never faced trial in the Soviet Union for his involvement in the murder of Poland's Jews.[49]

Choosing between Murder and Desertion

To illustrate the different ways Trawnikis at the Operation Reinhard camps acted, we can draw on the few surviving reports from the training camp, testimony by former guards in Soviet hearings, some interrogations of German perpetrators during West German criminal investigations, and the memoirs and statements of Jewish survivors. The latter in particular mention many details and sometimes include references to specific names. These sources show that a wide range of actions was available to these men.

There are numerous stories of extremely brutal men such as Zugwachmann Christian Schmidt, an ethnic German from the Soviet Union, who in the course of his everyday duties at Belzec committed countless acts of extreme violence and murdered Jews out of "sheer bloodlust."[50] After the war, Belzec survivor

Rudolf Reder recalled the NCOs Schmidt, Schneider, Kunz, and Trautwein as the "biggest murderers."[51] Yet the sources also provide ample evidence of how unreliable these auxiliaries could be. An entire squad of eleven Trawnikis deserted Belzec on March 3, 1943, by which point the camp was being dismantled. In the Germans' view, the company of Trawnikis that replaced that squad likewise gave signs of open mutiny after about two weeks on-site, namely on April 10.[52]

A similar pattern existed at Treblinka. Ivan Marchenko, who worked at Treblinka's gas chambers, was known among the Jewish forced labor details as "Ivan the Terrible" because of the numerous individual murders and atrocities he committed. Here, too, however, individual Trawnikis rebelled or deserted.[53] The same can be said for accounts regarding Sobibor.

Only rarely do these sources yield the names of rank-and-file Trawnikis who warrant mention as a result of some particularly memorable incident. The names of the NCOs among the auxiliaries emerge with much greater frequency, especially in statements by Sobibor survivors. It is much the same with regard to witness accounts from Belzec. Their names likely were indelibly etched upon the memories of survivors because of the prominent role of the NCOs and because NCOs' names were mentioned often in everyday settings as opposed to those of the rank and file. Some evidence also suggests that the predominantly Soviet-German NCOs harbored a greater affinity for National Socialism and its perceived enemies. That may explain why they committed antisemitic atrocities with greater frequency and intensity.

Contacts with Jewish Prisoners and the Outside World

The sources include numerous accounts that illustrate how the Trawnikis at Sobibor communicated with victims and how they interacted with the world beyond the camp. Samuel Lerer stated in 1968 that some members of the guards had been "good" to the Jews, while Dov Freiberg testified that he had felt "a connection" with individual Trawnikis. For less brutal treatment, some of the auxiliaries demanded money, while others balked at the violence "for idealistic reasons." Acting on their convictions, they even passed on information in defiance of regulations.[54] The historical record likewise makes clear that other guards shared valuable news with Jews only in exchange for payment.[55] Attempts to bribe guards for grander schemes could go terribly wrong. When an adolescent from Warsaw paid a Trawniki for help with an escape attempt, the auxiliary accepted the money but betrayed the Jewish boy's intentions to the SS.[56]

Sometimes Jews and Trawnikis could enter into prolonged arrangements. Former prisoner Kurt Thomas in 1973 recalled how he regularly engaged in trade with a certain "Biarzar," an overseer in a section of the Sobibor camp called the "hereditary farm" (Erbhof). Every other day, Thomas gave the guard a part of the money that he regularly found on the square where Jews had to undress. In exchange, Thomas usually received a bottle of vodka and two pounds of sausage. Food and stimulants, such as alcohol and tobacco, were in high demand, and Thomas could in turn barter such items for other essential items.[57]

Other Trawnikis had a very obvious interest in acquiring valuables and cash from within the camp. They could exchange them for desirable goods and services outside the camp's confines, and this mixture of barter and cash facilitated daily contacts with the local population. Several residents from the greater Sobibor area consistently reported how the "black ones" redeemed their wages for food and drink in taverns or the company of prostitutes. These wages came officially in the form of Polish currency and unofficially in the form of valuables stolen from the murdered Jews or obtained through trade with members of the forced labor details. Practically every day, Trawnikis reportedly bartered gold teeth or pieces of valuable jewelry that they had pocketed at Sobibor.[58]

Barter with the locals in the surrounding villages created numerous opportunities for social interaction. Many of Sobibor's auxiliaries liked to frequent the village of Osowa, about four miles to the southeast, where they could attend dances. On such occasions, they told even casual acquaintances about the gas chambers at their place of work.[59] A switchman at the Sobibor railroad station recalled socializing regularly with a guard named "Vaska," who told him all kinds of details about conditions inside the camp.[60] Here and there, closer ties developed such that the sister of a Trawniki posted to Sobibor was able to stay with a nearby Polish resident when she visited her brother. During a shared evening together, the brother also spoke about the mass murder of the Jews and the burning of their corpses.[61]

According to credible statements, even Trawnikis whom the Germans deemed reliable were known to reveal details about what went on inside the camps. In his free time, Zugwachmann Alexander Kaiser reportedly told locals about conditions at Sobibor and discussed how cruelly certain individuals such as Karl Frenzel physically maltreated the auxiliaries.[62] Another guard once asked a local resident through the camp fence to come over and watch a shooting at the notorious "hospital," just beyond where the guard was standing. From his new vantage point, the Pole then observed the murder of ten to fifteen people.[63]

It also happened, here and there, that Trawnikis established more-enduring contacts with locals. For example, Kaiser kept a mistress, a Ukrainian woman by the name of Maria Saj from a nearby village. Kaiser visited her regularly. They even had a daughter together. Saj was likewise privy to Sobibor's ghastly significance.[64]

In light of such everyday contacts, people living near Sobibor soon began to recognize distinctions in the conduct of the auxiliaries and off-duty members of the SS personnel who frequented the bar at the railway station and other nearby vendors. While the Trawnikis often stood out because of their high consumption of alcohol and often appeared drunk in public, the Germans seemed to behave with much greater discipline outside the camp.[65]

Dereliction of Duty, Resistance, and Desertion

As noted at the outset, Trawnikis stationed at the Operation Reinhard camps often went absent without leave (AWOL). Frequently, desertions were successful. Every now and then, fugitive guards were recaptured. Mikhail Sharanov, who ran away from Treblinka on March 13, 1943, was caught a little later and shot in front of his assembled comrades to set an example.[66] Evaluations of personnel records for the auxiliaries as a whole suggest that at least a fifth of the roughly five thousand men evaded serving the Germans by deserting.[67] Such a high rate for this most extreme expression of dereliction of duty leads to a variety of conclusions.

The Trawnikis' frequent resort to desertion despite the death penalty recalls first and foremost the fact that, for those who had been former Red Army soldiers, their recruitment had taken place under life-threatening circumstances in POW camps. Furthermore, the desertions also indicate that the Nazis were unable to establish acceptable terms of employment for their non-German auxiliaries. In many cases, it was only the deterioration of the Wehrmacht's fortunes across several fronts in 1943 that prompted Trawnikis to vacate their posts and, in some cases, to change sides once again by joining the partisans. This in turn hints at both the guards' inherent fear of the Nazis and Soviets and their thoroughly opportunistic calculations regarding the future viability of each ruling system.

The rate of desertion among the Trawnikis also suggests that the desire to disengage from or repudiate their SS masters must have been even more pronounced, though it did not lead

in every case to the potentially life-threatening step of illegally leaving the camp. At Belzec, two Trawnikis reportedly demonstrated an open antipathy to the mass murder. For this, Camp Commandant Gottlieb Hering shot them both.[68]

Numerous indications of resistance on the part of Sobibor's auxiliaries in everyday life partly reflect the disgruntlement that actually existed. According to a postwar statement by a former guard, one of his fellow Trawnikis may have expressed a partial repudiation of the Nazis' logic of extermination when he secretly mailed a letter by a Jewish woman deported to Sobibor; German censors, the statement claims, discovered the letter, thereby triggering an investigation into the identity of the courier. By luck, the guard in question went undetected, but the investigation most likely diminished his readiness to repeat his risky act.[69]

Hersz Cukierman, a cook at Sobibor's Camp I, and his son Józef, his assistant, remembered Vladimir Kovshevatskii because he frequently supplied them both with information and treated them in an almost friendly manner. A native of the Kiev area, Kovshevatskii was detailed to Camp III. After making contact with the Cukiermans, he often reported about what went on at the gas chambers. For example, in 1942, the Germans shot a group of Jews belonging to the forced labor detail of Camp III. During the shooting, those who were spared had to sing the song "One day the sun will shine on me too." Kovshevatskii seems to have provided other prisoners with information as well and hinted that he had contacts to partisans in the area. The night before Kovshevatskii was to transfer out of Sobibor, he and several Trawnikis deserted.[70]

The guard Krupka, who cooked for the Trawnikis at Sobibor, apparently behaved somewhat like Kovshevatskii. He also shared news about the front with Jews. His motive, he frankly stated, was that he hated the Germans. Krupka is also said to have eventually deserted.[71] In the run-up to the Sobibor uprising, Stanisław Szmajzner, whose mission was to steal guns from the Trawnikis' barracks, characterized the auxiliaries as a cruel and brutal force devoted to the Germans, but he also recalled a detail at variance with that portrayal. He remembered a guard who told the Jews of the Jewish revolt at Treblinka in August 1943—doing so just days before he himself escaped. The Jews of course welcomed this information, which served as an additional incentive for planning their own insurrection.[72]

Moshe Bachir credibly reported that the Trawnikis at Sobibor had often acted "worse than the Germans." But he was also able to recall that he and others who had escaped during the Jewish uprising later encountered three fugitive auxiliaries from Sobibor in the woods. In the conversation that ensued, the former guards told the Jews about an escape tunnel that the Jewish forced laborers in Camp III had dug. Tragically, another Trawniki betrayed the tunnel's existence to the Germans shortly before its completion.[73]

For the Trawnikis, desertion was the most obvious way to repudiate their service with the Germans—but renewed capture meant the death penalty. Nonetheless, the fragmentary surviving personnel records contain the names of 114 guards who worked at Belzec, Sobibor, or Treblinka and ultimately opted for desertion. At least thirteen of them were killed for their effort. With few exceptions, however, these desertions took place only after the German defeat at Stalingrad, when German victory in the East began to look less likely. Furthermore, the overwhelming majority fled only during the dismantling of the killing centers or after redeployment out of the Operation Reinhard camps, when circumstances were more conducive to successful desertion.

Of the Trawnikis who served at Belzec, documents indicate a total of thirty-four cases of desertion, all of which occurred after 1942 and the end of the mass killing operations. By contrast, there are fifty-five cases of desertions by Trawnikis who served at Sobibor, but only seventeen of them occurred during the killing operations. This leads to the conclusion that from

late autumn 1943, as the front was approaching and Germany's defeat was increasingly foreseeable, more and more auxiliaries opted to change sides. They had begun to realize the dangers of being associated with working for the Germans. Moreover, during the final burning of corpses and the camp's dismantling, German supervision and security measures were probably more lax, which may have also facilitated desertion.

The desertions continued throughout the summer of 1943. Ivan Kakarash and Konstantin Dimida, who were mentioned at the outset of this chapter, had transferred to Sobibor together with Ivan Demjanjuk at the end of March 1943. Three months later, on July 1, they went AWOL.[74] From hearsay, a nearby Polish resident learned of the desertion of three Trawnikis, whose names he recalled. The men were then rumored to have joined the partisans.[75] Details surrounding the desertion of a certain "Vorodia" provide a hint as to how much the auxiliary guards hated individual Germans. Before slipping away from Sobibor, "Vorodia" reportedly pinned a caricature of SS-Oberscharführer Erich Bauer to the camp fence. The image depicted Bauer, who often worked at the gas chambers, with his eyes gouged out and the caption: "You'll go through the same thing you did to us."[76]

Even such cases of resistance and refusal sometimes had a dark side. By one account, several of the auxiliary guards at Sobibor offered to help Jewish forced laborers with an escape attempt and asked for a sum of money in advance in order to make arrangements. After the Jews had handed over a considerable sum of money, the offer was revealed to be a ruse. The Trawnikis in question, ultimately twelve in all, deserted, taking their rifles and the Jews' money with them. But they provided none of the assistance they had promised the slave laborers.[77]

Excessive Violence and Cruelty

Despite the diverse forms of dereliction of duty and resistance described above, Jewish survivors remembered the Trawnikis primarily as a group that ensured the functioning of the Operation Reinhard camps by enabling and indulging in mass murder. Numerous accounts of widespread avarice reveal the personal motives for some of the guards' conduct. Despite a strict prohibition on theft and the risk entailed if caught violating it, many auxiliaries nonetheless pocketed money, gold, or jewelry belonging to the Jewish victims whenever and wherever they could.[78] Moreover, the sources bear witness to such harrowing accounts of extraordinary violence and unrestrained readiness to kill that it seems the Trawnikis embraced German motives for the genocide to some extent, added their own personal rationale, and even derived some kind of personal gratification from maltreating and murdering their victims.

Survivors and local residents frequently mentioned auxiliaries in the context of innumerable incidents of excessive violence that shaped everyday life in the Operation Reinhard camps. As a rule, such witnesses could only vaguely recall names. At Sobibor, one guard acquired a certain renown among the Jews for being quick on the trigger when people strayed too close to the fence. Another, known as "Taras," gained notoriety for beating people regularly and brutally.[79] A certain "Michal" is also said to have committed violent excesses at Sobibor. He was known for sadistically refusing water to parched recent arrivals at the well, and for frequently forcing Jews into the latrine, where they became smeared with feces. Another story tells of a Trawniki nicknamed "Ruck-Zuck" (English: Jiffy), who used a bayonet to cut open the chest of a child.[80]

Starting during summer 1942, when the Germans began selecting women from the deportation trains to work as forced laborers at Sobibor, sexual assault and even rape on the part of individual Trawnikis became a regular feature of camp life. A guard named "Ivan" apparently stood out in this respect. Sexual violence seems to have escalated to such an extent that the SS personnel had to intervene.[81] Sobibor survivors also recalled watching an ordinary Wachmann by the name of Malinowski, together with some Germans, bludgeon to death numerous Jews, one by one, because the gas chambers were not operational at the moment.[82]

In addition, survivors were more likely to remember the names of certain Trawniki NCOs. For example, Gruppenwachmann Franz Podessa, usually detailed to Sobibor's Camp III, was seen in Camp I, smashing a water jug against the head of an elderly recent arrival, evidently killing the old man on the spot. And witness statements contain the story of how Zugwachmann Richard Klatt, who was killed in the uprising on October 14, snatched a baby, just born as its mother was arriving at Sobibor, and threw it into the latrine. Another survivor simply referred to Klatt as a "sadist" for his many cruelties.[83]

All these accounts, careful examination, consideration, and integration of the scattered and sometimes difficult-to-access sources concerning the auxiliaries who served at the Operation Reinhard camps yield a complex and largely reliable portrayal of their deployment. From the first killings in the gas chambers at Belzec in March 1942 to the suspension of murder operations at Sobibor in October 1943, these men worked unceasingly to guarantee that all three killing centers fulfilled the purpose for which the Germans had created them. Despite numerous disciplinary problems, despite the numerous instances of dereliction of duty and desertion, the Trawnikis never called into question the function of the camps.

In the end, only Jewish insurgents put an end to the killing at Treblinka on August 2, 1943, and at Sobibor, a little more than two months later, on October 14. Although the planners of these revolts originally nurtured the hope that the Trawnikis would join them in their uprisings or at least step aside and let the Jews escape, these hopes were dashed. Instead, the auxiliaries actively fought the Jewish insurgents and then helped hunt down the Jews who had escaped.[84]

The Trawnikis may well have suffered in many respects on account of their status, which was indeed precarious. They had to fear maltreatment and frequent punishment, including extensive beatings. For more serious infractions, they faced the death penalty. Such rigidly enforced measures, further influenced by arbitrariness and the Nazis' notions of racial superiority, certainly surpassed corresponding provisions of the disciplinary code as applied to members of the Wehrmacht, the SS, or Germany's various police forces. For cases of misconduct, such as going AWOL, consuming alcohol on duty, or engaging in corruption, there existed a repressive catalog of penal measures that courts-martial broadly applied to Germans in uniform. Individual Trawnikis certainly did lend noteworthy support to the few Jews selected for the forced labor details at the killing centers. But for those vast numbers of Jews condemned to death, the guards as a whole posed a life-threatening menace.

Even Grigorii Kniga, who had served at Belzec, characterized the status of the Jews in retrospect: "They performed all of the heavy and horrible tasks. Their living conditions were unbearable. On account of a transgression, any one of us, of the guards, could execute or kill any one of those Jews."[85] It is therefore unambiguously clear that one must understand the Trawnikis as perpetrators who contributed decisively to the Holocaust in German-occupied Poland. The Germans' failure to forge reliable adjuncts of Nazi extermination policy from this heterogeneous group does not change the basic fact of its complicity in Operation Reinhard. Niemann's photos of a trip to Berlin to reward twenty-two Trawnikis in the summer of 1943 show just how much officials in the German capital appreciated their services, which had proven so essential to them in implementing the murder of Poland's Jews.

Notes

1. In the main body of the chapter text, Russian names appear according to the transliteration system of the US Library of Congress. In the footnotes, the spellings remain as the author found them in the sources. A few typos in source material appear to have crept into the literature. In the most obvious cases, the more accurate form has been inserted in parentheses.

2. Report by Niemann to Wirth, July 1, 1943, FSB, K-779 (Trawniki). By circuitous means, it was possible to see certain documents for this volume but not the Trawnikis' original personnel records, held in Moscow. These would have been extremely helpful in identifying the men depicted in Niemann's photos. On the content of the record group in Moscow, see the valuable information in Black, "Police Auxiliaries," pp. 333–336.

3. Mission report Gendarmeriezug Cholm, January 7, 1943, NIOD, 804/23; statement by Hersz Cukierman, September 17, 1944, LNW, Q 234/4489.

4. Statement by Moshe Bachir, December 16, 1965, LNW, Q 234/4464; similar statement by Stanislaw Smajzner, April 25–26, 1968, NIOD, 804/18.

5. Black, "Police Auxiliaries," p. 366.

6. Rich, "Footsoldiers," p. 687.

7. See Benz, *Handlanger*, pp. 226–238; on the value of Soviet judicial records as source material, also Pohl, "Strafverfahren;" Black, "Police Auxiliaries," pp. 349–352. There is good reason to believe the statements given by some of the former Trawnikis. In the first years after the war, the Soviets captured and tried numerous Trawnikis, several of whom lied about their role in Operation Reinhard and thus, due to a lack of evidence, received only prison sentences instead of the death penalty. Subsequent to an amnesty in 1955, two years after Stalin's death, the same men were again questioned in the 1960s within the framework of new investigations into other suspects. Aware that they could not be prosecuted for the same offense twice, the witnesses openly admitted to earlier lies and testified in detail about Operation Reinhard and their own involvement; see interrogation of Grigorij Kniga, December 9, 1964, BArch, B 162/43904 (LG Bonn 28 KLs 8/10), Bd. Personenakte 2; interrogation of Grigorij Kniga, December 11, 1964, ibid.; interrogation of Mitrofan Klötz, August 9, 1965, ibid.; interrogation of Taras Olejinik (sic: Olejnik), July 23, 1966, ibid., Bd.

Personenakte 3; interrogation of Dimitrij Pundik, September 23, 1965, ibid.

8. Pohl, "Trawniki-Männer," provides valuable insights into the example of Belzec. See also Sandkühler, "Trawniki-Männer," a precise and exhaustive unpublished study written as an expert opinion for the investigation of former Zugwachmann Samuel Kunz, who had served at Belzec.

9. RFSS to SSPF Lublin, July 25, 1941, BArch, RW 41/4.

10. On recruitment and training, see Black, "Foot Soldiers," pp. 5–18.

11. Interrogation of Iwan Kozlovskij, April 6, 1949, BArch, B 162/43904 (LG Bonn 28 KLs 8/10), Bd. Personenakte 2; on content of schooling, see Sandkühler, "Trawniki-Männer," p. 68.

12. On designations, interrogation of Franciszek Sitarski, November 17, 1967, LNW, Q 234/4583; interrogation of Erich Bauer, December 10, 1962, LNW, Q 234/4266.

13. Benz, *Handlanger*, pp. 48–49.

14. The seminal work on this remains Streit, *Keine Kameraden*; see also Overmans, "Kriegsgefangenenpolitik."

15. Interrogation of Grigorij Kniga, December 9, 1964, B 162/43904 (LG Bonn 28 KLs 8/10), Bd. Personenakte 2.

16. Interrogation of Prokofij Businnij, November 18, 1974, LNW, Q 234/4467.

17. Interrogation of Jakob Engelhardt, August 7, 1975, HHW, 461-36346/39.

18. Interrogation of Alexandr Semigodow, May 24, 1973, LNW, Q 234/4469.

19. For basic information on recruiting, Black, "Police Auxiliaries," pp. 356–360; Black, "Trawniki-Männer," pp. 315–318; Benz, *Handlanger*, pp. 70–73.

20. This is based on an evaluation of the extensive biographical data compiled by Peter Black from available personnel forms, transfer lists, and transcripts of interrogations; see USHMM, PBP 61/14, 61/15, and 61/16.

21. Black, "Trawniki-Männer," pp. 324–327.

22. Interrogation of Timofeji Gurch, June 22, 1966, BArch, B 162/43904 (LG Bonn 28 KLs 8/10), Bd. Personenakte 2; interrogation of Alexander Ssemigodow, July 7, 1965, ibid., Bd. Personenakte 3.

23. On the use of the Trawnikis in Sobibor, see interrogation of Erich Bauer, December 10, 1962, LNW, Q 234/4266; interrogation of Erich Bauer, October 6, 1965, LNW, Q 234/4416.

24. Interrogation of Emanuel Schulz, September 8, 1961, LNW, Q 234/4486; also Benz, *Handlanger*, pp. 86–87. With regard to Belzec, another Trawniki provided precise information on the daily routine: at 06:00 reveille, 06:30–07:00 roll call, assignment of duties, 07:00–07:30 breakfast, 07:30–12:00 duty in the killing center, 12:00–13:00 lunch break, 13:00–18:00 or 19:00 additional duties, 21:00 or 22:00 lights out; see interrogation of Timofejewitsch Lynkin, July 27, 1966, BArch, B 162/43904 (LG Bonn 28 KLs 8/10), Bd. Personenakte 3.

25. Peter Black was able to establish the ethnicity of 162 Trawniki NCOs. His analysis yielded the following: 80 Soviet Germans, 40 Ukrainians, 21 Russians, 18 Balts, 1 Pole, and 2 men of Russian or Ukrainian origin. Several of the Balts, Russians, and Ukrainians also bore German names that suggest a corresponding German heritage, although this was not expressly noted.

26. On the varying size of platoons and squads, see Black, "Foot Soldiers," p. 21; Benz, *Henkersknecht*, p. 67.

27. Ibid., p. 66; Black, "Foot Soldiers," p. 8.

28. See USHMM, PBP 61/14, 61/15, and 61/16.

29. A roster from the US Office of Special Investigations claims that a maximum of 344 guards could have been deployed at Belzec from 1941 to 1943. This document, however, contains some unreliable information that encumbers verification of this group's size. Sandkühler, "Trawniki-Männer," p. 154, indicates a similar conclusion. Evaluation of Peter Black's more extensive research leads to a lower figure of at least 322 Trawnikis who were active in Belzec.

30. See ibid. Sobibor was in operation for about 18 months, while Belzec existed for nine months and Treblinka for 13 months. In Treblinka, the need for rotating Trawnikis seems to have been the lowest and thus their consistency the highest. This points to the camp's efficiency and the experience gained in handling the Trawnikis. It may also be that Treblinka, which was located farther west, faced less danger from partisans and thus experienced fewer disciplinary problems.

31. Berger, *Experten*, pp. 403, 408, 411; interrogation of Erich Lachmann, June 21, 1961, LNW, Q 234/4262; interrogation of Erich Bauer, December 11, 1962, LNW, Q 234/4266.

32. Interrogation of Werner Dubois, September 16, 1961, LNW, Q 234/3170; interrogation of Kurt Franz, September 14, 1961, ibid.

33. Excerpt Peter Black on interrogation of Mikhail Razgonayev, September 20–22, 1948, USHMM, PBP 58/1.

34. Interrogations of Hubert Gomerski, December 9, 1949, HHW, 461-36346/2; May 16, 1961, HHW, 461-36346/39; September 30, 1976, HHW, 461-36346/49.

35. Interrogation of Emanuel Schulz, September 8, 1961, LNW, Q 234/4486. Here, the former Trawniki mentions the brutal treatment on the part of the SS.

36. Interrogation of Jakob Engelhardt, March 14, 1984, LNW, Q 234/4491.

37. Ibid.

38. Excerpt Peter Black on the interrogation of Nikolaj Schalajew, USHMM, PBP 58/1.

39. Interrogation of Heinrich Unverhau, October 21, 1965, LNW, Q 234/4417.

40. Interrogation of Werner Dubois, September 16, 1961, LNW, Q 234/3170; interrogation of Kurt Franz, September 14, 1961, ibid.

41. Excerpts from Peter Black on the interrogations of Georgy Skydan, March 26, 1950, USHMM, PBP 58/1, and Prokofiy Ryabtsev, February 3, 1965, ibid.; on comparable systems, Cüppers, *Wegbereiter*, pp. 180–186.

42. Interrogation of Jakob Engelhardt, March 14, 1984, LNW, Q 234/4491.

43. Interrogation of Prokofij Businnij, August 8, 1975, LNW, Q 234/4467; on Dalke see statement by Hersz Cukierman, October 18, 1949, HHW, 461-36346/1.

44. Interrogation of Emanuel Schulz, September 8, 1961, LNW, Q 234/4486; statement by Moshe Bachir, December 16, 1965, LNW, Q 234/4464.

45. On the "hospital" see statement by Moshe Bachir, May 14, 1973, LNW, Q 234/4464; statement by Dov Freiberg, July 4, 1974, LNW, Q 234/4470; interrogation of Prokofij Businnij, August 8, 1975, LNW, Q 234/4488; interrogation of Jakob Engelhardt, March 14, 1984, LNW, Q 234/4491.

46. Transfer list, Trawniki training camp to Sonderkommando Sobibor, March 26, 1943, FSB, K-779 (Trawniki); on the particulars for Demjanjuk and the trial in Munich, see Benz, *Henkersknecht*.

47. Transfer list, Trawniki training camp to Sobibor "SS-Arbeitslager," September 16, 1943, FSB, K-779 (Trawniki).

48. Personnel list, Sonderkommando Sobibor, March 30, 1944, ibid.

49. Another published photo of Kaiser shows him during the burial on October 14, 1943 of the Germans who were killed during the Sobibor uprising (Schelvis, *Vernichtungslager*, p. 205). The photo depicting Kaiser in an SS uniform in Italy is published in Webb, *Sobibor*, p. 407; for biographical notes regarding this person, see Sandkühler, "Trawniki-Männer," p. 156 fn 92, p. 168.

50. Interrogation of Robert Jührs, October 12, 1961, NIOD, 804/49; statement of Rudolf Reder, January 26, 1960, BArch, B 162/8384. Schmidt seems to have committed suicide in Italy during the final phase of the war.

51. Ibid.

52. See Black, "Foot Soldiers," p. 35.

53. Willenberg, *Treblinka*, p. 53.

54. Statement of Samuel Lerer, May 10, 1968, LNW, Q 234/4474; statement of Dov Freiberg, July 25, 1945, LNW, Q 234/4470.

55. Statement of Josef Herszmann, January 21, 1966, LNW, Q 234/4472.

56. Eye-witness account by Hersz Cukierman, December 8, 1945, HHW, 461-36346/43.

57. Statement of Kurt Thomas, December 6, 1973, HHW, 461-36346/26. The identity of this Trawniki could not be clarified.

58. Interrogation of Jan Piwonski, April 22, 1975, LNW, Q 234/4478; interrogation of Stefan Stelmaszuk, April 23, 1975, LNW, Q 234/4486; interrogation of Franciszek Sitarski, May 15, 1984, LNW, Q 234/4480.

59. Interrogation of Katarzyna Grodzicka, October 5, 1978, LNW, Q 234/4489.

60. Interrogation of Jan Piwonski (son), May 10, 1984, LNW, Q 234/4396.

61. Interrogation of Franciszek Sitarski, May 15, 1984, LNW, Q 234/4480.

62. Interrogation of Boleslaw Pierzchowski, October 15, 1945, LNW, Q 234/4489.

63. Interrogation of Jan Krzowski, August 7, 1974, LNW, Q 234/8233.

64. Interrogation of Stefania Zatorska, October 18, 1945, LNW Q 234/4486. The relationship continued even after Kaiser transferred to Italy along with other perpetrators from Operation Reinhard. Kaiser wrote Saj that he and his comrades were operating in Italy as they had done in Sobibor (ibid.).

65. Interrogation of Franciszek Sitarski, May 15, 1984, LNW, Q 234/4480; interrogation of Jan Piwonski April 22, 1975, LNW, Q 234/4478.

66.   Excerpt Peter Black on the interrogation of Fedor Ryabeka, USHMM, PBP 58/1.

67.   Black, "Foot Soldiers," pp. 32–33; with even higher estimates, Benz, *Handlanger*, p. 238.

68.   Interrogation of Heinrich Unverhau, July 21, 1960, BArch, B 162/4427.

69.   Interrogation of Prokofij Businnij, August 8, 1975, LNW, Q 234/4467.

70.   Eye-witness account by Hersz Cukierman, December 8, 1945, HHW, 461-36346/43; statement of Hershel Cukiermann, December 13, 1973, LNW, Q 234/4568; statement of Hershel Cukiermann, November 2, 1965, LNW, Q 234/8234; statement of Josef Cukierman, December 2, 1949, HHW, 461-36346/2. See also statement of Ada Lichtmann, February 23, 1966, LNW, Q 234/4475; statement of Izchak Lichtmann, Oct. 1963, LNW, Q 234/4476; see also Benz, *Handlanger*, pp. 233–234.

71.   Statement of Abraham Margulies, undated, LNW, Q 234/4476.

72.   Statement of Stanislaw Szmajzner, February 9, 1961, LNW, Q 234/4480.

73.   Statement of Moshe Bachir, December 16, 1965, LNW, Q 234/4464; statement of Izchak Lichtmann, December 15, 1945, LNW, Q 234/4572.

74.   Report by Niemann to Wirth, July 1, 1943, FSB, K-779 (Trawniki); transfer list, Trawniki training camp to Sonderkommando Sobibor, March 26, 1943, ibid.

75.   Interrogation of Jan Piwonski, April 22, 1975, LNW, Q 234/4478.

76.   Statement of Samuel Lerer, May 8, 1950, LNW, Q 234/4479.

77.   See eyewitness account by Hersz Cukierman, December 8, 1945, HHW, 461-36346/43.

78.   Excerpts from Peter Black on the interrogation of Prokofiy Ryabtsev, February 3, 1965, USHMM, PBP 58/1, and Vasiliy Shuller, December 14, 1964, USHMM, PBP 58/7; statement of Wladislawa Göbel, December 17, 1959, BArch, B 162/3166.

79.   Statement of Ada Lichtmann, February 23, 1966, LNW, Q 234/4475, and May 19, 1959, ibid.

80.   Statement of Dov Freiberg, December 23, 1965, LNW, Q 234/4470; statement of Ada Lichtmann, February 23, 1966, LNW, Q 234/4475.

81.   Statement of Izchak Lichtmann, Oct. 1963, LNW, Q 234/4476; statement of Ada Lichtmann, February 23, 1966, LNW, Q 234/4475, and May 19, 1959, ibid.

82.   Statement of Ziss Meyer, October 18, 1965, LNW, Q 234/4477.

83.   Statement of Abraham Kohn, January 18, 1977, LNW, Q 234/4571; statement of Ada Lichtmann, February 23, 1966, LNW, Q 234/4475; statement of Abraham Margulies, November 18, 1965, LNW, Q 234/4476.

84.   Excerpt from Peter Black on the interrogation of Vladimir Sharan, July 5, 1947, USHMM, PBP 58/7.

85.   Interrogation of Grigorij Kniga, December 9, 1964, BArch, B 162/43904 (LG Bonn 28 KLs 8/10), Bd. Personenakte 2.

Reward for Genocide

A Trip to Berlin for Perpetrators from Operation Reinhard

MARTIN CÜPPERS AND STEFFEN HÄNSCHEN

The Brandenburg Gate in radiant sunlight, a leisurely walk down the boulevard Unter den Linden, past the New Guardhouse, on to the baroque Berlin Cathedral, and across the street to the Prussian dynasty's City Palace. Then a day in Potsdam with its historic city center, its parks, and of course Sanssouci Palace.

What sounds like the sightseeing schedule of innumerable visitors to Berlin in the twenty-first century in fact resembled that of an unusual tour group in the German capital in the summer of 1943. For this trip, Johann Niemann, two German SS noncommissioned officers (SS-Unterführer), and twenty-two auxiliary guards known as "Trawnikis" had taken a break from the daily killing operations at the Sobibor and Treblinka killing centers. They had driven by bus to Berlin to spend several relaxing days, with an attractive itinerary arranged. On this occasion, they also met with high-ranking superiors from the Chancellery of the Führer (*Kanzlei des Führers*, KdF), co-organizers of the Holocaust in the killing centers of German-occupied Poland, who, on at least one of the days in question, accompanied the group.

This astonishing scenario reveals itself in the pictures of a small photo album that Niemann later compiled as a personal memento. Unlike the first album, which addresses his early career, the green cardboard cover of this second album exhibits none of the embossed lettering that recalls his service in the SS. Instead, it corresponds to a product for private use that was commercially available at the time. Both albums were found among Niemann's possessions after the Jewish uprising at Sobibor in October 1943 and handed over to his widow along with other personal items some weeks later. The contents of the albums resemble one another in the choice of pictures and their arrangement.

The relatively short timeframe between the distribution of prints to interested parties soon after the trip in midsummer 1943 and Niemann's death that autumn suggests that it was Niemann himself who compiled the album at Sobibor.[1] The album contains eighty photos from the trip spread out over twenty pages. In addition to these photos, Niemann's collection contains an additional seventeen unmounted photographs from the journey to Berlin. Nine of these are duplicates of photos in the album. Eight are images that Niemann, for reasons unknown, chose not to glue into his album, even though there was enough space for them on four blank pages (see figs. 8.26–8.33). Not long after the trip, at least two photographers submitted collections to Niemann for viewing. From these, he seems to have chosen photos in the formats 5.5 cm × 8 cm and 5.8 cm × 8 cm and then combined them on the pages of his album according to his own taste.[2]

In doing so, Niemann did not adhere to chronology. Instead, he arranged the photos primarily according to aesthetic considerations. For example, in order to establish a visual conclusion for his journey, the album ends with a photo of the Old Airfield forced labor camp in the vicinity of Lublin. The camp, under the command of Christian Wirth, the inspector of all the Operation Reinhard (*Aktion Reinhard*) camps, served as a depot for the enormous amounts of plunder taken from the murdered Jews of Poland.[3] Niemann's journey to Berlin began at the Old Airfield, and it may well have ended there as well. As is immediately apparent, the final photo in the album reflects the same situation depicted in the first. This final photo clearly originated at the outset of the journey and was apparently glued into the album for lack of a more suitable image.

Such compositional preferences in the arrangement of the photos make it difficult to discern the actual route of Niemann's trip to Berlin at first glance. For Niemann, this aspect seems to have been secondary. Instead, Niemann combined his photos on the album's pages according to image features that have a close similarity or connection. The content of the album can thus be decoded by means of key concepts. Niemann does not state them in the form of captions, but upon examination, the basic narrative leaps off the page all the same. Page 1 conveys "travel," for example, "rest" follows on pages 2 and 4, while "tour bus" can be inferred from page 3. There follows "eating and drinking" (p. 5), "group photos" (pp. 6–8 and 11), "swimming pool and zoo" (p. 10), "streets" (p. 13), "imposing buildings" (p. 14), "gates, portals, columns" (p. 15), "Reich Chancellery, center of power" (p. 16), "facades on Unter den Linden" (p. 17), and "towers and palaces" (p. 18). The album ends with a combination of "group photos" on pages 19 and 20.

This kind of structure resembles practices common in many other albums created at the time. It had the advantage of offering a simplified visual message, even if the journey's route and the sequence of events had to be explained by way of a supplementary narrative. As in the "Brandenburg Album," Niemann's weakness for impressive buildings and their clear architectural lines becomes clear. The Berlin album contain numerous such photos with images from the capital and nearby Potsdam; however, in contrast to the first album, Niemann's explanatory captions are absent here.

Finally, in the arrangement of the Berlin photos, Niemann unmistakably drew on duplicate prints in three instances. In doing so, he apparently found these images—which showed him on Unter den Linden in the company of officials from the KdF, front and center in a group photo in front of Sanssouci, and in the tour group on the way to Potsdam's Garrison Church—so memorable that he used them twice in the same album (see figs. 8.24–8.25).

The selection of pictures also betrays Niemann's preferences with regard to format. Each time he placed a print in vertical format in the album, he supplemented it with another photo in vertical format either directly next to or diagonally across from it.

Composition of the Tour Group

The album's photographs show, on the one hand, some of the highlights from this organized vacation trip, such as numerous sights in the capital and neighboring Potsdam, as well as senior representatives from the seat of power in Berlin, along with more casual moments such as a rest stop and snack during the long journey in the summer heat. On the other hand, the tour group is represented in numerous posed group photos and spontaneous snapshots, each time in a different composition. Johann Niemann, a newly minted SS-Untersturmführer and thus a full-fledged member of the officer corps, posed repeatedly in the center of each group shot.

In some of Niemann's photos, senior officials from the Chancellery of the Führer in the persons of Werner Blankenburg and Dietrich Allers appear alongside the German SS men and the Trawnikis. Earlier in the war, Blankenburg and Allers had played pivotal roles in the murder of institutionalized patients in the Reich, the program known as "euthanasia" or Operation T4 (*Aktion T4*). By 1942, both men had taken on new responsibilities in perpetrating the Holocaust in occupied Poland.

In the summer of 1943, Blankenburg succeeded Viktor Brack as head of the KdF's political department and had jurisdiction over operations within the Operation Reinhard camps. In this capacity, he worked closely with the SS and police leader (*SS-und Polizeiführer*, SSPF) in District Lublin, Odilo Globocnik, who organized the deportations of Jews to the killing centers. Allers, one of Blankenburg's subordinates, served as managing director of the Berlin-based T4 head office and its cover organization, the Charitable Foundation for Institutional Care (*Gemeinnützige Stiftung für Anstaltspflege*), which coordinated the "euthanasia" operation in the Reich. His duties now covered the Operation Reinhard killing centers and the Germans who worked there. Some of the photos from the Berlin trip also appear to show Arnold Oels. Within the Chancellery of the Führer, Oels's position was that of personnel manager for the T4 and Operation Reinhard men.[4]

The Berlin album documents the remarkable fact that Blankenburg and Allers took time off to receive Niemann and his traveling companions, to stroll through the capital with them, and to engage in lively conversation with Trawnikis, the lowest level in the hierarchy of Operation Reinhard. Nominally, the KdF at first glance had nothing at all to do with these guards. This auxiliary force was subordinate to SSPF Globocnik in far-away Lublin. The photos and the evident spirit of cooperation on display now provide vivid evidence as to how, with regard to the Holocaust and the unprecedented tasks it posed, responsibilities and nominal chains of command were negotiated anew, distributed, and coordinated among different institutions.

Under Globocnik's command, the Trawnikis forced the General Government's Jews out of their ghettos and onto the deportation trains. While the Chancellery of the Führer guaranteed the operation of the three Reinhard camps—Belzec, Sobibor, and Treblinka—by providing its own mass murder experts, Globocnik placed at its disposal additionally needed guards in the form of Trawnikis. He did so because the smoothest possible operation of the Reinhard camps also lay in his interest.

Against this backdrop, Niemann's album documents the remarkable degree of recognition and well-meaning solicitude that the KdF demonstrated vis-à-vis the Trawnikis, who provided significant support to the Germans in the killing centers. The images of Blankenburg, Allers, Niemann, and the Trawnikis together symbolize the full arc of personnel involved in the operation of the Reinhard camps. From the leadership based in Berlin to the German SS men deployed in the camps to the auxiliary guards in the form of the Trawnikis, these photographs show all three levels of the hierarchy whose members implemented the Holocaust at Belzec, Sobibor, and Treblinka.

Available sources do not allow scholars to establish when and in what context the idea for this unusual trip originated. The KdF put considerable effort into making the trip possible. Officials in Berlin had arranged for a driver and a bus to pick up the men in the eastern reaches of the General Government. The in-house motor pool of the cover organization that transported patients to their deaths in the "euthanasia" operation, the Charitable Ambulance Society (Gekrat, *Gemeinnützige Krankentransportgesellschaft*), probably provided the bus.[5] The Chancellery of the Führer also arranged accommodations and organized the itinerary for Niemann's tour group.

In postwar interrogation, Fritz Bleich, an associate of Hitler's attending physician Karl Brandt who worked in the KdF in 1943, recalled this very unusual visit. He mentioned that "Cossacks," his choice of word for the Trawnikis, had traveled to Berlin as a kind of reward and had even been received at the Reich Chancellery, the heart of Nazi power and the official address of the KdF.[6] In addition to the itinerary, which made allowances for sightseeing, entertainment, and recreation, Blankenburg und Allers used the grand reception and their own presence during the visit to create an atmosphere that signaled appreciation and solicitude. Beyond the central aspect of reward, this kind of treatment aimed to impress the Trawnikis and bind them more closely to Nazi Germany.

Of all the Germans deployed to Poland for Operation Reinhard, Herbert Floß and Hubert Gomerski had also received permission to travel to Berlin with Niemann. These three men were bound together by their military training and membership in the Waffen-SS, the armed forces of the SS. This crucial distinction set them apart from most of the other German personnel in the camps, who had come primarily from civilian occupations. As an SS-Untersturmführer, Niemann held the highest rank of the three. By virtue of his rank, he was the tour group's undisputed leader, as is clearly evident in the photos.

Floß held the rank of SS-Oberscharführer and Gomerski that of SS-Scharführer, making the latter the junior of the two, with the second-lowest noncommissioned rank.[7] Their biographies and previous careers exhibit some parallels but also differences. While Floß and Niemann joined the Nazi Party in 1930 and 1931, respectively, Gomerski had already belonged to the Hitler Youth in 1927, before becoming a party member two years later. Niemann joined the SS at the Esterwegen concentration camp in the Emsland region in 1934. From there, he moved to the Sachsenhausen concentration camp near Berlin during the reorganization of the concentration camp system.

It was much the same with Floß, who in 1935 joined the 2nd SS-Death's Head Battalion "Elbe," which oversaw the Lichtenburg concentration camp in Saxony. After about two years in Lichtenburg, he transferred to the Buchenwald concentration camp near Weimar in Thuringia, where he worked in the commandant's office. Just slightly older than Niemann and Floß, Gomerski had already joined the General SS in 1930, much earlier than the others. But Gomerski, a lathe operator by trade, joined the Waffen-SS, the military branch of the SS, only at the outset of the war in 1939—and even trained briefly with a Death's Head formation stationed in occupied Cracow.[8]

In late 1939 or early 1940, Niemann, Floß, and Gomerski received orders transferring them to the Chancellery of the Führer and the nascent "euthanasia" program. All three worked as "burners" for disposal of the corpses.[9] When Hitler formally shut down this program, Niemann was among the very first T4 specialists ordered to the General Government, where he helped build the Belzec killing center. Initially in charge of the actual killing area with the gas chambers within the Belzec camp, he moved on to Sobibor as deputy commandant in the summer of 1942.

Floß and Gomerski were detailed to Operation Reinhard a few months after Niemann, reporting to Sobibor in April 1942. Once Floß had acquired the expertise urgently required for the cremation of bodies that autumn, he was reassigned to Belzec that same November. At his new posting, he continued working in the same capacity. Some three months later, he was applying his experience at Treblinka. Gomerski, by contrast, remained in Sobibor throughout Operation Reinhard. He worked at the ramp along the rail siding where the deportation trains stopped, guarded Jewish slave labor detachments, and carried out various duties within Camp III, where Sobibor's gas chambers were located.[10]

These tasks aside, all three men, as soldiers of the Waffen-SS, had additional responsibilities with regard to the Trawnikis. Niemann, Floß, and Gomerski each trained platoons that had been transferred to Sobibor from the training camp in Trawniki. Floß performed similar tasks following his transfer to Treblinka. Niemann, as deputy camp commander in Sobibor, also assigned the Trawnikis their duties and, when necessary, instructed guards prior to the arrival of deportation trains.[11] All this provides ample reason for the presence of the three men among those traveling to Berlin. Since Niemann, Floß, and Gomerski spent so much of their daily work routine with the auxiliary troops, these SS men had probably helped select participants for the trip, so that they themselves might receive permission to accompany the group to the capital.

The twenty-two Trawnikis provided the core group and thus the largest part of the visitors to Berlin.[12] Based on the number of stripes on the epaulets of their uniform jackets, it is clear from the photos that most of them were noncommissioned officers (NCOs). Thus, within the framework of their service as auxiliaries, these NCOs occupied key positions of responsibility in the killing process at the Operation Reinhard camps.

Niemann's prints make it possible to identify nine Zugwachmänner, with three stripes on their epaulets, which means that 45 percent of the Trawnikis in the tour group held this comparatively high rank. The size of this subgroup provides additional proof for a circumstance already suggested by the presence of Niemann and Floß. Since no more than 150 Trawnikis, approximately the size of a reinforced company and usually led by no more than five Zugwachmänner, served in any one of the three killing centers at any given time, Trawnikis from different Operation Reinhard camps must have traveled with Niemann to Berlin.

The tour group presumably consisted mainly of deserving personnel from Sobibor and Treblinka, as the mass killing in the gas chambers at these two locations was still under way at the time of the trip. The killing at Belzec had come to an end more than half a year earlier, and the Trawnikis from that camp were now serving elsewhere. However, important NCOs from among the Trawnikis, such as Alexander Kaiser, Richard Klatt, Franz Bienemann, and Boris Rogosa, had gained their

first experience at Belzec, before their transfer to Sobibor or Treblinka. And it is indeed possible to identify some of them in Niemann's album. Thus, Trawnikis from Belzec were also among those selected for the Berlin trip. After Belzec was shut down, the Zugwachmänner Christian Schmidt and Heinrich Schütz, both notorious among Jewish survivors, were posted to the Old Airfield forced labor camp, where, in recognition of their previous merits, they too may have received an invitation to board the bus to Berlin.[13] Thus, judging from the subgroup of nine Zugwachmänner alone, it is clear that Trawnikis who had served in all three Reinhard camps were among Niemann's traveling companions.

The relatively high number of Zugwachmänner aside, the Trawnikis who visited Berlin included three Gruppenwachmänner and four Oberwachmänner, each with two stripes or one stripe, respectively, on their epaulets. The lowest but by far most widespread rank among the Trawnikis as a whole, that of Wachmann, was held by just six of the visitors to Berlin. Thus, NCOs dominated the Trawnikis in the tour group, while the rank and file were underrepresented with less than a one-third share.

The disproportionate number of NCOs among the Trawniki tour group reflects the Germans' general treatment of auxiliary guards. For the most part, the Germans bestowed the rank of Zugwachmann on men of ethnic German origin who seemed reliable and favorable to Nazi goals. By contrast, German ethnicity, pro-Nazi sentiments and the discipline and reliability that often accompanied such political leanings were less common among the junior ranks. Accordingly, language barriers among the travelers would have been negligible, as a majority would have spoken German.

The makeup of this group with its large share of Zugwachmänner and diligently culled representatives of the lower ranks underscores the character of the trip as a reward primarily for senior Trawnikis or those entrusted with special tasks within

Operation Reinhard. This is precisely what Bleich, the official who witnessed the tour group's reception in the Reich Chancellery in the summer of 1943, stressed in his postwar statement.[14] The men in Niemann's photos represented a unique spectrum of Trawnikis: they very likely demonstrated an extraordinary degree of reliability in their cooperation with the Germans and fulfilled their terrifying duties with an energy and commitment that clearly exceeded that of the average auxiliary guard.

Despite a considerable amount of time and effort spent on research in German, American, and Ukrainian archives, an attempt to identify the Trawnikis in Niemann's photos by using comparison photos yielded only meager results. The fragmentary nature of the source material available and lingering restrictions on access to the original records made it impossible to find more than a handful of photos of Trawnikis who had been identified in the course of criminal investigations.[15] Voluminous judicial records, especially those from Soviet criminal investigations and trials, may provide multifaceted accounts of the Trawnikis' duties during the Holocaust, but they rarely contain photos that allow for comparison with the prints in Niemann's Berlin album. For most of the suspects or defendants whose cases could be reviewed, it was not possible to prove their presence in the Berlin photos, although the written records thus far inaccessible may well harbor some of the names of the twenty-two Trawnikis in the tour group, as well as details concerning their duties and their complicity in the crimes committed during Operation Reinhard.

Only three of the Zugwachmänner who feature in Niemann's album could be identified by name. They appear in other, previously known photographs. The first is Alexander Kaiser, a senior Zugwachmann, who shows up in two of Niemann's prints from Sobibor. Kaiser is also recognizable in a photo taken after the Jewish uprising at Sobibor. There, he is standing next to Niemann's coffin at the funeral of the German casualties from the uprising. In addition to the Niemann photos, he is seen in another print wearing an SS uniform while standing among former Operation Reinhard staff members during a mission in Italy in 1944 (see figs. 6.48–6.49 and 9.7).

Two additional Zugwachmänner from Niemann's Berlin album are recognizable in a studio portrait that originated close to the Treblinka camp and shows the German perpetrators August Hengst and Karl Pötzinger as well.[16] One of the Trawnikis in this photo was Franz Bienemann, who was also known by the nickname "Bomber." The second appears to be Alexander Jäger, whom prisoners at Treblinka considered no less fearsome. The photo album that belonged to Kurt Franz, the deputy commandant of Treblinka, also contains a photo that features Jäger. There, he is seen in shorts running across the grounds of Treblinka.[17]

As Zugwachmänner, all three of the identifiable Trawnikis from the Berlin tour group—Kaiser, Bienemann, and Jäger— held leading positions at Sobibor or Treblinka. References from the accounts of Jewish survivors and interrogations of former Trawnikis conducted by the Soviet investigators make it clear that all of them committed innumerable atrocities and individual acts of murder. As ethnic Germans in positions of responsibility for operations, at least Kaiser and Bienemann had already served as NCOs at Belzec before their transfer to Sobibor or Treblinka.[18]

Overall, the historical record contains relatively little information about the lives of these men. Born in Russia around 1918, all three of them belonged to the same age cohort, shared a German ethnicity, and hailed from what is now the Saratov administrative region, which includes most of what was once the Volga Germans' traditional area of settlement. Jäger seems to have worked as a farmer, while Bienemann may have completed training as a teacher. By contrast, Kaiser's vocation remains unknown. As soldiers of the Red Army, all three must have fallen into captivity not long after the German invasion of the Soviet Union in June 1941. Jäger's personnel number, 14, indicates that they were among the very first Soviet Germans to be selected from the prisoner of war camps and sent to the newly established training camp in Trawniki.

Jäger and Kaiser gained their first experience in the Holocaust and what would become Operation Reinhard in the Lublin ghetto in March 1942. Already Trawniki NCOs, they participated in a storm of terror, extreme violence, and individual murder lasting several days, as SS and police forces liquidated large parts of the ghetto and forced the Jews onto trains headed to Belzec. Bienemann had been deployed at Belzec since November 1941, one of the first Trawnikis posted there. In the spring of 1942, he moved on to Sobibor and subsequently to Treblinka, where he became one of the most senior Zugwachmänner. Jäger occupied a similarly pivotal position among the Trawnikis at Treblinka. He had transferred to Treblinka subsequent to a posting of several weeks in the Warsaw Ghetto. After a probationary period at Belzec, Kaiser was promoted to Zugwachmann and became lead Trawniki at Sobibor.

Together with the German perpetrators, these three Trawnikis subsequently deployed to Italy and ultimately survived the end phase of the war. While Bienemann's trail went cold, and details about Kaiser's fate remain unconfirmed, the Soviets tracked down and interrogated Jäger. He acknowledged his presence at Treblinka and confessed to killing at least two hundred persons. Condemned to death, he was probably executed in the Soviet Union in the early 1950s.[19]

Finally, Niemann's Berlin album allows us to identify a fourth group, consisting of four women. Their presence comes as a surprise. The women, seen in stylish summer dresses, are not administrative employees from the Berlin Chancellery of the Führer. Three of them are the wives of the three German SS soldiers: Henriette Niemann, Danida Floß, and Emilie Gomerski.[20] The identity of the fourth woman could not be determined conclusively. The three wives must have traveled

from their hometowns after receiving an official invitation and joined their husbands for part of their program in Berlin and Potsdam.[21] The disconcerting presence of women among this most unusual tour group of mass murderers raises questions: What kind of conversations did they have at the time? And to what extent did the young women really know about their husbands' activities?

It is known that, in the summer of 1942, Theresa Stangl, the wife of Franz Stangl, spent her vacation near a fishing pond just 2.5 miles from Sobibor. She had traveled to Poland to be close to her husband. From the remarks of one of Stangl's drunken subordinates, she learned the true extent of her husband's dreadful duties. Her response, reportedly, was one of shock and despair.[22] The wife of Erich Fuchs, who was also deployed at Sobibor, claimed that her husband, while at home on leave, broke down in tears as he confided the nature of his work to her.[23]

That women, despite all imaginable emotional consternation, could also become de facto accomplices was indicated in March 1946 during the search of the household where the spouse of Walter Nowak lived. On this occasion, the police confiscated thirteen watches, several gold rings, and other objects of value, which her husband, a former SS guard at Sobibor, had stolen from his victims and subsequently sent home to his wife.[24]

Whatever commitments to secrecy husbands may have made, such examples suggest that wives were confidantes and accessories to the genocidal crimes. In fact, the Holocaust could not be kept secret at all, even if labeled as "Secret Reich Business." The crimes regularly took place in public spaces where thousands of people became witnesses. And these witnesses in turn informed innumerable family members and acquaintances.[25] It stands to reason that the wives of Niemann, Floß, and Gomerski likewise came to possess such knowledge. One photo of Henriette Niemann within the greater Niemann collection shows her with her husband and other "euthanasia" perpetrators on a walk near the killing site in Bernburg in the winter of 1940–1941. In addition, after Hitler decreed the formal end of the murder of institutionalized patients in September 1941, the Niemanns and Flosses spent a vacation at the T4 recreation home Villa Schoberstein on the Attersee, east of Salzburg. It was then, if not earlier, that Henriette Niemann and Danida Floß first met, before their paths crossed again in Berlin two years later. And it was to this villa that the two, now widows, retreated in the summer of 1944 to rest and recover.[26]

As the perpetrators' social relations included their wives, these women became accessories and accomplices able to share knowledge among themselves.

During the official part of their husbands' visit to Berlin, the authority of the offices held by Blankenburg or Allers presumably would have precluded any careless talk about the camps and the details of what went on there—so long as these two men remained with the tour group. When these senior officials had bid farewell, however, Niemann and his traveling companions, gathered for a relaxed round of drinks, could very well have divulged particulars concerning their daily work routine in the Operation Reinhard camps.

Route and Itinerary

Niemann's photographs convey a diverse array of impressions of his journey and the various stops along the way, even though a precise chronology and sequence of events can no longer be reestablished with absolute certainty due to Niemann's sorting in the album.

The journey probably began in July 1943. A later timeframe seems impossible due to the Jewish uprising at the Treblinka killing center on August 2. This dramatic event, a caesura for Operation Reinhard as a whole, brought an enormous increase in activity for the planners and organizers in Lublin and Berlin,

as well as the executors on-site. From that point on, the personnel at Treblinka were dedicated to wrapping up the killing operations and preparing for the camp's demolition, while those farther up the chain of command expedited the conclusion of the Operation Reinhard program as a whole. A considerably earlier timeframe than July 1943 seems out of the question due to the volume of killing at Sobibor and Treblinka and the clear signs of midsummer in evidence among the album's photos.

As can be seen in the first photo, the Old Airfield forced labor camp in Lublin served as the point of departure. The group met there on a sunny day and stowed their luggage on a Daimler-Benz O 3750 bus registered with the Reich Postal Service.[27] Shortly thereafter, the Berlin-bound bus set off on its journey across occupied Poland. The destination sign bore the word *Sonderfahrt*, "special trip." Judging from the position of the sun in photos taken prior to boarding, the Reinhard men departed late in the morning at the earliest. The drive to the capital, more than 435 miles away, should have taken at least two days. It remains unknown where the tourists were accommodated upon arrival.[28]

The first actual day of the visit seems to have been filled with a program dedicated to the political and cultural center of Berlin. The first thing on the agenda that morning was the "official" reception at the KdF offices in the Reich Chancellery. SA-Oberführer Werner Blankenburg, the ranking official on hand, would have greeted the group.[29]

As the photos suggest, a stroll through the heart of Berlin followed. Blankenburg and Allers took valuable time away from their desks to join the visitors. Oels also appears to be among them. This astonishing tour group, at this point without the four women, started at the Reich Chancellery and passed other key junctions of Nazi power such as Joseph Goebbels's Ministry of Propaganda before reaching Pariser Platz and the Brandenburg Gate. A stroll down Unter den Linden led to the

New Guardhouse (*Neue Wache*), where the group was again photographed engaged in lively discussion.

Somewhere near the New Guardhouse, the officials and the tourists boarded the bus and headed west via Potsdamer Platz to visit the Berlin Zoo. Several prints in the album feature exotic animals. In one photo, Blankenburg and Niemann can be seen viewing the elephants (fig. 8.15, bottom left). Possibly that same evening or toward the end of another day, the SS men and Trawnikis returned to Pariser Platz. Niemann's photos show the Brandenburg Gate and Unter den Linden with the sun hanging low in the west. On this occasion, someone among them took additional photos of the Berlin Cathedral and the City Palace across the street.

Probably on the second day of their trip, the tour group started off the morning with a drive to Potsdam to visit the historic city center, palaces, and parks. Blankenburg and Allers no longer accompanied the tourists, but Oels was probably with them. It was also on this day that the women joined the group. As elsewhere, the position of the sun and geographic features make it possible to reconstruct a relatively clear sequence of events for that day.

Upon reaching the historic center of Potsdam, the group first viewed the City Palace on the Old Market Square and the nearby Nikolai Church. From there, they strolled west on Breite Street, passed the royal stables on the right, and headed toward the famous Garrison Church, which they probably also visited.

Back on the bus, the visitors subsequently rode to the northern edge of the palace grounds, where they examined agricultural equipment at the Bornstedt Crown Estate or some neighboring facilities. Afterward, they proceeded to the beer garden in front of the Dragon House and took a noon break. Several photos from the album show the Germans and Trawnikis engaged in a jovial round of beer during this stop. Not long thereafter, the group seems to have moved on to the royal park. The tourists passed the Orangery Palace and the historic windmill before reaching Sanssouci around 1 p.m. Here, they had the opportunity to view the palace exterior at the very least and pose on the outdoor staircase for more souvenir photos.

On the third day of the trip, rest and relaxation seems to have been in the foreground. Now on their own—absent any representatives from the KdF and without the wives, who may have already left the city—the men visited an outdoor swimming pool in the greater Berlin area around noon. A total of three photos show the Germans and Trawnikis in uniform in the midsummer heat standing awkwardly at the edge of the pool near the sunbathing area, posing for a group photo. Other Trawnikis, changed into swimming attire, seem to have enjoyed the water.

Either on this or another day, the tour group also attended the circus, which one of the prints not mounted in the album suggests (see fig. 8.33). Taken together, the photos give the impression that the itinerary was relatively densely packed and probably required at least three days. Allowing for arrival and departure, the entire visit to Berlin must have lasted at least five days under a tautly organized schedule. Realistically speaking, given the long hours spent driving, Niemann and his men arrived back in Lublin after an absence of six or seven days.

Back at their posts in Sobibor and Treblinka, the murderous daily work routine continued for Niemann and his traveling companions. In early August, Niemann must have spent several vacation days with Gomerski in Adersbach in the Sudetenland, from where he sent a postcard to his wife.[30] Probably just days after the tour group returned from Berlin, Jewish prisoners at Treblinka launched their uprising, leading to the swift end of that killing center's existence. Two months later, the Jewish uprising at Sobibor brought a hasty conclusion to Operation Reinhard in general. Beyond these revolts, which the perpetrators could not have foreseen, the photos from the

Berlin trip bear witness to a moment when the SS men and the Trawnikis could already expect an imminent end to the deportations. After all, they had already murdered almost all of the Jews of Poland. Therefore, there was plenty of reason to believe that the gigantic program of murder would soon end, in their view, as an unqualified success.

In a letter to his wife dated August 20, 1943, Niemann mentioned his impending transfer to the Italian city of Trieste.[31] Thus, Niemann's album on the journey to Berlin provides an eloquent testimony to this "success," as he and his comrades undoubtedly saw it. And it was for this success that the Chancellery of the Führer had shown its gratitude to the dedicated and devoted Trawnikis and the three SS men who had led them in the murder of 1.8 million people.

Notes

1. On Niemann's possessions in Sobibor, which lists both photo albums, see the document in the appendix 2.5. A letter from Arnold Oels to Henriette Niemann dated December 13, 1943, USHMMA, Acc 2020.8.1, mentions the intended transfer of his possessions.

2. A small series of an image included in the album and four additional photos, in contrast to all the other paper prints, has a smooth edge cut and higher image contrasts, and possibly originates from an additional photographer (see figs. 8.25, top left, and 8.29–8.33).

3. In the late summer of 1941, a Jewish forced labor camp was established on Lublin's Wrońska Street, in the buildings and hangars of a former airplane factory, which was initially subordinate to the Dachau-based clothing factory of the Waffen-SS. In 1942, the location became a central warehouse for the Operation Reinhard camps. Jewish forced laborers had to clean, sort, and pack the personal effects of the murdered victims before they were sent on for further use. For this task, 4,000 Jewish women and 1,200 Jewish men were deployed there in November 1942. The ramp at the Old Airfield nearby was the arrival site for deportations to District Lublin. Trains from the German Reich, Slovakia, and the Protectorate of Bohemia and Moravia stopped here on the way to the transit ghettos and to Sobibor, as well as transports from the ghettos in Warsaw and Bialystok to District Lublin. On November 3,

1943, the Jewish forced laborers were forcibly marched to the Majdanek concentration camp, 1.2 miles away, and shot there within the framework of Operation Harvest Festival (*Aktion Erntefest*)). See Hänschen, *Transitghetto*, pp. 258–261; on the economic context also, Kaienburg, *Wirtschaft*, pp. 540–542.

4. On the interrelation between the KdF and Reinhard operations, see chapter 4 in this volume; also Berger, *Experten*.

5. The bus with the license plate RP-102 322 was acquired by the Reich Postal Service in July 1941 and subsequently used in the Karlsruhe area. In an undated vehicle list of the Reich Post Central Office, the bus is noted under the rubric "front assistance," indicating that the vehicle was not deployed in the T4 murders between early 1940 and August 1941.

6. Interrogation of Fritz Bleich, November 27, 1946, BArch, Nbg. Doc. NO 860.

7. See their marriage documents, BArch, RS Personalakten RuSHA Niemann, Floß, Gomerski; also BArch, SSO Niemann.

8. Ibid., curriculum vitae of Herbert Floß, October 20, 1936, BArch, RS Herbert Floß; interrogation of Hubert Gomerski, April 11, 1950, HHW, 461-36346/2.

9. Interrogation of Hubert Gomerski, May 17, 1960, HHW, 461-36346/9 and November 19, 1973, LNW, Q 234/4471.

10. On Niemann, see appendix 2 in this book. On Floß and Gomerski, see the interrogations of Franz Rum, November 24, 1961, LNW, Q 234/4267; Hans-Heinz Schütt, June 7, 1961, LNW, Q 234/4263; Hubert Gomerski, December 9, 1949, HHW, 462-36346/2; Hubert Gomerski, May 16, 1961, HHW, 461-36346/39; Hubert Gomerski, September 30, 1976, HHW, 461-36346/49; as well as Angrick, "Aktion 1005," pp. 236, 248–251.

11. See excerpt from Peter Black on the interrogations of Michael Rasgonjajew, USHMMA, PBP 58/1, and Hubert Gomerski, December 9, 1949, HHW, 461-36346/2.

12. While individual guards are not shown in most of the group photographs, the photos in front of the façade of Sanssouci Palace as well as the image taken in front of the Berlin Cathedral show all 22 Trawnikis.

13. Sandkühler, "Trawniki-Männer," p. 236. The Zugwachmänner Schmidt and Schütz cannot be identified as possibly among the travelers, owing to a lack of corresponding photos for comparison.

14. Interrogation of Fritz Bleich, November 27, 1946, BArch, Nbg. Doc. NO 860.

15. For an informative overview of the sources in the historical record, see Black, "Police Auxiliaries," pp. 333–355.

16. Photo album for Sobibor trial in Hagen, LNW, Q 234/4564 (the Trawniki is labeled as no. 75).

17. Ibid., marked as no. 73; Franz-Album, LNR, RWB 18244.

18. Biographical information on Kaiser in chapter 7 of this volume. On Jäger and Bienemann see the biographical fragments and mentions in USHMMA, PBP 58/1; interrogation of Kurt Franz, June 28, 1962, LNW, Q 234/4364; Sandkühler, "Trawniki-Männer," p. 189.

19. Ibid.

20. See the photos in the respective marriage documents, BArch, RS Floß and Niemann.

21. Dietrich Allers confirms this in retrospect in his condolence letter to Henriette Niemann, October 21, 1943 (see app. 2 fig. 2.2)

22. Sereny, *Abgrund*, pp. 143–146.

23. Interrogation of Anna Fuchs, March 28, 1966, NIOD, 804/47.

24. The search protocol is reprinted in Böhm, "'Karrieren,'" p. 141.

25. On women as perpetrators and accessories in detail, Schwarz, *Frau*; Lower, *Helferinnen*; on the public nature of the mass crimes also, Bajohr and Pohl, *Holocaust*. See also Goldhagen, *Vollstrecker*, p. 288, where the infamous example of Vera Wohlauf, wife of the company commander Julius Wohlauf from Reserve Police Battalion 101, is described. Pregnant, Vera Wohlauf was present at the deportation of the Jewish community of Międzyrzec Podlaski in August 1942.

26. See the postcard from Danida Floß to her parents, September 19, 1941, as well as the documents from the T4 personnel director Arnold Oels to Henriette Niemann, March 9, 1944, und July 24, 1944, USHMMA, Acc 2020.8.1.

27. On the use of the bus with the license plate RP-102 322, see note 5.

28. Figures 8.3 and 8.14 possibly show the vicinity of an accommodation that served as overnight stay en route, since the same place was photographed at different times, and in one case Trawnikis on the roof of the tour bus also seem to be unloading baggage.

29. See the interrogation of Fritz Bleich, November 27, 1946, BArch, Nbg. Doc. NO 860.

30. See Niemann's postcard, August 9, 1943, USHMMA, Acc 2020.8.1.

31. See the reproduction of the August 20, 1943, letter; appendix 2 figure 2.1.

The Berlin Album and Additional Travel Pictures

Figures 8.1 and 8.2. Cover of the photo album for the Berlin trip in an 18 cm × 25 cm format.

Figure 8.3. *Top*, *left*, Lublin, the Old Airfield. Operation Reinhard forced labor camp and warehouse in July 1943. *Top*, *right*, scene in front of an accommodation, possibly during the trip. Atop the bus, Trawnikis are loosening the tarps that covered the luggage. In a light-colored jacket, the unidentified tour guide, on his right, Niemann. The group of three men next to the bus includes, at left, SS-Scharführer Herbert Gomerski. *Bottom*, *left*, group photo in front of the bus, a Type O 3750 Mercedes Benz, with about thirty seats. The license plate is clearly visible. Standing just above it is Zugwachmann Franz Bienemann. At far left, the driver. The group also includes the twenty-two Trawnikis. Niemann stands in the center, and on the right are Zugwachmann Alexander Kaiser, Hubert Gomerski, the tour guide, and, at far right, presumably Zugwachmann Alexander Jäger. *Bottom*, *right*, taking a break and enjoying a snack during the journey: from left, Gomerski, Niemann, the tour guide, and, kneeling, the driver.

Figure 8.4. Lublin, the Old Airfield, Operation Reinhard forced labor camp and warehouse in July 1943. Trawnikis stow their baggage before the trip. Zugwachmann Alexander Kaiser is looking straight at the camera. The setting is the same as that in the photo on the last page of the album.

Figure 8.5. *Top, left*, a rest break in the shade. Sitting at the top of the slope, in the center, is Niemann; at right is Gomerski, smoking; behind Niemann is Zugwachmann Kaiser. *Top, right*, during a break: Niemann at right; on the left, the tour guide. *Bottom, left*, Niemann with an unidentified man. *Bottom, right*, the tour group, with Niemann at the center, in front of the historic windmill near Sanssouci Palace. The photo album belonging to Kurt Franz contains the same photo.

Figure 8.6. *Top, left*, inside the tour bus. Front left, Niemann; on the right, SS-Oberscharführer Herbert Floß, beside him, his wife, Danida. The series of four photos showing the interior of the bus was probably taken on the day of the Potsdam visit, near the Prussian palaces. *Top, right*, inside the bus, with the doors open: from left, Mr. and Mrs. Niemann and Floß, as well as the tour guide and the driver. *Bottom, left*, the tour group in the bus. The occupants are seated largely in accordance with their rank. In front, Niemann; behind him, Floß and Gomerski with their wives, Danida and Emilie. Easily identifiable by the insignia of rank on their epaulets: men with the ranks of Zugwachmann, Gruppenwachmann, and Oberwachmann. At the very back: Trawniki enlisted ranks. *Bottom, right*, group photo at the rear of the bus. Far right, Gomerski; in the foreground, with his jacket unbuttoned, Niemann.

Figure 8.7. *Top*, *left*, snapshot taken while the travelers were getting off the bus. In the foreground, Danida Floß; at center, facing the camera, Niemann. *Top*, *right*, beer garden in front of the Dragon House in Potsdam. Front left, Gomerski; next to him, his wife, Emilie; with her back to the camera, Henriette Niemann; at her side, Danida Floß. On the right, at the table, is Zugwachmann Franz Bienemann, seen in a three-quarter view. *Bottom*, *left*, beer garden at the Dragon House in Potsdam. In the foreground, Herbert Floß, probably also Arnold Oels and Niemann. *Bottom*, *right*, view from the front of the bus. Front left, Henriette and Johann Niemann; behind them, Gomerski and his wife.

Figure 8.8. *Top*, *left*, Niemann during a rest break. *Top*, *right*, Niemann; behind him, at left, Zugwachmann Franz Bienemann. *Bottom*, *left*, Gomerski. The tour bus can be seen in the background. *Bottom*, *right*, Gomerski; at left, Danida Floß and Henriette Niemann.

Figure 8.9. *Top*, *left*, visit to a farmyard in the Potsdam area. At the center, evidently a guide with local knowledge. Behind him, on the left, is Niemann. At far left, the driver; next to him, the tour guide. Floß, turned away from the camera and wearing a visor cap and a camera bag, can be seen in the foreground on the right. This photo, which had become detached from the album, was unequivocally assigned to its proper place: the only empty spot in the album. *Top*, *right*, in front of the Neue Wache (New Guardhouse) in Berlin. In a light-colored suit with an arm sling, Dietrich Allers; on the left, Werner Blankenburg; and across from the latter, Zugwachmann Bienemann. In the foreground, wearing a suit, is presumably Arnold Oels; the man next to him is possibly Zugwachmann Alexander Jäger. *Bottom*, *left*, the tour group in a midmorning photo in the courtyard of the Potsdam City Palace; in the background, St. Nikolai Church. *Bottom*, *right*, at the west façade of the Potsdam City Palace. In the center, Niemann; Floß has a camera slung around his neck.

Figure 8.10. *Top*, *left*, an unidentified Trawniki; Zugwachmann Kaiser; Niemann in half profile; Zugwachmann Bienemann; turned away from the camera, Floß; wearing glasses, Blankenburg; the driver; another unidentified Trawniki (*from left to right*). The hood of the bus is visible in the foreground. *Top*, *right*, the tour group in the late afternoon, near the Opera on Unter den Linden Boulevard. The man in the foreground, second from left, is probably Arnold Oels; also seen in the photo are Werner Blankenburg, Dietrich Allers, and Hubert Gomerski. *Bottom*, *left*, officials from the Chancellery of the Führer, with Niemann in the center, on Unter den Linden. *Bottom*, *right*, the group on the flight of stairs in front of Sanssouci Palace.

Figure 8.11. Probably Arnold Oels, the personnel manager at the Chancellery of the Führer with responsibility for staffing Operation Reinhard and Operation T4. With his arm in a sling, Dietrich Allers, Oels's direct superior and manager of the T4 Central Office at 4 Tiergartenstraße in Berlin; wearing a visor cap, Niemann; in the foreground and wearing glasses, Werner Blankenburg, the head of Office II at the Chancellery of the Führer, in conversation with Zugwachmann Bienemann (*from left to right*).

Figure 8.12. *Top*, *left*, en route to the Garrison Church in Potsdam. *Top*, *right*, the tour group on the flight of stairs in front of Sanssouci Palace; in the center, Niemann. *Bottom*, *left*, beer garden at the Dragon House in Potsdam. In the foreground, Trawnikis drinking a toast; at the table behind them and to the left, Floß; with his back to the camera, Niemann, *Bottom*, *right*, group photo of German SS men and Trawnikis with the rank of Zugwachmann. In the foreground, wearing a light-colored jacket, is the tour guide. At left, Gomerski; standing and wearing a garrison cap, Kaiser; seated, Niemann; at the corner of the table, Floß.

Figure 8.13. On the flight of stairs in front of Sanssouci Palace. In the center: Niemann; behind him, at left, his wife; at right, Danida Floß; at right, next to Niemann, Emilie Gomerski; beside her, probably Arnold Oels.

Figure 8.14. *Top*, *left*, feeding a sea lion in the Berlin Zoo. *Top*, *right*, beer garden at the Dragon House in Potsdam. In the center, probably Arnold Oels; to the right, next to the tree, Niemann. *Bottom*, *left*, snapshot at an outdoor swimming pool, probably in Berlin. Taking a photo is the tour escort from the Chancellery of the Führer, observed on the left by Niemann. Several Trawnikis are wearing swim trunks. *Bottom*, *right*, Unidentified young women. This snapshot was taken at the same spot as figure 8.3, top right.

Figure 8.15. *Top*, *left*, scene at an outdoor pool; left, at the edge of the pool, Niemann in a visor cap. The photo must have been taken shortly before the one on the previous page, as the group on the left can still be seen in much the same position at the pool's edge. *Top*, *right*, baboons in the Berlin Zoo. *Bottom*, *left*, the elephant house at the Berlin Zoo. In the center, Niemann; around him, several Trawnikis. Second from left, probably Blankenburg. *Bottom*, *right*, feeding the sea lions in the Berlin Zoo, as in the photo on the previous page.

Figure 8.16. *Top*, *left*, group photo in front of Sanssouci Palace. In the center, Niemann. This snapshot resembles those in figures 8.12 and 8.25. *Top*, *right*, group photo taken from the side of the flight of stairs at Sanssouci Palace. It is similar to figure 8.10, bottom right. *Bottom*, *left*, snapshot of the tour group in the area of the Potsdam palaces and gardens. Second from right, Gomerski; next, facing away from the camera, is Floß; fifth from the left, Niemann. The photo shows the same setting as that in figure 8.9, top left. *Bottom*, *right*, the tour group boarding the bus. At center, waiting, is Niemann. This snapshot resembles the one on the first page of the album.

Figure 8.17. *Top*, *left*, Trawnikis on the way to the Orangery Palace in Potsdam; walking ahead of them, the wives. *Top*, *right*, in the Potsdam palace park; left, with a camera, Floß; in the center, Niemann and Gomerski. *Bottom*, *left*, Group photo of Trawnikis, Niemann, the tour guide, and the driver at the outdoor swimming pool, probably in Berlin. Far left: presumably, Zugwachmann Alexander Jäger. *Bottom*, *right*, Berlin, Unter den Linden. View of Friedrich Wilhelm University (now Humboldt University) in Berlin.

Figure 8.18. *Top*, *left*, Berlin, on Unter den Linden, looking down Friedrichstraße; visible in the background, the Friedrichstraße Railroad Station. *Top*, *right*, Potsdamer Platz (Potsdam Square) in Berlin; left, the suburban train station; right, the Pschorr Brewery. *Bottom*, *left*, Berlin, Pariser Platz (Paris Square), looking eastward at Unter den Linden; in the background, the tower of Rotes Rathaus (Red City Hall). *Bottom*, *right*, Berlin, Pariser Platz, in the shadow of the Brandenburg Gate.

Figure 8.19. *Top*, *left*, a side view of Sanssouci Palace, Potsdam. *Top*, *right*, Berlin, Unter den Linden, view of the Opera House. *Bottom*, *left*, Berlin, Wilhelmstraße. Left, the Borsig Palace; center, the annex building of the Old Reich Chancellery, with the "Führer Balcony" added by Albert Speer in 1935; right, the Old Reich Chancellery at 77 Wilhelmstrasse, the so-called Palais Schulenburg. *Bottom*, *right*, the Prinz-Karl-Palais on Wilhelmplatz in Berlin, used by Reich Propaganda Minister Joseph Goebbels as his offices.

Figure 8.20. *Top, left*, Brandenburg Gate, viewed from Pariser Platz. *Top, right*, Neue Wache in Berlin, on Unter den Linden. *Bottom, left.* Potsdam City Palace; in the background, St. Nikolai Church. *Bottom, right*, the Old Library on Unter den Linden. The Opernplatz, the square in front of the building, was the site of the book burning on May 10, 1933.

Figure 8.21. *Top*, *left*, looking down Voß Street; in the foreground, the portal of Villa Borsig; behind it, the New Reich Chancellery building. *Top*, *right*, New Reich Chancellery on Voßstrasse in Berlin. *Bottom*, *left*, entrance of the New Reich Chancellery. *Bottom*, *right*, New Reich Chancellery on Voß Street; looking eastward at the wing of the Presidential Chancellery.

Figure 8.22. *Top*, *left*, the Old Library with Opernplatz. At the bottom of the image, a lowered bus window can be seen indistinctly. *Top*, *right*, the Old Palace (Altes Palais), the former residence of Emperor Wilhelm I on Unter den Linden. *Bottom*, *left*, the Berlin Armory (Zeughaus) on Unter den Linden, at that time the National Socialists' war museum. B*ottom*, *right*, Berlin's Friedrich Wilhelm University, seen from the east.

Figure 8.23. *Top*, *left*, Berlin. Alexanderplatz, with a view of George Church (Georgenkirche) and the Minolhaus, a commercial building. A window frame of the bus is visible at the lower edge of the image. *Top*, *right*, Orangery Palace in Potsdam. In the background, the wives of the German SS men. *Bottom*, *left*, inner courtyard of the Potsdam City Palace. The tour group is walking toward the main wing. *Bottom*, *right*, beer garden at the Dragon House in Potsdam; right, at the table, Herbert Floß.

Figure 8.24. *Top*, *left*, group photo; a river can be seen in the background. In the center, Gomerski and Floß; at far left, with his back to the camera, Niemann. *Top*, *right*, the tour group on the way to the Potsdam Garrison Church. The photo is identical to figure 8.12, top left. *Bottom*, *left*, seven Trawnikis drinking beer; Floß is the third man from the right. The photo was taken at the same place as figure 8.12, bottom right. *Bottom*, *right*, officials from the Chancellery of the Führer, with Niemann, on Unter den Linden. With an arm sling, Dietrich Allers; in a visor cap, Johann Niemann; wearing glasses, Werner Blankenburg in conversation with Zugwachmann Bienemann. The photo is identical to figure 8.10, bottom left.

Figure 8.25. *Top*, *left*, group photo with all twenty-two Trawnikis in front of the Berlin Cathedral. *Top*, *right*, in front of Sanssouci Palace; same subject as figure 8.12, top, right. *Bottom*, *left*, Lublin, the Old Airfield. The tour group before departure, same time and place as in the first photo in the album. In the background, half concealed and with his back to the camera, Herbert Floß; far right, with a briefcase, the driver. The old hangars seen in the background served as warehouses for the possessions stolen in the extermination camps. *Bottom*, *right*, Trawnikis in the beer garden at the Dragon House in Potsdam. In the background, Zugwachmann Franz Bienemann; across from him, facing away from the camera, Hubert Gomerski.

Additional photos from the Berlin trip

Figure 8.26. Taking a rest break during the journey; similar to figure 8.5, top, left. The bus is visible in the background. At the top of the slope, Niemann; at right, next to him, Hubert Gomerski.

Figure 8.27. Taking a rest break during the journey. A similar photo appears on the first page of the album. In the foreground, eating, Gomerski; next to him, Niemann; standing, the bus driver.

Figure 8.28. Another scene from the rest break. Seated in the background, Gomerski and Niemann.

Figure 8.29. Group photo with six Trawnikis and Dietrich Allers (*right*). The photo was presumably taken near the tour group's accommodations in Berlin.

Figure 8.31. Group photo at the Emperor Wilhelm National Monument. In the background, the Berlin City Palace.

Figure 8.30. The tour group at the Emperor Wilhelm National Monument.

Figure 8.32. Feeding the animals in the Berlin Zoo.

Figure 8.33. In front of a circus, probably in Berlin. In the center, Niemann and Gomerski.

9

The Revolt at Sobibor and the End of the Death Camp

ANNE LEPPER, ANDREAS KAHRS,
ANNETT GERHARDT, AND STEFFEN HÄNSCHEN

On October 14, 1943, the Jewish prisoners in Sobibor dared the essentially impossible: they put into action their plan to launch an uprising and bring about their own liberation. The beginning of the revolt was designed to arouse no suspicion among the German camp personnel at first. The small clandestine group of organizers was relying on the well-known greed of the SS men and their propensity for personal enrichment.

Under the pretext of showing him a new coat, the rebels first lured Johann Niemann into the tailors' barracks in Camp I. Semion Rozenfeld, a Soviet prisoner of war who was actively involved in planning the insurrection, observed the events from barracks located just opposite:

"[We] sat at the window and looked out at the entrance to Camp I. We saw Niemann, on horseback, come riding through the gate, ride up to the tailors' workshop, jump off the horse, and go into the barracks. Inside every workshop were two of our men. [. . .] And five minutes after he had gone in, the horse suddenly started to whinny and rear up on its hind legs. [. . .] That worried Petscherskii and me. We didn't understand what had happened. The following had happened: Schubajew was inside, he was shorter than Niemann, and his blow with the axe landed awkwardly. Niemann cried out. He had not killed him. The horse heard this and reared up. [. . .] We were very anxious.

Then, a few minutes later, we saw someone come out of the tailors' workshop and run in our direction. He came over to us and handed us Niemann's pistol. [Then] we calmed down."[1]

After this, the revolt took its course. Other SS men who, like Niemann, had been lured to the workshops under a pretext appeared in Camp I. One after another, they were overpowered and killed by the Jewish prisoners: "We were counting on the German habit of punctuality. [. . .] I have to say that this plan succeeded very well. They came separately. While the SS man was inspecting the coat, he was immediately killed with an axe and hidden under the things. Our task was to eliminate all the SS men within one hour, so that they never noticed that one of the others was absent for an extended period of time. After that, at 4:30, the Kapo authorized to lead us ostensibly lined us up for going to work. [. . .] He leads us to the main gate, on the way we make a raid on the armory and proceed to the main gate."[2]

Escape and Resistance

From the outset, resistance in Sobibor took many forms, none of which can be disregarded in an examination of the prisoners' organized revolt on October 14, 1943. To make any opposition impossible, the camp leadership had created a system for comprehensive monitoring of the prisoner population. The permanent threat and experience of violence and draconian punishments made for an atmosphere of terror and perpetual fear. Despite—or perhaps precisely because of—the prisoners' hopeless situation, the thought of resistance and escape was ever-present in the minds of many. As Abraham Margulies remembered, "[we] wanted so very much to live. So it's not surprising that from the first day of our stay in the camp, our minds were crowded with various ideas and combinations of ideas about the possibility of an escape."[3] Margulies had been deported from Zamość to Sobibor in May 1942, at the age of twenty-one.

An early and significant site of spontaneous resistance was the so-called ramp. Upon arrival, the deportees were forced out of the trains and onto the ramp at the railroad station. Incoming Jews were to be deceived as to the true purpose of the camp and confirmed in the assumption that Sobibor was a labor camp. Often, however, the deportees realized what arrival in Sobibor meant for them. In light of their desperate situation, time after time they attacked their guards and put up a fight against the camp personnel who were intent on herding them through the "tube" and into the gas chambers. The survivor Moshe Bachir recalled a particular moment: "I can remember a transport of naked women who were holding their infants in their arms [. . .]. They didn't believe the lies that Oberscharführer Hermann Michel had told them. They attacked the guards with the baby bottles they held in their hands and managed to injure several officers. There was panic among the German heroes, and they called the Ukrainians to their aid. With great effort, the Ukrainians overpowered the naked women. Most of them were killed on the spot and never entered the gas chambers."[4]

Bachir described another event, which is representative of the story of a great many arrivals who rebelled against the violence at the ramp: an elderly Jewish man, he said, stood in front of the German guard Karl Frenzel and let a handful of sand trickle through his fingers. The Jew said that the time of the German perpetrators would fade away in just the same manner. After saying a prayer, the old man slapped the German SS man with all his might. Only the intervention of the camp commandant, Franz Reichleitner, kept Frenzel from losing control in the face of an act that, from the Germans' standpoint, was an almost unbelievable provocation. With stoic calm, the old man then surrendered himself to Reichleitner, who shot him in front of his family.[5]

Other deportees—primarily those from the countries of Western Europe—arriving at Sobibor did not yet know what sort of place it actually was. Those few among them who had been selected for forced labor in the camp soon became aware of what was going on, however. Their grief for all those who had arrived at the camp with them and then been murdered in the gas chambers only a few hours later was now mixed with their distress at being forced to work at such a place.

The Jewish prisoners in Sobibor soon realized that escape offered their only real chance of leaving the camp alive. Particularly during the first months of the camp's existence, attempts to escape were repeatedly made, both by individual prisoners and by relatively small groups. Only a few actually succeeded in leaving the camp unnoticed, however, as both the planning and the execution of an escape could hardly be kept secret; moreover, such actions entailed the greatest threats—and not only to their own lives. Under the extreme conditions, it was exceptionally difficult for the prisoners to build relationships of trust, and the risk of betrayal by a confidant prior to an escape attempt was substantial.

In addition, there was fear of the incalculable hazards that would await them outside the confines of the camp. To those Jews who had been deported to Sobibor from foreign countries, it seemed almost impossible to organize a life in hiding, owing to their lack of linguistic skills and local knowledge. Polish Jews were aware of the dangers to which they would be exposed after a successful escape. Before deportation to Sobibor, they had already experienced antisemitic violence or betrayal by the civilian population, and frequently they harbored little hope of obtaining the support that was crucial to survival in hiding. Several instances of escape provide evidence that Polish inhabitants of the region were a major factor in the Germans' ability to closely monitor the extensive area. On December 25 and 26, 1942, presumably three Jewish men and two Jewish women managed to escape from Camp III, and two Trawnikis also deserted at this time. After a manhunt of several days, the German police reported from Chełm that the two guards and a Polish Jewish woman named Pesia Liberman had been tracked down, thanks to the "resoluteness" of three Polish policemen, and had been killed in an ensuing firefight.[6] In the camp itself, the Germans reacted to this incident with great brutality. Hershel Cukierman assumed that all the remaining Jews in Camp III were shot in the wake of the escape.[7]

The memoirs and statements of the survivors provide impressive insights into the complexity of the attempts to escape. Several accounts contain references to a failed attempt to build a tunnel that would enable prisoners to escape from the killing area in Camp III. Also firmly fixed in the memory of various survivors was the escape of members of the so-called forest detachment, deployed outside the camp in order to obtain wood. Two Polish Jews, Salomon Podchlebnik and Josef Kopp, overpowered a Trawniki during their labor deployment in July 1943. After his corpse had been discovered by the other guards, additional Jews took to their heels.[8] Some of the members of the work detail who stayed behind were then shot in front of the other prisoners in the camp.[9]

After the first successful escape attempts, the German camp personnel had established a system of collective punishments. As a result, every prisoner in Sobibor was aware that after an escape, those who remained behind had to expect savage punishment. The mortal danger in which they placed their fellow sufferers prevented many prisoners from daring to escape. Jakub Biskubicz recalled, "I admit that I, too, dreamed all the time of escaping and looked for an appropriate opportunity [. . .]. But at the same time, it occurred to me that others would pay with their lives just for me, and I dismissed the thought."[10] This dilemma also fueled doubt and mistrust among the prisoners. Icchak Lichtman recalled that "escape attempts and instances of betrayal" occurred repeatedly.[11]

In addition to the various individual plans for escape, there were different resistance activities. They ranged from acts of sabotage and attacks on the camp personnel to at least one early plan for organizing a collective uprising, which, however, never came to fruition. Some prisoners hit on the idea of poisoning the camp's SS personnel as well as the Trawniki guard force. The poison needed for this purpose was to be procured, in small doses, from the Jewish workers in the camp "pharmacy" and passed on to workers in the kitchen who were privy to the plan. Ultimately, it was to be their task to prepare the food for the camp personnel without being detected. One confidant, however, betrayed the scheme before it could be put into action. Those who were accused of involvement in the plan were murdered.[12]

The atmosphere among the prisoners changed in the summer of 1943, when there was a noticeable decrease in the number of deportation trains arriving. The Jewish laborers sensed that an imminent shutdown of the death camp was becoming increasingly likely. Johann Niemann's reference to his upcoming transfer to Italy in a letter to his wife suggests that his redeployment was scheduled for the early fall.[13]

The Jewish prisoners obviously managed at the eleventh hour to implement their plans for a revolt. They were well aware that in the event of a termination of the systematic murder, the German guards would not take the risk of leaving alive the Jewish witnesses to their crimes. This premonition became bitter certainty at the end of June 1943, when a transport with the last members of the Jewish Sonderkommando from Belzec arrived in Sobibor. The Belzec camp, in the southern part of District Lublin, had already been closed around the end of 1942. The remaining members of the Jewish Sonderkommando, however, were forced to spend the next six months there burning the corpses from the mass graves and eliminating the traces of the crimes. After that, they were promised, they would be taken to a labor camp. But their transport left Belzec and headed for Sobibor. There, in contrast to the usual way of handling arriving transports, they were not received on the ramp by the Jewish prisoners working in the railroad station detachment (Bahnhofskommando), as the German camp personnel wanted to prevent all contact between the two groups. The prisoners from Belzec refused to get out of the freight cars, and in turn attacked the Germans at the ramp. Despite the mandated isolation in Camp I, the Jews in Sobibor learned of the group's arrival and heard a short time later that the members of the Sonderkommando had been shot.[14] In the clothing of the murdered men, the sorting detachment (Sortier-Kommando) found slips of paper with messages warning them against nurturing false hopes as to their fate: "We have worked in Belzec for a year. We don't know where they're taking us now. There are tables in the freight cars, we got bread for three days, canned goods, and vodka. If that was a deception, keep in mind that death awaits you too. Don't believe the Germans, avenge us!"[15]

Haltingly, but at regular intervals, information about the course of the war also reached the remaining Jews in Sobibor. They learned of the armed uprising in the Warsaw Ghetto, and there were rumors that partisan units were active on the other side of the Bug River, not far from the grounds of the camp.

October 14, 1943

In light of these developments and lessons learned, the thoughts of certain Jewish prisoners concerning an armed revolt in Sobibor took on a definite and specific shape. A small, secret resistance group was formed to plan an organized mass escape. This inner circle of ten to twelve prisoners was under the leadership of Leon Felhendler, a rabbi's son from Żółkiewka. Independently of this group, prisoners in Camp III had begun to dig a tunnel for a planned large-scale escape. Just before its completion, however, this project was disclosed to the Germans, presumably by fellow prisoners. As a result, most of the members of the Jewish Sonderkommando were murdered.[16]

The plans of the prisoners in Camp I gained additional momentum on September 23, 1943, when a transport from the Minsk ghetto reached Sobibor. Besides the last inhabitants of the ghetto, it brought a large group of Soviet Jewish prisoners of war (POWs) to the camp. The expansion and development of the new section known as Camp IV had just begun at this time, and various construction projects within the existing camp also were on the agenda. Because new manpower was needed for these purposes, SS-Oberscharführer Karl Frenzel selected approximately eighty men for forced labor in the camp. The failure of the German camp personnel to associate any security risk with the battle-hardened Jewish Red Army soldiers can be interpreted as negligence induced by arrogance. A few days after their arrival in Sobibor, some of the POWs, with thirty-four-year-old Lieutenant Aleksandr Pecherskii as their leader, aligned themselves with the already existing planning committee for the revolt.[17] Through this collaboration, the military expertise of the former Red Army men was combined with the strengths available in the group around Felhendler, including local knowledge as well as familiarity with the procedures and goings-on in the camp.

In long conversations, usually held in the women's barracks building in Camp I amid the utmost secrecy, the group headed by Felhendler and Pecherskii began in the following days to work out concrete plans for the revolt and a subsequent mass escape of the Jewish prisoners. Early thoughts about building an escape tunnel were scrapped because of the incalculable risks inherent in the marshy terrain. Eventually a strategy was developed; it involved luring the SS men into various workshops before the afternoon roll call at intervals of a few minutes, under the pretext of handing over to them—for their personal enrichment—articles of clothing from the belongings of murdered Jews. Once there, they were to be killed by preappointed prisoner groups, and their corpses were to be concealed. As many SS men as possible were to be killed in this manner, in as short a time as possible and unnoticed by the rest of the guards. At the same time, the rebel fighters planned to disrupt the power supply and loot the armory.

Just a few minutes before roll call, when the bulk of the Jewish prisoners would already be assembled as usual on the central square in Camp I, they were to be informed of the events in the camp and encouraged to escape. The Trawnikis, it was hoped, would fall in beside the fleeing mass of Jewish laborers, at least to some extent, rather than quell the rebellion.

Only approximately thirty to forty of the 500–600 Jewish prisoners[18] who were in Camp I at this point in time were privy to the plans.[19] Individuals who were deemed suitable and trustworthy were included in the preparations and took on concrete tasks; for most prisoners, however, the series of activities went unnoticed. Though it was the organizers' aim to help as many people as possible to escape during the revolt, the concealment of the arrangements meant that only a few had a chance to

prepare mentally and practically for the events by taking along valuables, warm clothes, and food. Thomas Blatt, who, as a backer of the revolt committee, was broadly informed though not directly involved in the plan's execution, had already made provisions in the days preceding the scheduled uprising: "I dug out from under the trash a beautiful, large, folded knife that I had hidden. [. . .] Next I dug up from my hiding place, under the documents waiting to be burned, the valuables I'd hidden in preparation for escape—a fortune in diamonds, gold and paper money."[20]

Others were informed about the goings-on in the camp by fellow prisoners to whom they were close. The Dutchwoman Selma Wijnberg learned about the planned revolt only a few hours in advance, from her Polish friend Chaim Engel, who was involved in the preparations. He urged her to equip herself for the upcoming escape with warm clothing and suitable boots from the sorting barracks.[21] Shortly before the start of the revolt, Leon Felhendler paid a visit to sixteen-year-old Moshe Bachir in the workshop barracks and thrust some valuables into his pocket, with these words: "I don't know what will happen in half an hour, which of us two will stay alive. Possibly neither of us will. But if God helps you and you survive, you'll certainly need these."[22] It was these gold coins given him by Felhendler that ensured Moshe Bachir's survival in the months following the escape: he used them to bribe peasants who otherwise would have betrayed him.

Felhendler's words reveal the tension that was the constant companion of the Jewish prisoners during this time. On the one hand, they were aware that only the revolt and a subsequent escape offered them the chance of survival. On the other hand, keeping a low profile in an unfamiliar environment in turn involved new dangers, risks which those concerned found hard to estimate. After the war Aleksandr Pecherskii recalled that a prisoner named Luka, a woman with whom he had become friends in the camp, was stricken with great fear and doubt after she learned of Pecherskii's plans to revolt: "She took my hand and asked me, Sasha, why are you doing this? There's no way back from here. And even if you manage to escape, we'll all be taken to Camp III. I'm so afraid of it. Even though the camp here is so terrible, I don't want to die, and on top of that such an agonizing death."[23]

On account of the anticipated absence of several SS men—especially the infamous Gustav Wagner, whose upcoming departure on leave had been announced, as well as Franz Reichleitner, the camp commandant—the date for the revolt was set at short notice: October 13, 1943. On the morning of that day, however, several SS men from the nearby Osowa labor camp arrived in Sobibor. At first, the organizers of the uprising suspected that their plan had been betrayed, but a short time later it turned out that the Germans were merely paying a visit to the camp and that the camp leadership was not aware of the secret activities in the camp. In the end, the revolt was postponed to the next day.

On October 14, the uprising began in the afternoon, as planned, with the killing of Johann Niemann, who was in command of the camp on this day because of Reichleitner's absence. After that, the resistance groups in various workshops, one after the other, killed ten more SS men. Only Karl Frenzel, whom the Jewish prisoners particularly loathed, failed to show up at the appointed time in the designated workshop.

While the individual labor detachments gradually returned to the camp from their deployments outside its confines and had to assemble for the afternoon roll call, the news of the revolt spread like wildfire among the other prisoners. In fact, the uprising was already under way. In the confusing situation, those who felt both physically and mentally able to prepare for escape began, in great haste, to do so. Euphoria spread, and cries of "Hooray" were heard from all sides.[24] The Trawnikis,

who now noticed both the absence of a large part of the SS personnel and also the unusual behavior of the Jewish prisoners, were asked to join in the escape attempt. Contrary to hopes, however, they opened fire on the fleeing prisoners, who by this time had already approached the fence at several places and in sizeable groups. Karl Frenzel, too, now appeared at the edge of the Camp I compound, where he sought cover behind a wooden barrel and fired a submachine gun into the crowd. Many prisoners ran across the camp street, trying to make a dash for freedom through the main gate, as planned. In the process, however, they came under fire from the guards, resulting in the death of a great many prisoners in this area.[25]

Others negotiated the barbed wire and the surrounding minefield and reached the forest, which protected them from the bullets fired from the camp. In the chaotic situation inside the camp, where the fleeing Jews were within close shooting range of the guards atop the towers, they found hardly any way of offering mutual support. In many accounts by survivors, memories of this experience come up. Kalmen Wewryk, who had been deported from nearby Chełm to Sobibor, recalled, "I could see some of our people kneeling down and shooting at the enemy [with the looted firearms]. Others dropped like flies when struck by the bullets that were flying through the air around us. A friend called out to me, 'Kalmen, please save me, I've been hit!' But who could stop and help somebody else?"[26]

The prisoners from Camp III and Camp IV could not get free; they stayed behind in Sobibor. Other Jews decided against trying to escape on this day, for various reasons. After months of suffering and hardship in the camp, they had no hope of escaping the bullets of the guards, did not believe they could survive outside the confines of the camp, or were simply overwhelmed by the situation.

Those who successfully negotiated the fence and the minefield had only one goal in mind, as Kalmen Wewryk recalled:

"Everyone rushed off in a mad dash for freedom. We ran like frightened animals, cutting across country and heading for the dense forest. [...] We were bent on only one thing: getting away, reaching the forest, and escaping the hell known as Sobibor. After what seemed an eternity but actually had lasted only a few minutes, the trees became bigger, and I ran headlong toward them, completely out of breath. I'll never understand where I got the strength to run like that. And then—at last—there were trees above me. Sobibor lay behind me. I was free."[27]

With their sensational operation, the rebels had largely succeeded in putting their plans into action. Simultaneously, the uprising represented the end of the killing center. A short time later, Operation Reinhard also was terminated.

The German Perpetrators after the Revolt

In the course of the uprising, eleven SS men were killed; only six of the Germans present on October 14 survived.[28] The German camp personnel were not the only ones completely surprised by the prisoners' revolt. In Lublin, too, those in authority were shocked at the events in Sobibor.[29] One day after the revolt, a group led by Jakob Sporrenberg, Globocnik's successor as Lublin SS and police leader, and Hermann Höfle, the head of the Reinhard Task Force (*Einsatzstab Reinhard*), reached the camp. The SS man August Preyssl reported later on the reaction of the small group that reached the camp on this morning: "The Jews remaining in the camp, there were women and men, about 150 in number, [were] rounded up at a large spot in the camp. [...] Around 10 persons at a time were singled out from the crowd and led about 100 meters away; there they were made to lie down on the ground, facedown, and then were shot in the back of the neck."[30]

The Austrian Preyssl described how the group, on the return trip to Lublin, encountered another Jew who had escaped;

he was caught off the road in a field. "Upon questioning, he admitted that he had run away from the Sobibor camp. An SS-Untersturmführer from Sporrenberg's team then led the man into the nearby forest. I heard a shot, and shortly thereafter the Untersturmführer came back, carrying a pair of boots."[31]

Only a few days later, along with the remaining camp personnel from Sobibor, a few men from the Lublin staff of Operation Reinhard gathered in a military cemetery in Chełm to bury the eleven SS men killed four days earlier in the uprising. Dietrich Allers and Werner Blankenburg, the two relevant officials from the Chancellery of the Führer, had made the long journey from Berlin to the General Government expressly to be present at the interment of "their" men.[32] The Niemann collection contains fourteen photos that show scenes from the burial and Niemann's grave (see figs. 9.1–9.14). The images testify to the Germans' effort to stage their dead comrades as heroes in the context of an elaborate ceremony and, by so doing, also to find an appropriate way of dealing with what had previously been unthinkable. Both the escape of such a large number of prisoners and the death of half of the German camp personnel undoubtedly meant a significant disgrace for those in authority. Tellingly, the letter of sympathy from the Chancellery of the Führer to Niemann's widow also contains an attempt to style the deputy camp commandant as an SS man who died a heroic death, killed in action (see app. 2 fig. 2.2).[33] The photos of the ceremony that were sent to Henriette Niemann, which she herself added to the collection of photos left behind when her husband died, were intended to record the tribute to the SS men for their families. In the summer of 1944, Henriette Niemann received a letter from the German local command in Chełm, along with three additional photos of her husband's grave, two of which also have survived. In the letter, she was informed that no further care of the grave could be provided, because of the advancing front.[34] Involuntarily, however, the

German perpetrators documented something else with the images of the military cemetery in Chełm: the success of Jewish resistance in Sobibor.[35]

Odyssey after the Escape

For many of the approximately three hundred prisoners who managed to escape from the camp, a veritable odyssey began immediately after the successful revolt. Until the region was liberated by Red Army units in the summer of 1944, they were exposed to countless dangers. It can be assumed that at least sixty fugitives from Sobibor survived the following months until the end of the war.[36] All the others, more than two hundred persons, lost their lives, and the fates of the majority remain unclear to this day. We know only that around one hundred of the Jewish escapees were captured and murdered during the very first days, within the framework of the large-scale manhunt initiated by the Germans. Among the participants in the hunt were SS and police units, as well as members of the Wehrmacht and the Customs Border Guards.[37] Dov Freiberg, a Polish Jew who was sixteen at the time, recalled, "Then we kept on the move for three days with nothing to eat or drink. Whatever Christian we came up to, we were told that here and there someone from Sobibor was shot."[38]

The aim of many of the fugitives was to join one of the Jewish partisan units operating in the forests around Lublin. Around thirty of the escaped prisoners managed in the end to make contact with partisan groups.[39] Because many Polish partisans refused to accept Jews and in some cases even persecuted them, the Jewish units represented the safest refuge in the underground.[40] In their efforts to establish contact with partisans, some of the fugitives inevitably had disillusioning experiences. Dov Freiberg, who attempted to leave the immediate vicinity of the camp grounds with a small group, of which

Semion Rozenfeld also was a member, told about an attack by Polish partisans who at first had feigned solidarity with the fugitives: "We're just sitting and eating, and [the partisans] ask us whether we have rifles and gold with us. They say that we should hand over our rifles to them, because it's customary to collect all the rifles at first and then distribute them again. [. . .] We give them our few rifles, and it was all over for us. [. . .] They reload the rifles and start shooting at us. Now we're trapped, we have nothing we could use to return fire, and now our bad luck is complete. Finally we are away from Sobibor, and now we're to be killed by these people."[41] While some of his comrades-in-arms were murdered in that incident, Freiberg succeeded—just barely—in getting away from the attackers. Together with two other fugitives, Rozenfeld and Abraham Reis, he continued his odyssey through the Polish provinces.

Searching for refuge, the escaped prisoners wandered around in the forests without knowing what places they would arrive at and whom they could turn to. Many banded together in small groups of two to four. Only a very few decided, after the traumatic experiences in the camp and the revolt, to continue the difficult and dangerous escape on their own. Gathering in larger groups, however—as it quickly became clear—was more likely to involve the risk of detection by search parties. Besides, the larger the group, the more difficult the decision-making process became. The members of a roughly forty-member group who had escaped together from Sobibor decided, for example, very shortly after leaving the camp to split up and continue their escape by separate routes. Thomas Blatt, who belonged to this group at first, along with Freiberg and Rozenfeld, recalled, "I looked around. We were being joined by more and more escapees. The moon was the only light as the exhausted survivors gathered in the forest. The head count revealed that close to forty Jews were in our group. [. . .] We were even more vulnerable as a larger group, but, on the other hand, we gained three rifles and a few revolvers. [. . .] Near a summit, I looked back and froze at the sight of a long thread of people stretching like a gigantic snake. I knew that it was impossible not to be discovered eventually, now when they were searching for us."[42]

In deciding who should undertake the getaway from the camp with whom, often chance played a role by bringing various individuals together when they left the confines of the camp. Primarily, however, age, origin, and personal relationships influenced the decision-making. Many people tried to band together with those whom they already knew from the camp, and the former Red Army soldiers were especially quick to form groups. Older and physically less resilient people had a harder time finding acceptance into a small group, as did women and all those who had been deported to Sobibor from Western European countries. Because the latter lacked a command of the language and were unfamiliar with the area, they had to rely on offers from native Poles to join company with them. Thus, it is not surprising that a large proportion of the survivors consisted of young Polish men, many of whom were able to find their way around in the region.

Selma Wijnberg was the only Dutchwoman who survived the Sobibor camp and lived to see the end of the war. Her story shows that the postescape situation, even among former prisoners, sometimes was no guarantee of solidly united action; rather, they all fought for their own survival. When the revolt broke out, Wijnberg joined her Polish lover, Chaim Engel, and fled into the forest along with several Polish Jews. Her presence obviously put the group at risk, as she spoke no Polish and therefore could be unequivocally associated with the camp by search parties. Later, she reported, "We ran and came across a group of Polish Jews. Chaim said to them, 'Can we stay together?' One member of the group had a gun and wanted to shoot Chaim because he was afraid of me, since I didn't speak any Polish. You know, they were afraid. I jumped in front of

Chaim, and he didn't shoot. We went on our way, the two of us, and left the group alone."[43]

But language skills and local knowledge, even for Polish Jews, were no guarantee that the fugitives would not lose their bearings during the escape. Mordechai Goldfarb describes how his group went astray on the journey: "We ran all night long, over some railroad tracks, and when we slowed our pace toward morning—because we thought we were already far away from the camp—we suddenly heard geese cackling! We had run in a circle all night and found ourselves near the damned place again."[44]

Ursula Stern,[45] the only German survivor of Sobibor, had a similar experience. Along with her friend Cathi Gökkes,[46] a Dutch Jew, she had teamed up with Eda Waldman (née Fiszer),[47] a native of Poland. Together, the three women ran "for two or three days" until they were forced to realize: "We had run in a circle and were still in the vicinity of the camp."[48] Despite the demotivating effect of this experience, they tried again. Like many others, they wanted to contact the local Jewish partisan units. Eventually, several days later, they managed to do so in an unexpected way: "Eda and I wanted to beg for food in a Polish village. A man in a black uniform with black boots approached us. Eda said, he's sure to be a Nazi. But we couldn't run away, because he had already seen us. We told him we had run away from a Polish labor camp. Eda had money. He immediately understood that we were from Sobibor. [. . .] He hid us in a little wooded area. [. . .] There was a great deal of antisemitism in Poland but this man came back to us with food, etc. He knew the Germans, including Frenzel, very well. He had often eaten together with Frenzel in the café. We were quite close to the camp, and all day long we heard the Germans' hysterical shouts coming from the camp. Toward evening, a Polish boy between the ages of 10 and 12 came; he told us the man was sitting in the tavern and drinking. In this state, the boy said, he might talk [about us]. The boy guided us all night until we reached a place deep in the forest. He said the partisans often came there. [. . .] Then, 2 or 3 days later, we met with the Jewish partisans."[49]

The women were accepted into the unit and fought there until the end of June 1944, when the Red Army liberated the area. While with the partisans, Eda Waldman came across her friend Icchak Lichtman again, whom she knew from Sobibor and who, in another small group, had also found the way to the partisans. Together, the couple spent the remaining months before liberation in the partisan unit, married shortly after the war ended, and eventually immigrated to Israel.

Icchak and Eda Lichtman were not the only twosome who met in the camp and began a future together after the war. Abraham Margulies and Hela Felenbaum (later Weiss) also met again and became a couple. Selma Wijnberg and Chaim Engel, too, stayed together after they had survived the months between the escape from the camp and the liberation by sharing a hiding place. Both had wandered, lost, through the area around Sobibor for ten days at first. Then, near the small town of Chełm, approximately thirty miles from Sobibor, they met a peasant couple who agreed to hide them in their hayloft in exchange for payment. There the two fugitives spent several months, during which Wijnberg—by that time pregnant—recorded her concerns in a diary.[50] In the dark hayloft, where there was not even room enough to stand, they both had to deal with the shortage of food, the loneliness, dirt, cold, and the constant fear of being discovered. Wijnberg and Engel knew, as did all the others who had survived the first few days after the uprising and continued to fight for their survival during the following weeks, how quickly this struggle could come to an end. Ursula Stern reported after the war that her friend Cathi Gökkes, who had spent time with the partisan unit along with her following the escape from Sobibor, was killed fighting the Germans on the day of liberation: "She was killed on the very last day, 10 minutes before liberation."[51]

Not only the German units but also Polish civilians presented a general threat. After the successful escape from the camp, the fugitives had no alternative but to contact the inhabitants of the region and ask for food, clothing, or a place to hide. To obtain the vitally necessary support, they had to reveal their identity in one way or another and, by doing so, risk being attacked or betrayed. Like Moshe Bachir and Thomas Blatt, many others with advance knowledge of the plans for revolt in Sobibor were well provided with valuables for the period in the underground. However, that also made them desirable targets for gangs of criminals or for ordinary Polish citizens who took advantage of the runaways' helpless situation. Not infrequently, the virulent antisemitism of the Polish population also played a role here. In addition, in the course of their hunt for the fugitives, the Germans held out the prospect of a high reward for those who handed over captured Jews to them—for the civilian population, marked by four years of war and German occupation, this incentive is not to be underestimated.

All the survivors' accounts of the period immediately after the successful escape from the death camp contain stories of the solidarity and the support they experienced, as well as of the verbal and physical attacks. To survive for any length of time outside the camp, the fugitives had to rely on help from numerous people who were mostly unknown to them and on the silence of these same people who thus would also put themselves and their families in danger. The diverse experiences of those who escaped from Sobibor show how random, and how dependent on coincidence, survival was under these circumstances.

As a small boy, one local resident saw forestry workers in Zbereże, only a few miles from Sobibor, reveal to the Germans the hiding place of six Jews who had fled from the camp. As a result, the captured fugitives were shot in the forest by the Customs Border Guards, together with two other Jews who until then had been forced to work in the village for members of the local German border guards post.[52] In contrast, there is the experience of Selma Wijnberg and Chaim Engel, who found shelter with a Polish family, who—admittedly, in exchange for payment but also directly risking their own lives—kept them hidden in their barn for more than eight months, until the Red Army liberated the region.

After Liberation

Not even the taking of the region by the Red Army in June 1944 put an end to the perilous situation in which the escapees found themselves. Widespread antisemitism continued to have an effect among the Polish population. The few Jews who returned to the villages and cities were frequently subject to aggression and attacks. Leon Felhendler, who had been in hiding until liberation, sheltered by peasants near his hometown of Żółkiewka, ultimately went to Lublin, where he first shared an apartment at 4 Kowalska Street with a few other survivors of Sobibor.[53] In November 1944, four months after the liberation of the city, the Jewish survivor Hersz Blank was killed there in an attack by a group of Poles.[54] Shortly thereafter, Felhendler and his wife moved into an apartment on Złota Street in the historic part of Lublin, where he was shot in early April 1945, also in an attack motivated by antisemitism.[55] Besides Felhendler and Blank, at least two other Sobibor survivors—Aron Licht and Josef Kopp—were murdered after the liberation of the region. Many survivors later remembered violent assaults to which they themselves were exposed. They also had learned that some of their fellow sufferers, after they had endured the time in the camp and the lengthy flight and period in hiding, were killed at a time when they had believed themselves already in safety.[56]

During the first days after liberation, the survivors alternated between despair and euphoria. After the months they had spent in concealment, sometimes under hair-raising conditions, many could scarcely comprehend that the end of the war had come and they could move about freely again. Selma Wijnberg, too, had difficulty grasping her regained freedom in the first days. In her diary, she wrote, "It's unbelievable! We really are free and I am really writing outside!! Is it true? We continuously have to tell ourselves that it is really true. We are human beings again and we can talk to other people! Chaim talked this morning with two Russians and he thanked them for giving us our freedom back."[57]

The few survivors, however, now faced the difficult task of finding their bearings in the extremely chaotic postwar situation and reorganizing their lives. For many, that included the search for family members and friends, in the hope that they were still alive. The desperate search was to take years, sometimes even decades. Besides the need to regulate their own lives and make plans for a future in freedom, however, the desire to participate in the fight against the retreating German troops continued to play a role for some. While some survivors, such as the Lichtman couple, Ursula Stern, and Cathi Gökkes, had successfully joined a partisan unit during the occupation period, others had to wait until the Red Army had liberated the region to continue their fight against the Germans. A few days after the Soviet troops arrived, Semion Rozenfeld, who, together with Dov Freiberg, had survived the months after the escape from Sobibor in various hiding places, went to the Red Army's temporary base in Chełm to volunteer for military service. Shortly thereafter, he headed westward with the unit assigned to him and eventually took part in the storming of Berlin, the capital of the Reich.[58]

The memory of the time in Sobibor never released its hold on the survivors. For many, it was hardly possible to overcome the unimaginable psychological and physical harm inflicted upon them and undertake a new beginning. After the war, they had to find a way of dealing with the fact that their former world no longer existed and most of their relatives and friends were no longer alive. Frequently the survivors also were confronted with the fact that Poles were now living in the former homes of their families, and these Poles were unwilling to surrender the homes after the war. Antisemitism, partly latent, partly overt, reached a new peak in the wake of the conflicts over the distribution of housing and other property that had been owned by Jews, exposing the survivors to a dangerous threat. For this reason, almost all decided not to return to their hometowns again. Only the hope of finding other survivors brought a few back, briefly, immediately after the war's end.

Selma Engel, after the liberation of Poland, her marriage, and the birth of her child in liberated Lublin, at first decided to return with her husband, Chaim Engel, to her old hometown of Zwolle in the Netherlands to learn whether other family members had survived. But after her husband, a native Pole, was repeatedly exposed to racist hostility and was not permitted to remain in the country, the couple decided to immigrate to Israel. Others, too, opted for emigration, not infrequently influenced by fresh experiences of ostracism and antisemitism.

Some of the survivors settled in the United States, and others immigrated to Israel, Canada, Australia, or Latin America. Five Jewish Red Army soldiers who had been deported from Minsk to Sobibor returned to the Soviet Union after the war. Only one of the Polish survivors, Leon Cymiel of Chełm, who had successfully escaped from the camp before the revolt, is known to have lived in Poland after the war until his death in the 1990s.

The Survivors' Testimonies against the Perpetrators

Despite the emotional strain inherent in a renewed examination of the experiences in the camp, many survivors decided shortly after the war's end to confront their past once again, in order to testify against the perpetrators who were apprehended by law enforcement authorities and placed on trial. The prospect that at least a few of the tormentors would be sentenced for their actions was sufficient incentive for them to face the difficult task of reconstructing their own memories, a task carrying the intrinsic risk of a potential retraumatization.

In 1948, two survivors of Sobibor, Samuel Lerer and Ester Raab, were decisively involved in the capture of a former tormentor. After they had coincidentally recognized the former SS-Scharführer Erich Bauer on the street in Berlin's Kreuzberg neighborhood and brought about his arrest, they both testified against him in the subsequent criminal proceedings. It was the first trial of one of the German camp personnel. Bauer, who had been in charge of the gas chambers at Sobibor, was sentenced to death in May 1950. After the death penalty was abolished, the sentence was changed to lifelong imprisonment, and Bauer was released from prison in 1971.[59] Also in 1950, Hubert Gomerski and Johann Klier stood trial in Frankfurt am Main for their actions in Sobibor. Ultimately Gomerski was sentenced to life in prison, while Klier was acquitted of the charges by the Frankfurt judges.[60]

But it was not only coincidence, as in Bauer's case, that led the survivors to work toward a prosecution of their former tormentors. In the same year, Kurt Thomas, by now a resident of Pittsburgh, Pennsylvania, sent a letter to the office of the chief prosecutor (Oberstaatsanwaltschaft) in Frankfurt am Main, in which he emphasized his willingness to cooperate in the prosecution of the perpetrators from Sobibor. At the same time, he provided important information about individual perpetrators. The letter went unanswered, but over the course of the following decades, Thomas and other survivors repeatedly played an active role in the apprehension and prosecution of the perpetrators. When Yehuda Lerner, a Warsaw native living in Israel, was asked in the late 1950s to testify about his time in Sobibor, he declined at first, saying that he was "trying to forget what happened and not inclined to review the bad things from the

Nazi era again."[61] Only when the investigator in charge phoned him to say that it was a matter of testifying against Gustav Wagner, who had been arrested in Brazil not long before, did Lerner spontaneously consent: "No, really! When would you like to see me, and give me your address [. . .] I'd be willing to go, even tomorrow, to the place where he lives, to teach him a lesson, and not wait until he's brought to court."[62] Before his extradition to Germany could be granted, Wagner was found dead in São Paulo, and the exact circumstances of his death were never fully explained.[63]

The biggest Sobibor trial, involving twelve German camp personnel, began in September 1965 in the regional court (Landgericht) in Hagen. It continued for sixteen months. More than twenty survivors traveled to Germany for the main trial, and twenty others were interrogated elsewhere for the proceedings. Providing many details, they described the horrible daily routine in the camp and testified against their former tormentors. Their information, however, reached the German public only to a very limited extent. Interest in the Nazi trials had already decreased perceptibly during the Frankfurt Auschwitz trials, which began in 1964, and the proceedings in Hagen aroused little attention, as the crimes of Operation Reinhard had found little place in the minds of the German public. At the end of the proceedings, only Karl Frenzel received a life sentence; of the other defendants, half were acquitted and the rest were given relatively light sentences of three to eight years.[64]

Hubert Gomerski's defense attorneys later succeeded in having his 1950 sentence changed to a 15-year prison term. He was released from prison in 1972, for the time being. When he was found incompetent to stand trial in further appeal proceedings, he left the courtroom as a free man in 1983. Three years later, he was awarded compensation for wrongful imprisonment in the amount of DM 63,632.[65]

Karl Frenzel managed to obtain a new trial, in which he was again sentenced to life imprisonment, but the sentence was never imposed because of his "poor state of health," and he was released.[66] In 1983, it was still Thomas Blatt's mission in life to contribute to the sentencing of the perpetrators and to inform the public about the history of Sobibor. On the periphery of the trial, he met and engaged in a discussion with Karl Frenzel that served as the basis for an article in Stern magazine, "Meeting with a Murderer" ("Begegnung mit einem Mörder").[67]

Admittedly, the German prosecuting authorities investigated the perpetrators of Operation Reinhard, including the defendants in the Sobibor case, more thoroughly than other Nazi criminals. Of fifty-five Germans deployed in Sobibor and known by name, sixteen stood trial between 1950 and 1981, in four proceedings in total. Nonetheless, the sentences imposed were incommensurate with the enormous crimes, and most survivors reacted with corresponding disappointment to the judges' decision.[68]

In the years 2009–2011, the trial of the Trawniki John Demjanjuk in Munich attracted international attention in this context for the last time. More than sixty-five years after the revolt in Sobibor, survivors such as Thomas Blatt, Philip Bialowitz, and Jules Schelvis made the history of the death camp known to a wider public through their testimonies. The trial of the native Ukrainian differed from the previous proceedings in one major point: for the first time, the judges considered mere presence in a death camp to be sufficient proof of shared responsibility for the crimes committed on-site, without requiring proof of individual participation in the criminal acts as well.[69]

This new legal interpretation would have led to different verdicts with harsher sentences in the earlier trials of the German camp personnel. Almost all the defendants in earlier proceedings availed themselves of the same defense strategy in court: in marked contrast to their former abundance of power and astonishing scope of action, they pretended to have been insignificant underlings, mere recipients of orders, who allegedly felt ill at ease in the camp and in their official positions and abstained from acts of violence of their own. Only the testimonies of the survivors made it possible nonetheless to prove individual participation in some instances.

Closing of the Sobibor Death Camp and Commemoration at the Site

Over the decades, the site of the former death camp has changed a great deal. Physical vestiges providing "evidence" of the crimes committed in the years 1942–1943 have vanished almost entirely. After the revolt of October 14, 1943, Heinrich Himmler decided to close and demolish the camp forthwith. The previous commandant of Belzec, Gottlieb Hering, was tasked with the dismantling process. Over the course of the following month, individual buildings in Camp I and all of Camp II were torn down; the gas chambers were blown up and the remnants of the structures were removed.[70] The burning of corpses was concluded, and the camp grounds were leveled and some areas converted into forest. Jewish prisoners from Treblinka were forced to carry out the work of dismantling the camp. After approximately one month, on November 23, 1943, they were shot on the camp grounds. Only the front compound was temporarily revamped. Shortly afterward, it was handed over to the Polish Construction Service in the General Government (*Polnischer Baudienst im Generalgouvernement*), which used it to house Polish laborers who were required to work for the German occupiers.

After the liberation of the region by the Red Army in July 1944, the site went largely ignored in official quarters. Only in the first few months resettled Ukrainians were housed in the still-existing buildings of the front camp. Then these structures passed into private hands, and the forested terrain was handed over to the forestry authorities and left to itself.

The state-run "Chief Commission for the Investigation of German War Crimes in Poland" (Główna Komisja Badania Zbrodni Niemieckich w Polsce), which conducted a short on-site visit as early as 1945 to throw light on the criminal offences, found an area that had been unsystematically and untidily searched. The remnants of human bones lay on the surface of the ground, and deep trenches had been excavated.[71] On September 26, 1950, members of the Voivodeship Committee of the Jews in Lublin reported that they had seen "excavated graves" at the site, "around which human remains are strewn." They had been told, they said, that "scavengers [had] searched for gold teeth" there.[72] For many years to come, residents of the area continued to open the mass graves, digging deep into the ground and searching through the mix of soil and ashes, looking for objects of value. Allegedly, on occasion as many as one hundred grave robbers at the same time divided the area into "claims."[73] In 1960, the prosecutor's office in Lublin initiated public proceedings against four "cemetery hyenas"[74] in order to deter copycats. Several grave robbers had been caught by the militia during the current year,[75] but actual convictions were obtained in only a few cases.

Jewish survivors, too, inevitably learned of the conditions at the former death camp. Leon Felhendler visited the grounds several times before his murder in April 1945. While in hiding during the months after his escape, he had conceived a different idea of what would become of the scene of the crimes after liberation. What he now saw in Sobibor filled him with rage and pain: "I can't reconcile myself to the fact that no one is interested in erecting a monument here, putting up a fence."[76]

In fact, it was a long time before an appropriate commemoration took place at the site. Not until 1960, sixteen years after the war's end, was there a plaque with information about the mass graves on the former camp grounds, but the area continued to be left unsupervised. A debate about the future of the site began but very slowly and gradually. On June 27, 1965, government representatives officially dedicated the first monument, which had been designed by Mieczysław Welter. It consisted of various elements—a symbolic mound of ashes at the site of the mass graves, a block of stone marking the site of the gas chamber, and a sculpture depicting a grieving mother with her child in her arms. The information on a board at the entrance to the memorial site, however, did not correspond to the historical facts. There was no mention of the fact that the camp had been built exclusively for the purpose of murdering Jews.[77] Instead, the text read as follows: "In this camp, 250,000 Soviet prisoners of war, Jews, Poles, and Gypsies were murdered."[78] It was owing to the efforts of the Sobibor survivor Thomas Blatt that this text was changed in 1993.[79]

Responsibility for the grounds of the memorial site continued to rest with the local forestry authorities during the 1960s. They decided in 1974, after the number of visitors from foreign countries had increased, to create a parking lot and build a wooden structure with a space that invited people to pause and spend some time there. Two rooms were to offer the possibility of an overnight stay.[80]

The newly built wooden house was never used as a place for learning and commemoration, however. It served first as a training center for the forestry authorities and later as a kindergarten with a playground. Not until 1993, when the memorial site became affiliated with the district museum in the neighboring town of Włodawa, was a museum established in the little building. In 2003, at the initiative of the Bildungswerk Stanisław Hantz and the Sobibór Memorial Site, the Trail of Memory project was launched.[81] Today, more than three hundred memorial stones on the grounds of the memorial site serve as reminders of the individual fates of Jews from Poland, Czechoslovakia, Germany, France, and the Netherlands who were murdered in Sobibor.

Until 2012, the memorial site continued to be a branch of the district museum. Then, as a branch of the Majdanek State Museum, it became a state-operated memorial site, and the planning for a redevelopment of the grounds began. In 2014, the area was expanded to a size of almost sixty-two acres. The former housing compound of the German SS guards, with the only building still standing from the camp period, the "Green House," and parts of former Camp I—the camp area for the Jewish prisoners, where they boldly launched their revolt on October 14, 1943—remained privately owned, however.

An international commission, with Poland, Israel, the Netherlands, and Slovakia as sponsoring partners, held a competition to choose a design for the memorial complex. The winner was named in July 2013. In December 2018, the area of the mass graves was covered with white stones. Protected in this way, it can no longer be entered by the public. A new museum building was constructed. Nonetheless, questions about the future of the Sobibor memorial site and the neighboring land remain unresolved. Since 2017, three places in the forest have been discovered, quite near the former camp grounds, where ashes and other human remains are located. It stands to reason that these are spots where, after the war, grave robbers searched through the contents of the mass graves and the ashes, looking for valuables. How these and other finds are to be dealt with must be determined by future discussion about the Sobibór memorial site.

The place where the German perpetrators were interred after the revolt is no longer in existence today. The following section documents the photos sent to Henriette Niemann after the events, showing the German military cemetery and the burial of the SS men in Chełm.

Notes

1. Interview by Anne Lepper with Semion Rozenfeld, November 23, 2017 (all statements in this chapter translated from the German edition of this book). See also Freiberg, *Survive*, p. 293; statement of Jehuda Lerner, December 1, 1959, NIOD, 804/17.

2. Statement of Alexander Petscherskii, July 17, 1974, NIOD, 804/19.

3. Statement of Abraham Margulies, November 15, 1965, LNW, Q 234/4419; joint statement of Eda and Itzaak Lichtman, Symcha Bialo-wicz, Abraham Margulies, Dov Freiberg, and Jakub Biskubicz, September 1963, LNW, Q 234/4570.

4. Statement of Moshe Bachir, January 28, 1985, NIOD, 804/13. See also Bem, *Sobibor*, p. 239, and Arad, *Belzec*, pp. 188–190.

5. Statement of Moshe Bachir, January 28, 1985, NIOD, 804/13.

6. Mission report, Cholm Gendarmerie platoon, January 7, 1943, NIOD, 804/23.

7. Statement of Hersz Cukiermann, September 17, 1944, LNW, Q 234/8234; similarly, interrogation of Bolender, December 3, 1963, LNW, Q 234/4320.

8. Statement of Salomon Podchlebnik, October 10, 1965, LNW, Q 234/442. Also among those who survived the war were Adam Wang, Chaim Korenfeld, and Simon Honigmann. Josef Kopp, who had es-caped with Podchlebnik, was murdered in Poland shortly after the war ended.

9. Schelvis, *Sobibór*, p. 163.

10. Joint statement of Lichtman, Bialowitz, et al., September 1963, LNW, Q 234/457.

11. Cited in Bruder, *Helden*, p. 76.

12. See, for example, statement of Simcha Bialowitz, October 26, 1965, LNW, Q 234/4466.

13. Niemann wrote on August 20 that his transfer to Trieste was scheduled to take place in six weeks (letter from Johann Niemann to Henriette Niemann, August 20, 1943, USHMMA, Acc 2020.8.1.; see app. 2 fig. 2.1).

14. Statement of Adam Wang, June 11, 1974, HHW, 461-36346/36.

15. Statement of Leon Felhendler, 1944, LNW, Q 234/4432. Also see statement of Philip Bialowitz, October 25, 1965, LNW, Q 234/4623.

16. Bialowitz, *Promise*, pp. 102–104; Bem, *Sobibor*, p. 192, pp. 248–250; Arad, *Belzec*, p. 304.

17. See, for example, the statement of Alexander Petscherskii, July 17, 1974, LNW, Q243/4478; Petscherskii, *Bericht*; Wewryk, *Sobibor*, pp. 77–79; Freiberg, *Survive*, pp. 286–288.

18. In addition to the Jews in Camp I, Schelvis, *Sobibór*, p. 197, esti-mates the number of members of the Sonderkommando in the killing sector in Camp III on the day of the uprising at fifty, and in the new Camp IV sector at sixty. As there was no contact between these two sectors, and because no prisoner from the killing sector or Camp IV

survived the uprising, it is impossible to determine with any certainty, based on the state of current research, how many prisoners there were in total in the camp.

19. See statement of Chaim Engel, July 19, 1945, LNW, Q 234/4452.

20. Blatt, *Ashes*, p. 146 ff.

21. Selma Engel cited in Markham Walsh, *Dancing through Dark-ness*, p. 87 and p. 116.

22. Statement of Moshe Bachir, January 29, 1985, NIOD, 804/13.

23. Cited in Bruder, *Helden*, p. 39; cf. Petscherskii, *Bericht*, p. 81 and p. 96. In his account, Pecherskii also claims that other prisoners had seen Luka escape during the revolt. After that, her trace is lost, however. Presumably, the young woman either died in the vicinity of the camp during the revolt or was caught and murdered in the course of her subsequent flight.

24. See, for example, Freiberg, *Survive*, p. 295.

25. Blatt, *Sobibor*, pp. 118–120.

26. Wewryk, *Sobibor*, p. 86.

27. Ibid., pp. 100–101.

28. At first nine SS men were believed to be dead, one wounded, and one, SS-Unterscharführer Josef Wolf, missing. See NIOD, 804/1; also Blatt, *Sobibor*, p. 121.

29. Schelvis, *Sobibór*, p. 200.

30. Interrogation of August Preyssl, May 3, 1962, LNW, Q234/4291.

31. Ibid.

32. On the burial, see also the interrogation of Erich Bauer, Novem-ber 30, 1965, NIOD, 804/46.

33. Letter from Dietrich Allers to Henriette Niemann, October 21, 1943, USHMMA, Acc 2020.8.1 (see app. 2 fig. 2.2).

34. Letter from Local Command (Ortskommandantur; OK) Cholm to Henriette Niemann, July 1, 1944, USHMMA, Acc 2020.8.1.

35. Thus far, two photos of the interment are known that undoubt-edly come from the same series (published in Schelvis, *Sobibór*, app. XL).

36. The exact number can no longer be determined. The list of forty-seven names in Schelvis, *Sobibór*, pp. 273 ff., is certainly incom-plete. A list from the investigation proceedings against Frenzel suggests that there were other survivors, who had died in the meantime, how-ever, or were unwilling to testify (file note, December 5, 1983, LNW, Q243/4451). Bem, *Sobibor*, p. 298, lists 93 names.

37. Situation report Bug section, October 25, 1943, NIOD, 804/1.

38. Statement of Dov Freiberg, July 25, 1945, LNW, Q234/4573.

39. See in detail Bruder, "Partisanenkampf."

40. In the statements of the survivors about attacks by Polish partisans, the designation of the units they encountered in the forests is often inexact. Frequently they are referred to as *Armia Krajowa* (Home Army), but they may also have been ordinary partisan bands.

41. Statement of Dov Freiberg, July 25, 1945, LNW, Q234/4573.

42. Blatt, *Ashes*, p. 155 ff.

43. Interview with Selma Engel, July 16, 1990, USHMMA, RG-50.030.0067.

44. Statement of Mordechai Goldfarb, January 29, 1962, LNW, Q234/4472.

45. Later she took the name Ilona Safran.

46. Called "Käthi," see Bruder, *Helden*, p. 145.

47. In the statements called Eda or Ada, later Ada Lichtman.

48. Statement of Ursula Stern, November 8, 1965, LNW, Q234/4623.

49. Ibid.

50. See Selma Wijnberg diary, 1943–1944, USHMMA, Acc 1999.A.0201 (Selma Engel papers).

51. Statement of Ursula Stern, November 8, 1965, LNW, Q234/4623, and statement of Selma Engel, August 29, 1946, LNW, Q234/4268. Selma Engel already knew Cathi ("Käthi") Gökkes and Ursula Stern from the camp and met the latter in Lublin after the liberation.

52. Interview with Jan Doliński, April 30, 2011, Marek Bem collection, Centrum Archiwistyki Społecznej Warsaw.

53. Many survivors tried after liberation to reach the cities as soon as possible, as the atmosphere in smaller towns and villages continued to be dangerous for them, and the circumstances compelled them to fear being discovered, threatened, and murdered. See Hänschen, *Izbica*, pp. 441–453.

54. Blank, like others living in the apartment, was from Izbica but presumably had not been in Sobibor; rather, he had survived the war in a different place. Some accounts, however, include Blank, too, among the Sobibor survivors. The story based on the description by Thomas Blatt is found in Krall, *Tanz auf fremder Hochzeit*, pp. 104–105; on this incident and on the anti-Jewish violence in the Lublin region see also Kopciowski, "Anti-Jewish Incidents."

55. See Kopciowski, *Felhendler*. Before his murder, Felhendler testified in Lublin about his time in Sobibor. His statement was subsequently used in the trials of the perpetrators (see statement of Felhendler, 1944, LNW, Q234/4432).

56. Statement of Esther Raab, Hagen, October 10, 1977, LNW, Q234/4572. See also Freiberg, *Survive*, p. 419.

57. Cited in Markham Walsh, *Dancing through Darkness*, p. 141. For the original handwritten (Dutch) quote see Selma Wijnberg's diary, USHMMA, Acc 1999.A.0201.

58. See, for example, Freiberg, *Survive*, pp. 397–399.

59. Berger, *Experten*, p. 370.

60. Verdict by Frankfurt jury court (Schwurgericht), October 28, 1950, HHW, 461-36346-4.

61. Cited from Tuwia Friedman (Israeli investigator), in Bruder, *Helden*, p. 90.

62. Ibid., p. 91.

63. See Stahl, *Nazi-Jagd*, pp. 263–271. The theory of Wagner's lawyer that he had taken his own life was repeatedly called into question, in part because the former SS man was found with stab wounds to his torso.

64. See list in Berger, *Experten*, pp. 366–367. Kurt Bolender committed suicide during confinement.

65. Berger, *Experten*, p. 370. Gomerski died in 1999.

66. Frenzel was released from prison in 1982 and died in 1996.

67. "Begegnung mit einem Mörder," in: *Der Stern*, 13/1984.

68. The trial of Franz Stangl, the first commandant of Sobibor, must also be included. The Treblinka death camp was indeed at the center of the proceedings, but Stangl's actions in Sobibor also played a part in his sentencing to life imprisonment. Besides the eleven SS men killed in the uprising in Sobibor, other German camp personnel, such as the camp commandant, Franz Reichleitner, and Herbert Floß, had lost their lives before the end of the war (Berger, *Experten*, pp. 371–376).

69. On the trial see Douglas, *Demjanjuk*; Wefing, *Fall Demjanjuk*; Benz, *Henkersknecht*.

70. The foundations were laid bare again in the context of the renovation of the memorial complex in 2015.

71. Also the journalist Mordechaj Canin in his report on a visit to the grounds in 1945; see Canin, *Ruiny*, pp. 459–466.

72. Wojewodzki Komitet Żydow w Lublinie do Centralnego Komitetu Żydow w Polsce [Voivodeship Committee of Jews in Lublin to the Central Committee of Jews in Poland], September 26, 1950, ŻIH, 355/38, 22.1.9.

73. See Utz, "Sobibor nach den Deutschen," p. 294.

74. *"Hieny cmentarne"*—"cemetery hyenas" (burial-ground scavengers) is the Polish term for grave robbers at sites associated with the Holocaust.

75. Report of *Rada Ochrony Pomników Walk i Męczeństwa*, November 8, 1960, ROPWiM, Sign. 1/100. For the evidence photos see APL, Gruppe 988 (Lublin Voivodeship court), Sig. 4/711 (IVk 90/60). An inspection by the Voivodeship in May 1962 revealed that grave robbery was still taking place: "During our visit we noticed, near the former crematorium, traces indicating that approximately 10 holes had been dug by 'cemetery hyenas.'" A member of the militia who was present reported that people looking for gold came even from Lublin, fifty miles away. Report by Stefan Guirard and Jozef Kowalik, May 7, 1962, ROPWiM, Sign. 52/6, pp. 2–6.

76. Based on the report of the wife of Leon Felhendler, Ester Muterperel, December 1945; see Kopciowski and Kuwałek, "Relacja żony Leona Feldhendlera."

77. It remains unclear whether and how many Roma and Sinti were among the victims.

78. Complete text: "At this place, a Nazi killing center existed from May 1942 to October 1943. In this camp, 250,000 Soviet prisoners of war, Jews, Poles, and Gypsies were murdered. On October 14, 1943, an armed uprising broke out in the camp. After fighting the Nazi guards, several hundred prisoners escaped."

79. Kuwałek, *Miejsca pamięci*, p. 26. Over the years, plaques in the various languages were put up. In the course of the redevelopment of the Sobibor memorial site, the wall was torn down in 2014. The mound of ashes was covered with stones in 2017, and since 2014 the statue has stood at a remote spot. After construction work is complete, it is to be moved to the place dedicated to the uprising.

80. See report by Jerzy Przymanowski, December 12, 1974, ROPWiM, Sign. 52/6.

81. Now a joint project in partnership with the Dutch foundation Stichting Sobibor, which is being continued in the redesigned memorial complex.

Photos of the Burial of the SS Men Killed in the Revolt and Niemann's Grave

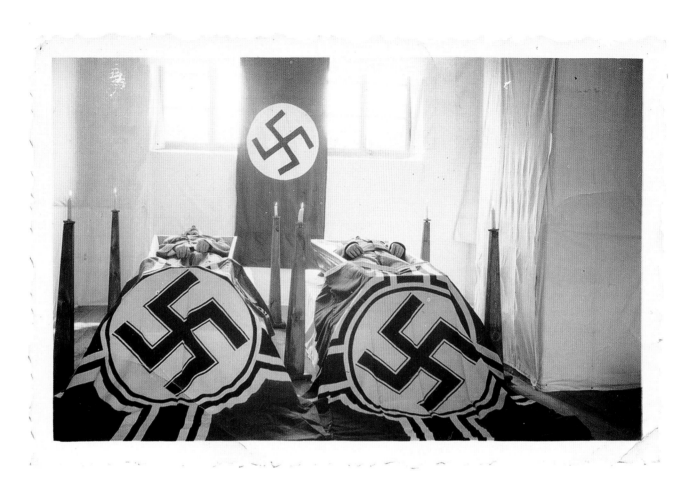

Figure 9.1. Viewing room at the German military cemetery in Chełm, October 18, 1943. The marking "Niemann" on the back of the print suggests that his body is in the coffin on the right. This photo and the thirteen following ones show scenes from the burial ceremony and Niemann's grave. The copies were sent to the widow, Henriette Niemann.

Figure 9.2. SS men carry wreaths and the coffin of a man killed in the Sobibor revolt out of the viewing room. On the left and right, Trawnikis form a guard of honor.

Figure 9.3. SS soldiers, presumably stationed locally in Chełm, carry coffins of the Germans killed in the Sobibor revolt to the burial ground.

Figure 9.4. Niemann's coffin. The words "Ustuf [Untersturmführer] Johann Niemann" are apparent on the piece of paper attached to the coffin.

Figure 9.5. Members of the Waffen-SS, Trawnikis, and German members of the Sobibor camp SS carry wreaths to the caskets. Fourth from right, SS-Scharführer Karl Richter; the ninth man is Zugwachmann Alexander Kaiser; at the rear, on the left, probably SS-Unterscharführer Ernst Zierke.

Figure 9.6. The 11 coffins of the Germans killed in the revolt are arranged in three rows. At the center front is Niemann's coffin.

Figure 9.7. Germans and Trawnikis at the burial ceremony for the Germans killed in the Sobibor revolt. In the foreground on the right is SS-Obersturmführer Gottlieb Hering, the previous commandant of the Belzec death camp. Behind him on the left, with tinted glasses, is SS-Hauptsturmführer Ernst Lerch, the adjutant of the Lublin SS and police leader; next to him, in SA uniforms, Werner Blankenburg and Dietrich Allers. Next to them on the left, wearing overcoats, are SS-Unterscharführer Willi Wendland, Zugwachmann Alexander Kaiser, SS-Unterscharführer Ernst Zierke, and SS-Unterscharführer Franz Wolf.

Figure 9.8. The attendees at the ceremony, giving the Nazi salute. In front, second from the right, SS-Untersturmführer Gottfried Schwarz, Niemann's "comrade" from the T4 program and the Belzec camp. Behind him on the left is Lerch, next to Blankenburg, Allers, and Hering.

Figure 9.9. In the foreground, Gottlieb Hering with a wreath, facing the caskets. On his left is SS-Scharführer Karl Richter, who was in charge of the staff club in Sobibor. On the right, presumably the men of a Waffen-SS honor guard from Chełm.

Figure 9.10. Werner Blankenburg, head of Office II at the Chancellery of the Führer, holding a wreath and facing the coffins. Behind him on the left, Hering.

Figure 9.11. Giving the Nazi salute, Blankenburg places a wreath at the coffins of the Germans. Following this, the SA-Oberführer also delivered the eulogy.

Figure 9.12. Standing in front of the coffins of the Germans who were killed are (*from left to right*) Gottlieb Hering, Werner Blankenburg, Dietrich Allers, and Ernst Lerch. Blankenburg, the only one not giving the Nazi salute in this situation, was possibly just completing his eulogy. After the ceremony, he traveled to Sobibor with Allers to conduct an on-site inspection. Both men had already visited the extermination camp several times, on previous occasions.

Figure 9.13. The burial ground in Chełm, where Niemann also was buried, in the summer of 1944. At Henriette Niemann's request, the local command in Cholm sent her this photo and the following one of the military cemetery on July 1, 1944.

Figure 9.14. Niemann's grave in the summer of 1944, with this inscription on the cross: "SS Ustuf. Johann Niemann, Sobibor Special Unit [*Sonderkommando*], born August 4, 1913, in Völlen, Leer District, East Frisia, died October 14, 1943, in Sobibor." On the right is the grave cross of an SS-Oberscharführer also killed during the revolt.

10

Henriette Niemann

Wife and Mother, Confidante and Profiteer

ANNE LEPPER AND MARTIN CÜPPERS

A look at the photos in the Niemann collection reveals that Henriette, Johann Niemann's wife, is pictured with unexpected frequency: unexpected because her presence in photographs is not limited to the private context of the family in Völlen but extends also to Johann Niemann's deployment sites. Henriette Niemann's repeated willingness to place herself, at least in geographical terms, in the immediate vicinity of her husband's criminal activities raises questions about her character and her own life. Particularly relevant here is the fact that only her decision to preserve her late husband's effects over the decades made it possible to present the collection of photos and documents to the public today.

Studies on wives of Nazi perpetrators remain relatively rare to this day. Although several studies on the broader role of women in the Nazi state have now been published, they justifiably focus on the issue of their direct involvement in perpetration, while wives of perpetrators usually are only a marginal topic in the research.[1] A few works are devoted to examining the role of spouses or partners in the Nazi system and in the individual subjective and emotional world of specific perpetrators. Especially noteworthy in this connection is the groundbreaking work of Gudrun Schwarz, who for the

first time demonstrated in the late 1990s that the systematic crimes arising from and sustained by Nazi society can be truly understood only with due consideration of all those who contributed to them—an "ensemble of women and men."[2] Several works give attention also to individual wives of high-ranking Nazi perpetrators, in order to shed light on these women's role and significance in the context of their husbands' actions.[3] The inadequate body of source material, however, often frustrates attempts at in-depth analysis or compels researchers to refer to the surviving ego-documents of the husbands.

Precisely for that reason, the Niemann collection must be regarded as unique. Numerous sources with direct reference to Henriette Niemann and her role as a de facto single mother with responsibility for managing a farm, on the one hand, and as the wife of an SS man highly involved in the Nazis' mass crimes, on the other hand, make it seem worthwhile to view her as an independent person and, in so doing, to present her life history before, during, and after her marriage to Johann Niemann. In the process, we will focus on pursuing questions of her personal development and her role as a possible confidante and accomplice. Furthermore, some surviving documents permit conclusions about her life after 1945 and thus grant us the altogether rare opportunity to sketch a cohesive biographical portrait.

East Frisia

Henriette Frey, born in Völlen on June 27, 1921, was the second child of August Frey and his wife, Janna. Her only sister, Auguste, was five years older. The girls' parents had a small farming operation,[4] and in the 1920s and early 1930s, the family's life was characterized by a daily routine geared to the duties of farm life. Earlier, like millions of his contemporaries in Europe, the father had served as a young soldier in the First World War. Apparently deployed on the western front—as indicated by a postcard he sent home from France as late as April 1918—he returned to his East Frisian homeland after Germany's defeat.[5] His war experience and abiding ties to former comrades seem to have had a lasting effect on him, as his membership in the Kyffhäuser League, a right-wing conservative war veterans' association, suggests.[6]

The Kyffhäuser German Warriors' League (*Deutscher Reichskriegerbund Kyffhäuser*), still in existence today, is a coalition of veterans' groups with origins that go back to the late eighteenth century. It was established as a loosely organized league in 1900. Finally, in 1922, it became the only official umbrella organization of the military and veterans' associations; as such, it offered a platform for nationalist and antidemocratic ideas and expressions of loyalty to the German empire and its ruling political elite. During the First World War, the association had attempted to keep ideological differences among the soldiers at a low level, in the interests of a nonpartisan comradeship in the battlefield. But after Germany's defeat, perceived as a humiliation, and the Treaty of Versailles, it developed into a gathering point for supporters of antidemocratic and nationalistic ideologies.[7] In early May 1933, its president, General von Horn, openly committed to Adolf Hitler and thereby ensured the continued existence of the league within the Nazi system.[8]

August Frey was a Kyffhäuser member through the local veterans' association, which was firmly established in the region, and in which the ideological orientation of the umbrella organization was not necessarily shared. Among adult males in Völlen and the surrounding area, membership in the group was the rule rather than the exception. But because Frey personally made it a point to keep issues of *Parole-Buch,* the Kyffhäuser association's nationwide newspaper, there is reason to conjecture that nationalist ideas were already present in the family before January 30, 1933, and that the transfer of power to the National Socialists was more likely welcomed. At this time, the Freys' younger daughter, Henriette, had just turned eleven; thus, for all practical purposes, it was National Socialism, rather than the earlier influences of a democratic society, that shaped her entire political socialization. Even for a girl in remote East Frisia, life must have changed perceptibly under the Nazi dictatorship. In Völlen, as everywhere else in the Reich, the new holders of power probably reduced the influence of the Protestant church, still one of the determining factors in rural everyday life, while Nazi ideology also must have been accorded increasing importance in the schools.

In its beginnings, this transformation can be reconstructed with the aid of a little notebook in which the young girl started writing at the time of the Nazi takeover. She may have used it in school as well. On the first few pages, carefully numbered, are five Christmas carols; this suggests that it was started at some point during Advent.[9] The songs are followed by writings with different content dealing with Germany, its geographical expanse and history but no longer mentioning religion at all. One short note has to do with the "old Germanic peoples," whom the schoolgirl described in idealized terms: "Tall and strong, blue eyes, blond hair. Brave and bold."[10] Such attempts at writing, still childish, can hardly be evaluated as indications of solidifying National Socialist convictions on the part of Henriette Frey, however; rather, they are merely evidence of an obvious fundamental interest in geography and history and an apparent musical inclination. In early 1937, at the age of fifteen, she pursued that inclination outside school hours as well by joining Concordia, the choral society in Völlen.[11] One photo from the Niemann collection probably dates from this period. It shows the choir standing before a fully occupied auditorium beneath the gigantic motto, "Sing, my people!" A popular collection of songs by the Nazi author Heinrich Anacker had been published under that same title, *Singe, mein Volk!*, in 1935. Still, we cannot assess with any certainty the extent to which the body of song rehearsed and presented under the given banner influenced the young member of the chorus.

But diligence and conscientiousness, character traits already implied in the compositions in her little notebook, were also confirmed at her school-leaving ceremony, where she received special recognition for excellence. The event stuck in her memory; even years later, in recording her life history, Frey stated naively and at the same time with unmistakable pride that she was the only pupil to whom the teacher had "presented a picture" on account of her good scholastic achievements.[12] This side of her personality is also seen in her relationship with her parents. The surviving sources indicate a close relationship on an ongoing basis, in which conflicts surely existed but evidently were by no means decisive. As an adolescent, Henriette did not give priority to going her own way, as her sister Auguste unmistakably appears to have done. The elder sister had married early and left the farm, and as part of this step had been "equipped in full" by her parents, as stated in their will.[13] By contrast, the younger daughter worked to the best of her ability in the household and on the farm and thus showed herself to be far more engaged with her parents. Her successful completion of

primary school was followed by employment. She was forced to give up her job after only two years, however, after her mother, as she later wrote, had suffered a "misfortune." Whether this referred to an accident or a serious illness remains unclear, but after this event Janna Frey was scarcely able to work anymore.[14] This incident forced Henriette Frey in 1938 to return to her parents' farm, where she was to assume the role of her mother from then on.[15] For all practical purposes' this basic constellation remained virtually unchanged in the decades that followed.[16]

Marriage to an SS Man Entrusted with Government Secrets

As an adolescent, Henriette Frey had known her neighbor Johann Niemann, eight years older than she, for quite some time. Their parents' farms were barely more than a stone's throw apart, and thus the two must have frequently encountered each other in day-to-day life in the village. The point at which the neighborly relationship between the young people developed into a romantic one is not part of the historical record. What is certain is only that Henriette, still a minor, became pregnant by Johann Niemann around the end of 1938 or beginning of 1939. At that time, he was already working at the Sachsenhausen concentration camp as a member of the headquarters staff and was back home in Völlen only when on leave.

To avoid an illegitimate birth, the parents-to-be submitted a marriage application to the SS Race and Settlement Main Office (*SS-Rasse- und Siedlungshauptamt*) in the early summer of 1939. Both had to work through a time-consuming bureaucratic process, during the course of which their "racial" backgrounds and "genetic fitness" were examined for Himmler's SS. Both must have quickly realized that the procedures would take weeks, if not months, to complete. As in numerous other cases, it proved to be practically impossible to obtain some of the required certifications and verifications of ancestors long since deceased. The time pressure sensed by the expectant mother is evident in a letter that she wrote to the pastor in Völlen in July 1939. In it, she expressly asks the clergyman to have the remaining proofs of descent sent to her and closes with three exclamation points intended to emphasize the urgency of the matter.[17]

In contrast to many others wanting to get married, however, the young woman did not try to present herself as a model National Socialist in the life history she wrote for the SS evaluators. Instead, avoiding empty phrases, she chose to emphasize certain items from the Nazis' ideological repertoire: her diligence and her good scholastic achievements. In addition, the ideal of fulfillment of duty echoed in the conclusion of her essay. At the same time, however, Frey was well aware that National Socialism assigned a high value to this quality, and that the SS in particular promoted doing one's duty as a defining ideal. With a certain calculation and unusual pathos, when describing the necessity of taking care of her mother and her parents' farm—and her resulting decision to forego her own career development—she wrote, "And this duty of running our farm household still calls me every day."[18]

After several delays due to missing documents, the marriage was finally "given temporary approval" by the SS evaluators on September 21, 1939; the remaining documents still had to be obtained, however.[19] In the midst of this protracted process, on October 8, 1939, Henriette Frey gave birth to her first child, her son August. In the end, the young parents could not exchange their wedding vows at the civil registry office until December 26. Although Henriette Niemann continued to belong to the Protestant church, no church wedding took place because her husband, conforming to the typical practices of the SS, had left the church and was regarded thereafter as "believing in God" without belonging to a church (gottgläubig). The young couple,

in view of their shared peasant origin, were endowed with very modest financial means and had no cash assets at all. Early the following summer, they sought to obtain a marriage loan, intended to help newlyweds start a life together. The subsidy of RM (Reichsmark) 500, finally granted to the Niemanns only in June 1941, did not lead to the establishment of a home of their own, however.[20] Instead, the young mother continued to live on her parents' farm, where she took care of her invalid mother and kept the farming operation and the household going. When her husband, who otherwise was generally absent, had leave, he obviously stayed at the farm of his parents-in-law. Soon, however, his visits were made even more complicated by the long journeys needed to reach Völlen.

Before his marriage, Niemann, an SS noncommissioned officer, had already signed on to assist with the Nazi "euthanasia" program of systematic murder, and he was deployed in Grafeneck, in southern Germany, from early 1940 at the latest. His relatives too, lacking any deep knowledge of the precise circumstances, are likely to have welcomed the move as a promotion and sizeable career step. For Henriette Niemann, already familiar with her husband's absence from the time when he was working at the Sachsenhausen concentration camp, the new assignment probably brought no fundamental change. Only the physical distance between husband and wife had clearly increased again with the move to his new place of employment: Grafeneck Castle.

While Johann Niemann was going about his tasks at several T4 killing centers, the war brought changes even to the East Frisian provinces. Unexpectedly, the Freys and their daughter Henriette were required to house soldiers at the farm in the late summer of 1940. The men billeted there, members of a Wehrmacht engineer unit, were possibly intended for use as reserve troops for Hitler's planned landing operation in England. For a number of weeks, the soldiers waited in Völlen and the surrounding area for their deployment, until the military operation was abandoned and the Wehrmacht troops disappeared from the East Frisian village. Interestingly, the event left traces in Niemann's photo collection. One of the men seemed to have brought along a 35 mm camera, with which he photographed the women who provided the accommodations. Apart from the previous prints from the studio in Papenburg and an early vacation shot, these photos represent the first private photographic documentation in the family, and thus they differ quite materially from Niemann's photographic record from his circle of comrades. Tellingly, Niemann also pasted some of the prints into his first photo album and labeled individual images with comments such as "Billeting, 1940." His wife, Henriette, is seen in several of the photos, going blithely about her chores in her usual environment and laughing in an unstudied manner as she looks toward the amateur photographer's camera (see app. 1 fig. 1.23, bottom right; app. 1 fig. 1.24, bottom right; and app. 1 fig. 1.25, bottom left). The photographs show scenes from everyday life on the farm. The young woman is seen carrying two large water buckets with a yoke and hanging out the laundry in the yard. Months later, one of the soldiers wrote a heartfelt letter to the Frey family, thanking them at length for the friendly reception and the pleasant stay he and his "comrades" enjoyed.[21]

In the winter of 1940/41, Henriette Niemann escaped from her maternal duties and the daily farm routine to pay a short visit to her husband at his new deployment site in Bernburg, on the River Saale. Presumably this was the first time she was in direct proximity to the T4 killings in which her husband was involved. A photo from the Niemann collection shows the couple with some of Johann Niemann's colleagues strolling through the town and obviously in a jovial mood (see fig. 3.9). It is hardly conceivable that, during the visit, there was no mention of what was simultaneously taking place in the T4 killing center. From the winter of 1940/41 at the latest, therefore, Henriette Niemann probably was informed at least in part

about the nature of the "euthanasia" program and her husband's activities.

In addition, the mass crimes, which were officially subject to absolute secrecy, may also have come up for discussion on another occasion, at a time when the young woman met other colleagues of her husband. Shortly after Hitler had ordered the official termination of the extermination program in August 1941, a few participants had an opportunity to vacation once more at Haus Schoberstein, the T4 recreation facility in Austria's Salzkammergut region. The men went there at the invitation of the Chancellery of the Führer, which was in charge of both T4 and its "rest home." Henriette Niemann, as the spouse of one of the vacationers, was also allowed to travel to the facility, located in a charming lakeside setting on the Attersee. The couple's son, August, appears to have stayed at home with the family in Völlen. At this time, if not earlier, the mother became acquainted with at least one other wife of a T4 perpetrator: Danida Floß, who was married to Herbert Floß, a colleague of Niemann's from the T4 program. The two couples seem to have made friends during their first joint stay on the Attersee. Several photos and a postcard from Danida Floß to her parents serve as evidence of happy, carefree days spent together. In one of the photos, the wives and Herbert Floß stand side by side, close and visibly relaxed, during a walk, with an unbroken view of the Alps in the background. Johann Niemann, not seen in the image, may have taken the photo. In a postcard dated September 19, 1941, Danida Floß told her parents about wonderful days spent together in the mountains and the "aching muscles that followed" (see fig. 3.19).[22] The bond forged between the two couples at that time and the friendly relationship between the wives in particular persisted throughout the coming years and even survived the death of their husbands.

Finally, a few weeks after the return from the Salzkammergut, Niemann was transferred to Poland, where he was one of the first to begin work on Operation Reinhard. Meetings between Niemann and his wife undoubtedly became even less frequent as a result. Nine months after the Attersee vacation, the couple's second child, their daughter Johanne, was born in Völlen on May 25, 1942.[23] It is highly probable that the father experienced the event only from afar. Niemann quite likely set eyes on his daughter, not yet eighteen months old when he died, on only a few occasions. Despite all the sacrifice on the personal level, the career path Niemann was pursuing in the SS was surely appreciated by the Frey family. The income of their son-in-law increased yet again upon his transfer to Poland and guaranteed a better financial situation in Völlen too, an outcome that must have boosted the standing of the SS soldier in the family and in the village milieu. Individual Niemann photos also show his father-in-law and suggest an uncomplicated relationship (see app. 1 fig. 1.23, bottom middle). And soon the rural household even profited substantially from the son-in-law's activities in Poland.

In July 1943, the couple celebrated a reunion in Berlin. The Chancellery of the Führer, which organized a trip to Berlin to reward the Trawnikis deployed in the Operation Reinhard killing centers, had even invited the wives of the three German SS men who came along on the journey. Henriette Niemann and Danida Floß also met again on this occasion. Together with Emilie Gomerski, they most likely rejoiced at the presence of their husbands and enjoyed the capital in midsummer, as well as the palaces and parkland in Potsdam. The surviving photos of the trip frequently show the women together. During these outings, they may also have exchanged ideas about their roles at the side of SS men deployed in Poland and involved in the genocide of the Jews.

After the welcome diversion, Henriette Niemann returned to the East Frisian provinces and to her children and her parents' farm, where a postcard reached her a few weeks later. "Too bad you're not still here," Niemann wrote on August 9, 1943.[24] Emotional closeness and a naturally associated longing,

feelings that absolutely seem to have existed between the two, also are clearly expressed in a letter that the SS-Untersturmführer wrote from Sobibor on August 20.[25] It was the last surviving sign of life received by his wife. In the letter, he thanked her for the apples she had sent. Her obviously affectionate gesture was a reminder of his rural home and symbolic evidence that the world was in good order there, and the fruit appears to have accomplished its purpose. The deputy camp commandant at Sobibor inquires solicitously about his children and emphasizes that, of course, it is always "a relief when you know whether all is well at home."[26]

That Henriette Niemann organized things so that "all [was] well at home" is part of the historical record at another level as well. Surviving documents provide evidence of the personal avarice of SS soldiers, beyond the mass murders, and attest to the role of the wife as accomplice. Jewish survivors, in a great many memoirs, have put on record the vast extent of the private corruption that was rampant among the Germans in Sobibor and elsewhere. Eda Lichtman, for example, described how she was forced to sew dolls' clothes for the children of her tormentors and to secretly put together packages that the SS men took home with them when they went on leave.[27] And Stanislaw Szmaijzner, who worked in Sobibor as a goldsmith, reported several times that he had to hide gold and melt it down for individual Germans on a regular basis, to satisfy their greed.[28] However, the perpetrators' enrichment, which was described as being multifaceted, has thus far been provable in only a few, relatively trivial-seeming individual cases.[29] For the Niemanns, astonishingly concrete evidence of enrichment is now available, and it leads to correspondingly significant insights.

While Niemann was still deployed at the Belzec killing center, suspiciously high cash deposits began to appear in his wife's savings book. It documents an initial receipt of money for August 11, 1942. On that day, Henriette Niemann deposited RM 971 in her account, which equated to almost four times the lavish monthly salary paid by the Chancellery of the Führer to the German SS men in the Operation Reinhard camps.[30] For October of that year, after Niemann had already moved to the Sobibor death camp, a further deposit of RM 800 is documented, and in December an additional RM 400 appeared in the savings book. The cash deposits continued in 1943: RM 700 in March, and RM 1,000 on October 6 (see app. 2 fig. 2.3).[31]

All that, however, still does not account for the entire stream of cash. In fact, additional suspicious deposits into the savings account of Henriette's father, August Frey, during the same time period can be discerned. On May 12, 1943, the sum of RM 1,100 was added to his previously rather meager savings of RM 104. The very same day, there was another deposit—this time, RM 3,000—and toward the end of the year, other large cash deposits followed (see app. 2 fig. 2.4).[32] The recording of such large cash deposits in August Frey's account also is evidence that Henriette Niemann seemingly was well aware of the criminal nature of her actions. The use of her father's account was an attempt to conceal, if at all possible, the private profit resulting from plunder during the Holocaust. Because deposits in just one rural savings account evidently seemed too conspicuous to her with the passage of time, and she no longer knew what to do with the large amounts of money, Henriette Niemann began to distribute the cash among several accounts. The sudden streams of cash were incommensurate with the previous income of the family. Niemann's repeated plundering of Jewish valuables in Belzec and Sobibor suggests itself as the sole explanation. Fundamentally, such robbery has been described consistently and in detail by many survivors, but is rarely, if ever, reflected in traceable documentation created by the families of perpetrators. By depositing cash in different savings accounts, opening new accounts of different types, and distributing the new wealth, beginning in the summer of 1942, Henriette Niemann took the significant step from wife and presumptive confidante to accomplice and active Holocaust profiteer.

Also against this backdrop, Niemann wrote to his wife in August 1943, in what was presumably his last letter from Sobibor, to say that personally he was doing "very well." Expressing his yearning for the family in Völlen in surprisingly clear terms, he added, "only my thoughts are always with you all, I'd like so much to see August and Hanne once again." He made plain the foreseeable unlikelihood of an imminent visit, however, by informing his wife about plans of his Berlin superiors to transfer him and other men from Sobibor to southern Europe. "Trieste is up at the top of Italy," he wrote, and in conclusion intimated vague discontent at the prospect of being separated from the family in the coming months as well. "But Henny," he continued, "what can one do, we have to do our duty wherever they put us."[33] Henriette Niemann was no stranger to such a sense of duty. Years earlier, she had emphasized this attitude on her own behalf when communicating with the SS evaluators who controlled the selection of wives. At least the prospect of Italy as a new deployment site, far from all front lines, may have seemed to her to be a safe option for her husband. However, as we know, the SS-Untersturmführer never undertook the intended deployment to Italy. Less than two months after his last letter to his wife, he was killed during the revolt of the Jewish prisoners in Sobibor.

Widow, Mother, and Farmer, 1943–1978

By late October 1943, Henriette Niemann in Völlen must have received a letter from Berlin in which Dietrich Allers of the Chancellery of the Führer informed her of her husband's death. With empathetic words, the trained lawyer and senior civil servant (*Regierungsrat*) attempted to convey to the young woman, personally known to him from the Berlin trip, the circumstances of a heroic death—by fabricating battles that never took place. After delivering the shocking news, he addressed existential matters, generously holding out the prospect of support, without any red tape, from the Chancellery of the Führer for the first months (see app. 2 fig. 2.2).[34]

The letter announcing Niemann's death must have shaken Henriette Niemann's life plan and that of her family to the core. The twenty-two-year-old mother of a son barely four years old and a daughter not yet eighteen months old had lost her husband, to whom she had been married for only four years and whom she probably believed to be safe, by and large, in the Lublin District. A family photo that the young widow had made some months later, in the Papenburg studio known to her from previous visits, still reveals clear signs of the sorrow felt by her and her children (see fig. 10.4).

The widow, in her search for consolation and an active way of dealing with grief, did not limit herself to her family members and her circle of friends in Völlen. In addition, she invited Danida Floß, a fellow sufferer, to East Frisia. Having known Floß for several years, the two women could look back on carefree days together with their husbands. Floß had been widowed shortly after Henriette Niemann, a few days after the Sobibor revolt, when her husband was trying to take some Trawniki guards back from there to their training camp. The Trawnikis overpowered him and shot him with his own firearm. At Niemann's invitation, the two widows met in Völlen in March 1944 at the latest. During the following summer, there was even another opportunity to avail themselves of the hospitality of the Chancellery of the Führer. Both women spent a lengthy vacation on the Attersee in Haus Schoberstein—the recreation facility where they had enjoyed happy days in September 1941 with their husbands, who were involved in the T4 program at that time.[35]

While there, Niemann received a letter from her sister Auguste, asking affectionately how her younger sister was feeling, and telling about life at home in Völlen.[36] Both children had stayed in Völlen and were being cared for by their aunt and grandparents, Auguste wrote reassuringly, saying how well August and Johanne were sleeping and how seldom they asked about their mother. In addition, the letter contained the explicit encouragement to indulge in some downtime and take the opportunity, amid all the grief, also to recharge her batteries. The written evidence of sisterly affection closes with the words, "Give my regards to Mrs. Floß, see you again soon." Thus, family members from Völlen knew Danida Floß from her earlier visit to the village. Not least of all, the letter also shows the family's awareness that the privilege of a vacation in the Alps had been made possible for the two widows once again by top-level institutions in Berlin.[37]

Support for the grieving widow did not come solely from her immediate private sphere and the Chancellery of the Führer. Other agencies of the Nazi bureaucracy also made an effort to give Henriette Niemann the impression that she would continue to be in good hands with the Nazis' Führer state. In April 1944, exactly six months after Niemann's death, the widow received a letter from an employee of Lebensborn's Main Department of SS-Combatants' Orphans (Hauptabteilung SS-Kriegerwaisen). The letter states that Himmler has tasked the SS organization with making its "experience in youth care available to the survivors of our comrades killed in action."[38] Far more substantial than such gestures of emotional support and dubious advice on raising Nazi children, however, was the continued financial support from the Chancellery of the Führer. The promise made by Dietrich Allers shortly after Niemann's death—to keep paying the husband's salary for the time being—was a promise kept. As a result, regular payments in the amount of his previous earnings, as well as an additional transfer of RM 2,395 from Berlin, were made. In June 1944, after the customary bureaucratic delay, the official monthly payments of the widows' and orphans' pension from the Pension Office of the Waffen-SS (Versorgungsamt der Waffen-SS) finally commenced. However, in comparison with the deposits in family accounts—proceeds of the private spoils of Operation Reinhard—the RM 367 pension that was meant to secure a livelihood actually represented a cash flow of only secondary importance.[39]

In 1944, when there were growing indications of an end to the Nazi dictatorship, Henriette Niemann, still in Völlen, made further efforts to safeguard the assets resulting from her husband's Nazi spoils. She set up savings accounts for both children, with unusually large deposits of more than RM 1,500 apiece.[40] In addition, she opened another savings account of her own and deposited fresh large sums in her father's account, bringing his balance to a generous RM 15,700.[41] Besides all the economic transactions involving the valuables stolen in the death camps, Henriette Niemann also tried to honor the memory of her deceased husband. Through the Chancellery of the Führer, she showed concern for the tending of grave "No. 399" in the military cemetery in Chełm. In late July 1944, however, Arnold Oels, Niemann's former personnel officer, informed her with regret that the Red Army had occupied the area. The Nazi official considerately added that it was now necessary "to wait until a later point in time" to see to the further care of the grave.[42]

On May 8, 1945, the Allies finally compelled the unconditional surrender of Nazi Germany. Whether Henriette Niemann experienced the day and the following months as a profound transformation, a true sea change, or failed to see any such far-reaching alterations to her everyday world in the East Frisian provinces, remains an open question. Later, however, she was taken completely by surprise when West Germany adopted a new fiscal course. The currency reform of June 21, 1948, was intended to bring about a massive reduction of the money supply, which the Nazis had artificially increased for their conduct of the war, and thereby to create a more appropriate relationship between goods and monetary value. As a result,

on the effective date, the bank seized a large part of Henriette Niemann's assets. Of her approximately RM 40,000, still deposited in the various accounts of the family at the time, only around 2 percent remained after the reform. Thus, the currency reform not only put an end to consequences of the Nazi economy but also, in Niemann's case, simultaneously eliminated assets accrued through the murder of Jews during the Holocaust. Henriette Niemann, as a temporary profiteer, therefore seems to have begun her life in the Federal Republic with only modest financial means. It is certainly conceivable, however, that the widow was still hoarding jewelry or other valuables of the victims in her home, in addition to her bank deposits. Such objects of value may have made the family's life in postwar Germany an easier one after all.[43]

During those years, greater attention undoubtedly had to be given to securing the family's livelihood once again. In the young Federal Republic, it was uncertain for a long time how the pensions of the widows and orphans of former Waffen-SS members should be handled. As a result, Henriette Niemann engaged in a protracted exchange of letters with the relevant authorities, in which she attempted to assert her alleged right to financial support. Into the early 1960s, payments were alternately awarded and then revoked again, so that ultimately it can scarcely be determined what funds were actually paid out to her and her children.[44]

After 1945 Henriette Niemann continued to live on her parents' farm and take care of the household and some farming chores. In 1954 her mother died, and her father, owing to his age, was increasingly unable to manage the strength-sapping tasks of farming by himself. Forced to seek additional male assistance as a result, August Frey hired the Dutch citizen Jan Hayo Klimp, presumably in the early 1950s. Initially Klimp worked illegally on the farm, but from 1954 there was an official permit from the Regional Employment Office of Lower Saxony for the employment of the trained farmer.[45] Klimp, born in Siddeburen in the Netherlands in 1910, had joined the SS during the Nazi occupation of his country; after the war he had been sentenced there to a twelve-year prison term for "collaboration with the enemy." In 1951, he escaped from the prison in Veenhuizen and took shelter on the Frey family's farm in East Frisia. For many years after Klimp was already officially employed on the farm in Völlen, he continued to be sought as one of approximately 350 Nazi perpetrators in the Netherlands. Evidently the Dutch authorities finally became aware of his whereabouts only at the end of the 1970s. Several newspapers, including the Dutch *Leidisch Dagblad* and *Neues Deutschland*, based in East Germany, reported on Klimp's possible extradition to the Netherlands, which never came to pass, however.[46]

At that time, Klimp and Henriette, who was for all practical purposes his boss, had already been in a relationship for many years. "Uncle Jan" had long since been introduced into and accepted by the family. The widow's new relationship, which evidently had begun soon after Klimp came to the farm, allows us to draw cautious conclusions as to her political sympathies. After all, Klimp was the second staunch Nazi and SS man whom Henriette Niemann chose as a partner. While her first relationship choice had been made under the Nazi dictatorship, she decided on Klimp in the political context of the young West German democracy. Together, the two looked after the farm and took care of all the associated farming duties, while Henriette raised her two children in addition. Her decades of dedication to her parents' farming operation finally found belated recognition in the summer of 1961. Her father, now more than eighty years old, signed the farm over to his daughter Henriette in the presence of a notary and had it expressly stated in the notarial deed what share she had already earned for herself through her long years of unpaid work on the farm.[47] Together with her new partner, she continued to run the agricultural operation for more than two decades. In the late 1970s, Henriette

Niemann was diagnosed with cancer, which finally claimed her life on February 20, 1980.

Conclusion

The surviving sources permit amazingly multifaceted insights into Henriette Niemann's path in life, on the one hand; on the other hand, however, unanswered questions remain. In particular, her political convictions and personal attitude toward National Socialism seem vague at best, and unambiguous indications of steadfast Nazi sentiments are only indirectly a part of the historical record. A number of biographical details suggest that the young woman did not distance herself from National Socialism and its goals in any way. Her marriage to the concentration-camp guard Niemann, the visit to the T4 killing center in Bernburg, repeated stays at the T4 recreation facility on the Attersee, and her participation in the Berlin trip at the invitation of the Chancellery of the Führer represent evidence of her sympathy with the Nazi regime. That suggests that, as a wife, she also was not just the devoted mother of her husband's children but more of a genuine partner and emotional prop for him.

It is beyond dispute that Henriette Niemann was prepared to profit from National Socialism and the crimes of her husband. Corresponding evidence is available in exceptional detail. Without knowledge of Niemann's work in Operation Reinhard, all her efforts to conceal the funds derived from the plunder in Belzec und Sobibor in her own savings accounts and even in those of family members are inconceivable. Therefore, as in scarcely any other case, there exists proof of how the corruption of the SS, often described by Jewish survivors, had an economic benefit for the perpetrators and their family members.

Henriette Niemann presents the noteworthy example of a young woman who, as the result of a romantic relationship in her native village, came into direct contact with Himmler's self-appointed Nazi elite. Her life from that point on was to be decisively shaped by that development. Comparatively modest family prospects changed rapidly when her husband was transferred out of the concentration-camp system, first to the T4 program and then, most notably, to Operation Reinhard. Upon her husband's death, however, all the privileges she experienced were probably put into perspective, at least from her point of view. They ended with the Allied victory over the Nazi dictatorship and the liberation of Europe from National Socialism—a liberation that Henriette Niemann, like the majority of German postwar society, most likely never experienced as such. Because she was unable, once the currency reform was introduced, to protect the assets stolen from Holocaust victims, the widow began life in the Federal Republic of Germany as a peasant woman, a smallholder: the same status she had held before the Nazis' policy of extermination. For Henriette Niemann, the years from 1939 to 1945 were absolutely precedent setting; the wartime was probably the most significant phase of her life. Whether she ever thought deeply and carefully about her husband's crimes and her own involvement in them, or might have raised this topic with her children, is not indicated anywhere in the historical record.

Notes

1. See Lower, *Hitler's Furies*; Harvey, *Germanization*; Steinbacher, *Volksgenossinnen*; Kompisch, *Täterinnen*.
2. Schwarz, *Frau*, p. 7; also Kramer, *Volksgenossinnen*.
3. Matthäus, "Auszüge"; Kämmer, "Lina Heydrich."
4. In 1968 the farm had "livestock numbering ten sheep and barnyard fowl." It stands to reason that this was the size decades earlier as well; see Decision of the Aurich Social Court in the employment dispute between Jan Hayo Klimp and the Hannover Employers' Liability Insurance Association, February 25, 1970, USHMMA, Acc 2020.8.1.
5. Picture postcard from August Frey, April 7, 1918, ibid.

6. See several issues of the association's newspaper, *Parole-Buch,* ibid.
7. Fricke and Bramke, "Kyffhäuser-Bund"; Hein, *Elite*, p. 136.
8. In late 1933 the association was finally incorporated into the SA. In 1934, according to a Nazi press directive, it had more than three million members in 32,500 local groups. Approximately 1.6 million of these members belonged to the SA Reserve, and around 200,000 were in the active SA. Furthermore, at that time approximately 360,000 NCOs and 70,000 officers of the Wehrmacht were association members; see Toepser-Ziegert, *NS-Presseanweisungen*, p. 519.
9. Notebook of Henriette Frey, USHMMA, Acc 2020.8.1.
10. Ibid.
11. Membership card of Henriette Niemann, ibid.
12. Life history of Henriette Frey, undated, summer 1939, BArch, RS Johann Niemann.
13. Will of August and Janna Frey, May 7, 1950, USHMMA, Acc 2020.8.1.
14. Notarial recording of the conveyance of the Frey farm to Henriette Niemann, June 14, 1961, ibid.
15. Life history of Henriette Frey, undated, summer 1939, BArch, RS Johann Niemann.
16. Notarial recording of the conveyance of the Frey farm to Henriette Niemann, June 14, 1961, USHMMA, Acc 2020.8.1.
17. Letter from Henriette Niemann to the pastor in Völlen, July 14, 1939, ibid.
18. See life history of Henriette Frey, undated, summer 1939, BArch, RS Johann Niemann.
19. Excerpt from kinship file (*Sippenakte*) of Johann Niemann, BArch, RS Johann Niemann.
20. Certificate of indebtedness of the couple, August 5/7, 1939, BArch, RS Johann Niemann; Administrative notice of the granting of a marriage loan, Niederbarnim Tax Office, June 4, 1941 USHMMA, Acc 2020.8.1.
21. Letter from Willi N. to the Frey family, November 19, 1940, USHMMA, Acc 2020.8.1.
22. Postcard from Danida Floß (née Grams) to the family of Albert Grams, September 19, 1941, ibid. Presumably Floß brought the postcard with her to a subsequent reunion and gave it to Henriette Niemann as a memento.

23. Copy of the birth certificate of Johanne Niemann, March 14, 1944, ibid.

24. Postcard from Johann to Henriette Niemann, August 9, 1943, ibid.

25. See letter from Johann to Henriette Niemann, August 20, 1943, ibid.

26. Ibid.

27. Letter from Kurt Thomas, December 15, 1949, LNW, Q 234/4481; statement of Eda Lichtman, March 3, 1964, NIOD, 804/17.

28. Statement of Stanislaw Szmajzner, June 4, 1976, LNW, Q 234/4572.

29. See the chapter by Martin Cüppers and Steffen Hänschen on the trip to Berlin.

30. RM 971 was worth about $380 at the time and nearly $7000 in 2021 dollars.

31. Savings book of Henriette Niemann 1942–1954, USHMMA, Acc 2020.8.1.

32. Savings book of August Frey 1929–1952, ibid.

33. Letter from Johann to Henriette Niemann, August 20, 1943, ibid.

34. Letter from Dietrich Allers to Henriette Niemann, October 21, 1943, USHMMA, Acc 2020.8.1.

35. Letter from Arnold Oels to Henriette Niemann, March 9, 1944, ibid.; letter from Arnold Oels to Henriette Niemann, July 24, 1944, ibid.

36. Letter from Auguste Griepenburg to Henriette Niemann, July 23, 1944, ibid.

37. Ibid.

38. Letter from Lebensborn, Hauptabt. SS-Kriegerwaisen, to Henriette Niemann, April 4, 1944, ibid.

39. Savings book of Henriette Niemann, 1942–1954, ibid.

40. Savings book of August Niemann, 1944–1961, ibid. For the daughter Johanne Niemann see Settlement of the settlement bank, Raiffeisenkasse Ihrhove, September 15, 1984, ibid.

41. Savings book of August Frey, 1929–1952, ibid. On Henriette Niemann's second savings book see Settlement of the settlement bank, Raiffeisenkasse Ihrhove, September 15, 1984, ibid.

42. Letter from Arnold Oels to Henriette Niemann, July 24, 1944, ibid; letter from local commandant's office (Ortskommandantur) in Chelm, July 1, 1944, ibid.

43. On "Zero Hour" see Winkler, Weg; on the economy Buchheim, "Währungsreform"; also Settlement Raiffeisenkasse Ihrhove, September 15, 1948, USHMMA, Acc 2020.8.1.

44. Administrative notice of assessment of widows' and orphans' receipt of benefits, Oldenburg Pension Office, February 8, 1952, ibid; Administrative notice, Regional Pension Office for Lower Saxony, Pension Department, April 23, 1952, ibid; Hanover Regional Insurance Institution, disability insurance of Henriette Niemann, September 19, 1953, ibid; Certification of ruling on legal relationships, Regional Pension Office for Lower Saxony, Pension Department, January 11, 1956, ibid; letter from the Federal Insurance Institution for Employees to Henriette Niemann, November 2, 1956, ibid.

45. Employment permit of the Regional Employment Office of Lower Saxony for Jan Hayo Klimp, October 15, 1954, ibid.

46. "Niederlande suchen weitere Kriegsverbrecher in der BRD" [Netherlands looking for more war criminals in the FRG], in Neues Deutschland, July 27, 1978; "Oorlogsmisdadiger Klimp woont vlak over de grens" [The war criminal Klimp lives just on the other side of the border], in Leidisch Dagblad, July 26, 1978.

47. Notarized transfer agreement, June 14, 1961, USHMMA, Acc 2020.8.1.

Henriette Niemann in the Photo Collection

Figure 10.1. Henriette Frey as a 13-year-old during a stay in the Eifel region. "As a memento of Monschau! August 16, [19]34" is noted on the back. The photo is thus one of the earliest in the collection.

Figure 10.2. Henriette Niemann, presumably in 1940, on her parents' farm in Völlen. "Water carrier," was the caption Niemann wrote beneath it in his album.

Figure 10.3. Studio portrait, taken between May 1939 and July 1941. The older brother, Gerhard Niemann, his wife Johanna, Henriette, and Johann Niemann as an SS-Scharführer (*from left to right*).

Figure 10.4. Studio portrait of the widow with her children, August and Johanne, in the early summer of 1944.

11
Living with the Memory
Meetings with Semion Rozenfeld

ANNE LEPPER

I met Semion Rozenfeld for the first time on November 23, 2017, in the small town of Gedera, around eighteen miles south of Tel Aviv. He had lived in Israel since 1990, when he, his wife, and his two adult sons emigrated from Odessa in Ukraine. Ninety-five years old in late 2017, he lived in a retirement home on the edge of town, and his son Mikhail visited him there as often as possible. Mikhail was present on this day too, to coordinate the meeting and, as quickly became clear, to take care of his father.

For what lay ahead of us was not easy for Rozenfeld. Once again, he had to dig into the past and summon up memories; once more, he had to face and deal with his ordeal in Sobibor. This time his task would be especially challenging, as he had agreed to review with me and give an opinion on the Niemann photographs. At the time of our meeting, he was one of only three survivors of the German death camp and the only one from this group able to place the photos in context on the basis of his own experiences.

As he sat before me in his room in the residence, sitting up straight in a chair, the wheeled walker parked at his side, with an eyepatch and a crooked smile on his face, the words of the survivor Dov Freiberg, who described Rozenfeld in his book *To Survive Sobibor*, inevitably came into my mind. Rozenfeld and Freiberg, after their successful escape from the camp during the revolt, had met one another in the forest by chance. Initially on the move in a large group of approximately forty fleeing Jews, the two, along with another fugitive—Abraham Reiss, who was murdered in the very last days of the war—decided to continue their journey together. Freiberg and Rozenfeld survived the months of flight and concealment until the summer of 1944, when they finally were liberated in Chełm by the Red Army. Freiberg, a Warsaw native who had just turned sixteen, was deeply impressed by his Soviet companion: "Large, tall and twice as wide as I was. He moved heavily, like a bear, and I thought he personified the typical Russian soldier."[1]

And in fact, Rozenfeld identified strongly with his role as a Red Army soldier. A few days after the Soviet troops had arrived in Chełm in the summer of 1944, he rejoined the ranks of the Red Army and set out to fight against the Nazis once more. Freiberg recalled, "[He] said that he had to hurry and rejoin the Soviet army so that he could still manage to fight the Germans. When we tried to argue that he shouldn't leave so quickly, that we should stay together a bit so that we could enjoy our liberty, he replied that he was a Soviet soldier and his place was with the army."[2]

After being wounded in the fight for Puławy and undergoing a subsequent hospital stay in Łódź, Rozenfeld's personal end to the war finally came in early May 1945 in Berlin, where he had experienced the final battles for the Reich capital. Like a great many other Soviet soldiers, he too wrote on the walls of the conquered Reichstag, recording the names of the places which had shaped his personal experiences of the war: "Baranovichi–Sobibor–Berlin."[3] To learn whether any of his relatives had managed to survive the war, he quickly started on his way back home.

Semion Rozenfeld was born in 1922 in the small village of Ternivka in the Vinnytsia administrative district, at the center of what is now Ukraine. In 1940, just eighteen years old, he joined the Red Army. One year later he found himself a German prisoner of war after being wounded in fierce fighting. He was sent to a labor camp in Minsk, and from there, in September 1943, he was put into a transport with approximately two thousand Jews from the labor camp and the Minsk ghetto and deported to Sobibor. He was part of a large group of Jewish Soviet POWs who arrived at the camp, including Alexander Pechersky (Aleksandr Pecherskii) and several others who later were to play a defining role in organizing the revolt. Only a few of the Jews from the transport—among them some of the Soviet POWs—were selected for forced labor upon arrival in the camp. All the others were murdered in the gas chambers immediately after they reached Sobibor.

At the outset of my talks with Semion and Mikhail Rozenfeld, I told the two men that the photo albums I brought with me had once belonged to Johann Niemann, the former deputy camp commandant of Sobibor. Semion Rozenfeld thought for a moment, and then he remembered:

Niemann. . . . When our train arrived in Sobibor, this Niemann was standing on the ramp and shouting, "Carpenters, cabinetmakers, out of the train!" My friend Sasha Kupchin from Kiev was not a carpenter, but nevertheless he said to me, "My father is a carpenter, I remember a few things. Come on, you'll be my helper." But I replied, "I can't do anything. I don't want to make a fool of myself." Sasha answered, "Fine, but I'm getting out of the train. We'll see each other this evening in the barracks." When he was gone, some kind of power took hold of me and told me, "Get out, get out." I raised my hand and said, *"Ich bin Glasermeister."* ["I'm a master glazier."]

And Niemann heard it, came over to me, and asked, "Are you a Communist?" I said, "No." He said, *"Raus, verfluchtes Schwein"* ["Out, you bastard."] I got out and joined Sasha Kupchin. We had to pivot to the left and were led away. Then they herded us into Camp I. That's how it was.[4]

In addition to this first disturbing meeting, which at least meant that the new arrival was saved for the time being, Rozenfeld has another specific memory of Niemann; at the same time, it is the last one. At the beginning of the revolt on October 14, 1943, he and Alexandr Pecherskii were positioned in a barracks building in Camp I, opposite the building in which Niemann was killed. From that vantage point, the two observed the course of events:

[We] sat at the window and looked out at the entrance to Camp I. We saw Niemann, on horseback, come riding through the gate, ride up to the tailors' workshop, jump off the horse, and go into the barracks. Inside every workshop were two of our men. [. . .] And five minutes after he had gone in, the horse suddenly started to whinny and rear up on its hind legs. [. . .] That worried Pecherskii and me. We didn't understand what had happened. The following had happened: Schubajew was inside, he was shorter than Niemann, and his axe blow landed awkwardly. Niemann cried out. He had not killed him. The horse heard this and reared up. [. . .] We were very anxious. Then, a few minutes later, we saw someone come out of the tailors' workshop and run in our direction. He came over to us and handed us Niemann's pistol. [Then] we calmed down.[5]

When I showed him a photo of Niemann, a signed portrait dating from 1939, Rozenfeld seemed somewhat irritated: "Here he looks young, very young. In the camp, he was older."[6] Looking at other photos in which various members of the German guard force are pictured, I pointed to Gustav Wagner and asked Rozenfeld whether he recognized him. "No, I can't. It's not possible, it's simply too many years ago." Wagner's atrocities, however, he remembered only too well: "The man was very brutal. He could kill a person with his fist. I think he was a former boxer."[7]

We looked at the first photo in which parts of the camp topography can be identified. Taken from the guard tower at the main entrance to the camp, facing northwest, it shows the entrance gate, the ramp, and the forward section of the so-called front compound (*Vorlager*), with the guards at the entrance and the houses where the German guards lived. Using his finger, Rozenfeld pointed to more details in the photo: "Here were the houses in which the Germans lived. Here was the rail line. Here was the gate. The trains came in here. Here they were stopped and unloaded onto the ramp. On the gate were the words *Sonderlager SS* [SS Special Camp]. The sign was fairly large. But I didn't see these banners. As I recall it, there were only the words *Sonderlager SS*."[8]

Already obvious in this statement is a problem that accompanied our talks at all times. The photographs from the Niemann collection were made between the fall of 1942 and the summer of 1943, but Rozenfeld did not arrive in Sobibor until September 22, 1943. Particularly during the months preceding his arrival in the camp, however, the physical structure of the grounds had been substantially altered by a considerable number of reconstruction and expansion projects. Therefore, many of the things we see in the photos could not have been seen by him or would have looked different. That applies especially to the section known as Camp I, the compound with the prisoners' barracks, where Rozenfeld spent most of his time

in Sobibor. Extensive reconstruction work was still under way here during the summer of 1943, work in which he himself was forced to participate after his arrival in late September. "We put up a lot of barracks there. The barracks were isolated, standardized. We hammered in posts and laid foundations. We assembled the little ready-made houses that came from Norway. They stood half a meter above the ground."[9]

During our meeting, these changes sometimes made it difficult for Rozenfeld to recognize the familiar places in the photos. When we looked at the overview, which was shot from the southwest end of the camp and shows part of Camp I to the east (see fig. 6.6), he could scarcely recognize this area: "Sector I. Yes, it was in this corner. But what are those little heaps? What is that? Where these little heaps are, there was a shed. Shoes were piled up in it. Children's shoes, all together. [. . .] When we were brought into the camp, everything had already been built. There were little houses everywhere, this long toilet room next to the carpenters' workshop. And in the middle was the roll call square, where we were counted four times a day."[10]

It was amazing to me how much Rozenfeld nonetheless remembered after all the years and, despite the relatively short time he spent in the camp, could recognize in the photos. I asked him whether, from Camp I, it was possible for him to see the houses in the front compound (Vorlager). "Yes, we saw them, because we were separated from the officers' little houses by only a row of three meter [ten feet] fencing. While the barracks in Camp I were being built, we could see them from above. On the same occasion, I also saw the roofs of Camp III."[11]

Camp III was the place where the victims were murdered and then, at first, hastily buried in mass graves by Jewish forced laborers. Later on, the corpses were burned there. For the prisoners in Camp I, Camp III was, on the one hand, far away and, on the other hand, quite near. The roof of the gas chambers was always visible and the smoke from the burning bodies was omnipresent, as was the fear of being sent to work in that part of the camp—a punishment favored by the German guards, which was, as everyone knew, tantamount to a death sentence.

When I showed him a photo of the *Altes Kasino* (old staff club) in which both Niemann and the camp commandant, Reichleitner, were temporarily quartered, Rozenfeld recognized it at once: "Yes, those are the little houses in which the Germans lived. They were behind the fence. The first sector was separated by a row of barbed wire.[12] On the far side there were three rows of barbed wire, three meters high. And behind it were the little houses in which the Germans lived. There were many of them."[13]

While looking at the images from the front compound, Rozenfeld was already trying to situate them within the camp topography and pinpoint the position from which he had been able to see the buildings in question during his time in the camp. He tried the same thing with the next photos showing the area between sections I and II of the camp (see fig. 6.7). Visible in the center of the image is the tall fire lookout tower, built before the war, which rose into the sky in the middle of the camp. Rozenfeld recognized the angle of the shot immediately; at a slightly different spot, he himself had made his way between Camp I and Camp II on several occasions. To give me a better explanation of the angle from which the photo was taken, he reached for some paper and started drawing a map of the camp for me. On it, besides the overall camp structure, he marked all the places that held special significance for him. He pointed to the barracks building in which he waited for the SS man Frenzel on the day of the uprising, the man whom the organizers had assigned him to kill.[14] He also pinpointed the place at which that same Frenzel, at a later point in the revolt, positioned himself behind a barrel and fired a submachine gun at the escaping prisoners. Then, referring to the drawing, he told me about the spot at which he tried to sever the barbed wire of the camp fence and—when this attempt failed—decided to climb over it. With his finger, he traced a line showing his way into the forest, which he finally reached, his clothing torn by the fence and a gunshot wound in his leg.

"Frenzel had already grasped what was going on. He also hadn't come to the carpenters' workshop, he was somewhere else. It was clear to him that we might take over the armory. That's why he started firing a submachine gun at us, to keep us away from the gun room. He fired and cut us off from the armory, and, carrying the axe, I ran straight to the barbed wire. I wanted to cut the barbed wire off the fencepost, but I didn't manage to do so. Then I wanted to cut the fencepost down, but I wasn't successful there either. I threw the axe away, climbed over the barbed wire. At that spot there was only one row of barbed wire. I jumped over the barbed wire, which was three meters high. I tore my coveralls. Under the coveralls I was also wearing trousers and clothing, I had good shoes. I ran like a soldier. And the forest was 150 meters [about 500 feet] from the camp. [. . .] My coveralls were a little damaged, but that didn't bother me. I ran like a soldier, fell, crawled, jumped. Then a bullet pierced my leg here [he points to a place on his leg]. Here I have a scar. But it didn't touch the bone. I didn't notice until I was in the forest that it was wet here. I saw that there was blood everywhere. My blood clots well, and my wound stopped bleeding. And then in the forest . . . that's another story."[15]

Another story, the next one. There followed perilous, energy-sapping months, which he spent together with Freiberg in various hiding places in the forest and with Polish civilians who had agreed to take the fugitives into their homes. Then he went back into the army, was wounded, and took part in the storming of Berlin. The stories Rozenfeld had to tell are so full of brutality, grief, and courage that it was sometimes hard to believe that this friendly, good-humored old man with the mischievous smile has experienced them all himself. His son Mikhail also told me how difficult it was for him, when he was young, to piece together the mosaic of all his father's incomprehensible experiences and end up with a complete picture. Like many children of survivors, the sons of Semion Rozenfeld too had to spend a long time collecting the fragments of their traumatized father's stories in order to understand: "From childhood I remember that, as soon as the conversations shifted to the time in the camp, the escape [. . .], everybody started hissing and immediately switched to Yiddish. As I grew older, I began to understand their secrets. I always listened open-mouthed to my father's reminiscences."[16]

After the war ended, when Rozenfeld had finally succeeded in returning to his small home town of Ternivka, he was forced to realize that almost his entire family had been killed during the war. When he learned that a brother of his father had survived and was staying with his family in the nearby town of Khashchuvate, he set out to meet what he thought were his last remaining relatives. Not long after that, on January 15, 1946, he married his uncle's daughter, Yevgeniya (Evgeniia), who had served as a soldier in the Red Army during the war. They moved to the small town of Haivoron, around eighteen miles south of Ternivka, where their two sons grew up.

For the Rozenfelds' children, the fragments from their father's tales did not join together to form a clearer picture until many years later, in the early 1960s, when something happened that caused him to bring up the memories from the depths of his mind:

> In the early 1960s, in Odessa, my father and I were relaxing at the 16th station of [Big] Fountain [an area of city beaches and resorts] in the course of a long walk. Next to my father, a young man from Kiev was resting. The two got into a conversation with one another. I noticed my father's agitation and started to listen. From the few sentences I overheard, however, I didn't understand what was going on. Later, when the whole family was sitting together, he told us about the conversation with the man from Kiev, who had told

him that he had read about the revolt in Sobibor and its leader, Pecherskii, in *Komsomol'skaia Pravda* [a Russian newspaper]. My father told us all this with tears in his eyes, tears of joy and pain. Soon a letter reached us from Kiev, with the article in question. Papa immediately wrote a letter to the editors of the newspaper and received a reply right away, containing, among other things, the address of Uncle Sasha [Pecherskii] and many questions. The letter was from Tomin and Sinel'nikov, who later published the book *Return Is Undesirable*.[17] The publication of the book marked the beginning of a new life for my father. First the meeting with Pecherskii, and then we also found [Arkadii] Vaispapir. Papa was invited to schools and businesses all over the country. Other prisoners from the camp were being found all the time, and at the last meeting there were already six of them.[18]

Before these developments, Rozenfeld had not known that other Red Army soldiers who were included in his transport from the Minsk labor camp had survived the end of the war. Only now, twenty years later, did he finally have the opportunity to exchange views and try to find a way of dealing with his memories. The Soviet survivors agreed to meet every five years to commemorate the revolt and those who died in Sobibor. Later, in the 1990s, after immigration to Israel, contacts with other survivors were added, including Dov Freiberg.

Even in Gedera in 2017, in his room in the retirement home, Rozenfeld still made the impression described by Freiberg in his book. He was friendly, courteous, and pleased with the flowers and candy we brought him. Almost apologetically, he bade goodbye to me at our first meeting, when his solicitous son noticed, after two full hours, that his father was tired. "I'm sorry, but at the age of ninety-five I can't sit for such a long time anymore. I have to lie down for a bit." But I had permission to come back in order to continue delving into the difficult memories with him.

Semion Rozenfeld passed away on June 3, 2019. He was the last known survivor of the camp, following the deaths of

Arkadii Vaispapir in Ukraine and Selma Engel-Wijnberg in the United States the previous year. His memories are of incalculable value. What good fortune that, although sitting and talking for so long placed a visible strain on him, he was nonetheless willing to share those memories with us.

Notes

1. Freiberg, *To Survive Sobibor*, p. 305.

2. Ibid, p. 385.

3. In Baranovichi (Baranavichy), a Belarusian town southwest of Minsk, Rozenfeld was taken prisoner by German troops in October 1941. See statement of Rozenfeld, February 24, 1966, LNW, Q 234/4486 (translated from German).

4. Interview with the author, Gedera, November 23, 2017 (translated from Russian). See also the statement made by Rozenfeld in 1966 in which he also said that he had been selected by Niemann at the ramp, erroneously referring to him as "Heumann." The statement reads, "The deputy head of the camp, Heumann [sic], whose name and official position I did not learn until later, singled out carpenters, glaziers, and cabinetmakers from the people who had arrived. There were approximately 80 to 90 [persons selected]. I also succeeded in getting into this group." Statement of Rozenfeld, February 24, 1966, LNW, Q 234/4486 (translated from German).

5. Interview, November 23, 2017 (translated from Russian).

6. Ibid.

7. Ibid.

8. Ibid. In fact, the inscription on the entrance gate was a little different from Rozenfeld's memory. As we can see in the picture from the Niemann collection, it read "SS Sonderkommando" (see fig. 6.4).

9. Interview, December 5, 2017 (translated from Russian).

10. Interview, November 23, 2017.

11. Ibid.

12. This is a reference to Camp I.

13. Interview, November 23, 2017.

14. Karl Frenzel was the only one of the SS men who had not shown up in the workshop at the arranged time and therefore could not be killed during the revolt. As Rozenfeld later reported, he had replied as follows when Pecherskii asked whether he was able to kill someone with an axe: "I'm not able to kill a human being. But I can certainly kill a Nazi."

15. Interview, December 5, 2017.

16. Email from Mikhail Rozenfeld to the author, November 26, 2017 (translated from Russian).

17. V· Tomin and A. Sinel'nikov, *Vozvrashchenie nezhelatel'no*, Moscow, 1964.

18. Email from Mikhail Rozenfeld to the author, November 26, 2017.

Photos with Semion Rozenfeld and a Map of Sobibor Drawn by Him

Figure 11.1. The author (*left*), Semion Rozenfeld, and translator Daniel Hizkiyahu (*right*) look at the photographs from Niemann's collection during one of their meetings in Gedera, Israel, in November 2017.

Figure 11.2. Semion Rozenfeld and Dov Freiberg with two acquaintances, the brothers Yozhik and Monyek Serchuk (*left to right*), in Chełm during the summer of 1944, shortly after their liberation. Like Rozenfeld and Freiberg, the Serchuk brothers too had stayed in hiding in the forests around Chełm after the revolt in Sobibor. Together, the four men got through the last weeks before liberation by the Red Army. Shortly after this photo was taken, Rozenfeld resumed his service in the Red Army, while Monyek Serchuk joined the Polish armed forces. Both are already in uniform in this photo.

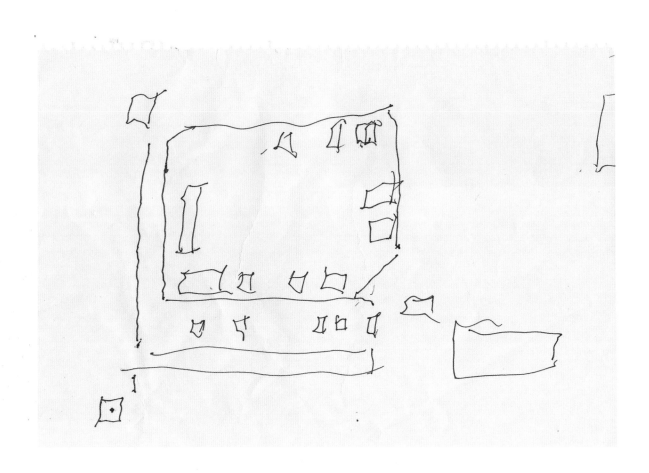

Figure 11.3. Map drawn from memory by Semion Rozenfeld, giving an overview of the Sobibor camp, during an interview with the author on December 5, 2017.

Appendix 1
The Brandenburg Album

Appendix 1 Figure 1.1. 2nd SS Death's Head Unit "Brandenburg"

Appendix 1 Figure 1.2. Inside front cover

Appendix 1 Figure 1.3. Page 1. Note that 1.3–1.26 are right-hand pages. The album's left-hand pages held no photos.

Appendix 1 Figure 1.4. Page 3

Appendix 1 Figure 1.5. Page 5 The photos with red corners were removed from the album at some point and their original positions were reconstructed by the editors for this volume.

Appendix 1 Figure 1.6. Page 7

Appendix 1 Figure 1.7. Page 9

Appendix 1 Figure 1.8. Page 11

Appendix 1 Figure 1.9. Page 13

Appendix 1 Figure 1.10. Page 15

Appendix 1 Figure 1.11. Page 17

Appendix 1 Figure 1.12. Page 19

Appendix 1 Figure 1.13. Page 21

Appendix 1 Figure 1.14. Page 23

Appendix 1 Figure 1.15. Page 25

Appendix 1 Figure 1.16. Page 27

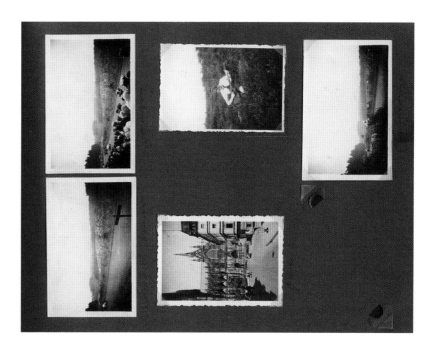

Appendix 1 Figure 1.17. Page 29

Appendix 1 Figure 1.18. Page 31

Appendix 1 Figure 1.19. Page 33

Appendix 1 Figure 1.20. Page 35

Appendix 1 Figure 1.21. Page 37

Appendix 1 Figure 1.22. Page 39

Appendix 1 Figure 1.23. Page 41

Appendix 1 Figure 1.24. Page 43

Appendix 1 Figure 1.25. Page 45

Appendix 1 Figure 1.26. Page 47

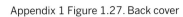

Appendix 1 Figure 1.27. Back cover

Appendix 2
Documents from the Niemann Collection
(translations from German)

Sobibor, August 20, 1943

Dear Henny,

I received your letter and the parcel with thanks, all the apples were still good. Now Henny, how are you? Are you still fit and well, it's a relief to know whether all is well at home, I'm doing very well personally, only my thoughts are always with you all I'd so much like to see August and Hanne again at some point, but I think it won't happen so quickly. Yesterday we got notification from Berlin that we're going to Italy in 5 weeks and specifically to Trieste. Trieste is up at the top of Italy. Now Henny, if that's true then it will be quite some time before we meet again. But Henny, what can you do, we have to do our duty wherever they put us. Now something else, do you already have the grain at home as well as the hay, because the weather is really very good. Henny, be a dear and send me my uniform tunic, because I need it now, Henny be a dear now in conclusion I wish you and all the others all the best, I hope it won't be much longer with love and kisses [two words illegible]

Your Jonny

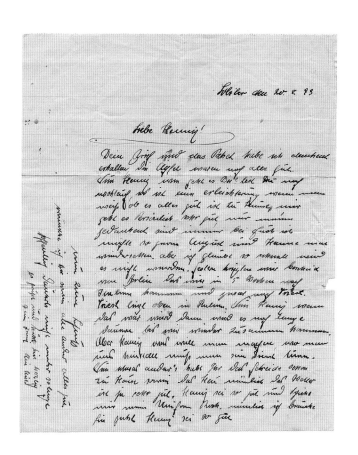

Appendix 2 figure 2.1. Presumably the last letter from Johann Niemann to his wife, Henriette.

317

Oberregierungsrat D. Allers
Berlin W. 35
4 Tiergartenstrasse   Berlin, October 21, 1943

Dear Mrs. Niemann,

I made your acquaintance during your husband's visit to
Berlin with his men. Now I must write to you today with very
sad news.

Your husband was killed in action while doing his duty
in an exemplary manner, in the course of heavy fighting
against insurgents. His men, for the most part, died with him.
Together with the 10 comrades killed in action along with
him, your husband was laid to rest in the heroes' cemetery in
Cholm on Monday, October 18, 1943. Oberführer Blankenburg [and I] had the opportunity to take part in the ceremony. During the ceremony your husband in particular was
explicitly mentioned as having been an outstanding soldier
and comrade, always ready to do his duty and lend his full
support. In fighting against the rebels, too, he proved himself
a good leader by leading the way for his men.

Mrs. Niemann, please be assured of the warmest sympathy of all those associated with our office and of my personal
concern as well. I have instructed Mr. Oels to call on you and
discuss with you everything that is required. At the same
time, please refrain from attending to claims for entitlement
to maintenance for the time being, as the requisite documents
first have to be obtained. Besides, responsibility for salary
payments for the next 3 months will be assumed by us in any
event.

> With my warmest sympathy and
> Heil Hitler!
> Yours, [signature]

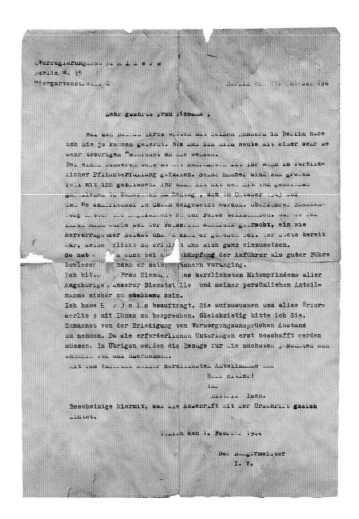

Appendix 2 figure 2.2. Certified copy of letter
from Dietrich Allers to Henriette Niemann.

Appendix 2 figure 2.3. Page from activity record for Henriette Niemann's account.

The account was opened in June 1942 and closed in July 1958. The page shown above covers the period between August and December 1942. At midmonth (August 14, September 18, October 14, November 13, December 11), salary payments from the Chancellery of the Führer are deposited into the account. Each payment is for approximately 260 Reichsmarks (RM); in addition, there is a special payment of RM 243.44 shortly before Christmas. Apart from those transactions, Henriette Niemann herself made several larger deposits of cash, a different amount each time, into the account: on August 11, RM 971; on October 21, RM 800; and on December 23, RM 400. There is reason to suspect that these deposits resulted from assets that her husband had stolen from the murdered victims in Belzec and Sobibor and then possibly brought to Völlen in person when on home leave.

Appendix 2 figure 2.4. Page from August Frey's savings account passbook.

The passbook for the savings account opened by Henriette Niemann's father in June 1929 reflects the financial situation of the peasant family for the following years. In June 1930, the money on account totaled merely RM 36.33. The page reproduced above shows the cash flows between December 1940 and October 1944. In May 1943, there was still only RM 104.93 in the account, but in the following months, deposits of large sums of cash began, ultimately bringing the small farmer's account to the handsome total of RM 15,796.53. Identifiable on the two pages shown here are five deposits: on May 12, 1943, RM 1,100; on the same day, RM 3,000 more; on November 19, RM 900; on December 20, RM 1,300; and on October 31, 1944, RM 1,150. Until the late summer of 1943, deposits in the accounts of both the wife and the father-in-law of Johann Niemann correspond with possible leave dates for Niemann, who thus could have brought the sums of money in person from the General Government. But because cash deposits continued even after Niemann's death in October 1943, it stands to reason that the family in Völlen was keeping additional stolen cash at home and depositing it into the accounts bit by bit.

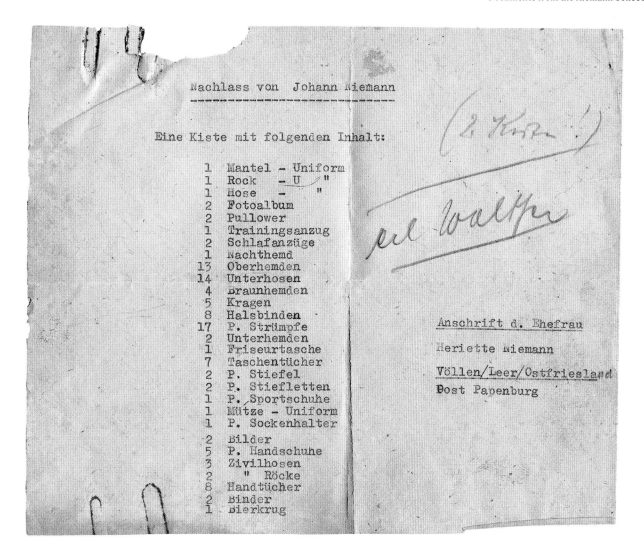

Nachlass von Johann Niemann

Eine Kiste mit folgenden Inhalt:

```
 1  Mantel - Uniform
 1  Rock   - U "
 1  Hose   -     "
 2  Fotoalbum
 2  Pullower
 1  Trainingsanzug
 2  Schlafanzüge
 1  Nachthemd
13  Oberhemden
14  Unterhosen
 4  Braunhemden
 5  Kragen
 8  Halsbinden
17  P. Strümpfe
 2  Unterhemden
 1  Friseurtasche
 7  Taschentücher
 2  P. Stiefel
 2  P. Stiefletten
 1  P. Sportschuhe
 1  Mütze - Uniform
 1  P. Sockenhalter

 2  Bilder
 5  P. Handschuhe
 3  Zivilhosen
 2   "  Röcke
 8  Handtücher
 2  Binder
 1  Bierkrug
```

Anschrift d. Ehefrau

Heriette Niemann

Völlen/Leer/Ostfriesland
Post Papenburg

Appendix 2 figure 2.5. List of the personal effects of Johann Niemann, made by Arnold Oels, the personnel official responsible for Operation Reinhard men at the Chancellery of the Führer, after the revolt of the Jewish prisoners and the killing of twelve German members of the camp SS on site in Sobibor. The list includes two photo albums (line 4).

Appendix 3
Short Biographies of Survivors of the Sobibor Camp

COMPILED BY THE BILDUNGSWERK STANISŁAW HANTZ

Included here are those survivors whose statements are mentioned in the book.

Bachir (Bahir), Moshe, born Szklarek on July 19, 1927, in Płock (Poland), was deported along with his mother and two brothers from the town of Komarów near Zamość to Sobibor in early May 1942. He was the only member of his family to be selected for forced labor upon arrival at the camp. He was deployed in the train station detail and also in the sorting detail for foodstuffs. In addition, he had to cut off the women's hair before they were murdered. After escaping from the camp during the revolt on October 14, 1943, he and another escaped prisoner stayed in the surrounding forests until liberation. After a period in a camp for displaced persons in Italy, he immigrated to Israel. Bachir testified several times against German perpetrators, including serving as a witness in the Eichmann trial in 1961. He died in Israel in 2002.

Bialowitz (Białowicz), Philip (Fiszel), born on December 25, 1925, in Izbica (Poland), together with his brother and two sisters, was deported to Sobibor in April 1943 in a group of the last Jews living in Izbica. At the camp, he worked in the sorting and train station details and also had to cut off the women's hair before they were killed. After escaping from the camp during the prisoner revolt, he and his brother managed to hide near their home town, in the house of a farmer whom they knew, until liberation. After the war Philip Bialowitz immigrated first to West Germany and later to the United States. He testified on several occasions against German perpetrators. In 2008 he published his memoirs, *A Promise at Sobibór*. He died in New York on August 6, 2016.

Bialowitz (Białowicz), Symcha, born on February 16, 1912, in Izbica (Poland), together with his brother and two sisters, was deported to Sobibor in April 1943 in a group of the last Jewish residents of Izbica. At the camp, he was deployed in the forest detachment and in the camp pharmacy. Symcha Bialowitz played an active role in the revolt on October 14, 1943. After escaping, he and his brother managed to hide in the home of a farmer whom they knew, near Izbica, until they were liberated by the Red Army. Following liberation, he went to Berlin; in 1949, he immigrated to Israel. There he married Lea Reyzner, a Jewish survivor from Zamość. He died in Israel on February 14, 2014.

Biskubicz, Jakub (Jakób), born on March 17, 1926, in Hrubieszów (Poland), was deported, with his family, from his home town to Sobibor in May 1942. He and his father were selected for work in the camp. His father was later shot there; his sister, mother, and grandmother were murdered in the gas chambers immediately after arrival. In the camp, he was deployed in the train station detail and in the carpenters' workshop. After escaping from the camp during the revolt on October 14, 1943, he spent weeks in the surrounding forests. At some point he was able to join a partisan unit and eventually the Red Army. Shortly after the war, Biskubicz immigrated to Israel. He gave testimony several times in trials of the German perpetrators. He died in Ramat Gan, Israel, in 2002.

Blatt, Thomas (Toivi), born on April 15, 1927, in Izbica (Poland), was deported to Sobibor on April 28, 1943, with his parents and his younger brother. Upon arrival, he was the only member of his family selected for forced labor in the camp. His task there was to burn the victims' papers—documents, photos, and letters—that had been taken away from them before they were murdered. After he had fled the camp during the prisoner revolt, he and two other escaped prisoners initially found refuge with a farmer, in exchange for payment. A few months later, however, their hiding place was betrayed. The other prisoners were killed. Blatt, though wounded, managed to escape and survive in the forests until liberation came, some weeks later. In the 1950s, he immigrated, first to Israel, and later to the United States. He published two books about his experiences and served as a witness in several trials of Nazi perpetrators, including the trial of John Demjanjuk in 2009. Thomas (Toivi) Blatt died in Santa Barbara, California, on October 31, 2015.

Cukierman, Hershel (Hersz), born on April 15, 1893, in Kurów (Poland), with his wife, Sara Cukierman, and his four children, was deported from the Opole Lubelski ghetto to Sobibor in May 1942. His wife and the three youngest children were killed immediately after arrival at the camp. He and his eldest son, Josef, were selected for forced labor in the camp. Hershel Cukierman worked in the camp as a cook; his son worked as a helper in the kitchen and the SS mess hall and as a shoeshine boy. After escaping from the camp during the revolt on October 14, 1943, they both were able to make their way back to their hometown, where they finally paid Polish farmers whom they knew to give them a hiding place. In May 1944, the son joined a partisan unit in the surrounding forests. After the war, the father and son reunited in Lublin, and later they immigrated together to West Germany. Both testified at trials of Erich Bauer in Berlin and Hubert Gomerski and Johann Klier in Frankfurt. Hershel Cukierman immigrated to the United States in the 1950s; his son Josef stayed in Germany, where he died of a heart attack on June 15, 1963. Hershel Cukierman took the witness stand once again in 1965, in the Sobibor trial in Hagen. He died in Irvington, New Jersey, in 1979.

Cymiel (before the war: Szymiel), Leon, born on February 20, 1924, in Chełm (Poland), was deported to Sobibor from a labor camp in Chełm in spring 1943, in a transport consisting of only a few cars. His father had already been deported to the killing camp at an earlier date. Upon arrival, Cymiel and twenty to thirty other deportees were selected for forced labor, to help with the further expansion of the camp. He was initially assigned to the train station detail. Leon Cymiel died in Warsaw in 1997.

Engel, Chaim, born on January 10, 1916, in Brudzew (Poland), was deported from Izbica to Sobibor on November 6, 1942. He met his future wife, Selma Wijnberg, a native of the Netherlands, in the camp. The two succeeded in escaping from Sobibor together during the revolt. Until they were liberated by the Red Army, they were hidden by a Polish farmer and his wife near Chełm. A few days after the liberation, Selma gave birth to a son, Emielchen. The young family spent a few more months in Poland before finally immigrating to the Netherlands. Their son, only a few months old, died on the voyage to Marseille. Fresh experiences of antisemitism and racism led the couple to leave Holland in the early 1950s, first for Israel and later for the United States. Chaim Engel testified several times in trials of German perpetrators. In addition, together with his wife, Selma Wijnberg-Engel, he regularly spoke to school classes about his experiences in Sobibor. Chaim Engel died in New Haven, Connecticut, on July 4, 2003, from injuries incurred in a car accident.

Felenbaum-Weiss, Hela (Hella), née Felenbaum, born on November 25, 1924, in Lublin (Poland), was deported from the Staw labor camp, which was being closed, to Sobibor at the end of December 1942, together with her two brothers. Their parents had been deported to Sobibor and murdered there several weeks earlier. One of her brothers, Shimek Felenbaum, tried to jump off the horse-drawn cart that was taking them to the camp but was shot by one of the German guards. At the Staw labor camp, Hela Felenbaum had already met Zelda Metz, Ester Terner (married name: Raab), and Riwka Feldman (married name: Zieliński), women whom she reencountered in Sobibor. Upon arriving at Sobibor, she was selected for forced labor. Her remaining brother, Heniek Felenbaum, was murdered immediately after arrival. In Sobibor, Hela Felenbaum was deployed in the knitting workshop, the laundry, and the gardening center. After she escaped during the prisoners' revolt, she first spent several days with Abraham Margulies in surrounding forests. Later, the two met other survivors from Sobibor, with whom they continued their journey. In the spring of 1944, Hela Felenbaum managed to join a Soviet partisan unit. After the Red Army arrived, she joined the Soviet armed forces and took part in the advance into the German Reich. After the war, she lived

at first in the territory of the former Czechoslovakia, where she met her future husband, Josef Weiss. Together, the couple later immigrated to Israel. Hela Felenbaum-Weiss testified several times in trials of German perpetrators. She died in Gedera, Israel, in 1998.

Felhendler (Feldhendler), Leon (Lejb/Lejbl), born on June 1, 1910, in Turobin (Poland), was deported with his wife, Toba Felhendler, and two sons from Izbica to Sobibor in January 1943. His wife and children were murdered upon arrival at the camp. Leon Felhendler had a leading role in organizing the revolt on October 14, 1943. After escaping, he and another fugitive from Sobibor, Majer Ziss from Hrubieszów ("Majorkiem"), returned to his previous place of residence, Żółkiewka, where he was hidden by a Polish couple. When neighbors became suspicious, he had to move to a different hiding place in the same village. After liberation, Felhendler moved to Lublin and married again. He lived with his second wife in the old quarter of Lublin, at 6/4 Złota Street, where he was shot by unidentified antisemites on April 3, 1945. Three days later, on April 6, 1945, Leon Felhendler succumbed to his wounds.

Freiberg, Dov (Berek), born on May 15, 1927, in Warsaw (Poland), was deported from the Warsaw Ghetto via Krasnystaw to Sobibor in May 1942. He arrived at the camp on May 14, one day before his fifteenth birthday. His mother and his siblings remained behind in Warsaw and were later murdered. In the camp, Dov Freiberg was deployed in various labor detachments: he worked in construction and forestry details, he polished shoes, and he helped to cut the women's hair before they were murdered. After escaping from the camp on October 14, 1943, he and another escaped prisoner, former Red Army soldier Semion Rozenfeld, managed to survive in the nearby forests and in various hiding places for months, until liberation. After the war, he went first to Germany and prepared for immigration to Palestine. An initial attempt to immigrate failed, however, when the ship *Exodus* was turned away by the British and sent back to Germany. Finally, in 1948, he was able to emigrate. Dov Freiberg gave testimony against German perpetrators on several occasions, including the Eichmann trial in 1961. In 2007 he published his memoirs, *To Survive Sobibor*. Dov Freiberg died in Israel in 2008.

Goldfarb, Mordechai (Mordechaj), born on March 15, 1920, in Piaski (Poland), was deported from the Piaski ghetto to Sobibor at the end of October 1942. In the camp, the trained painter had to produce pictures and signs for the camp staff. In addition, he was assigned to the train station detail. After escaping from the camp during the revolt on October 14, 1943, he joined a Jewish partisan unit, in which he fought until liberation. After the war, Mordechai Goldfarb immigrated to Israel. He testified several times at trials, providing information about his time in Sobibor. He died in Israel on June 8, 1984.

Kohn, Abraham (Abram), born on July 25, 1910, in Łódź (Poland), had to leave his home town with his family in early 1940. They went to relatives in Wysokie. In May 1942, they were deported to Sobibor, where Abraham Kohn performed forced labor in the sorting and forestry detachments and in the kitchen. After the revolt, he was hidden, along with Eda Waldman (married name: Lichtman) and Samuel Lerer, by a Polish farmer in Janów near Chełm until liberation. He immigrated to Australia after the war, and from there gave sworn evidence for the trial of Gomerski. Abraham Kohn died in Australia in 1986.

Lerer, Samuel, born on October 1, 1922, in Żółkiewka (Poland), together with his parents, a sister, and three brothers, was deported from his home town via Krasnystaw to Sobibor in early May 1942. His parents, youngest brother, and sister were murdered in the gas chambers upon arrival. In the camp,

Samuel Lerer worked in the horse stables, and his two brothers were deployed in the clothes-sorting detachment. Both brothers were killed in the prisoner revolt on October 14, 1943; he himself, along with two other prisoners, Ester Terner (married name: Raab) and Abraham Kohn, managed to escape. In Janów near Chełm, they were hidden in the barn of acquaintances, a peasant family, until liberation. After the war, the three lived together for a few weeks in Chełm and Lublin, but at the end of 1945, repeated antisemitic attacks on survivors in Poland caused them to go to Berlin. There, at a fair in Berlin-Kreuzberg in 1949, Samuel Lerer and Ester Raab came across the SS man Erich Bauer. They filed a report with the police and brought about his arrest, which led to his conviction one year later. Lerer subsequently immigrated to the United States and started a family. He gave evidence several times in trials of German perpetrators. Samuel Lerer died in New Jersey on March 3, 2016.

Lerner, Jehuda Leon, born on July 22, 1926, in Warsaw (Poland), was deported from Minsk in September 1943, after the forced labor camp there and the affiliated ghetto had been liquidated. His family had already been deported to Treblinka and murdered there several months earlier. In Sobibor, Jehuda Lerner was deployed at construction work for Camp IV. He participated actively in planning the revolt on October 14, 1943, and during its course, he killed the SS man Graetschus. After escaping from the camp, he fought in a partisan unit until liberated by the Red Army. After the war, he served for six months as vice-commander of the police force in Radom. Following several attacks on him by Polish antisemites from the *Armia Krajowa* milieu, he finally went to Wałbrzych (Waldenburg, Silesia), where he met his future wife. They went to West Germany and lived there in a DP camp, where their first daughter was born. In 1949, the family immigrated to Israel, where Lerner worked as a policeman. Claude Lanzmann interviewed Lerner in 1979 as part of the work on the film *Shoah*. In

2001, the powerful interview received special recognition due to a separate documentary film by Lanzmann, *Sobibor, 14 octobre 1943, 16 heures.* Jehuda Lerner died in Israel in 2007.

Lichtman, Eda (Ada), née Fiszer (married name: Waldman), born on January 1, 1915, in Jarosław (dual monarchy of Austria-Hungary, now Poland), was deported from Hrubieszów to Sobibor in June 1942. Her first husband had already been murdered in the Pustków labor camp in 1941. Along with two other women from her transport, she was among the first female forced laborers in the death camp. In Sobibor, she met Icchak Lichtman, whom she later married. After the escape, she, together with Cathi Gökkes and Ursula Stern (later Ilona Safran), joined a Jewish partisan unit, where she met Icchak Lichtman again. After liberation, they married and, in 1950, immigrated to Israel, where they settled near Tel Aviv. Eda Lichtman gave evidence several times in trials of German perpetrators, including the Eichmann trial in 1961. Eda Lichtmann talked about her experiences in Sobibor in Claude Lanzmann's documentary film *Four Sisters / Les Quatre Soeurs* (2018). She died in Israel in 1993.

Lichtman, Icchak (Itzaak/Yitzchak), born on December 10, 1908, in Żółkiewka (Poland), was deported to Sobibor in mid-May 1942 with his wife, his six-year-old son, his parents, three brothers, and a sister. After reaching the camp, he was the only member of his family selected for forced labor. His son was torn from his hands on the ramp and, together with his mother, forced into the gas chamber. In the camp, Icchak Lichtman was assigned to work in the cobblers' workshop. In Sobibor, he also met the woman who became his second wife, Eda Waldman (later Eda Lichtman). He had an active role in planning the revolt, in the course of which he killed the SS man Vallaster. After escaping from the camp, he fled across the Bug River and joined a partisan unit. There he met Eda Waldman,

also an escapee, again. Together, they stayed with the partisans until they were liberated by the Red Army. They married after the war and immigrated to Israel in 1950. They made their home in the vicinity of Tel Aviv. Icchak Lichtman died in Holon, Israel, in 1992.

Margulies, Abraham, born on January 25, 1921, in Żyrardów near Warsaw (Poland), was deported from the Zamość ghetto to Sobibor in May 1942. Upon arrival, he was selected for forced labor in the camp. He spent most of his time there in the train station detail, but he also had to sort clothes and work in the kitchen. After escaping during the revolt, he joined a partisan unit and fought there until he was liberated by the Red Army. Later he immigrated to Israel, where he worked as a printer. On several occasions, he gave evidence in trials of German perpetrators, including the Sobibor trials in Hagen. Abraham Margulies died in Israel in 1984.

Pechersky (Pecherskii), Alexander (Aleksandr), born on February 22, 1909, in Kremenchuk (Ukraine), a Jewish soldier in the Red Army, was deported from the POW camp in Minsk, upon its closure, to Sobibor in September 1943. At the ramp in Sobibor, along with sixty other Jewish Red Army men, he was selected for forced labor in the camp. Then Pechersky and other Soviet soldiers made contact with prisoners who had already been in the camp for some time. Together they began to lay plans for a revolt. After escaping, he and a few other Red Army men managed to cross the nearby Bug River and join a Russian partisan unit. After he was liberated by Soviet forces, he rejoined the Red Army and fought until he suffered a leg injury in August 1944. In the military hospital, he met his future wife, Olga. Once he had recovered, he returned to his former place of residence, Rostov on the Don River. In the 1960s, he published his memoirs of the revolt in book form. Pechersky testified against former Trawnikis in several trials, including proceedings in Kiev and Krasnodar. He was invited to testify at the Sobibor trials in Hagen but was denied permission to leave the Soviet Union; the court then had him deposed in Rostov on the Don. The Sobibor survivors living in the Soviet Union met regularly after the war. Alexander Pechersky died on January 19, 1990, in Rostov on the Don, Soviet Union.

Raab, Ester (Estera/Esther), née Terner, born on June 11, 1922, in Chełm (Poland), along with her brother, was deported to Sobibor from the Staw labor camp, upon its closure, in December 1942. During the journey, her brother managed to escape by jumping off the horse-drawn vehicle taking them to the camp. In Staw, Terner had met Hela Felenbaum, Zelda Metz, and Riwka Feldman, whom she later reencountered in Sobibor. Upon arrival at the camp, Terner was selected for forced labor by Gustav Wagner. She was assigned at first to the knitting workshop and later to the clothes-sorting detail. After the escape, she, together with Samuel Lerer and Abraham Kohn, found refuge in the barn of a Polish peasant family whom she knew, in Janów near Chełm. There she was reunited with her brother. After she was liberated by the Red Army, she first returned to her hometown of Chełm, where she ran across Irving Raab, her future husband, whom she had known before the war. They lived in Chełm and Lublin for several weeks before moving to Berlin at the end of 1945 in reaction to repeated antisemitic assaults in the region. The couple married in Berlin in 1946. In 1949, while at a local fair in Berlin-Kreuzberg, Ester Raab and Samuel Lerer happened to see the SS man Erich Bauer. They filed a report with the police and brought about his arrest, which led to his conviction one year later. In 1950 Ester Raab and her husband immigrated to the United States. She returned to Germany on several occasions to testify in trials of Nazi perpetrators. Ester Raab died in Vineland, New Jersey, on April 15, 2015.

Rotenberg, Ajzik (Aisik), born in 1925 in Włodawa (Poland), was deported to Sobibor in May 1943, when the ghetto in Włodawa was terminated. He was forced to make the trip on foot. In the camp, he was assigned to build barracks and houses. After the revolt he was captured in Adampol but managed to escape once more. He then joined a group of Jewish partisans. After liberation, he immigrated to Israel, started a family, and worked as a plasterer. He testified in both trials in Hagen involving the German perpetrators at the Sobibor camp. In 1994 he was seriously injured in an attack in Israel and died.

Rozenfeld (Rosenfeld), Semion (Shimon/Semjon), born on October 1, 1922, in Ternivka (Ukraine), a Jewish soldier in the Red Army, was deported to Sobibor from the Minsk POW camp upon its closure in September 1943. In the selection process at the ramp, he and around sixty other Jewish Red Army men were singled out for forced labor in the camp. His main task there was to build barracks in Camp I. He played an active part in the revolt on October 14, 1943, and had been assigned to kill the SS man Frenzel. Frenzel was not to be found, however, and survived. After escaping from the camp, Rozenfeld joined other escaped prisoners, including Dov (Berek) Freiberg, in the forest. Together with Freiberg, he survived until liberation by the Red Army, spending the intervening months in various hiding places in the forest and in the homes of Polish farmers. A few days after liberation, Rozenfeld rejoined the Red Army. After being wounded and spending a short time convalescing, he took part in the march on the Reich capital. In Berlin, like hundreds of other Soviet soldiers, he scrawled a message on a wall of the Reichstag. After the war, he, his wife, and their two sons spent many decades in Ukraine. In 1990, the family immigrated to Israel. Simeon Rozenfeld died in Gedera, Israel, on June 3, 2019.

Safran, Ilona, née Ursula Stern, born on August 28, 1926, in Essen (Germany), was deported to Sobibor in April 1943 via the Vught and Westerbork concentration camps in the Netherlands. Upon arrival at the ramp, she was selected for forced labor in the camp. She was initially assigned to the clothes-sorting detail and later moved to a construction detail for Camp IV, the new section of Sobibor. After escaping on October 14, 1943, she, together with Eda Waldman (married name: Lichtman) and Cathi Gökkes, joined a partisan unit and fought there until liberated by the Red Army. Cathi Gökkes was killed by retreating German Wehrmacht units shortly before the Soviet troops arrived. Ursula Stern and Eda Waldman survived. After the war ended, she traveled to Odessa via Lublin and Czernowitz with two other survivors, Selma Wijnberg and Chaim Engel. From there they continued their journey by ship to Marseille and reached the Netherlands in early 1946. There she met her future husband, Horst Martin Buchheimer, who also had emigrated from Germany during the war and had survived the German occupation of the Netherlands in the underground. At the end of 1947 the couple immigrated to Israel, where Ursula Stern took the name Ilona Safran. They started a family and had two children. Ilona Safran died in Israel in 1985.

Szmajzner, Stanisław (Szlomo), born on March 13, 1927, in Puławy (Poland), was deported to Sobibor from Opole Lubelskie in May 1942. At the beginning of his time in the camp, he was deployed as a goldsmith and forced to make jewelry for the German camp personnel from the precious metals looted from the victims and from the dental gold of the dead. Following that assignment, he headed a detachment of prisoners working in the skilled crafts and trades. Szmajzner took an active part in planning the revolt of October 14, 1943. After escaping from the camp, he hid at first, along with other escapees, in the forests around Sobibor, where the fugitives were attacked by

nationalist Polish partisans. Most of the approximately sixteen members of the group were murdered at that time. Then Szmajzner fought in a Jewish partisan unit until the war ended. In 1947, he immigrated to Brazil, where his book *Inferno em Sobibor* was published in 1968. In 1978, in São Paulo, he identified the former "camp sergeant" of Sobibor, SS-Oberscharführer Gustav Wagner, and brought about his arrest. Szmajzner died in the small town of Goiânia on March 3, 1989.

Thomas (Ticho), Kurt, born on April 11, 1914, in Brno (dual monarchy of Austria-Hungary, today Czechia), was deported to Sobibor from the Piaski transit camp in early November 1942. His parents, his sister, and his aunt had already been taken there several weeks earlier and murdered. He was forced to work in the camp's clothes-sorting detachment at first, and from the spring of 1943, he was deployed as a medical orderly in the newly created infirmary. After escaping from the camp during the revolt on October 14, 1943, he was able to find refuge with a Polish farmer whom he knew, near Piaski. There he spent the following months until he was liberated by the Red Army. After liberation, Thomas joined a Czech legion of the Red Army, and after the war's end he returned to his homeland. As early as 1946, he put together a report about his experiences in Sobibor for the Red Cross in Amsterdam. In 1948, Thomas immigrated to the United States, where he met his future wife, Tena. On several occasions he testified in trials of German perpetrators. He published his memoirs under the title *My Legacy*. Kurt Thomas died in Columbus, Ohio, on June 8, 2009.

Waispapir (Weispapir/Wajspapier), Arkadii (Arkady) Moiseevich, born in 1921 in Tver' (Ukraine), became a prisoner of war in 1941 and was imprisoned in Minsk for almost two years, until he was deported to Sobibor in September 1943. In the camp, he worked primarily on the construction of barracks. He was involved in the planning for the prisoner revolt and ultimately in the killing of two guards, Graetschus and Klatt. In a group of escaped prisoners, he fled across the Bug River, joined the partisans, and later rejoined the advancing Red Army. After the war, he started a family, worked as a technical engineer, and testified in several trials of German perpetrators. Arkadii Waispapir died in Kiev in January 2018.

Waizen, Aleksej, born on May 30, 1922 in Chodoriw (then Poland, now Ukraine), was made a prisoner of war by the Germans in 1941 and was deported to Sobibor in May/June 1942. In the camp he was forced to work in the sorting detachment. After escaping, he joined a group of Jewish partisans and later joined the Red Army. After the war he married and continued for many years to serve in the Red Army. For a very long time, he said nothing to anyone, particularly his family, about his experiences. He was interrogated several times for proceedings against the Trawnikis and German perpetrators. Aleksej Waizen died in Riazan' (Ryazan), Russia, on January 14, 2015.

Wewryk (Weweryk), Kalmen, born on June 25, 1906, in Chełm (Poland), was deported to Sobibor from his hometown in November 1942. His wife, Jocheved, his eight-year-old son Jossele, and his three-year-old daughter Pesha had already been deported to Sobibor in the summer of 1942 and murdered there. Selected for forced labor upon arrival at the camp, the trained carpenter was assigned primarily to work on building barracks and houses. After the revolt, Kalmen Wewryk, on his own at first, fled through the surrounding forests and tried to reach his hometown, approximately 12.5 miles away. Later he succeeded in joining a partisan unit near Chełm and fought with the unit until he was liberated by the Red Army. After the war, Kalmen Wewryk went to Wrocław, where he met his second wife, an Auschwitz survivor. The couple started a family,

and in 1956, the antisemitic climate in Poland led them to emigrate from Poland and settle first in France and then, in 1968, in Canada. Kalmen Wewryk died in Quebec, Canada, in 1989. In 1999, his story, *To Sobibor and Back: An Eyewitness Account*, was published.

Wijnberg-Engel, Selma (Saartje), née Wijnberg, born on May 15, 1922, in Groningen (Netherlands), was discovered in her hiding place and deported to Sobibor in early April 1943 via the Vught concentration camp and the Westerbork transit camp. After her arrival in the camp on April 9, 1943, she was selected for forced labor and assigned to the clothes-sorting detachment. She met her future husband, Chaim Engel, in Sobibor. With him, she succeeded in escaping from the camp during the revolt on October 14, 1943, and hiding in the home of a Polish peasant couple near Chełm until liberation by the Red Army. A few days after liberation, Selma Wijnberg gave birth to a son, Emielchen. The young family remained in Poland a few months longer, until finally moving to the Netherlands. During the sea voyage to Marseille, Emielchen, only a few months old, died. Fresh experiences of antisemitism and racism in the early 1950s led the couple to immigrate, first to Israel and later to the United States. Selma Wijnberg-Engel, together with her husband, testified several times in trials of German perpetrators. With her husband, Chaim Engel, she also spoke to school classes on a regular basis about her experiences in Sobibor. Selma Wijnberg-Engel died in East Haven, Connecticut, on December 4, 2018.

Zieliński, Regina, born Riwka (Rywka) Feldman on September 2, 1924, in Siedliszcze (Poland), was deported to Sobibor from the Staw labor camp, upon its closure, with her parents, her sister, and her brother at the end of December 1942. In Staw, her cousin Zelda Metz was a fellow prisoner, and she had already come to know Hela Felenbaum and Ester Terner (married name: Raab) there. She reencountered all three women in Sobibor. Her parents and sister were murdered upon arrival in the camp; her brother was selected for forced labor in Camp III, the killing area of Sobibor, and murdered after an attempt by a group of prisoners to escape in the summer of 1943. Regina Zieliński herself was assigned at first to the knitting workshop in Sobibor, and later she also had to work in the laundry, the sewing room, and the clothes-sorting detachment. After escaping during the revolt on October 14, 1943, she, Zelda Metz, and a male prisoner kept together at first but parted ways in the following weeks. In early 1944, she went back to her hometown of Siedliszcze, where she used false papers provided by friends of her parents to obtain a work permit. Disguised as a non-Jewish Pole, she worked as a nanny in Frankfurt am Main until the war ended. There she met her future husband, Kazimierz Zieliński, whom she married in 1945. In 1949, the couple immigrated to Australia. In the 1970s and 1980s, Regina Zieliński gave evidence several times in trials of German perpetrators. In her new homeland, she regularly gave talks to school classes about her experiences in Sobibor. She died in Australia in September 2014.

Appendix 4
Short Biographies of German Perpetrators

COMPILED BY MARTIN CÜPPERS

Included here are those who could be identified in the photos of the Niemann collection with certainty or with some degree of confidence.

Allers, Dietrich, born May 17, 1910, in Kiel; died March 22, 1975, in Munich.
As a teenager, he belonged to the antidemocratic youth organization "Jungsturm" from 1923 to 1927. After graduation from secondary school, he studied law in Berlin and Jena and became an administrative civil servant in 1937. Allers joined the NSDAP and the SA in 1932. He fought in the war in 1940, and then was exempted from military service and recruited for the T4 program by Werner Blankenburg, an acquaintance from the SA. From early 1941, he served as general manager of the Berlin Central Office of T4 and, in that capacity, also visited the killing facilities. From 1942, he also had a comparable function for Operation Reinhard and inspected the death camps in the General Government on several occasions. After Christian Wirth's death in 1944, Allers became his successor in Italy, with an office in Trieste. In 1945, he escaped to Austria but was captured there by British troops and interned until 1947. Afterward he worked as a lumberjack and in other jobs. In 1952, he ran for election as a member of the far-right Socialist Reich Party (*Sozialistische Reichspartei*). Then he found employment as a company lawyer with Deutsche Werft, a shipbuilding firm in Hamburg, and practiced law once again. Among other things, he advised the Sobibor perpetrator Kurt Bolender. He also maintained personal contact with other T4 and Operation Reinhard perpetrators. In the trial of leading officials in the T4 program, he was sentenced to eight years in prison by the Regional Court (*Landgericht*) in Frankfurt/Main in late 1968 for complicity in thousands of murders. Because he was credited with time spent in investigative custody, however, he did not have to serve the sentence. Proceedings initiated in the early 1970s concerning his responsibility for crimes committed in Italy were abandoned because of his death.

Barbl, Heinrich, born March 3, 1900, in Sarleinsbach, Austria; date of death unknown.
Barbl, a plumber by trade, joined the SA in 1933. The following year, he was under arrest in Austria for three weeks for distributing Nazi publications. He joined the SS in 1938. Barbl evidently came to Hartheim to join the T4 program in 1940 at the request of Christian Wirth. In Hartheim, he helped to build the gas chamber and later embossed the names of murder victims on urns. At the beginning of 1942, he was transferred

to Belzec with the rank of SS-Unterscharführer. There, using his previous expertise as a plumber, he installed pipes in the first stationary gas chambers. Together with Erich Fuchs, Barbl did the same work at Sobibor in the spring of 1942. Frequently drunk on the job, it appears, he was regarded as simple-minded by his German comrades. After the end of Operation Reinhard, Barbl was deployed in the Trieste area of Italy to "fight against partisans." Once the war was over, he lived in Austria again. He was repeatedly interrogated as a witness but was never charged himself.

Bauer, Erich, born March 26, 1900, in Berlin; died February 4, 1980, in Berlin.

After an apprenticeship as a lathe operator, Bauer fought in World War I and was taken prisoner by the French forces. After the war, he trained as a driver. He worked as a streetcar conductor in Berlin from 1933 to 1940. Bauer joined the SA in 1933 and the NSDAP in 1937. Detailed to the T4 program as a result of his membership in an SA Storm Unit in Berlin, his duties there included serving as a driver for lead physicians. He was transferred to Sobibor with the rank of SS-Oberscharführer in the spring of 1942 and worked there both in Camp III and as a driver. Following the revolt in late 1943, he was transferred to Italy. After the war and a brief period as a prisoner of war in US hands, Bauer lived in Berlin again, beginning in 1946. There he was recognized by the Sobibor survivors Ester Raab and Samuel Lerer, who chanced to see him on the street in August 1949 and filed a police report. Bauer was arrested, charged, and then sentenced to death in one of the early Operation Reinhard trials, for the crimes he had committed in Sobibor. In the newly established Federal Republic of Germany, the sentence was changed in 1951 to life in prison. Subsequently, Bauer testified as a witness in other Sobibor trials.

Beckmann, Rudolf, born November 21, 1904, in Buer/Westfalen; died October 14, 1943, in Sobibor.

After training as a farmer, Beckmann joined the SA. He was then detailed to the T4 program in 1940 and also worked in Grafeneck and Hadamar as a farmer. With the rank of SS-Oberscharführer, he was transferred in the spring of 1942 to Sobibor, where he commanded the sorting detachments in Camp II. In addition, he was responsible for managing the horses on the "hereditary farm" (Erbhof) and worked in the forester's lodge for the camp administration. It was in this building that he was killed by Chaim Engel and the Kapo Pożyczki during the revolt.

Blankenburg, Werner, born June 19, 1905, in Caputh/Brandenburg; died November 28, 1957, in Stuttgart.

Blankenburg joined the NSDAP and the SA as early as April 1929. From 1938, as the deputy of Oberdienstleiter Viktor Brack, the head of Office II, Blankenburg was Oberbereichsleiter of Department II a of the Chancellery of the Führer, where plans for implementing the "euthanasia" program for adults were being accelerated in the summer of 1939. In addition to Brack, Blankenburg had a key role in the T4 program from the outset. After Brack left in the summer of 1942, Blankenburg took over the position and thus was also responsible for the implementation of Operation Reinhard in the Belzec, Sobibor, and Treblinka camps until the program ended; he visited the sites on several occasions. After the war, he lived in Stuttgart under the assumed name of Werner Bieleke and had various jobs in Ludwigsburg, Freudenstadt, and elsewhere. Attempts by law enforcement authorities to learn his whereabouts continued, apparently with very little vigor, until his death. Former members of the T4 program and associates from the Chancellery of the Führer, apparently including Allers, took part in his funeral service.

Bolender, Kurt, born May 21, 1912, in Duisburg; died October 10, 1966, in Hagen (suicide while in custody).

Following training, Bolender worked as an iron inspector for Thyssen. In 1931, he joined the NSDAP and the SA, and the next year he switched to the SS. In 1939, Bolender was a soldier in an SS Death's-Head regiment (*Standarte*), and from there he was detached to the T4 program for work as a "burner" in Brandenburg, Hartheim, and Sonnenstein. In the winter of 1941/42, the Chancellery of the Führer assigned him to Medical Service East (*Sanitätsdienst Ost*) at the front. In his next assignment, Bolender, now with the rank of SS-Scharführer, went to Sobibor in April 1942. There, he supervised Jewish labor detachments at the gas chambers and mass graves in Camp III and was responsible for countless atrocities. At the end of the year, he was sentenced by the German Police Court in Cracow to several months of imprisonment for incitement of perjury in his divorce proceedings. After the revolt in Sobibor, he continued to be deployed for the dismantling of the camp and was then sent to Italy with other key players from Operation Reinhard. After the war ended, he temporarily used the alias "Heinz Brenner," in an allusion to his former work duties. Later, he lived in Hamburg under the name "Wilhelm Kurt Vahle." He maintained contact with Dietrich Allers, who also gave him legal advice. In the course of judicial investigations regarding Sobibor, Bolender was tracked down in 1961 and, beginning in 1965, brought to trial in the Sobibor trial in Hagen. Before the sentence was proclaimed, he hanged himself in his cell.

Dachsel, Arthur, born March 11, 1890, in Böhlen/Saxony; pronounced dead in 1958.

Dachsel worked first as a blacksmith and then as a medical orderly. He joined the NSDAP in 1933. In 1940, he was detailed to Operation T4 and assigned to Sonnenstein as a medical orderly. In the fall of 1942, he was transferred to Belzec as one of the oldest actors from the Chancellery of the Führer to participate in Operation Reinhard. In Belzec, he supervised the sorting of the looted items. In the summer of 1943, he was transferred to Sobibor, where his duties included helping to build Camp IV. After the revolt, he was sent to Italy with other Germans at the end of 1943. Details of his life after 1945 are not known.

Floß, Herbert, born August 25, 1912, in Reinholdshain/Saxony; died October 22, 1943, near Chełm.

After an apprenticeship as a dyer, Floß was temporarily unemployed. In 1930, he joined the NSDAP, and the following year he also became a member of the SA. In 1935, he switched from the SA to the SS. From that time on, he worked first as a guard for the SS Death's-Head unit in the Lichtenburg concentration camp and then in the Buchenwald concentration camp. At the end of 1939, he was ordered to work in the T4 program and deployed as a "burner" in several killing facilities. In April 1942, now holding the rank of SS-Oberscharführer, he was transferred to Sobibor, where he was responsible also for the further training of the Trawnikis. Beginning in the fall of 1942, Floß acquired special knowledge of cremation. With this expertise, he transferred to Belzec in late 1942 and Treblinka in the spring of 1943, to guide the process of efficiently cremating the murder victims at each camp and, as a secondary duty, to train the Trawnikis. Following the revolt, he returned to Sobibor. Tasked with escorting a group of guards back to the village of Trawniki, he was overpowered by them near Chełm and shot with his own firearm.

Franz, Kurt, born January 17, 1914, in Düsseldorf; died July 4, 1998, in Wuppertal.

After his school years, Franz worked first as an errand boy. He began a culinary apprenticeship in 1929 and worked in various positions. In 1932, he established connections to the Steel

Helmet (*Der Stahlhelm*), a veterans' organization. In 1935, Franz was in the military, serving in an artillery regiment. In 1937, he joined the SS and became a guard in the SS Death's-Head Regiment "Thüringen" in the Buchenwald concentration camp. From there, in the fall of 1939, he was detailed to the T4 program and deployed primarily as a cook at the Grafeneck, Brandenburg, Hartheim, and Sonnenstein killing facilities and in the staff dining room at the Chancellery of the Führer in Berlin. With the rank of SS-Oberscharführer, Franz was sent to Belzec in May 1942; in September he was transferred to Treblinka as deputy camp commandant under Franz Stangl. At Treblinka, he was known among the prisoners by the nickname "Lyalke" (Yiddish: doll) and greatly feared as a result of countless acts of cruelty. After the dismantling of Treblinka, he was ordered to Italy as a trainer. In May 1945 Franz escaped to Germany. Captured shortly thereafter by US forces, he took flight again. Subsequently he found work in his hometown, first as a bridge-builder and then as a cook once again. Franz was arrested and charged in late 1959 in the course of judicial investigations relating to Treblinka. In 1965, in the Düsseldorf Treblinka trial, he was sentenced to lifelong imprisonment. He became a day-release prisoner in the late 1970s and was granted full release in 1993.

Frenzel, Karl, born August 20, 1911, in Zehdenick/Brandenburg; died September 2, 1996, near Hanover.
After training as a carpenter and a period of temporary unemployment, Frenzel found work in the agricultural sector and as a driver. He joined the NSDAP and the SA in 1930, and after changing jobs several times, he was detailed to the T4 "euthanasia" program in early 1940 at the recommendation of his SA superiors. In T4, he was deployed as a "burner" in Grafeneck, Bernburg, and Hadamar. In April 1942, he was deployed to Sobibor with the rank of SS-Oberscharführer. There, as head of Camp I, he was infamous for his countless acts of cruelty.

Having frustrated the prisoners' plan to kill him during the revolt, he subsequently played a part in the dismantling of the camp until the end of 1943, when he was transferred to Italy and deployed in Trieste and Fiume. When the German forces retreated, he was briefly in US captivity. After that, in civilian life in Göttingen, he was ultimately employed as stage manager at a film studio. In the course of the investigations regarding Sobibor, Frenzel was arrested and brought to trial in 1965. Sentenced in Hagen to life imprisonment, he was released at the end of 1975 but later arrested again. In his appeal proceedings in 1985, he received the same sentence, although it was not imposed because of his poor health.

Gomerski, Hubert, born November 11, 1911, in Schweinheim/Lower Franconia; died December 28, 1999, in Frankfurt/Main.
Gomerski apprenticed and found employment as a lathe operator. He joined the Hitler Youth in 1925, the NSDAP in 1929, and the SS in 1930. He received military training in the fall of 1939 in an SS Death's-Head regiment in German-occupied Cracow and was subsequently detailed to Operation T4 in 1940. Initially he was deployed to Hartheim in an administrative job, and later he worked as a "burner." In Hadamar, he also worked as a "burner" and in the metalworking shop until his transfer to Sobibor in April 1942. There, as a member of the Waffen-SS, he was responsible for the further training of Trawnikis and worked primarily at the gas chambers in Camp III. In addition to Wagner and Frenzel, Gomerski was one of the most greatly feared Germans. When the revolt occurred, he was home on leave, but returned briefly to Sobibor to take part in the dismantling of the camp. At the end of 1943, he was ordered to Italy, where he was stationed in Fiume. In the Hadamar trial in 1947, he was acquitted; however, in one of the early Sobibor trials in Frankfurt/Main in August 1950, he was sentenced to life in prison. In the course of appeal proceedings in the 1970s, he was released from imprisonment. A last attempt to prosecute

him ended in 1984 with the abatement of the action because he was incompetent to stand trial.

Graetschus, Siegfried, born June 9, 1916, in Tilsit/East Prussia; died October 14, 1943, in Sobibor.

After elementary school, Graetschus worked on his parents' farm. In 1934, he served in the military. From 1936, he was a member of the NSDAP and the SS, and was a guard at the Sachsenhausen concentration camp at the time when Niemann was part of the headquarters staff there. From there, at the end of 1939, Graetschus was detailed to Operation T4 and evidently was deployed as a "burner" at the same time as Niemann in Grafeneck, Brandenburg, and Bernburg. In early 1942, now with the rank of SS-Oberscharführer, he was transferred to Belzec and then shifted to Treblinka during the construction phase in the spring. In September 1942, he was finally ordered to Sobibor, where he was responsible from then on for the further training of the Trawnikis. Another promotion in the summer of 1943 awarded him the rank of SS-Untersturmführer. Graetschus was killed by Arkadii Waispapir and Jehuda Lerner during the revolt in Sobibor.

Groth, Paul, born presumably in 1913 in Hamburg; date of death unknown, pronounced dead in 1951.

Groth probably was apprenticed and then employed as a butcher. It is likely, but not absolutely certain, that he joined the NSDAP and the SA. After being detailed to the T4 program, he worked as a "burner" and in other capacities. In the spring of 1942, after promotion to SS-Scharführer, he was assigned to Operation Reinhard and initially deployed in Belzec. After the camp was largely dismantled in the spring of 1943, he was transferred to Sobibor, where his duties included supervision of the sorting detachments in Camp II. Several survivors described him as extremely violent. In addition, descriptions of sexual assaults on Jewish women are part of the historical

record of his character. What became of him after the revolt in Sobibor and the dismantling of the camp is not known.

Hengst, August, born April 25, 1905, in Bonn; died 1963.

Hengst apprenticed as a baker, and in civilian life also worked as a cook and a building superintendent. He joined the NSDAP in 1933. After he became part of Operation T4, he worked as a cook. Then, with the rank of SS-Unterscharführer, he was transferred to Treblinka in the spring of 1942 for assignment to Operation Reinhard. His deployment there continued until the camp was closed in September 1943. For the purpose of supplying the SS personnel at the camp, he operated in part from Warsaw. Then, until 1945, he was ordered to Italy with other Operation Reinhard actors and stationed in Trieste and Udine. In the Düsseldorf Treblinka Trials, Hengst gave evidence but was not charged himself.

Hering, Gottlieb, born June 2, 1887, in Warmbronn; died October 9, 1945, in Stetten; both towns are in Württemberg.

After first working as a farmhand, Hering served in the military for six years, from 1907 to 1912. He then joined the police force in Heilbronn. He fought in World War I, and in 1919 entered a training program for the criminal police (*Kriminalpolizei*). By 1929 he had attained the rank of detective chief superintendent (*Kriminaloberkommissar*). Though sympathetic to the Social Democratic Party, Hering remained in police service in 1933 with the support of his colleague Christian Wirth; in May of that year he joined the NSDAP. After the onset of the war in 1939, he worked at first in Gotenhafen and then, in 1940, moved over to Operation T4, where he served as office manager in Sonnenstein, Bernburg, and Hadamar. Temporarily he worked as a security-police trainer at the leadership training facility (*Führerschule*) in Prague. In the summer of 1942, Hering was assigned to Operation Reinhard to succeed Wirth as commandant in Belzec. After the camp was vacated, he served as commandant of the Poniatowa forced labor camp until the mass shootings that were part of Operation Harvest Festival (*Aktion Erntefest*). In addition, he was tasked with the dismantling in Sobibor. After that, he commanded former Operation Reinhard men in Trieste, Italy, where he was simultaneously head of the San Sabba concentration camp. After the war, Hering returned to his native region but soon fell ill and died under suspicious circumstances.

Hödl, Franz, born August 1, 1905, in Aschach near Linz; date of death unknown.

Hödl was employed as a driver. He joined the NSDAP in 1937 and the SS in 1938. He was detailed to T4, probably as a result of his acquaintance with Franz Reichleitner, and worked as a driver in Hartheim. In the same function, he was sent by the Chancellery of the Führer to the Russian front, to the Medical Service East (*Sanitätsdienst Ost*), in the winter of 1941/42 before he was transferred to Sobibor with the rank of SS-Scharführer. There, Hödl was deployed at the gas chambers in Camp III. After the revolt, together with other Operation Reinhard actors, he was transferred to Italy, where he served as Reichleitner's driver. He survived the war, and in 1947 was sentenced in Linz to three years in prison for his actions at the T4 killing facility in Hartheim.

Kamm, Rudolf, born September 28, 1905, in Settenz/Bohemia; date of death unknown.

Kamm, as trained craftsman, joined the NSDAP at the end of 1938. After he was assigned to T4, he worked as a "burner" at the Sonnenstein killing facility. In the summer of 1942, now with the rank of SS-Unterscharführer, he was ordered to Belzec. In the spring of 1943, following the dismantling of the death camp, Kamm was sent to Sobibor. There, he worked in Camp II, overseeing the sorting detachment and, during its deployment outside the camp, the forest detachment. At the end

of the year, he was posted to Italy, where he was apparently stationed in Fiume until the war was over. Information about his life after that time is unavailable.

Klier, Johann, born July 15, 1901, in Stadtsteinach; died 1955.

Klier was apprenticed and employed as a baker. In early 1933, he joined the SA and the NSDAP. From 1938 to 1940, he worked as a Nazi block warden (*Blockleiter*). After assignment to the T4 program in Hadamar, he worked first as an unskilled laborer and then was put in charge of the heating. In August 1942, with the rank of SS-Unterscharführer, he was transferred to Sobibor, where he worked as a baker and, as a secondary duty, oversaw the sorting of shoes. Some survivors remembered him as "the good Klier" for humane gestures and a less violent manner. Following the revolt in Sobibor, he was transferred to Italy in late 1943 and stationed in Trieste. After the war, he was in detention until 1948. Soon thereafter, he was charged in one of the early Sobibor trials in Frankfurt/Main but acquitted in 1950.

Konrad, Fritz, born presumably around 1900; died October 14, 1943, in Sobibor.

Konrad, a trained male nurse or orderly, in 1940 became associated with the T4 program, where his duties included escorting transports to the killing facilities. In the spring of 1943, with the rank of SS-Unterscharführer, he was assigned to Operation Reinhard and worked in Sobibor, overseeing the sorting of clothing in Camp II, until the revolt.

Lerch, Ernst, born November 19, 1914, in Klagenfurt, Austria; died 1997 in Klagenfurt.

After completing secondary school, Lerch entered the university but did not graduate. He worked as a waiter and, until 1938, was employed in his father's café, which had a dance floor, in Klagenfurt. The café was a popular meeting places for Austrian Nazis. Lerch himself joined the NSDAP in the early 1930s and in 1934 became a member of the Austrian SS. From 1938 to 1941, he worked for the security service of the SS in Berlin and then was brought to Lublin by Odilo Globocnik, whom he knew from Austria, and assigned to Globocnik's staff as his personal assistant. In this capacity, Lerch was intensively involved with Operation Reinhard and also was present at Niemann's burial service in Chełm before he was sent to join Globocnik in Italy. He was imprisoned by British forces after the war but escaped and disappeared for several years. In the 1960s, he was interrogated on several occasions with regard to Operation Reinhard. He was not charged in Austria until 1971, however. His trial in Klagenfurt in 1972 ended without a conviction, after only two court sessions. Subsequently, he continued to operate his Tanz-café Lerch in the city.

Müller, Adolf, born possibly in 1902 in Berlin; died March 10, 1949, in Berlin.

After his school days, Müller worked as an unskilled laborer. He joined the NSDAP and, in 1931, the SA. He fought in the Wehrmacht in France in 1940 before he was recruited for T4 and worked as a superintendent and janitor. Promoted to the rank of SS-Unterscharführer, he was transferred to Sobibor in the spring of 1943 and deployed primarily in Camp II, overseeing the sorting detachments, and with the forest detachment. After the revolt at the end of 1943, he was sent to Italy. He escaped from there to Germany in late 1945. Details of his life after that time are not known.

Oels, Arnold, born June 16, 1908, in Leipzig; date of death unknown.

After his time in school, Oels worked as a traveling salesman. He joined the NSDAP in May 1933, and after the war began in 1939, he volunteered for the Waffen-SS. In 1940, on the recommendation of a female acquaintance at the Hartheim killing facility, he successfully applied for employment in the Chancellery of the Führer and from then on was assigned to the personnel department of the T4 Central Office in Berlin. From October 1942, he served as head of the department and was also in charge of the German Operation Reinhard men in the three death camps. After the revolt in Sobibor, Oels was on-site himself. He settled Niemann's estate, most likely arranged for his photos to be sent to his widow, and supported her in additional matters. He remained an employee of the Chancellery of the Führer until Germany's defeat in 1945. After the war, he worked as a commercial clerk in the textile trade in Hanover. In the 1960s, he gave evidence on several occasions in various investigation proceedings in the Federal Republic of Germany concerning T4 and Operation Reinhard. Proceedings instigated against him by the public prosecutor's office in Frankfurt/Main were abandoned in 1972.

Pötzinger, Karl, born October 28, 1908 in Marktredwitz/Upper Franconia; died December 22, 1944, in Italy.

Pötzinger was apprenticed and employed as a brewer. In May 1932, he joined the NSDAP and the SA. At the end of 1939, he was recruited for Operation T4 and assigned to the Brandenburg and Bernburg killing facilities as a "burner." In May 1942, with the rank of SS-Scharführer, he was ordered to Treblinka, where he worked predominantly in the area of the gas chambers and, from September 1943, also was involved in the dismantling of the death camp. Afterward, he was transferred to Italy. Pötzinger was stationed in Udine and died there during an aerial attack.

Reichleitner, Franz, born December 2, 1906, in Ried/Tyrol; died January 3, 1944, near Fiume/Italy.

Reichleitner was trained and employed as a police detective. After the 1938 *Anschluss*, he worked for the Gestapo in Linz. He knew Franz Stangl from his official duties and in private life. In the early 1930s, he was already active in the Austrian

Nazi movement, and several future actors in T4 and Operation Reinhard, such as Franz Hödl and Gustav Wagner, came from his local NSDAP group. He was detailed to the T4 program in 1940 and assigned to the office staff of the Hartheim killing facility. After Stangl's departure, he became office head there. In the course of personnel changes for Operation Reinhard, Reichleitner was among those transferred to the General Government in the late summer of 1942. From that time on, he served as commandant of Sobibor; from the standpoint of Jewish survivors, his presence attracted little notice in the everyday life of the camp. He was on leave when the revolt took place, and shortly thereafter he was ordered to Italy. He served as commander of the Operation Reinhard men in Fiume for a few weeks, until he was shot in that region by partisans in early 1944.

Richter, Karl, born probably in 1914 in Karlsbad/Bohemia; died in August 1944 in Italy.
In civilian life, Richter worked as a butcher and a driver. No proof of his membership in the NSDAP has survived. After going to work for the T4 program, he was employed as a driver. In the fall of 1942 at the latest, with the rank of SS-Unterscharführer, he was transferred to Operation Reinhard in Sobibor. There he worked in the kitchen, the staff club, and, when needed, at the ramp and at the undressing site. Following the revolt in Sobibor in late 1943, he was ordered to Italy and stationed in Fiume. He was killed during an operation in the region.

Rost, Paul, born June 12, 1904, in Deutschenbora/Saxony; died March 21, 1984, in Dresden.
After apprenticing and working as a butcher, Rost entered police school in 1925. Upon completion of the training, he was employed by the Dresden police service. He joined the NSDAP in 1937 and the SS in 1940. That same year he was detailed to Operation T4 and assigned to the Sonnenstein killing facility as transport manager for the pickup of those selected for "euthanasia." In October 1942, if not earlier, he was promoted to SS-Untersturmführer and assigned to Operation Reinhard. With his police training, his formal role in Sobibor was to fight corruption, working primarily in Camp II. After Operation Reinhard ended, he was sent to Italy and stationed in Trieste. In 1945, he was briefly a captive of the US forces and then returned to Dresden. The following year he was placed in investigative custody because of his responsibilities in the T4 program, but he was never convicted. After that, he worked in Dresden as an unskilled laborer.

Schmiedgen, Otto, born July 15, 1892, in Dorfchemnitz; date of death unknown.
After his school years, Schmiedgen worked as a salesclerk. He joined the NSDAP in the spring of 1933 and was also an SA member. After being detailed to Operation T4, he was assigned to work as a driver at the Bernburg and Hartheim killing facilities. In his case, there was no order to take part in Operation Reinhard in 1942; rather, Schmiedgen appears to have continued to work in Hartheim. Nothing is known about his life after 1945.

Schulze, Erich, born March 3, 1902, in Adlershof/Berlin; date of death unknown.
Schulze worked as a farmhand. He became an NSDAP member in 1937, and after assignment to Operation T4, he took part in the systematic murder as a guard and a "burner." From September 1942 at the latest, he was involved in Operation Reinhard and deployed as an SS-Scharführer in Treblinka. From there, he was ordered to Sobibor the following year. Schulze's duties in the Sobibor camp included supervising the so-called

forest detachment of Jewish forced laborers. After the revolt in late 1943, he was transferred to Italy and stationed in Trieste. Further details of his life history are not known.

Schwarz, Gottfried, born May 3, 1913, in Fürth; died June 19, 1944, in San Pietro.

Schwarz, a professional brewer, joined the NSDAP and the SS in September 1932. Beginning in 1934, he was a member of the SS Death's-Head Regiment "Brandenburg" in the Sachsenhausen concentration camp. In the fall of 1939, he signed on to the T4 program in the Chancellery of the Führer; then, similarly to Niemann, he was deployed as a "burner" in Grafeneck, Brandenburg, and Bernburg. With Niemann and other Waffen-SS soldiers with the rank of SS-Oberscharführer, he was posted to Belzec in the late fall of 1941 to work on constructing the camp. There he served as deputy camp commandant under Wirth and later under Hering. When Belzec was dismantled, Schwarz became commandant of the Dorohucza forced labor camp in the spring of 1943. At the end of 1943, he was transferred to Trieste where he was killed by Italian partisans the following summer.

Unverhau, Heinrich, born May 26, 1911, in Vienenburg near Goslar; died 1983.

Forced to abandon his apprenticeship as a plumber because of an eye injury, Unverhau then trained and worked as a musician in Königslutter. He joined the Steel Helmet veterans organization in 1932 and temporarily worked full-time in a band associated with the *Stahlhelm*. In 1934, he began training for employment as a male nurse. He joined the SA in 1933 and the NSDAP in 1937. At the end of 1939, he was detailed to the T4 program as a nurse and assigned to work in Grafeneck and Hadamar. In the winter of 1941/42, the Chancellery of the Führer sent him to work for the Medical Service East (*Sanitätsdienst Ost*). In the summer of 1942, with the rank of SS-Unterscharführer,

Unverhau was transferred to Belzec, where he oversaw the sorting of clothing. There he was hospitalized with epidemic typhus, which led to the surgical removal of one eye in the fall of 1942. After convalescing, he was transferred in the early summer of 1943 to Sobibor, where he also supervised the clothes-sorting detachment. Toward the end of the year, he was posted to Italy, and in March 1944, he was drafted for service in the Wehrmacht. After the war ended, he was a prisoner for several months and was arrested in 1948 for his service in Grafeneck. Unverhau freely admitted to the charges, and he was acquitted in the trial. Investigation of him in the Belzec trial in Munich was discontinued. Unverhau was also acquitted in the Sobibor trial in 1966.

Wagner, Gustav, born July 18, 1911, in Vienna; died 1980 in São Paulo/Brazil, apparently by suicide.

Wagner apprenticed as a commercial employee. He was inducted into the Austrian army in 1930 but was discharged three years later for "moral unsuitability" and found himself temporarily unemployed. In early 1931, he had already joined the NSDAP, which was banned in Austria two years later. He joined the SS in 1933. Arrested for illegal party activities, he fled to Germany in 1936. He went to work for Operation T4 in 1940, presumably as a result of his acquaintance with Reichleitner through their mutual connection with the local NSDAP group in Austria, and was assigned to administrative work at the Hartheim killing facility. Wagner was transferred to Sobibor in the spring of 1942, with the rank of SS-Scharführer. There he functioned as the "sergeant" (*Spieß*) in charge of the camp organization. Among the Jewish prisoners, he was almost universally the most feared of the German personnel, owing to his omnipresence and brutality. Absent on leave when the revolt took place in Sobibor, he helped later on with the dismantling of the camp. Then Wagner was transferred to Italy and stationed in Fiume. After the war, he did construction work at first. He and Franz Stangl, with the assistance of Walther Rauff, working in Rome, and of the Vatican, fled initially to Syria and later to Brazil, where he lived under a false name. The Nazi hunter Simon Wiesenthal successfully tracked him down. He was arrested on May 30, 1978, and identified by Sobibor survivor Stanisław Szmajzner in person. The Brazilian courts, however, rejected requests for extradition made by several countries, and released Wagner.

Wendland, Willi, born presumably on January 27, 1903, in Berlin; died in December 1944 in Italy.
Possibly Wendland apprenticed and worked as a baker. He joined the NSDAP in 1933 and probably belonged to other Nazi organizations as well, but verified information has not survived. He was engaged by the T4 program in 1940 and deployed as a kitchen helper and as a "burner" at the Brandenburg, Bernburg, and Sonnenstein killing facilities. He was transferred from there to Sobibor, with the rank of SS-Unterscharführer, only in the spring of 1943. His duties in the Sobibor camp included supervising work in the sorting barracks and overseeing various labor detachments outside the camp. In addition, Wendland also worked in Camp III. Like most of the other men from Operation Reinhard, he was transferred to Italy at the end of 1943. One year later he was killed there during a military operation.

Wirth, Christian, born November 24, 1885, in Oberbalzheim/Württemberg; died May 26, 1944, near Trieste/Italy.
Wirth was trained as a sawyer. From 1905 to 1910, he was in the military, serving with Württemberg's Grenadier Regiment 123. After that, he was a constable in Heilbronn and underwent further training with the Stuttgart criminal investigation force (*Kriminalpolizei*). In 1914, he volunteered for service in the First World War and soon was wounded. From 1917 he served in the military police in Stuttgart. After the war, he returned to the criminal investigation force in Stuttgart. He joined the NSDAP as early as 1922–1923 and rejoined in early 1931. From 1933, he also belonged to the SA, and he became an SS member in 1939. He was detached to the Chancellery of the Führer for service in the T4 program in the fall of 1939, and in January 1940, he took part in the experiments with killing by gas in Brandenburg. Next he set up the office sections at the Brandenburg, Grafeneck, and Hartheim killing facilities, which meant that Wirth was responsible, in each case, for the practical organization of the murders. From approximately mid-1940 he acted as the overseer of all the killing facilities. With this expertise and now with the rank of captain of the protection police (*Schutzpolizei*) and SS-Obersturmführer, he was appointed in late 1941 to head one of the first groups of SS soldiers charged with building the Belzec camp. He then served as the first commandant of the death camp and, in the summer of 1942, rose to become the inspector in charge of all the Operation Reinhard camps, with an office in Lublin. Simultaneously, he headed the Old Airfield camp in the Lublin area. After transfer to Italy in September 1943, he directed the deployment of the Operation Reinhard men from his headquarters in Trieste until May 1944, when he was killed in an attack by partisans.

Wolf, Franz, born April 9, 1907, in Krummau/Bohemia (Český Krumlov); date of death unknown.
After training as a forester, he went to work in his father's photographic shop in 1926. Following his father's death in 1937, he and his two brothers ran the shop. In 1936, Wolf joined the Sudeten German Party (*Sudetendeutsche Partei*). After the breakup of Czechoslovakia, he was drafted into the Wehrmacht. In 1939 and 1940, he fought in the war in Poland and in France, respectively, and in became affiliated with Operation T4 in 1940. Wolf worked as a photographer in Hadamar and later in Heidelberg; in each place, for purposes of documentation, he took photos

of patients about to be killed. In the spring 1943, now with the rank of SS-Unterscharführer, he and his brother Josef were posted to Sobibor, where he served as an overseer in the sorting barracks and with the forest detachment. At the end of 1943, he was transferred to Italy. After the war, he was on the run at first but was arrested by US forces and interned. Later, he lived in the vicinity of Heidelberg. He was charged in the Sobibor trial in Hagen and, in 1968, was sentenced to eight years in prison.

Zierke, Ernst, born May 6, 1905, in Krampe/Pomerania; died May 23, 1972, in Celle.

After his school days, Zierke was employed as a forestry worker before apprenticing as a blacksmith and then working in this trade on various large farms. Following a period of unemployment, he was hired to work as a nurse in Neuruppin, Brandenburg. He joined the NSDAP and the SA in 1930. At the end of 1939, along with other nurses from Neuruppin, he was detached to the T4 program and deployed to escort transports in Grafeneck and then in Hadamar. In the winter of 1941/42, the Chancellery of the Führer assigned him to the Medical Service East (*Sanitätsdienst Ost*). The following summer, after promotion to SS-Unterscharführer, he was transferred to Belzec, where he also was involved in the shooting of ill or elderly victims. After the camp was dismantled, he was transferred to the Dorohucza forced labor camp. Following the revolt in Sobibor, Zierke temporarily remained in the camp to help with its dismantling. From late 1943 to the end of the war, he served in Fiume, Italy. In the course of judicial investigations regarding Hadamar in 1947, he was held in investigative custody but acquitted in the ensuing trial. Zierke was also under investigation in subsequent proceedings concerning Belzec and Sobibor but was not charged.

Sources and Bibliography

Sources

Archiwum Instytut Pamięci Narodowej, Oddział w Lublinie (AIPN Lu) (Archive of the Institute of National Remembrance, Lublin Division)
Lu 1/15/105 Investigation file, Bełżec extermination camp

Archiwum Muzeum-Miejsca Pamięci w Bełżcu (AMMPB) (Archive of the Bełżec Museum and Memorial Site, a branch of the State Museum at Majdanek)
Interviews and reports

Archiwum Państwowe w Lublinie (APL) (State Archive in Lublin)
Gruppe 988 Voivodeship Court in Lublin

Archiwum Rady Ochrony Pomników Walk i Męczeństwa (AROPWiM) (Archive of the Council for Protection of Sites of Struggle and Martyrdom, Warsaw)
Sign. 1/100 Activities of the council, 1960–1969
Sign. 52/6 Protection of the former Nazi camps in Bełżec and Sobibór, 1962–1975

Archiwum Żydowskiego Instytutu Historycznego (AŻIH) (Archive of the Jewish Historical Institute, Warsaw)
Bestand 301 Statements of survivors
Bestand 302 Personal narratives

Arolsen Archives (International Tracing Service)
1.2.7.07 General Government

Behörde des Bundesbeauftragten für die Stasi-Unterlagen, Berlin (BStU) (Agency of the Federal Commissioner for Stasi Records, Berlin)
HA IX "Euthanasia" trials

Bundesarchiv (BArch) (German Federal Archives), Berlin
NS 19 Personal staff of the Reichsführer-SS
NS 32 SS Leadership Main Office
R 58 Reich Security Main Office
RS Personnel files, Race and Settlement Main Office
SA SA personnel files
SSO SS officer personnel files
NSDAP-ZK/GK Central and Gau card file of the NSDAP

Bundesarchiv (BArch) (German Federal Archives), Koblenz
All.Proz. 1 Nuremberg documents

Bundesarchiv (BArch) (German Federal Archives), Ludwigsburg Branch
B 162/1270-1273 Trial of Karl Streibel et al., Trawniki training camp
B 162/2209-2213 Trial of Dietrich Allers, responsibility for Operations T4 and Reinhard
B 162/3164-3173 Trial of Josef Oberhauser et al., Belzec death camp
B 162/3848 Photograph file with copies of the photo album of Kurt Franz, photo collection of Willi Mentz
B 162/4426-4432 Trial of Kurt Bolender et al., Sobibor death camp
B 162/8381-8388 Trial of Heinrich Krone et al., Central Construction Administration in Lublin

B 162/18252-18253 Photograph files for San
Sabba/Trieste and "Euthanasia" trials
B 162/27199-27203 Trial of personnel of
the Chancellery of the Führer
B 162/30386 Photograph file for Sobibor

Bundesarchiv (BArch) Militärarchiv (German Federal Archives—
Military Archives), Freiburg)
RW 41 Military commander, Ukraine

Fundacja Ośrodka KARTA (KARTA Center Foundation), Warsaw
Archive group: History of the Sobibór train station

Ghetto Fighters House, Lohamei Hagetaot (GFH)
Photo archive

Hessisches Hauptstaatsarchiv, Wiesbaden (HHW) (Hessen Central State
Archives, Wiesbaden)
461-36346 Trial of Hubert Gomerski and
Konrad Klier, Sobibor death camp
469-1373 Trial of Hoffmann et al.
631a-1488-1491 Trial of Arnold Oels et al.

Landesarchiv Nordrhein-Westfalen, Abteilung Rheinland, Duisburg
(LNR) (North Rhine-Westphalia State Archive, Rhineland Division,
Duisburg)
Gerichte Rep. 388/-796 Trial of Kurt Franz
et al., Treblinka death camp
RWB 18244a und 18248a Photo album of Kurt
Franz and photo collection of Willi Mentz

Landesarchiv Nordrhein-Westfalen, Abteilung Westfalen, Münster
(LNW) (North Rhine-Westphalia State Archive, Westphalia Division,
Münster)
Q 234/1839-1843 Trial of Kurt Bolender, Karl Frenzel, et al.
Q 234/4241-4261 Sobibor death camp
Q 234/5243-5245
Q 234/8231-8242
Q 234/11419, 11822-11823, 12870, 12917
Q 234/7883 Investigation of members of
Reserve Police Battalion 67

National Archives and Records Administration (NARA), College Park,
Maryland
Aerial images of the Wehrmacht, predominantly
from 1940 and 1944

NIOD Instituut voor Oorlogs-, Holocaust- en Genocidestudies,
Amsterdam (NIOD) (NIOD Institute for War, Holocaust, and Genocide
Studies, Amsterdam)
804/13-49 Posthumous papers of Jules Schelvis,
extensive court records concerning Sobibor

Sammlung Marek Bem (Marek Bem Collection)
Interview with Jan Doliński, April 30, 2011

Sammlung Bildungswerk Stanisław Hantz (Bildungswerk Stanisław
Hantz Collection)
Interview with Hermann Adams, January 20, 2019

Staatsarchiv Hamburg (StAH) (State Archives of the Free and Hanseatic
City of Hamburg)
NSG 213.12 0039/1-70 Trial of Karl Streibel
et al., Trawniki training camp

Staatsarchiv München (StAM) (Munich State Archives)
Staw 33033 Trial of Josef Oberhauser et al., Belzec death camp

Tsentral'nij Derzhavnij Istorichnij Arkhiv Ukrayini (TS-Davo) (Central
State Archive of the Government of Ukraine, Kyiv)
3676-4/327-331 Trawniki personnel files

United States Holocaust Memorial Museum Archives (USHMMA),
Washington D.C.
RG 31.018M Trials of Trawnikis in the Soviet Union
PBP Papers of Peter Black, Acc 2008.331.1
Steven Spielberg Film and Video Archive

Yad Vashem Archives, Jerusalem (YVA)
Photo archives

Zentrale Stelle der Landesjustizverwaltungen, Ludwigsburg (ZSL)
(Central Office of the Land Judicial Authorities [for the Investigation of
National Socialist Crimes], Ludwigsburg)
Central card file

Bibliography

Adams, Hermann. *Geboren in Ihrhove, Westoverledingen–Im Holocaust umgekommen. Lebens-und Todeswege jüdischer Frauen und Männer.* Westoverledingen: pro print. 2017.

Angrick, Andrej. *"Aktion 1005." Spurenbeseitigung von NS-Massenverbrechen 1942–1945.* 2 vols. Göttingen: Wallstein, 2018.

———. "'Experiment Massenmord.' Zu den Überlegungen des NS-Regimes, welche Tötungstechniken bei der Vernichtung der europäischen Juden anzuwenden waren." In *Gewalt und Alltag im besetzten Polen 1939–1945*, ed. Jochen Böhler and Stephan Lehnstaedt, 117–137. Osnabrück: Fibre, 2012.

Arad, Yitzhak. *Belzec, Sobibor, Treblinka: The Operation Reinhard Death Camps.* Bloomington: Indiana University Press, 1987.

Bajohr, Frank. *Parvenüs und Profiteure. Korruption in der NS-Zeit.* Frankfurt: Fischer, 2001.

———. Dieter Pohl. *Der Holocaust als offenes Geheimnis. Die Deutschen, die NS-Führung und die Alliierten.* Munich: Beck, 2006.

Beddies, Thomas, and Kristina Hübener, eds. *Kinder in der NS-Psychiatrie.* Berlin: be.bra, 2004.

Bem, Marek. *Sobibór. Niemiecki obóz zagłady 1942–1943.* Lublin: Oto Agencja Producencka, 2009.

———, ed. *Sobibór.* Warsaw: Ośrodek Karta, 2010.

Benz, Angelika. *Handlanger der SS. Die Rolle der Trawniki-Männer im Holocaust.* Berlin: Metropol, 2015.

———. *Der Henkersknecht. Der Prozess gegen John (Iwan) Demjanjuk in München.* Berlin: Metropol, 2011.

Benz, Wolfgang, and Barbara Distel, eds. *Der Ort des Terrors. Geschichte der nationalsozialistischen Konzentrationslager.* 9 vols. Munich: C. H. Beck, 2005–2009.

Benzenhöfer, Udo. *Der Fall Leipzig (alias Fall "Kind Knauer") und die Planung der NS-"Kindereuthanasie."* Münster: Klemm & Oelschläger 2008.

———. *"Kinderfachabteilungen" und "NS-Kindereuthanasie."* Wetzlar: Peter Lang, 2000.

Berger, Sara. *Experten der Vernichtung. Das T4-Reinhardt-Netzwerk in den Lagern, Belzec, Sobibor und Treblinka.* Hamburg: Hamburger Edition, 2013.

Bialowitz, Philip, with Joseph Bialowitz. *A Promise at Sobibór: A Jewish Boy's Story of Revolt and Survival in Nazi-Occupied Poland.* Madison: University of Wisconsin Press, 2010.

Bildungswerk Stanisław Hantz e. V. *Texte zur Aktion Reinhard. Berichte von Rudolf Reder und Chaim Hirszman.* Kassel: Bildungswerk Stanisław Hantz e.V, 2018.

Birg, Herwig. *Die demographische Zeitenwende. Der Bevölkerungsrückgang in Deutschland und Europa.* Berlin: C. H. Beck, 2001.

Black, Peter. "Die Trawniki-Männer und die 'Aktion Reinhard.'" In *"Aktion Reinhardt,"* ed. Bogdan Musial, 309–352. Osnabrück: Fibre 2004.

———. "Foot Soldiers of the Final Solution: The Trawniki Training Camp and Operation Reinhard." *Holocaust and Genocide Studies* 25, no. 1 (2011): 1–99.

———. "Police Auxiliaries for Operation Reinhard: Shedding Light on the Trawniki Training Camp through Documents from Behind the Iron Curtain." In *Secret Intelligence and the Holocaust,* ed. David Bankier, 327–366. New York: Enigma, 2006.

Blatt, Thomas T. *Nur die Schatten bleiben. Der Aufstand im Vernichtungslager Sobibór.* Berlin: Aufbau, 2000.

———. *Sobibór. Der vergessene Aufstand.* Hamburg and Münster, 2004. English edition: *Sobibor, the forgotten revolt. A survivor's report.* Issaquah: H. E. P., 1998.

———. *From the Ashes of Sobibor: A Story of Survival.* Evanston, IL: Northwestern University Press, 1997.

Bodek, Andrzej, and Thomas Sandkühler, eds. *Der Katzmann-Bericht. Bilanz des Judenmordes im Distrikt Galizien.* Berlin: Hentrich, 1995.

Böhm, Boris. "'Karrieren.' Von der 'Euthanasie'-Anstalt Sonnenstein in die Vernichtungslager im besetzten Polen." In *Von den Krankenmorden auf dem Sonnenstein zur "Endlösung der Judenfrage" im Osten*, ed. Kuratorium Gedenkstätte Sonnenstein e.V., 109–144. Pirna: Gedenkstätte Sonnenstein, 2001.

Boll, Bernd. "Vom Album ins Archiv. Zur Überlieferung privater Fotografien aus dem Zweiten Weltkrieg." In *Mit der Kamera bewaffnet. Krieg und Fotografie*, ed. Anton Holzer, 167–178. Marburg: Jonas, 2003.

Bopp, Petra, and Sandra Starke. *Fremde im Visier. Fotoalben aus dem Zweiten Weltkrieg.* Bielefeld: Kerber, 2009.

———. "Images of Violence in Wehrmacht Soldiers' Private Photo Albums." In *Violence and Visibility in Modern History*, ed. Jürgen

Martschukat and Silvan Niedermeier, 181–197. New York: Palgrave Macmillan, 2013.

Browning, Christopher. *The Origins of the Final Solution: The Evolution of Nazi Jewish Policy, September 1939–March 1942*. With contributions by Jürgen Matthäus. Lincoln: Nebraska University Press, 2004.

———. *Ganz normale Männer. Das Reserve-Polizeibataillon 101 und die "Endlösung" in Polen*. Hamburg: Rowohlt, 1997. English edition: *Ordinary men: reserve police battalion 101 and the final solution in Poland*. New York: HarperCollins, 1992.

———. "Genocide and Public Health: German Doctors and Polish Jews, 1939–1941," *Holocaust and Genocide Studies*, 3/1 (1988), 21–36.

Bruder, Franziska. "Die jüdischen Aufständischen im NS-Vernichtungslager Sobibór und der Partisanenkampf. Ein Fallbeispiel für das Gebiet Parczew/Włodawa und Brest." In *Partisanen im Zweiten Weltkrieg. Der Slowakische Nationalaufstand im Kontext der europäischen Widerstandsbewegungen*, ed. Martin Zückert, Jürgen Zarusky, and Volker Zimmermann, 203–223. Göttingen: Vandenhoeck & Ruprecht, 2017.

———. *Hunderte solcher Helden. Der Aufstand jüdischer Gefangener im NS-Vernichtungslager Sobibór. Berichte, Recherchen und Analysen*. Hamburg and Münster: Unrast, 2013.

Bruttmann, Tal, Stefan Hördler, and Christoph Kreutzmüller, *Die fotografische Inszenierung des Verbrechens. Ein Album aus Auschwitz*. Darmstadt: WBG Academic, 2019.

Buchheim, Christoph. "Die Währungsreform 1948 in Westdeutschland." *Vierteljahrshefte für Zeitgeschichte* 36, no. 2 (1988): 189–231.

Busch, Christophe, Stefan Hördler, and Robert Jan van Pelt, eds. *Das Höcker-Album. Auschwitz durch die Linse der SS*. Darmstadt: WBG, 2016.

Canin, Mordechaj. *Przez ruiny i zgliszcza. Podróż po stu zgładzonych gminach żydowskich w Polsce*. Warsaw: Żydowski Instytut Historyczny, 2018.

Cüppers, Martin. *Walther Rauff—in deutschen Diensten. Vom Naziverbrecher zum BND-Spion*, Darmstadt: WBG, 2013.

———. *Wegbereiter der Shoah. Die Waffen-SS, der Kommandostab Reichsführer-SS und die Judenvernichtung 1939–1945*. Darmstadt: WBG, 2005.

———. "Täter vergessener Orte." In *Im Schatten von Auschwitz*, ed. Martin Langebach and Hanna Liever, 414–427. Bonn: Waxmann, 2017.

Der Dienstkalender Heinrich Himmlers 1941/42, edited, annotated, and introduced by Peter Witte, Michael Wildt, Martina Voigt, Dieter Pohl, Peter Klein, Christian Gerlach, Christoph Dieckmann, and Andrej Angrick. Hamburg: Hamburger Edition, 1999.

Dokumentation Leer 1933–1945, compiled by Menna Hensmann. Leer: City of Leer, 2011.

Douglas, Lawrence. *The Right Wrong Man: John Demjanjuk and the Last Great Nazi War Crimes Trial*. Princeton, NJ: Princeton University Press, 2016.

Dziuban, Zuzanna. "(Re)politicising the dead in post-Holocaust Poland: The afterlives of human remains at the Bełżec extermination camp." In *Human Remains in Society: Curation and Exhibition in the Aftermath of Genocide and Mass-Violence*, ed. J.-M. Dreyfus and E. Gessat-Anstett, 38–65. Manchester: Manchester University Press, 2017.

Eimers, Enno. "Die Eroberung der Macht in den Rathäusern Ostfrieslands durch die Nationalsozialisten: Die Bürgermeister zwischen Partei- und Kommunalinteresse." In *Ostfriesland im Dritten Reich. Die Anfänge der nationalsozialistischen Gewaltherrschaft im Regierungsbezirk Aurich 1933–1938*, ed. Herbert Reyer, Aurich: Ostfriesische Landschaft, 1999.

Eliach, Yaffa, ed. *Hasidic Tales of the Holocaust*. New York: Oxford University Press, 1982.

Faulenbach, Bernd, and Andrea Kaltofen, eds. *Hölle im Moor. Die Emslandlager 1933–1945*. Göttingen: Wallstein, 2017.

Fings, Karola. "Sinti und Roma—eine Reise am Abgrund." In *Im Schatten von Auschwitz*, ed. Martin Langebach and Hanna Liever, 386–399. Bonn: Waxmann, 2017.

Freiberg, Dov. *To Survive Sobibor*. Jerusalem: Geffen, 2007.

Fricke, Dieter, and Werner Bramke. "Kyffhäuser-Bund der Deutschen Landeskriegerverbände." In *Lexikon zur Parteiengeschichte. Die bürgerlichen und kleinbürgerlichen Parteien und Verbände in Deutschland (1789–1945)*, vol. 3, ed. Dieter Fricke, 325–344. Leipzig: Bibliographisches Institut, 1985.

Friedlander, Henry. *Der Weg zum NS-Genozid. Von der Euthanasie zur Endlösung*. Munich, 2001. English edition: *The origins of Nazi genocide: From euthanasia to the final solution.* Chapel Hill: University of North Carolina Press, 1995.

Gerlach, Christian. *Kalkulierte Morde. Die deutsche Wirtschafts- und Vernichtungspolitik in Weißrußland 1941–1944.* Hamburg: Hamburger Edition, 1999.

———. "Die Wannsee-Konferenz, das Schicksal der der deutschen Juden und Hitlers politische Grundsatzentscheidung, alle Juden Europas zu ermorden." In *Krieg, Ernährung, Völkermord. Forschungen zur deutschen Vernichtungspolitik im Zweiten Weltkrieg,* ed. Christian Gerlach, 10–84. Hamburg: Hamburger Edition, 1998.

Glazar, Richard. *Trap with a Green Fence: Survival in Treblinka.* Evanston, IL: Northwestern University Press, 1995.

Goldhagen, Daniel Jonah. *Hitlers willige Vollstrecker. Ganz gewöhnliche Deutsche und der Holocaust.* Berlin, 1996. English edition: *Hitler's willing executioners: ordinary Germans and the Holocaust.* New York: Knopf, 1996.

Gottwaldt, Alfred. "Warum war die Reichsbahn nicht auf der Wannsee-Konferenz vertreten?" In *Die Wannsee-Konferenz am 20. Januar 1942,* ed. Norbert Kampe and Peter Klein, 341–354. Cologne: DeGruyter, 2013.

———. Diana Schulle. *Die "Judendeportationen" aus dem Deutschen Reich 1941–1945.* Wiesbaden: marix 2005.

Grabowski, Jan. *Hunt for the Jews: Betrayal and Murder in German-Occupied Poland.* Bloomington: Indiana University Press, 2013.

Greve, Michael. *Die organisierte Vernichtung "lebensunwerten Lebens" im Rahmen der "Aktion T4." Dargestellt am Beispiel des Wirkens und der strafrechtlichen Verfolgung ausgewählter NS-Tötungsärzte.* Pfaffenweiler: Centaurus, 1998.

Gutman, Israel, and Bella Gutterman, eds. *The Auschwitz Album: The Story of a Transport.* Jerusalem: Yad Vashem, 2002.

Hänschen, Steffen. *Das Transitghetto Izbica im System des Holocaust.* Berlin: Metropol, 2018.

Hamburger Institut für Sozialforschung. *Vernichtungskrieg. Verbrechen der Wehrmacht 1941 bis 1944,* ed. Hannes Heer and Birgit Otte. Hamburg: Hamburger Edition, 1996.

———. *Verbrechen der Wehrmacht. Dimensionen des Vernichtungskrieges 1941–1944,* ed. Ulrike Jureit. Hamburg: Hamburger Edition, 2002.

Harvey, Elizabeth. *Women and the Nazi East: Agents and Witnesses of Germanization.* New Haven, CT: Yale University Press, 2003.

Hein, Bastian. *Elite für Volk und Führer? Die Allgemeine SS und ihre Mitglieder 1925–1945.* Munich: Oldenbourg, 2012.

Heinemann, Isabel. "*Rasse, Siedlung, deutsches Blut." Das Rasse- und Siedlungshauptamt der SS und die rassenpolitische Neuordnung Europas.* Göttingen: Wallstein, 2003.

Heinen, Franz Albert. *Ordensburg Vogelsang. Die Geschichte der NS-Kaderschmiede in der Eifel.* Berlin: Chr. Links, 2014.

Hembera, Melanie. "Die Rolle der Kanzlei des Führers beim Genozid an der jüdischen Bevölkerung im Generalgouvernement." In *Die "Aktion Reinhardt,"* ed. Stephan Lehnstaedt and Robert Traba, 27–44. Berlin: Metropol, 2019.

Hensmann, Menna, ed. *Dokumentation "Leer 1933–1945."* Leer: Stadt Leer, 2001.

Herbert, Ulrich, Karin Orth, and Christoph Dieckmann, eds. *Die nationalsozialistischen Konzentrationslager.* 2 vols. Göttingen: Wallstein, 1998.

Hinz-Wessels, Annette. *Tiergartenstraße 4. Schaltzentrale der nationalsozialistischen "Euthanasie"-Morde.* Berlin: Chr. Links, 2015.

Hohendorf, Gerrit. "Die Selektion der Opfer zwischen rassenhygienischer 'Ausmerze,' ökonomischer Brauchbarkeit und medizinischem Erlösungsideal." In *Die nationalsozialistische "Euthanasie"—Aktion T4 und ihre Opfer,* ed. Maike Rotzoll et al., 310–324. Paderborn: Schöningh, 2010.

Holler, Martin. *Der nationalsozialistische Völkermord an den Roma in der besetzten Sowjetunion (1941–1944). Gutachten für das Dokumentations- und Kulturzentrum Deutscher Sinti und Roma.* Heidelberg, 2009. http://www.sintiundroma.de/uploads/media/GutachtenMartinHoller.pdf, February 10, 2022.

Hördler, Stefan. "Die Ermordung der 'Unproduktiven'—Zwangsarbeiter als Opfer der NS-Euthanasie." In *Zwangsarbeit im Nationalsozialismus,* ed. Stefan Hördler, Volkhard Knigge, et al., 232–243. Göttingen: Wallstein, 2016.

Jäger, Herbert. *Verbrechen unter totalitärer Herrschaft. Studien zur nationalsozialistischen Gewaltkriminalität.* Freiburg: Walter, 1967.

Justiz und NS-Verbrechen (JNSV). Sammlung deutscher Strafurteile wegen nationalsozialistischer Tötungsverbrechen, 1945–1969, ed. C. F. Rüter, D. W. de Mildt. 29 vols. Amsterdam: University Press Amsterdam, 1968–2003.

Kämmer, Lisa Sophie. "Lina Heydrich (1911–1985). Selbstdarstellung und Fremdzuschreibung im Spannungsfeld weiblicher Täterschaft." *Zeitschrift der Gesellschaft für Schleswig-Holsteinische Geschichte* 139 (2014).

Kaienburg, Hermann. *Der Militär- und Wirtschaftskomplex der SS im KZ-Standort Sachsenhausen-Oranienburg. Schnittpunkt von KZ-System, Waffen-SS und Judenmord.* Berlin: Metropol, 2015.

———. *Die Wirtschaft der SS.* Berlin: Metropol 2003.

Kampe, Norbert, and Peter Klein, eds. *Die Wannsee-Konferenz am 20. Januar 1942. Dokumente, Forschungsstand, Kontroversen.* Cologne: DeGruyter, 2013.

Karski, Jan. *Story of a Secret State: My Report to the World.* Washington, DC: Georgetown University Press, 2014.

Kepplinger, Brigitte, and Irene Leitner, eds. *Dameron Report. Bericht des War Crimes Investigating Teams No. 6824 der U.S. Army vom 17. 7. 1945 über die Tötungsanstalt Hartheim.* Innsbruck: StudienVerlag, 2012.

Kershaw, Ian. *Hitler.* 2 vols. Stuttgart, 1998–2000. English edition: *Hitler.* 2 vols. London: Penguin Press, 1998–2000.

Klee, Ernst. *"Euthanasie" im NS-Staat. Die "Vernichtung lebensunwerten Lebens."* Frankfurt: Fischer, 1997.

———. *Was sie taten—Was sie wurden. Ärzte, Juristen und andere Beteiligte am Kranken- oder Judenmord.* Frankfurt: Fischer, 1986.

Klee, Ernst, Willi Dreßen, and Volker Rieß, eds. *"Schöne Zeiten." Judenmord aus der Sicht der Täter und Gaffer.* Frankfurt: Fischer, 1988. English edition: *The good old days: The Holocaust as seen by its perpetrators and bystanders.* New York: Free Press, 1991.

Klein, Peter. "Kulmhof/Chelmno." In *Der Ort des Terrors. Geschichte der nationalsozialistischen Konzentrationslager,* vol. 8: *Riga, Warsaw, Vaivara, Kaunas, Płaszów, Kulmhof/Chełmno, Bełżec, Sobibór, Treblinka,* ed. Wolfgang Benz and Barbara Distel, 301–328. Munich: C. H. Beck, 2008.

———. *Die "Wannsee-Konferenz" am 20. Januar 1942. Eine Einführung.* With a foreword by Hans-Christian Jasch. Berlin: Metropol, 2017.

Klukowski, Zygmunt. *Tagebuch aus den Jahren der Okkupation 1939-1944,* ed. Christine Glauning and Ewelina Wanke. Berlin: Metropol, 2017.

Knoch, Habbo. "Die Emslandlager 1933-1945." In *Der Ort des Terrors. Geschichte der nationalsozialistischen Konzentrationslager,* vol. 2: *Frühe Lager, Dachau, Emslandlager,* ed. Wolfgang Benz and Barbara Distel, 532–570. Munich: C. H. Beck, 2005.

Kompisch, Kathrin. *Täterinnen. Frauen im Nationalsozialismus.* Cologne: Böhlau, 2008.

Kopciowski, Adam. "Anti-Jewish Incidents in the Lublin Region in the Early Years after World War II." *Holocaust. Studies and Materials* (English edition) 1 (2008): 177–205.

———. Robert Kuwałek. "Relacja żony Leona Feldhendlera." *Zagłada Żydów. Studia i Materiały* (2011): 470–484.

———. *Lejba (Leon) Felhendler: A Biographical Sketch.* Lublin: Museum Majdanek, 2018.

Kowitz-Harms, Stephanie. *Die Shoah im Spiegel öffentlicher Konflikte in Polen. Zwischen Opfermythos und Schuldfrage (1985–2001).* Berlin: DeGruyter, 2014.

Krakowski, Shmuel. *Das Todeslager Chełmno/Kulmhof. Der Beginn der "Endlösung."* Göttingen: Wallstein, 2007.

Krall, Hanna: *Tanz auf fremder Hochzeit.* Munich: btb, 1997.

Kramer, Nicole. *Volksgenossinnen an der Heimatfront. Mobilisierung, Verhalten, Erinnerung.* Göttingen: Vandenhoeck & Ruprecht, 2012.

Krauss, Marita. "Kleine Welten. Alltagsfotografie—die Anschaulichkeit einer 'privaten Praxis.'" In *Visual History. Ein Studienbuch,* ed. Gerhard Paul, 57–75. Göttingen: Wallstein, 2006.

Kuwałek, Robert. *Główne miejsca pamięci po wymordowanym narodzie żydowskim (Chełmno-Kulmhof, Bełżec, Sobibór, Treblinka) oraz miejsca wspólnej polsko-żydowskiej martyrologii (Auschwitz-Birkenau, Majdanek, Stutthof)—ich funkcje i potencjał edukacyjny.* Lublin: Museum Majdanek, 2011.

———. "Belzec." In *Der Ort des Terrors, Geschichte der nationalsozialistischen Konzentrationslager,* vol. 8: *Riga, Warsaw, Vaivara, Kaunas, Płaszów, Kulmhof/Chełmno, Bełżec, Sobibór, Treblinka,* ed. Wolfgang Benz and Barbara Distel, 329–371. Munich: C. H. Beck, 2008.

———. *Das Vernichtungslager Belzec.* Berlin: Metropol, 2013.

———. "Nowe ustalenia dotyczące liczby ofiar niemieckiego obozu zagłady w Sobiborze." *Zeszyty Majdanka* 26 (2014): 17–60.

Langebach, Martin, and Hanna Liever, eds. *Im Schatten von Auschwitz. Spurensuche in Polen, Belarus und der Ukraine: Begegnen, Erinnern, Lernen.* Bonn: Waxmann, 2017.

Lehnstaedt, Stephan. *Der Kern des Holocaust: Bełżec, Sobibór, Treblinka und die Aktion Reinhardt.* Munich: C. H. Beck, 2017.

Lehnstaedt, Stephan, and Robert Traba, eds. *Die "Aktion Reinhardt." Geschichte und Gedenken.* Berlin: Metropol, 2019.

Ley, Astrid, and Annette Hinz-Wessels, eds. *Die Euthanasie-Anstalt Brandenburg an der Havel. Morde an Kranken und Behinderten im Nationalsozialismus.* Berlin: Metropol, 2012.

Ley, Michael. *Genozid und Heilserwartung. Zum nationalsozialistischen Mord am europäischen Judentum.* Vienna: Picus, 1993.

Libionka, Dariusz, ed. *Obóz Zagłady w Bełżcu w relacjach ocalonych i zeznaniach polskich świadków.* Lublin: Museum Majdanek, 2013.

———. *Zagłada Żydów w Generalnym Gubernatorstwie. Zarys problematyki.* Lublin: Museum Majdanek, 2017.

Lichtenstein, Heiner. "Franz Paul Stangl. Kommandant eines Vernichtungslagers." In *Im Namen des Volkes? Eine persönliche Bilanz der NS-Prozesse*, ed. Heiner Lichtenstein, 196–210. Cologne: Bund, 1984.

Lokers, Jan. "Boykott und Verdrängung der jüdischen Bevölkerung aus dem Wirtschaftsleben Ostfrieslands (1933–1938)." In *Ostfriesland im Dritten Reich*, ed. Herbert Reyer, 63–82. Aurich: Ostfriesische Landschaft, 1999.

Longerich, Peter, ed. *Die Ermordung der europäischen Juden. Eine umfassende Dokumentation des Holocaust.* Munich: DTV, 1989.

———. *Heinrich Himmler. Biographie.* Munich: Siedler, 2008. English edition: *Heinrich Himmer. A life.* Oxford: Oxford University Press, 2011.

———. *Hitler. Biographie.* Munich: Siedler, 2015. English edition: *Hitler: A Life.* Oxford: Oxford University Press, 2019.

Lower, Wendy. *Hitlers Helferinnen. Deutsche Frauen im Holocaust.* Frankfurt: Fischer, 2014. English edition: *Hitler's furies: German women in the Nazi killing fields.* New York: Houghton Mifflin Harcourt, 2013.

Mallmann, Klaus-Michael. "Der qualitative Sprung im Vernichtungsprozeß. Das Massaker von Kamenez-Podolsk Ende August 1941." *Jahrbuch für Antisemitismusforschung* 10 (2001): 239–264.

———. "Die Türöffner der 'Endlösung.' Zur Genesis des Genozids." In *Die Gestapo im Zweiten Weltkrieg. "Heimatfront" und besetztes Europa*, ed. Gerhard Paul and Klaus-Michael Mallmann, 437–463. Darmstadt: WBG, 2000.

Mallmann, Klaus-Michael, and Bogdan Musial, eds. *Genesis des Genozids: Polen 1939–1941.* Darmstadt: WBG, 2004.

Markham Walsh, Ann. *Dancing Through Darkness. When Love and Dreams Survived a Nazi Death Camp. Based on the Diary and Recorded Memories of Selma (Saartje Wijnberg) Engel.* Nashville: Dunham, 2013.

Matthäus, Jürgen. "'A Plan behind These Measures.' Aktion Reinhardt in the Context of Reports by the Geneva Offices of the World Jewish Congress and the Jewish Agency." In *Die "Aktion Reinhardt,"* ed. Stephan Lehnstaedt and Robert Traba, 137–160. Berlin: Metropol, 2019.

———. "Operation Barbarossa and the Onset of the Holocaust, June–December 1941." In *The Origins of the Final Solution,* ed. Christopher Browning, 244–308. Lincoln: University of Nebraska Press, 2004.

———. "'Es war sehr nett.' Auszüge aus dem Tagebuch der Margarete Himmler, 1937–1945." *WerkstattGeschichte* 25 (2000): 75–93.

Morsch, Günter, and Bertrand Perz, eds. *Neue Studien zu nationalsozialistischen Massentötungen durch Giftgas. Historische Bedeutung, technische Entwicklung, revisionistische Leugnung.* Berlin: Metropol, 2012.

———. *Sachsenhausen. Das "Konzentrationslager bei der Reichshauptstadt." Gründung und Ausbau.* Berlin: Metropol, 2014.

———. "Von Esterwegen nach Sachsenhausen. Die Neuordnung des KZ-Systems 1934–1937." In *Hölle im Moor. Die Emslandlager 1933–1945.*, ed. Bernd Faulenbach and Andrea Kaltofen, 87–98. Göttingen: Wallstein, 2017.

———, ed. *Die Konzentrationslager-SS 1936–1945: Exzess- und Direkttäter im KZ Sachsenhausen. Eine Ausstellung am historischen Ort.* Berlin: Metropol, 2016.

Münkel, Daniela. *Nationalsozialistische Agrarpolitik und Bauernalltag.* Frankfurt: Campus, 1996.

———. "Bäuerliche Interessen versus NS-Ideologie. Das Reichserbhofgesetz in der Praxis." *Vierteljahrshefte für Zeitgeschichte* 44/4 (1996), 549–580.

Musial, Bogdan, ed. *"Aktion Reinhardt." Der Völkermord an den Juden im Generalgouvernement 1941–1944.* Osnabrück: Fibre, 2004.

———. *Deutsche Zivilverwaltung und Judenverfolgung im Generalgouvernment. Eine Fallstudie zum Distrikt Lublin 1939–1944.* Wiesbaden: Harrasowitz, 1999.

———. "Ursprünge der 'Aktion Reinhardt.' Planung des Massenmordes an den Juden im Generalgouvernement." In *"Aktion Reinhardt,"* ed.

Bogdan Musial, 49–85. Osnabrück: Fibre, 2004. English edition: "The origins of 'Operation Reinhard': the decision-making process for the mass murder of the Jews in the Generalgouvernment." In: *Yad Vashem Studies* 28 (2000), 113–153.

Orth, Karin. *Die Konzentrationslager-SS. Sozialstrukturelle Analysen und biographische Studien.* 2nd ed. Göttingen: Wallstein, 2001.

Overmans, Rüdiger, "Die Kriegsgefangenenpolitik des Deutschen Reiches 1939 bis 1945." In *Das Deutsche Reich und der Zweite Weltkrieg*, vol. 9/2, ed. Jörg Echternkamp, 729–875. Munich: DVA 2005.

Paul, Gerhard. "Kriegsbilder-Bilderkriege." *Aus Politik und Zeitgeschichte* 31 (2009): 39–46.

——, ed. *Die Täter der Shoah. Fanatische Nationalsozialisten oder ganz normale Deutsche?* Göttingen: Wallstein, 2002.

——. *Das visuelle Zeitalter. Punkt und Pixel.* Göttingen: Wallstein, 2016.

Perz, Bertrand. "Warum Österreicher? Zum Personal der Dienststelle des SS- und Polizeiführers Odilo Globocnik in Lublin." In *Die "Aktion Reinhardt,"* ed. Stephan Lehnstaedt and Robert Traba, 45–70. Berlin: Metropol, 2019.

Perz, Bertrand, and Thomas Sandkühler. "Auschwitz und die 'Aktion Reinhard' 1942–1945. Judenmord und Raubpraxis in neuer Sicht." *Zeitgeschichte* 26/5 (1999): 283–316.

Peter, Janusz. "W Bełżcu podczas okupacji." In *Tomaszowskie za okupacji.* Tomaszów Lubelski: Nakł. Tomaszowskiego Towarzystwa Regionalnego, 1991.

Petscherski, Alexandr. *Bericht über den Aufstand in Sobibor,* ed. and trans. Ingrid Damerow. With a contribution by Stephan Lehnstaedt. Berlin: Metropol, 2018.

Pohl, Dieter. *Nationalsozialistische Judenverfolgung in Ostgalizien 1941–1944. Organisation und Durchführung eines staatlichen Massenverbrechens.* 2nd ed. Munich: Oldenbourg, 1997.

——. "Sowjetische und polnische Strafverfahren wegen NS-Verbrechen—Quellen für den Historiker?" In *Vom Recht zur Geschichte. Akten aus NS-Prozessen als Quellen der Zeitgeschichte*, ed. Jürgen Finger, Sven Keller, and Andreas Wirsching, 132–141. Göttingen: Vandenhoeck & Ruprecht, 2009.

——. "Die Trawniki-Männer im Vernichtungslager Belzec 1941–1943." In *NS-Gewaltherrschaft. Beiträge zur historischen Forschung und juristischen Aufarbeitung*, ed. Alfred Gottwaldt, Norbert Kampe, and Peter Klein, 278–289. Berlin: Hentrich, 2005.

Pyta, Wolfram. *Hitler. Der Künstler als Politiker und Feldherr. Eine Herrschaftsanalyse.* Munich: Siedler, 2015.

Rauh, Philipp. "Medizinische Selektionskriterien versus ökonomisch-utilitaristische Verwaltungsinteressen. Ergebnisse der Meldebogenauswertung." In *Die nationalsozialistische "Euthanasie"-Aktion T4 und ihre Opfer*, ed. Maike Rotzoll et al., 297–309. Paderborn: Schöningh, 2010.

Reder, Rudolf. "Bełżec, Kraków 1946. Deutsche Übersetzung: 'Bericht über Bełżec.'" In *Nationalsozialistische Zwangslager. Strukturen und Regionen—Täter und Opfer*, ed. Wolfgang Benz, Barbara Distel, and Angelika Königseder, 351–373. Berlin: Metropol, 2011. English edition: *Bełżec*, Oświęcim: Fundacja Judaica, Państwowe Muzeum Oświęcim-Brzezinka, 1997.

von Reeken, Dietmar. "Elitenrevolution, Elitenverschmelzung oder Elitenbündnis? Die Verwaltungselite in Ostfriesland 1932–1937." In *Ostfriesland im Dritten Reich. Die Anfänge der nationalsozialistischen Gewaltherrschaft im Regierungsbezirk Aurich 1933–1938*, ed. Herbert Reyer, Aurich: Ostfriesische Landschaft, 1999.

Reemtsma, Jan Philipp. *Vertrauen und Gewalt. Versuch über eine besondere Konstellation der Moderne.* Hamburg: Hamburger Edition, 2008.

Reinicke, David. "Die 'Moor-SA.' Selbstverständnis und Gewalt." In *Hölle im Moor*, ed. Bernd Faulenbach and Andrea Kaltofen, 143–155. Göttingen: Wallstein, 2017.

Reyer, Herbert. "Der bedrohliche Alltag unterm Nationalsozialismus. SA- und SS-Terror in Ostfriesland in den Jahren 1933–1935." In *Ostfriesland im Dritten Reich*, ed. Herbert Reyer, 83–96. Aurich: Ostfriesische Landschaft, 1999.

——, ed. *Ostfriesland im Dritten Reich. Die Anfänge der nationalsozialistischen Gewaltherrschaft im Regierungsbezirk Aurich 1933–1938.* Aurich: Ostfriesische Landschaft, 1999.

Rich, David. "Reinhard's Footsoldiers. Soviet Trophy Documents and Investigative Records as Sources." In *Remembering for the Future: The Holocaust in an Age of Genocide*, vol. 1, ed. John K. Roth and Elizabeth Maxwell, 688–701. London: Remembering for the Future, 2001.

Riedle, Andrea. *Die Angehörigen des Kommandanturstabs im KZ Sachsenhausen. Sozialstruktur, Dienstwege und biografische Studien.* Berlin: Metropol, 2011.

Rieger, Berndt. *Creator of Nazi Death Camps. The Life of Odilo Globocnik.* London: Vallentine Mitchell, 2007.

Ring, Klaus, and Stefan Wunsch, eds. *Bestimmung Herrenmensch. NS-Ordensburgen zwischen Faszination und Verbrechen.* Dresden: Sandstein, 2016.

Roitsch, Bianca. *Mehr als nur Zaungäste. Akteure im Umfeld der Lager Bergen-Belsen, Esterwegen und Moringen 1933–1960.* Paderborn: Schöningh, 2018.

Roseman, Mark. *Die Wannsee-Konferenz. Wie die NS-Bürokratie den Holocaust organisierte.* Munich: Propyläen, 2002. English edition: *The Wannsee Conference and the final solution: a reconsideration.* London: Folio, 2012.

Roth, Markus. *Herrenmenschen. Die deutschen Kreishauptleute im besetzten Polen. Karrierewege, Herrschaftspraxis und Nachgeschichte.* Göttingen: DeGruyter, 2009.

Rother, Bernd. *Die Sozialdemokratie im Land Braunschweig 1918 bis 1933.* Bonn: Dietz, 1990.

Rotzoll, Maike, Gerrit Hohendorf, Petra Fuchs, Paul Richter, Christoph Mundt, and Wolfgang U. Eckart, eds. *Die nationalsozialistische "Euthanasie"-Aktion T4 und ihre Opfer. Geschichte und ethische Konsequenzen in der Gegenwart.* Paderborn: Schöningh, 2010.

Rückerl, Adalbert, ed. *NS-Vernichtungslager im Spiegel deutscher Strafprozesse. Belzec, Sobibor, Treblinka, Chelmno.* 2nd ed. Munich: DTV, 1978.

Sachslehner, Johannes. *Zwei Millionen ham'ma erledigt. Odilo Globocnik—Hitlers Manager des Todes.* Vienna: Styria, 2014.

Sakowska, Ruta. *Die zweite Etappe ist der Tod. NS-Ausrottungspolitik gegen die polnischen Juden, gesehen mit den Augen der Opfer.* Berlin: Hentrich, 1993.

Sandkühler, Thomas. "Die Trawniki-Männer, die 'Aktion Reinhardt' und das Vernichtungslager Belzec. Sachverständigengutachten zum Ermittlungsverfahren StA Dortmund 45 J5 11/09," unpublished (2010). In BArch, B 162/43904.

Schelvis, Jules. *Vernichtungslager Sobibór.* Münster, 2012. English edition: *Sobibor: a history of a Nazi death camp.* New York: Bloomsbury, 2007.

Schulze, Dietmar. *"Euthanasie" in Bernburg. Die Landes-Heil- und Pflegeanstalt Bernburg/Anhaltische Nervenklinik in der Zeit des Nationalsozialismus.* Essen: Klartext, 1999.

Schwarz, Gudrun. *Eine Frau an seiner Seite. Ehefrauen in der "SS-Sippengemeinschaft."* Hamburg: Hamburger Edition, 1997.

Sereny, Gitta. *Am Abgrund: Gespräche mit dem Henker. Franz Stangl und die Morde von Treblinka.*: Frankfurt: Ullstein, 1980. English edition: *Into that darkness. An examination of conscience.* New York: McGraw-Hill, 1974.

Silberklang, David. *Gate of Tears. The Holocaust in the Lublin District.* Jerusalem: Yad Vashem, 2013.

Sofsky, Wolfgang. *Die Ordnung des Terrors: Das Konzentrationslager.* Frankfurt: Fischer, 1993.

Stahl, Daniel. *Nazi-Jagd. Südamerikas Diktaturen und die Ahndung von NS-Verbrechen.* Göttingen: Wallstein, 2013.

Starl, Timm. *Knipser. Die Bildgeschichte der privaten Fotografie in Deutschland und Österreich von 1880–1980.* Munich: Koehler & Amelang, 1995.

Steinbacher, Sybille. *Volksgenossinnen. Frauen in der NS-Volksgemeinschaft (Beiträge zur Geschichte des Nationalsozialismus 23).* Göttingen: Wallstein, 2007.

Stöckle, Thomas. *Grafeneck 1940. Die Euthanasie-Verbrechen in Südwestdeutschland.* Tübingen: Silberburg, 2012.

Streit, Christian. *Keine Kameraden. Die Wehrmacht und die sowjetischen Kriegsgefangenen 1941–1945.* Bonn: Dietz, 1997.

Taffet, Gerszon. "Die Vernichtung der Juden von Żółkiew." In *Nach dem Untergang. Die ersten Zeugnisse der Shoah in Polen 1944–1947. Berichte der Zentralen Jüdischen Historischen Kommission*, ed. Frank Beer, Wolfgang Benz, and Barbara Distel, 307–353. Berlin: Metropol, 2014.

Ticho, Kurt. *My Legacy. Holocaust, History and the Unfinished Task of Pope John Paul II.* Columbus, OH: K. Ticho, 2006.

Toepser-Ziegert, Gabriele. *NS-Presseanweisungen der Vorkriegszeit. Edition und Dokumentation*, vol. 2: *1934.* Munich: K. G. Saur, 1985.

Tomin, Valentin, and Aleksandr Sinel'nikov. *Vozvrashchenie nezhelatel'no.* Moscow: Molodaia Gvardiia, 1964.

Tuchel, Johannes. "Planung und Realität des Systems der Konzentrationslager 1934–1938." In *Die nationalsozialistischen Konzentrationslager. Entwicklung und Struktur*, vol. 1, ed. Ulrich Herbert, Karin Orth, and Christoph Dieckmann, 43–59. Göttingen: Wallstein, 1998.

Utz, Raphael. "Sobibór nach den Deutschen: Vom Tatort zum Friedhof?" In *Die "Aktion Reinhardt." Geschichte und Gedenken,* ed.

Stephan Lehnstaedt and Robert Traba, 291–313. Berlin: Metropol, 2019.

Die Verfolgung und Ermordung der europäischen Juden durch das nationalsozialistische Deutschland 1933–1945 (VEJ), ed. on behalf of the German Federal Archives, the Institute for Contemporary History, et al., 16 vols. Munich: Oldenbourg, 2008–2018.

Vojta, Tomáš. "'A True Inferno Was Created There.' Eradicating Traces of Mass Murder at Treblinka." In *Orte und Akteure im System der NS-Zwangslager. Ergebnisse des 18. Workshops zur Geschichte und Gedächtnisgeschichte nationalsozialistischer Konzentrationslager*, ed. Michael Becker, Dennis Bock, and Henrike Illig, 198–224. Berlin: Metropol, 2015.

Webb, Chris. *The Sobibor Death Camp. History, Biographies, Remembrance.* New York: Columbia University Press, 2017.

Wefing, Heinrich. *Der Fall Demjanjuk. Der letzte große NS-Prozess.* Munich: C. H. Beck, 2011.

Weitkamp, Sebastian. "Brechung des Widerstands und Machtsicherung des NS-Systems. Die Konzentrationslager im Emsland 1933–1936." In *Hölle im Moor*, ed. Bernd Faulenbach and Andrea Kaltofen, 25–37. Göttingen: Wallstein, 2017.

Wewryk, Kalmen. *To Sobibor and Back: An Eyewitness Account.* Włodawa: Muzeum Pojezierza Łęczyńsko-Włodawskiego, 2008.

Wienert, Annika. *Das Lager vorstellen. Die Architektur der nationalsozialistischen Vernichtungslager.* Berlin: Neofelis, 2015.

Willenberg, Samuel. *Surviving Treblinka.* Oxford: Basil Blackwell, 1989.

———. *Treblinka. Lager, Revolte, Flucht, Warschauer Aufstand.* Hamburg, Münster: Unrast, 2009. English edition: *Revolt in Treblinka.* Warsaw: Wydawnictwo Skorpion, 1992.

Winkler, Heinrich August. *Der lange Weg nach Westen*, vol. 2: *Deutsche Geschichte vom "Dritten Reich" bis zur Wiedervereinigung.* Munich: C. H. Beck, 2000.

Wirth, Andrzej, ed. *Der Stroop-Bericht, "Es gibt keinen jüdischen Wohnbezirk in Warschau mehr!"* Neuwied: Luchterhand, 1960.

Witte, Peter, and Stephen Tyas. "A New Document on the Deportation and Murder of Jews during 'Einsatz Reinhardt' 1942." *Holocaust and Genocide Studies* 15, no. 3 (2001): 468–486.

Index

Page numbers in *italic* refer to illustrations.

About the Authors and Editors

Martin Cüppers, academic director of the Ludwigsburg Research Center and professor of modern history at the University of Stuttgart. Among his book publications is *Walther Rauff—in deutschen Diensten. Vom Naziverbrecher zum BND-Spion* (Darmstadt: WBG, 2013).

Annett Gerhardt, affiliate of the Bildungswerk Stanisław Hantz e.V. (BSH), where she escorts educational trips to sites associated with Operation Reinhard and is in charge of the biographies for the Memorial Stones in Sobibor project (www.sobibor.de).

Karin Graf, pedagogue and founding member of the BSH, for which she has accompanied educational trips to the Auschwitz-Birkenau Memorial since 1995. She is the editor of the life story of former Auschwitz prisoner Stanisław Hantz, titled *Zitronen aus Kanada*, and curator of the exhibition *Nur die Sterne waren wie gestern*, telling the story of Henryk Mandelbaum, one of the prisoners in the Sonderkommando at Auschwitz-Birkenau.

Steffen Hänschen, affiliate of the BSH, where he organizes educational trips to various sites of the Holocaust in Poland, Ukraine and Lithuania. A literary studies scholar and translator, he is the author of the monograph *Das Transitghetto Izbica im System des Holocaust* (Berlin: Metropol, 2018) and one of the editors of *"Aktion Erntefest." Berichte und Zeugnisse Überlebender* (Berlin: Metropol, 2022), which includes testimonies of survivors of the euphemistically named "Harvest Festival."

Andreas Kahrs, project coordinator and historian affiliated with the BSH. He organizes educational trips to various sites of the Holocaust in Poland and is also Managing Director of the NGO *What Matters*. He is one of the editors of *"Aktion Erntefest." Berichte und Zeugnisse* Überlebender (Berlin: Metropol, 2022), which includes testimonies of survivors of the euphemistically named "Harvest Festival."

Anne Lepper, historian, educational consultant, and project coordinator affiliated with the BSH. She is the representative of the International School for Holocaust Studies at Yad Vashem in the German-speaking countries. Her dissertation examines transnational Jewish aid and rescue networks during World War II. In her work with the BSH, she organizes educational trip on the Holocaust in Lithuania.

Jetje Manheim, came into contact with Jules Schelvis while looking into the fate of her father's family, and then became active in the Stichting Sobibor. In that capacity she organized the commemoration journeys of the Foundation, and she participated in several journeys to the Operation Reinhard sites with the BSH. She also accompanied the 27 Dutch co-plaintiffs at the trial of Ivan Demjanjuk in Munich.

Jürgen Matthäus, historian and director for Applied Research at the USHMM's Jack, Joseph and Morton Mandel Center. He has published several books, and is the editor of the center's source volume series *Documenting Life and Destruction* (14 vols.).

Florian Ross, founding member of the BSH, where he has escorted educational trips to the Auschwitz-Birkenau memorial site since 1995 and to Operation Reinhard sites since 1998. In addition, he coordinates various joint BSH projects with local partners in Poland.